D1218829

THE
CINDERELLA
CAMPAIGN

FIRST CANADIAN ARMY AND THE
BATTLES FOR THE CHANNEL PORTS

MARK ZUEHLKE

THE
CINDERELLA
CAMPAIGN

Douglas & McIntyre

DOUGLAS AND MCINTYRE (2013) LTD.
P.O. Box 219, Madeira Park, BC, V0N 2H0
www.douglas-mcintyre.com

Editing by Kathy Vanderlinden
Dust jacket typesetting by Shed Simas/Onça Design
Jacket photographs: Author's collection
Maps by C. Stuart Daniel/Starshell Maps
Photos used by permission of Library and Archives Canada
Printed on 100% PCW
Printed and bound in Canada

Canada

Douglas and McIntyre (2013) Ltd. acknowledges the support of the Canada Council for the Arts,
which last year invested $153 million to bring the arts to Canadians throughout the country. We
also gratefully acknowledge financial support from the Government of Canada and from the
Province of British Columbia through the BC Arts Council and the Book Publishing Tax Credit.

LIBRARY AND ARCHIVES CANADA CATALOGUING IN PUBLICATION

Zuehlke, Mark, author
    Cinderella campaign : First Canadian Army and the battles for the Channel
ports / Mark Zuehlke.

(Canadian battle series)
Includes bibliographical references and index.
Issued in print and electronic formats.
ISBN 978-1-77162-089-5 (hardcover).--ISBN 978-1-77162-090-1 (HTML)

    1. Canada. Canadian Army. Army, First. 2. World War, 1939-1945--
Campaigns--France, Northern. 3. World War, 1939-1945--Regimental
histories--Canada. I. Title. II. Series: Canadian battle series

D768.153Z84 2017   940.54'2142   C2017-905466-x
                                                   C2017-905467-8

During September, while the main Allied forces were driving for the German frontier, General Crerar's First Canadian Army was the Cinderella of Eisenhower's forces.

—*Chester Wilmot, Australian correspondent*

The further east you go, the less important death becomes. The Japanese have no fear of death at all, and the Russians have almost none. In England and America life is very precious, and everything is done in wartime to preserve it and prevent its needless waste. We Germans stand in the middle.

—*Generalleutnant Ferdinand Heim, Commandant Fortress Boulogne*

War narrows a person's horizon and the most important person in a soldier's scope of vision is himself. One does not think too much about another person's sacrifices, although one realizes that the next person is sacrificing as much [as] or more than yourself.

—*Captain Joseph Greenblatt, Medical Officer, 3rd Canadian Infantry Division, September 18, 1944*

[CONTENTS]

I N 2006, I completed a two-volume set about D-Day and the six pivotal days that followed, wherein the Juno beachhead and the success of the Normandy invasion itself were secured by the Canadian soldiers who, on June 6, 1944, had landed on that thin strip of sand. I recognized at the time that the fighting described in *Juno Beach* and *Holding Juno* constituted what is generally considered the turning point in World War II and was therefore the part of this great conflict best known by Canadians and most other Western readers. Canada's army had, of course, fought in scores of other battles in the Northwest Europe Campaign, but many of these were largely forgotten by all but a few specialists.

While researching the two Normandy titles, because of flight scheduling I had landed in Amsterdam, rented a car, and driven south to Juno Beach. The route took me through the Scheldt Estuary—the heartland of a forgotten campaign. I paused here for several days to tour this fascinating battlefield, which had cost so many Canadian lives and been so important to the Allied effort. That initial tour hooked me. I drove toward Normandy knowing that when the two books I was researching there were completed, the Scheldt Estuary Campaign would be the subject of the next Canadian Battle Series volume.

And so it was. But in researching and writing *Terrible Victory*, I was haunted for much of the time by the problem of how to treat a closely aligned part of the story—what is generally called the Channel Ports

Campaign. In September 1944, the Allies desperately needed a port in either northern France or Belgium to resolve the growing problem of supplying the rapidly advancing troops still getting supplies from the Normandy beachheads. Separated from the sea by the Scheldt Estuary, Antwerp was the largest such port and the most desired. Opening that port to Allied shipping led to First Canadian Army's hard-fought battles from September 13 to November 6, which became the focus of *Terrible Victory*.

Between the last part of August and the end of September, however, the Canadians had been engaged in wresting several French and Belgian ports from German control for use by the Allies. In many ways the campaign to open Antwerp and the one to open Le Havre, Dieppe, Boulogne, Dunkirk, Calais, and Ostend were two parts of a whole. But it was such a large whole that the story couldn't be captured in a single book without skimping on the level of detail that was a hallmark of the Canadian Battle Series. A compromise was needed. And so I dealt with the Channel Ports Campaign as a sidebar to the larger and more costly Scheldt Estuary Campaign.

When *Terrible Victory* was finished, my attention was pulled elsewhere, to other campaigns that I felt needed immediate attention. But the channel ports remained at the back of my mind, awaiting the right moment. When I floated the idea of a book based solely on the channel ports, other historians expressed doubt that there was enough of a story there. I have met such skepticism before with other Canadian Battle Series subjects, so I was not dissuaded.

It was time to dig. So I dug into the research materials held at Library and Archives Canada, the Department of National Defence's Directorate of History and Heritage archives, and the United Kingdom's National Archives. And I found treasure. Dozens upon dozens of reports—some hefty, some no more than a half page hastily written by an officer on the spot. As a whole, this wealth of material set out a gripping story of a fateful period in the Allied war on Germany. It was a time when many aspects of the war hung in the balance and the course that Allied higher command would pursue remained undecided.

And so here we are with *Cinderella Campaign*.

As always with a Canadian Battle Series title, I have tried hard to incorporate into the story many personal veteran accounts, from the viewpoints of privates to generals. Unfortunately, the time of the World War II veteran is passing. The couple of interviews I did have were too uncertain on detail to be fitted into events. I am fortunate, however, that many veterans had spoken about this campaign to others in earlier years—fortunate also that many had written small relevant accounts. And there were the historical officers and unit war diarists of the day who had interviewed soldiers just returned from the smoke and fire of battle with fresh and vibrant stories to tell. Literally hundreds of documents have been consulted to carefully piece together what happened when First Canadian Army emerged from the slaughterhouse of the Falaise Gap and marched toward the Seine River and the channel ports. Many Canadian, British, and other Allied soldiers fighting as part of First Canadian Army died or were wounded in what, for reasons that will soon become apparent, I have titled *The Cinderella Campaign*. This is their story—one written to honour them.

ACKNOWLEDGEMENTS

I AM BLESSED TO have many people who go out of their way to assist in the writing and researching of the Canadian Battle Series titles. Right at the top stands my Dutch colleague and long-time friend Johan van Doorn. When I was researching *Terrible Victory*, he came across a mention of this on my website and immediately got in touch. The wealth of his knowledge about the Scheldt Estuary Campaign and indeed every other campaign that Canada fought in Northwest Europe has been of tremendous value over the years. For this book, we toured from the Falaise Gap to Ostend in order to thoroughly come to know this diverse and intriguing battleground. Johan is a terrific project manager. His skills at assembling Excel spreadsheets listing all the hundreds of files at archives that required consulting kept me grounded and streamlined the research effort significantly.

In the United Kingdom, John Howes spent many hours at Kew Archives photographing files that were unavailable in Canada. Many of these regarded the operations of 1 British Corps and 79th British Armoured Division brigades and regiments and were a great help to me in telling their story. Ian Mitchell also weighed in on this front. Thank you, gentlemen.

At the Canadian War Museum, Carol Reid was, as always, a solid supporter and directed me to files that might have been missed. Ditto Dr. Steve Harris and staff at the Directorate of Heritage and History, Department of National Defence, who always go above and beyond the call of duty to bring forward my massive wish list of files. Staff at Library and Archives Canada are consistently courteous and diligent in trying to assist this researcher from the west coast who needs to do so much work in such a constrained timeline. The University of Victoria Military Oral History interviews are always a godsend.

Writing of this book was made possible in part by a grant from the British Columbia Arts Council.

My agent, Carolyn Swayze, keeps the business side of my career ticking along efficiently enough that I need not give it undue attention, which frees me for the creative side of things. Douglas & McIntyre (2013) staff, from the editorial side through production to marketing and publicity, are all to be treasured for their attention to matters and their obvious love of publishing. Kathy Vanderlinden stepped up to once again journey with me through the editing of the book. There is much truth to the old cliché that a book is only as good as its editor— something too many publishers seem to be forgetting. Also pitching in again was copy editor Merrie-Ellen Wilcox. Mapmaker C. Stuart Daniel of Starshell Maps started collecting source maps for this book as soon as I told him about it. I am fortunate to be able to draw upon his abilities for those so-necessary maps.

The subject of maps leads to a caveat about the spelling of place names. For consistency, these names have been spelled according to the maps and documents of the period and may be inconsistent with contemporary spellings. Also, a good number of small places mentioned no longer exist, having been swallowed up within the expanding boundaries of larger communities nearby.

I have the pleasure of walking through this life with my partner Frances Backhouse alongside. Often she literally walks the battle-grounds with me and is a pillar of support for my efforts to honour our World War II veterans by bringing their stories to life for modern readers. We will walk more battlefields, love.

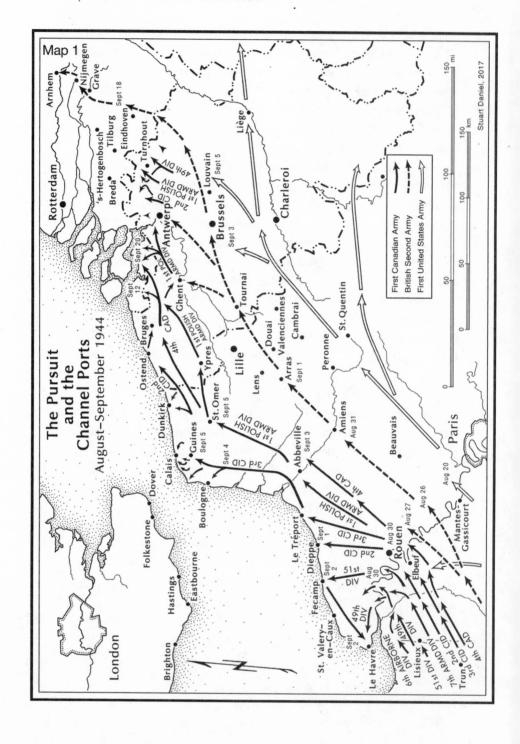

Map 1

The Pursuit
and the
Channel Ports
August–September 1944

Stuart Daniel, 2017

First Canadian Army
British Second Army
First United States Army

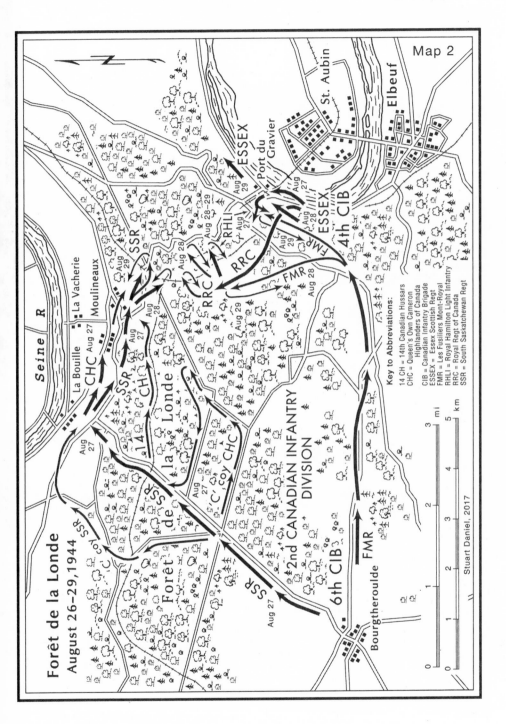

Map 2

Forêt de la Londe
August 26–29, 1944

Seine R

La Bouille
La Vacherie
Moulineaux
CHC Aug 27

St. Aubin
Elbeuf

ESSEX
Port du Gravier
ESSEX
4th CIB

2nd CANADIAN INFANTRY DIVISION

Forêt de la Londe

6th CIB

Bourgtheroulde

SSR
CHC
14 CH
C. coy CHC
FMR
RRC
RHLI
FMR

Aug 27
Aug 28
Aug 29
Aug 28–29

Stuart Daniel, 2017

Key to Abbreviations:

14 CH = 14th Canadian Hussars
CHC = Queen's Own Cameron
     Highlanders of Canada
CIB = Canadian Infantry Brigade
ESSEX = Essex Scottish Regt
FMR = Les Fusiliers Mont-Royal
RHLI = Royal Hamilton Light Infantry
RRC = Royal Regt of Canada
SSR = South Saskatchewan Regt

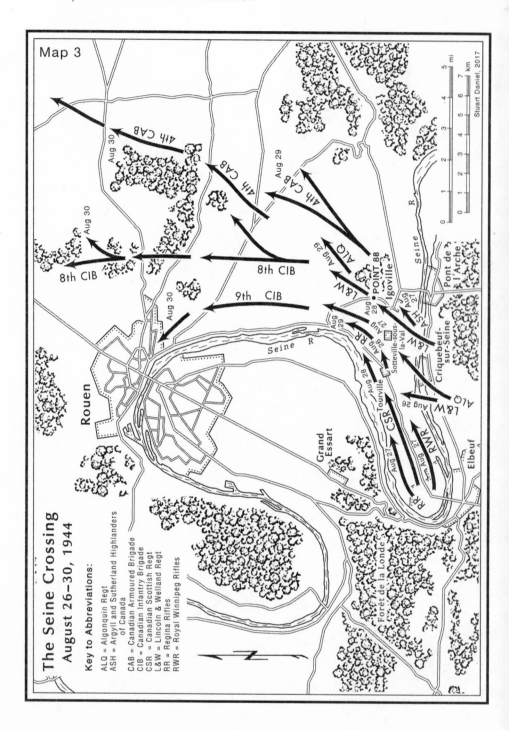

Map 3

The Seine Crossing
August 26–30, 1944

Key to Abbreviations:

ALQ = Algonquin Regt
ASH = Argyll and Sutherland Highlanders
          of Canada
CAB = Canadian Armoured Brigade
CIB = Canadian Infantry Brigade
CSR = Canadian Scottish Regt
L&W = Lincoln & Welland Regt
RR = Regina Rifles
RWR = Royal Winnipeg Rifles

Stuart Daniel, 2017

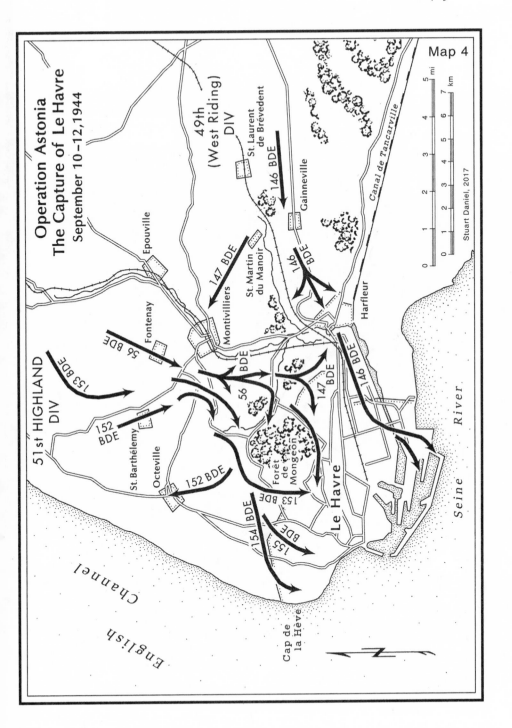

Map 4

Operation Astonia
The Capture of Le Havre
September 10–12, 1944

49th (West Riding) DIV

51st HIGHLAND DIV

Stuart Daniel, 2017

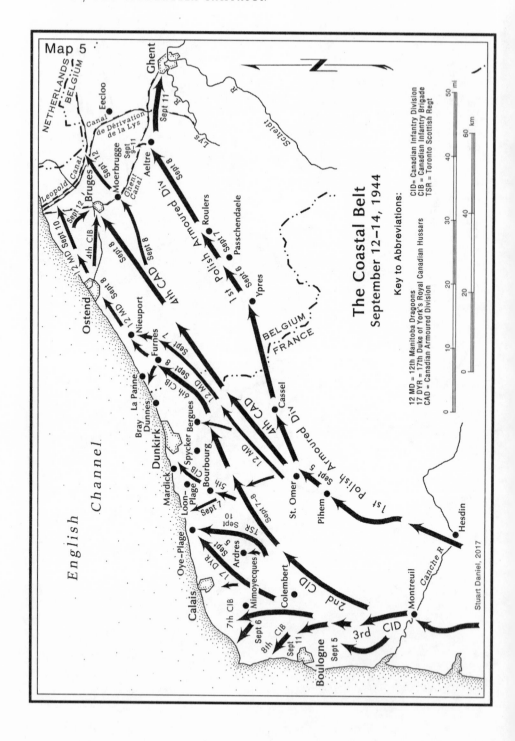

Map 5

The Coastal Belt
September 12–14, 1944

Key to Abbreviations:

12 MD = 12th Manitoba Dragoons
17 DYR = 17th Duke of York's Royal Canadian Hussars
CAD = Canadian Armoured Division

CID = Canadian Infantry Division
CIB = Canadian Infantry Brigade
TSR = Toronto Scottish Regt

Stuart Daniel, 2017

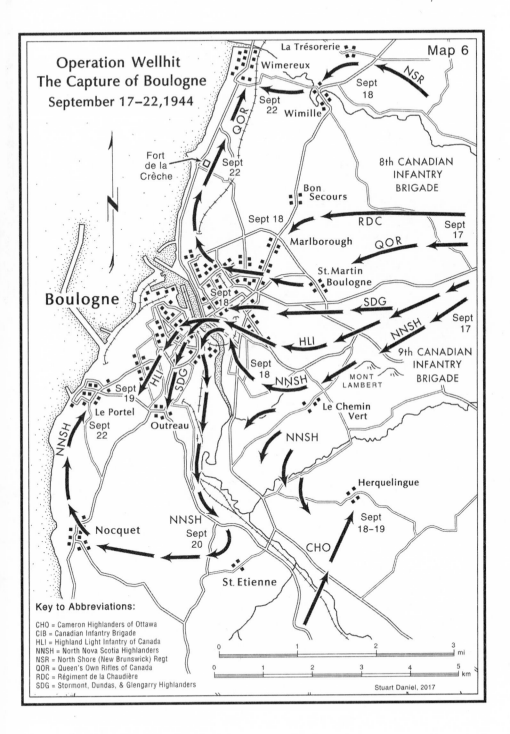

Operation Wellhit
The Capture of Boulogne
September 17–22, 1944

Map 6

La Trésorerie
Wimereux
NSR
Sept 18
Sept 22
Wimille

8th CANADIAN
INFANTRY
BRIGADE

Fort
de la
Crèche
Sept 22

Bon
Secours

Sept 18
RDC
QOR
Sept 17

Marlborough

St. Martin
Boulogne

SDG
Sept 17

Boulogne

Sept 18

HLI
NNSH

9th CANADIAN
INFANTRY
BRIGADE

MONT
LAMBERT

Sept 18

NNSH

Le Chemin
Vert

HLI
SDG

Sept 19
Le Portel
Sept 22
Outreau

NNSH

NNSH

Herquelingue

Sept
18–19

NNSH

Nocquet
Sept 20

CHO

St. Etienne

Key to Abbreviations:

CHO = Cameron Highlanders of Ottawa
CIB = Canadian Infantry Brigade
HLI = Highland Light Infantry of Canada
NNSH = North Nova Scotia Highlanders
NSR = North Shore (New Brunswick) Regt
QOR = Queen's Own Rifles of Canada
RDC = Régiment de la Chaudière
SDG = Stormont, Dundas, & Glengarry Highlanders

Stuart Daniel, 2017

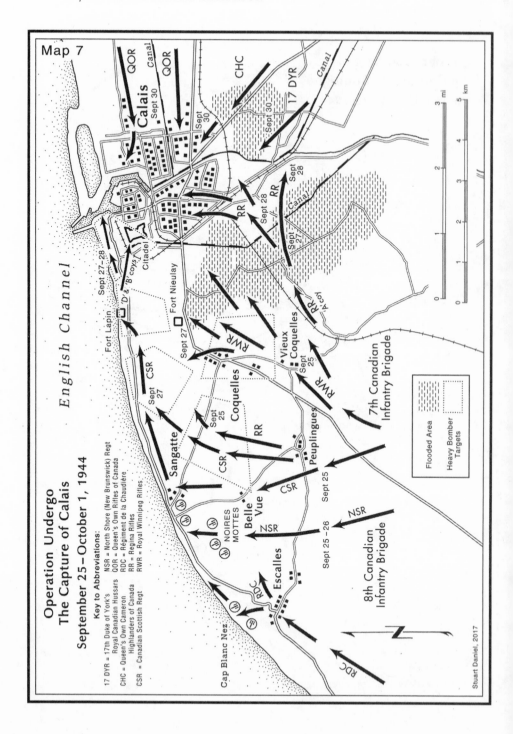

Map 7

Operation Undergo
The Capture of Calais
September 25–October 1, 1944

Key to Abbreviations:

17 DYR = 17th Duke of York's
Royal Canadian Hussars
CHC = Queen's Own Cameron
Highlanders of Canada
CSR = Canadian Scottish Regt

NSR = North Shore (New Brunswick) Regt
QOR = Queen's Own Rifles of Canada
RDC = Régiment de la Chaudière
RR = Regina Rifles
RWR = Royal Winnipeg Rifles

English Channel

Flooded Area

Heavy Bomber
Targets

Stuart Daniel, 2017

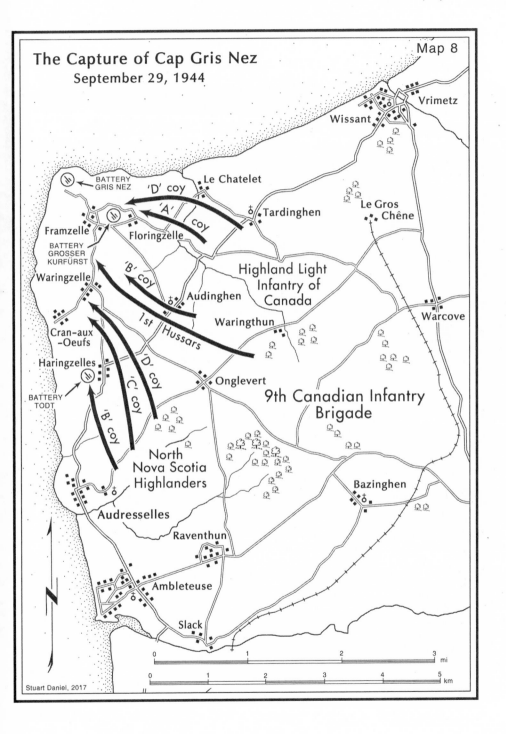

The Capture of Cap Gris Nez
September 29, 1944

Map 8

Vrimetz

Wissant

Le Gros
Chêne

BATTERY
GRIS NEZ

Le Chatelet

'D' coy

'A' coy

Tardinghen

Framzelle

Floringzelle

BATTERY
GROSSER
KURFÜRST

'B' coy

Waringzelle

Audinghen

Highland Light
Infantry of
Canada

Warcove

1st Hussars

Waringthun

Cran-aux
-Oeufs

Haringzelles

'D' coy

Onglevert

9th Canadian Infantry
Brigade

BATTERY
TODT

'C' coy

'B' coy

North
Nova Scotia
Highlanders

Bazinghen

Audresselles

Raventhun

Ambleteuse

Slack

0   1   2   3
                              mi
0   1   2   3   4   5
                                   km

Stuart Daniel, 2017

No Time Could Be Wasted

I N THREE DAYS, the hell of war was to engulf the old French port of Boulogne. Just as its German garrison was instructed to defend Boulogne to the last bullet and breath, Allied high command had made its capture and opening to shipping a matter of the highest priority. As First Canadian Army advanced out of Normandy on the left flank of the Allied juggernaut headed for Germany, taking Boulogne fell to two brigades of its 3rd Infantry Division, supported by artillery, tanks, and specialized siege equipment.

Interrogation of German prisoners, information from the Forces Françaises de l'Intérieur (French Forces of the Interior—FFI) resistance movement, and aerial photography analysis led Canadian intelligence staff to believe that Boulogne was defended by 5,500 to 7,000 German army, Luftwaffe, and marine personnel. While the relatively small garrison was considered to be a poor-quality affair afflicted by low morale, the city's fortifications were daunting. One Canadian report stated that the city was "completely surrounded by high features which [form] a very strong all round defensive system covering the port from landward attack. These defences [are] mutually supporting to a marked degree and command all the approaches to the city." Each defensive position was encircled by barbed-wire entanglements and minefields, and enclosed at least one large concrete gun emplacement protected by concrete dugouts linked together by underground passages. All roads approaching the city had been thoroughly mined. Every bridge had either been blown or was wired with explosives for destruction when the inevitable attack was launched.[1]

Just to the north of the city, the defences were anchored on an old French fort—Fort de la Crèche—that the Germans had extensively modernized and strengthened with thick-walled concrete pillboxes and defensive works. It bristled with light guns that protected two powerful 210-millimetre guns and four 105-millimetre heavy guns. Despite being designed primarily to face seaward, these six guns could rotate to fire landward, where the destructive weight of their massive shells posed a major threat to any attacker.

Fort de la Crèche was designed to protect Boulogne's main fortifications from northern attack and to threaten the right flank of any force approaching the city from the east. The fort itself was protected by another major strongpoint a short distance to the northeast. Called La Trésorerie, it formed the outermost defensive work in all of Boulogne's fortifications. Its coastal battery of three 12-inch guns were positioned on a dominating hill. Although these guns could not fire landward, the strongpoint's other defences made it a potent threat—so much so that the Canadians had decided La Trésorerie must be eliminated prior to the major assault on Boulogne. This task was given to the North Shore (New Brunswick) Regiment of 8th Canadian Infantry Brigade.[2] On September 8, 1944, the regiment moved to a pre-attack position well beyond the range of the German guns and initiated a program of aggressive patrols around La Trésorerie and other strongpoints north of Boulogne that would also have to be taken.

One such strongpoint was the hamlet of Wacquinghen, about a mile and a half northeast of La Trésorerie. On September 14, Lieutenant Victor Soucisse's scout platoon crept up to Wacquinghen's outskirts. As this move drew only sporadic machine-gun fire, Soucisse was convinced the hamlet was only lightly held. The moment Soucisse reported this possibility to Lieutenant Colonel Ernie Anderson, the North Shores commander decided to kick off operations early with a stealthy and hurried assault on Wacquinghen.

Consequently, at dusk on September 15, a small squad of infantrymen rushed toward the hamlet. Drawn from 'D' Company, the men were led by its Major O.L. "Otty" Corbett. Having joined the North

Shores in the midst of the Normandy Campaign's bitter early-July fight for Carpiquet Airfield, Corbett had emerged from that campaign as one of the battalion's most experienced company commanders. This night, he also hoped to be one of its luckiest. Just getting to the hamlet undetected would be no mean feat. The company was starting from high ground known locally as Bancres, about two miles east of Wacquinghen.[3] Advancing along the road to the hamlet would be folly because it was overlooked by La Trésorerie. Instead, Corbett led his assault squad in a wide cross-country sweep to approach from the northeast.

Only Corbett's most experienced men accompanied him—men he could trust not to silhouette themselves on a crest or make any other bad move that would betray their presence. As an added precaution, everybody had left behind equipment likely to rattle. Their wide sweep took them across gently rolling farm country, hugging every row of trees, delving into any fold of ground, or using the banks of a creek bed for cover. Precisely as night fell, Corbett's squad reached a small rise overlooking the hamlet. Everything, Corbett later said, "sounded peaceful and quiet." But he had a problem: the squad's wireless set had failed. If they kicked over a hornet's nest, there would be no calling for backup. Yet Corbett figured that if he were to "beat the Jerries to the village, no time could be wasted."

Corbett led his men down from the high ground and into a couple of the backyard gardens. They then dashed silently through the streets to the other side of the hamlet. "This move was successful. We got [there] ahead of the enemy and quickly sent back for the remainder of the company. Wacquinghen was in our hands."[4] It was 0130 hours. The race had been narrowly won. Just a few minutes later, a three-man German patrol approached and was sent fleeing by a volley of gunfire.[5]

The rest of 'D' Company soon arrived, and Corbett deployed the men into defensive positions that mostly faced toward the German line of approach. Still unable to establish wireless contact with battalion headquarters, Corbett felt increasingly uneasy. This was not because he expected the Germans to counterattack. Corbett was confident his men could repel that. His worries fixed on a hill about a half mile away called Pas de Gay that Soucisse had reconnoitred during the same patrol that convinced him Wacquinghen was ripe for plucking.

Soucisse had noted several concrete dugouts on the summit that he suspected sheltered a German observation post. The hill "looked high and menacing in the starlight and I commenced to think what a beautiful time we were going to have when it got daylight with an enemy observation post looking into our mess-tins and seeing every move." Corbett could easily imagine the Germans calling down deadly accurate artillery and mortar fire.

After another unsuccessful attempt to contact Lieutenant Colonel Anderson, Corbett decided to send a platoon to discover if Pas de Gay was occupied. Summoning Lieutenant Hobart Staples of No. 10 Platoon, Corbett ordered him to climb the hill and secure the dugouts. Hoping to complete the mission before daylight, Staples hurried his men along a road and then across a broad field to where a raised railway hugged the hill's southern base. "It was hard going," he related, "as we did not want to make any noise and yet we had to get over some wire fences. They proved a problem, but by holding the wires for each in turn we managed the job without raising any disturbance and finally reached the mouth of a re-entrant . . . Then we came upon a small dried-up brook and started up the left side—a mistake. But we had nothing to guide us . . . we simply had to grope along as best we could and trust to luck.

"It was very dark and we didn't seem to be getting anywhere except further away from the company, so I decided to withdraw to the mouth of the re-entrant. By that time it was getting near to morning and I left the men under Sergeant [Percy Fielsing] Mitchell and [Corporal Leonard Kenney] Dunne and went back to report to Major Corbett."

Wanting the hill badly, Corbett ordered Staples to try again and promised to also send No. 11 Platoon up in a left-flanking manoeuvre. Because it would be daylight, Corbett told Staples to lead with just a small fighting section rather than having the entire platoon strung out inside the gully. When Staples called for volunteers, ten trusted men stepped forward. They started climbing at 0700 hours. "Things looked very different in the daylight," Staples said. "We found and crossed the dried-up brook and this time we started up the right side instead of the left, came to barbed wire entanglements and concrete dugouts set in the hillside. These we had missed entirely in the darkness. We were almost to the top when I saw a German sentry on the skyline 25 yards away." Staples hissed at his Bren gunner to take out the German, but the soldier was unable to spot him. In the few seconds it took for Staples to point out the sentry's position, the German noticed the Canadians and ducked from sight.

Staples signalled his men to fan out and then led them up the slope at a run. Scrambling forward, Staples spotted another German and sighted his Sten gun on the man. When he squeezed the trigger, nothing happened. "I pressed the trigger again and again, decided safety was the better part of valour and went to ground. A few minutes later the enemy started to mortar the top of the hill and we were forced part way down the hillside where we had refuge in the concrete dugouts. We waited there and soon the enemy was coming over the top of the hill. We fired everything we had, Brens, rifles and mortar, and it slowed them up. I sent Sergeant Mitchell back to Major Corbett for reinforcements . . . and we waited there. Luckily the enemy didn't realize our predicament and Major Corbett came."

Emerging from their dugouts to charge Staples exposed the Germans to No. 11 Platoon closing from the left flank. The battle quickly deteriorated into a confused melee that allowed Staples and a few men to break into the summit fortifications. Private Eldon Wright got so close to one concrete dugout that grenades thrown by the Germans inside sailed well past him. Wright quickly exhausted his own grenade supply and shouted for more. Another man crawled over with a clutch of No. 36 grenades, and Wright threw two through an embrasure. With Staples closing fast on the dugout from the rear, the Germans suddenly vanished by way of an underground tunnel the Canadians discovered only after the position was overrun. At 0800 hours, Corbett arrived with more reinforcements. "We had the hill," he reported, "a beautiful observation post which gave control of the ground right to the sea coast north of Wimereux, bomb-proof sleeping quarters, a tunnel leading in the direction of La Trésorerie, and a cable junction box leading toward Cap Gris Nez and Calais. The tunnel entrance was blown to prevent any counterattack and we also used some grenades on the cable box."

After settling in the two platoons, Corbett went to battalion headquarters. He found Anderson "pacing the floor and ready to explode," for the battalion commander had heard nothing from 'D' Company since it went off into the darkness toward Wacquinghen. The adjutant, Captain Bob Ross, had spent the night and early morning assuring Anderson that the lack of news meant there was nothing to worry about, but he refused to accept this. "Now he was so happy over the success of the operation that he didn't give [me] the chewing out I deserved for not getting some messages back," Corbett noted.[6] Battalion head-quarters staff failed to record 'D' Company's casualty rate or probable German losses. But for what had been gained, North Shore losses were considered well within acceptable bounds.

In fact, when Anderson learned that Corbett had secured not only the hamlet but also Pas de Gay, he realized that a major obstacle to the forthcoming attack on La Trésorerie and the other main fortifica-tions guarding the northern flank of Boulogne had been taken. The destruction of the junction cable box was particularly welcome. Corbett had counted a total of 210 different wires leading from it. Anderson realized the box must have provided a secure communication link between all the German positions north of Boulogne. Had it remained in enemy hands, the Germans' ability to communicate would surely have compromised the planned operation. With the link severed, the Canadians had gained a critical and unforeseen advantage.[7]

Still, Anderson was deeply worried about the coming engagement. As the North Shores' Padre R. Miles Hickey later wrote, while men in other battalions usually knew their commander by "names that couldn't be written on . . . paper, Colonel Ernie received the endear-ing title of 'Uncle Ernie'" because he cared so much about his men's welfare.[8] Here at Boulogne, Anderson faced the disturbing reality that these men, and indeed the Canadians as a whole, had no experience in assaulting such heavily constructed and mutually supporting fortifi-cations. Breaking through them to capture Boulogne promised to be a slow and costly affair. But it was also a vital and necessary undertaking that must be accomplished with the greatest speed. Indeed, it seemed that the longer it took them to win this and the other channel ports so urgently assigned to First Canadian Army, the more likely that what had seemed an opportunity to win the war before the end of 1944 would slip from the Allied grasp.

PART ONE

PURSUIT TO THE SEINE

1

Getting on with the Business

I N THE MID-AFTERNOON of August 21, 1944, Canadian and Polish troops literally shook hands and finally closed the Falaise Gap—an action that brought the drawn-out and costly Normandy Campaign to an end. Although a large number of Germans managed to escape through the gap to the northeast, their losses since the Allied landings on June 6 were devastating. No accurate tally exists, but most reports confirm Supreme Headquarters Allied Expeditionary Force (SHAEF) commander General Dwight D. Eisenhower's statement that by August 25 about 400,000 Germans had died, been wounded, or been taken prisoner. The number captured stood at about 200,000. In the campaign's closing days, the remnants of two German armies had been herded into a pocket around the ancient city of Falaise. These survivors numbered approximately 100,000. About 10,000 were subsequently killed and another 40,000 to 50,000 either surrendered or were listed as missing and presumed dead. No more than 50,000 Germans escaped through the gap. Most of these were supply and service personnel rather than front-line fighting troops. Those who escaped took with them very little equipment, particularly anything mechanized.[1] Within the pocket, Britain's No. 2 Operational Research Section counted 187 tanks and self-propelled guns, 157 lightly armoured vehicles, 1,779 lorries, 669 cars, and 252 guns. Artillery losses over the course of the entire campaign were estimated at 1,500 field and heavier guns. Overall tank losses were believed to number about 1,300.

The campaign had cost the Allies dearly as well—206,703 soldiers. Of these, 124,394 were American and 82,309 British and Canadian. Canadian losses suffered from the landings on Juno Beach to the gap's closing numbered 18,444, with 5,021 being fatal. Of the many divisions fighting as part of the British Twenty-First Army Group, it was 3rd Canadian Infantry Division that suffered the highest number of casualties, with 2nd Canadian Infantry Division taking second place.[2]

First Canadian Army emerged from the smoke and fire of the Normandy Campaign battered and exhausted. But there was to be no time to rest or rebuild. The Germans were on the run, trying to reach and regroup beyond the Seine River. Across a wide front, the Allies were in pursuit. Believing the Allied intent was to surround and bag what remained of the retreating Fifth and Seventh Armies before they could reach the river, II ss Panzer Corps issued orders on August 22 to its 9th ss Panzer Division, 85th Infanterie-Division, and 21st Panzer Division to "fight a delaying withdrawal back over [the Seine] in four bounds, and . . . prevent the enemy from breaking through . . . The beginning of withdrawal from one line of resistance to the next as well as the length of time spent on individual lines of resistance will be ordered by the division individually."

Soon after this order was issued, a copy fell into the hands of Allied intelligence officers. Even though the German divisions it addressed were far too disorganized and weak to put the instructions into action, the xvth and xixth Corps of First United States Army struck out immediately to gain the Seine between Mantes-Gassicourt and Elbeuf. First Canadian Army would, meanwhile, continue to block the east side of the Falaise Gap and contain those Germans still in the pocket, while British Second Army drove "through to the Seine" west of the Americans. The American line of advance, along which they moved at a stunning pace, was such that it actually cut across the British front. But as the latter closed on the Seine, the Americans were to let them pass through and then withdraw to a boundary line farther east.[3]

The captured order had been issued in response to Hitler's instruction on August 20 to Oberbefehlshaber West [Commander in Chief of German armed forces in northwest Europe] Generalfeldmarschall Walter Model. Hitler had insisted that Model must hold Paris, "prevent an enemy breakthrough between Seine and Loire towards Dijon . . . reform the badly battered Armies between the Touques sector . . . and if the area forward of the Seine could not be held, to fall back and defend the line: Seine—Yonne—Canal de Bourgonge—Dijon—Dol—Swiss border."

Model replied the following day that "Paris could not be defended with the forces on hand." Lacking reinforcements from either Germany or Holland, Model had therefore initiated the reconnoitering of an emergency line north and east of Paris. Lapsing into one of his increasingly delusional rants, Hitler insisted on August 23 that the "defence of the Paris bridgehead is of decisive military and political importance. Its loss tears open the entire coastal front north of the Seine and deprives us of the basis for the long-range operations against England.

"In the course of history the fall of Paris has hitherto ever been followed by the fall of the whole of France.

"The Führer therefore reiterates his order to defend Paris in the blocking belt forward of the city. In this connection attention is drawn to the reinforcements announced for O.B. West.

"At the first indications of revolt within the city steps must be taken to intervene with severe measures, e.g. dynamiting of blocks of houses, public execution of ringleaders, evacuation of the city quarters involved, as the best means of preventing the further spread of revolt.

"Preparations are to be made for blowing up the Seine bridges. Paris must not fall into the hands of the enemy, or, if so, only as a field of rubble."

The reinforcements Hitler alluded to were far too few and scheduled to arrive much too late to enable Model to defend Paris or hold anywhere on the Seine. Two veteran units that Hitler had promised could arrive immediately—the 3rd and 15th Panzer Grenadier Divisions— were still in Italy. On August 25, the former concentrated at Verona for transfer to France, while the latter prepared to move to France via the Brenner Pass. Neither could possibly reach Model until September 2. Nor could any of the three green divisions or independent panzer brigades Hitler promised to send immediately from Germany. Any hope of stemming the Allied advance ultimately depended on the quantity and quality of what Model could salvage from his two armies retreating across France from Normandy.[4]

AMONG THE ALLIES, meanwhile, the mood was euphoric. On August 20, General Bernard Montgomery issued *General Operational Situation and Directive* M519 to his Twenty-First Army Group, outlining immediate plans that brimmed with confidence. With the Falaise Gap closing, he wrote, the German "divisions have ceased to exist as effective fighting formations.

"We will now complete the destruction of such of his forces as are still available to be destroyed, and we will then proceed to other matters.

"I must impress on all commanders the need for speed in getting on with the business.

"The Allied victory in N.W. Europe will have immense repercussions; it will lead to the end of the German military domination in France; it is the beginning of the end of the war.

"But if these great events are to be brought about, we must hurl ourselves on the enemy while he is still reeling from the blow; we must deal him more blows and ever more blows; he must be allowed no time to recover.

"This is no time to relax, or to sit back and congratulate ourselves. I call on all commanders for a great effort. Let us finish off the business in record time."

Montgomery's intention was to "complete the destruction of the enemy forces in north-west France. Then to advance northwards, with a view to the eventual destruction of all enemy forces in north-east France . . . As a first step we have got to cross the SEINE, and to get disposed beyond it—tactically and administratively—so that we can carry out quickly the orders of the Supreme Allied Commander."[5]

The original SHAEF plan developed in England well before the invasion had foreseen a need for the undoubtedly exhausted and much reduced Allied armies to pause at the Seine for possibly as long as thirty days. On August 17, this remained SHAEF's operational intention. Two days later, seeing the way the battle had developed, Eisenhower cancelled the pause.[6] Every effort would be made to press hard on the heels of the retreating Germans, overrun them if possible, and then destroy them in detail. Too often the Germans had proven their ability, when provided the slightest opportunity, to quickly regroup into ad hoc formations. They would then establish some form of coherent defensive line that forced the facing Allied troops to deploy and be drawn into a fixed and bloody action that could last for mere hours or persist for days. These were days the Germans could then use to rush reinforcements forward in support or to prepare more heavily defended positions behind this first defensive line. It would be far easier to sweep up disorganized and retreating forces than face any who managed to regroup. This point was being proven daily as the Allies advanced away from the Normandy battlefield, capturing a steady stream of prisoners from units unable to outpace them.

To the Allies, it was blatantly obvious that Paris and the rest of France were soon to be theirs. The Germans were simply too out-manned and outgunned to prevent this. Not only were Allied troops breaking out of Normandy, but just before dawn on August 15, the Seventh U.S. Army had landed three infantry divisions on beaches in southern France between St. Tropez and Cannes. And ahead of the amphibious assault, the U.S. 1st Provisional Airborne Division—a predominantly American formation supported by one British brig-ade—had dropped a short distance inland.7

Operation Dragoon achieved complete success. By nightfall, some 86,000 American troops were ashore. The following day, two French divisions joined them. The Germans in France suddenly faced op-ponents on two fronts. In southern France, German Army Group G's Generaloberst Johannes von Blaskowitz could offer only token resistance against American–Franco forces, because over the past two months most of his reserves had been sent to Normandy. His remaining eleven divisions were stretched across the breadth of the Riviera beaches and along the Biscay coast. On August 18, immediate battle obviously lost, Hitler ordered Von Blaskowitz to leave weak garrisons to defend the deep-water ports of Toulon and Marseilles while withdrawing the majority of his divisions to the Vosges Mountains in northeastern France.

Dragoon—originally code-named Anvil—had been a highly con-troversial operation. Eisenhower, with the firm backing of American chief of staff General George C. Marshall, badly wanted to open Marseilles. This port could then support the passage into southern France of forty to fifty divisions idling in the United States but "ready for action."[8] British Prime Minister Winston Churchill vehemently opposed the operation because the troops for it must be drawn away from the campaign in Italy. Without those divisions, it was unlikely that the remaining forces in Italy could effectively continue the Allied Mediterranean strategy, which was to advance up the length of Italy and break into central Europe via the Balkans. On August 5, Churchill lunched with Eisenhower at his temporary SHAEF headquarters near Portsmouth to press his case.

Capturing Marseilles, he argued, was now unnecessary, as the divisions from America could be delivered directly to deep-water ports in Brittany—particularly Cherbourg. Further, invading southern France offered no tactical advantage, as the campaign in the north was so far developed that the Allies would likely be pushing against the German border before the armies that landed there could catch up. Better to leave those troops in Italy. There they could continue the drive toward the Balkans, where the communist Josip Broz Tito's Yugoslav Partisans were in open revolt and tying down many German divisions. Operations in Italy would also prevent a German withdrawal of divisions from there that might otherwise be sent to reinforce OB West or deployed to the Russian front.

Eisenhower was not to be swayed. He needed two major ports, he insisted, one on each flank of the Allied advance. The left flank could be serviced by Antwerp, and Marseilles was the only candidate for the right flank. All afternoon the debate continued. While Churchill managed to win over First Sea Lord Admiral Sir Andrew Cunningham and, somewhat to his surprise, Eisenhower's chief of staff Lieutenant General Walter Bedell Smith, there was no moving the supreme commander. As one observer later wrote, "Ike said no, continued saying no all afternoon and ended by saying no in every form of the English language."

Neither Eisenhower nor Marshall in Washington cared about the Mediterranean strategy. Both considered it a distraction from the primary goal of defeating the Germans in France and then advancing directly into Germany. However, although Toulon and Marseilles would both fall on August 28 and soon be open to shipping, Dragoon's initial successes quickly lost luster in the face of reversals suffered by the American and French divisions driving up the Rhône valley. All along the way, they met a skilfully offered rearguard defence that prevented the overrunning of the retreating German divisions and blocked their ability to rapidly link up with the Allies advancing out of Normandy.[9] Not until September 15 would the Seventh U.S. Army come up alongside General George S. Patton's Third Army.[10]

Meanwhile, as Churchill had feared, the lessening of Allied operations in Italy gave the Germans there time to regain their breath and enabled Hitler to withdraw three divisions for service elsewhere. The Hermann Göring Division was transferred to Poland, while the 15th Panzer Grenadier and 5th Mountain Divisions moved to France.[11]

By the time these divisions departed Italy, however, the Germans were losing their grip on Paris, despite Hitler's demands for either a heroic defence or the city's destruction. Most of the defensive lines Hitler outlined during the days immediately following the Falaise Gap closure were already lost when his orders reached the affected formations. Patton's Third Army out on the right flank was steamrolling along, delayed more by shortages of fuel for the tanks than by German resistance. The American army was the most highly mechanized in the world—a fact Patton proved every day. Having finally wrested free of Normandy's *bocage* country, with its small fields ringed by dense earthen thickets atop high earthen banks, the Americans barrelled along largely undamaged roads that led directly to Paris. In just eleven hours on August 15, the 79th Infantry Division charged sixty miles from La Mêle-sur-Sarthe to Nogent-le-Roi. The following day, however, Patton's divisions stalled on a line running from Orléans to Chartres to Dreux—having literally run out of gas. Refuelled on the 18th, Patton again released his divisions. By dark, the 79th Division was three miles from the Seine and just a little west of Paris. The next morning, the division won a bridgehead across the river. The initial Allied intention had been only to surround Paris rather than enter it. Accordingly, Patton won a second crossing over the Seine to the city's southeast on August 23.

But events within the city forced a change of plan. On the 19th, the Paris police force had gone on strike, and this was followed by a general FFI uprising. During the ensuing night, the resistance won control of the city centre. The following morning, German military commander General Dietrich von Cholitz—not willing to oversee the city's destruction—negotiated an armistice to enable withdrawal of his troops from the rest of the city in exchange for recognizing the FFI as belligerents, leaving them in possession of the city centre and allowing entry of relief food convoys. The armistice was to extend to the 23rd but lasted barely into the night of the 20th, because the FFI proved incapable of exerting control over all its fighters. Sniping and skirmishing broke out across the city. German-controlled Paris Radio issued a broadcast that "irresponsible elements in Paris have taken up arms against the occupation authorities. The revolt will be rigorously suppressed."

As fighting intensified, the FFI leadership appealed to the Americans to come to the rescue. On August 22, Twelfth Army Group commander Lieutenant General Omar Bradley ordered v Corps commander Major General L.T. Gerow to enter the capital, as soon as the crumbling armistice ended on August 23, with his 2nd French Armoured and 4th U.S. Infantry Divisions. They were told, however, to avoid heavy fighting. Gerow advanced on the 24th, but was held up by German rearguard forces and roadblocks. The next day, the French entered Paris from the west and the Americans the south. German resistance collapsed, and by 0830 hours on August 25, French tanks were rolling triumphantly down the Champs Élysées. By nightfall, German resistance throughout the city had ceased. But the night was rent by gunfire as FFI bands hunted down collaborators and pro-Nazi militias. Morning found the streets filled with thousands of Parisians revelling in freedom after four years of occupation. As far as they were concerned, the Battle of France was won.[12]

WELL DISTANT FROM Paris, the battle for northern France was far from over. The same morning that Bradley had tasked v Corps with liberating Paris, several Canadian infantry battalions descended warily into the chaos of the Falaise Gap to round up any lingering

Germans. At 0900 hours on August 22, two companies of Argyll and Sutherland Highlanders of Canada formed on a ridge overlooking the valley through which, only the day before, thousands of Germans had been frantically trying to escape. Lance Corporal Harry Ruch, serving in 'A' Company's No. 7 Platoon, wrote that the Argylls had been ordered to "administer the death blow," so went forward supported by Staghound armoured cars manned by squadrons of the 12th Manitoba Dragoon Regiment. Nobody knew what to expect, "so we prepared for anything."[13]

'B' and 'C' Squadrons of the 12th Manitoba Dragoons accompanied the Argylls. The raison d'être of armoured reconnaissance (recce) regiments was to dash ahead of the main forces to test enemy resistance and blaze trails for the rest of their division to follow, so the Dragoons considered the day "a very dull time . . . without much excitement."[14]

'D' Squadron drew livelier duty, independently probing into unknown territory on an easterly heading beyond the gap. Discovering that the Germans had blown all bridges across the Vie River, the squadron's scout troop moved along the shore until it found a workable ford that the 26,600-pound wheeled Staghounds could cross without getting stuck. As the first car started across, a few diehard German infantry opened up with small-arms fire. This was easily suppressed by the armoured car's 37-millimetre turret-mounted gun and two .30-calibre machine guns. With the river behind them, the Dragoons raced onward and soon forded the Touques River. From there it was a two-mile dash through open fields to the village of Le Sap. Here they received "a rousing welcome" from the citizenry while also being sniped at by "a few Hun." The three lieutenants commanding the 'D' Squadron troops told the locals that they could not linger to clean up the Germans because they must continue advancing until recalled by battalion headquarters to their initial start line to replenish with fuel and ammunition. Just before they set off, "a local stalwart, a lady, stated that she would round up about fifty people and keep the Hun busy for the night if our patrols would return in the morning. Lieutenant [Frederick James] Bowes assured the Madame he would return and just to prove that he thought she was a big help, he gave her a few grenades to chuck at the Jerries. She was very happy to receive them."[15]

Meanwhile, several miles back and to the west, the Argylls with supporting Dragoons had continued their gruesome task. "As we progressed through the valley," Harry Ruch realized "the beating Jerry had taken. It must have been pure Hell for him. Wrecked tanks, truck[s], and wagons everywhere. Jerry dead all over the place. Horses both dead and living by the hundreds. We captured about 500 Jerries that survived the battle. They were dazed and had no fight in them. It took us all day to go through the valley. We swept through 15 miles and arrived back at our original positions about 1800, hungry, tired and a little sick from the smell of battle and the dead we went through. Found out that there is no rest for the wicked and we are to chase after the Jerries that got away. Starting tonight. We have been on the go steady for 27 days and we are beginning to feel the strain a little."[16]

Sweeping through the valley on one flank of the Argylls were also several companies of the Lincoln and Welland Regiment. The Argylls and Lincs constituted two of the three infantry battalions comprising 4th Canadian Armoured Division's 10th Infantry Brigade. Sergeant Rudy Horwood had wrangled leave from his position in the anti-tank platoon to accompany a long-time friend who served with the battalion's scouts. "I'd like to go out on this patrol . . . to see how he's doing," Horwood had told his platoon commander.

Horwood and fourteen other men advanced with only their rifles and some extra ammunition. "We didn't have pouches, grenades, Bren guns. We were going to check out a village. And so we started out and we moved very quickly. We were running, and we went over and . . . the village was empty. And then we were running back . . . somebody spotted some Germans . . . so three of us went around one side of the wood and the other twelve went around the other side. And the three on the right hand side of the wood were myself and [Private Ronald Dennis] McPherson and [Private] Billy Tucker, who was my personal friend."

Horwood was leading, between twenty and thirty feet ahead of the others, when a group of Germans marching with rifles on their shoulders appeared right ahead. "I fired a shot . . . and they were more surprised than I was, because . . . they scattered." Seeing that his compatriots had taken cover behind a large log, Horwood joined

them, and the three fired shots at the fleeing Germans. When the rest
of the platoon arrived, the Lincs rounded up about fifteen Germans
who had decided to surrender. They were in the process of persuading
these Germans to drop their weapons when another man backed
out of a cluster of trees with a rifle in his hands. "Harry Field . . .
shot . . . him through the back and killed him. And when the other
Germans saw that, they all put their weapons down . . . So we rounded
them up . . . and then . . . we checked . . . farmhouses and we found
Germans sleeping in barns and in houses. So we rounded them up."
Having captured thirty Germans, the Lincs confiscated their wallets
and divvied the cash found. Each man pocketed about 1,500 francs.
Horwood estimated their individual take at about thirty dollars, "more
than a month's pay."

By nightfall, the Canadian units clearing the gap had completed
their grisly task. None who descended into the valley that day would
ever forget the carnage. In his personal diary, the Lincoln's 'A' Company
commander, Major Johnny Farmer, succinctly described the experience. "All day sweep for prisoners. Bloody Gory!"[17]

THESE SWEEPS BY 4th Canadian Armoured Division within the gap
on August 22 accorded with Montgomery's general plan for Twenty-
First Army Group set out two days earlier. While he had immediately unleashed British Second Army for a glamorous chase to the
Seine River and beyond to the Somme, where it was to establish a
broad front stretching from Amiens to the sea, Montgomery handed First Canadian Army a more mundane role. In the short term,
the 11 Canadian Corps was to keep the Falaise Gap "bottle securely
corked." Meanwhile, 1 British Corps—which had been attached to First
Canadian Army throughout the Normandy Campaign to bolster its
strength to army size—would continue an advance begun on August
15 up the Normandy coast toward Lisieux and then swing east to Rouen
on the Seine.

For 11 Canadian Corps, Montgomery expected the bottling task to
be short-lived. Once "the cork is removed from the 'bottle,'" he intended
for all the "Canadian Army [to] advance to the Seine . . . cross the river,
and . . . operate to clear the whole Havre peninsula to the west . . . It

is important to secure the port of [Le Havre] very early. The railway communications from the port, eastwards and northwards, will be required for the maintenance of the armies and much time will be saved if they are secured intact, together with all possible rolling stock."[18]

Seldom given to sentiment or symbolic gesture, Montgomery included both in this order. Just up the coast from Le Havre was a small port called St. Valery-en-Caux. From June 10 to 12 in 1940, the 51st (Highland) Infantry Division had made a gallant, but doomed, stand here while hoping for possible evacuation by sea. The Germans had quickly boxed in and started crushing the defenders with superior forces. Fog obscuring the coast thwarted the evacuation attempt and contributed to several ships being sunk. With the Germans occupying cliffs overlooking the port, divisional commander Major General V.M. Fortune ordered his men to surrender on June 12. Remembering this event, Montgomery asked First Canadian Army's Lieutenant General Harry Crerar to assign the honour of liberating this town to the reconstituted Highland division. "All Scotland will be grateful," he wrote.

At the same time, he also suggested that 2nd Canadian Infantry Division should "deal very suitably with Dieppe."[19] On August 19, 1942, this division had been decimated during the infamous raid in which it suffered 3,367 casualties from a force of 4,963 Canadians committed. During the nine-hour battle, 913 Canadians died and another 1,946 were taken prisoner. The division was so badly mauled that it had barely concluded rebuilding before deploying from England to Normandy on July 9. Having lost so many officers and core non-commissioned officers at Dieppe, the division had entered the Normandy fighting with serious leadership deficiencies only exacerbated by the heavy casualties suffered through the July and August fighting.[20] News that it was to have the privilege of driving the Germans out of Dieppe was well received throughout its ranks.

In a phone call to the First Canadian Army Chief of Staff Brigadier C. Churchill "Church" Mann at noon on August 22, Montgomery made clear that he wanted to get 11 Canadian Corps moving away from the Falaise Gap. Ringing off, Mann immediately called 11 Canadian Corps headquarters and was assured by Chief of Staff Brigadier Elliot Rodger that all resistance inside the gap and within the pocket itself had ceased. He reported that Lieutenant General Guy Simonds was already visiting his divisions with orders that anticipated their being imminently released to join the advance toward the Seine. Mann then passed on this news to Montgomery, who declared "the restrictions . . . now removed and that as soon as possible, and as quickly as could be arranged, the advance was to be started to the river Seine." Mann said that 11 Corps could start a general advance the following morning, but that 2nd Infantry Division and the reconnaissance elements of 4th Armoured Division would set out "at once."[21]

While 11 Canadian Corps had been fully engaged in pinching shut the Falaise Gap, Crerar had left this operation's overall management to Simonds and focused his attention instead on planning the army's advance beyond the Normandy battleground. Through the early part of August, 1 British Corps had guarded the Canadian army's seaward flank by facing eastward and maintaining a holding posture. Only its right flank moved forward as necessary to keep aligned with the advance of 11 Canadian Corps. The largely static role this corps played was due to its having to cover such a large swath of frontage with fewer divisions than would normally be involved. Until it was reinforced by the arrival of the Royal Netherlands Brigade (Princess Irene's) and the 1st Belgian Infantry Brigade from England, the corps consisted only of the 49th (West Riding) Infantry Division, the 51st (Highland) Infantry Division, and the 6th Airborne Division.

Originally, this last division was to have been withdrawn to regroup in England in order to avoid its elite troops being whittled down by casualties suffered in extended ground-fighting operations. But the shortages 1 British Corps faced resulted in that plan being abandoned and the division having to absorb the feared casualties.

The experience of 1st Canadian Parachute Battalion, one of the three battalions comprising 3rd Parachute Brigade, was typical. From its nighttime drop on June 5–6 at the onset of D-Day, the Canadians had suffered three hundred casualties. A draft of seven officers and one hundred infantrymen drawn from the Canadian Base Reinforcement Battalion barely sufficed to enable the paratroops to maintain sustained operations. That the reinforcements were not trained parachutists, one report stated, "mattered little. Indeed, for the role in which the battalion was to be engaged during the remainder of its stay in France, well-trained and equipped infantrymen provided the most valuable acquisition that could have been supplied." After a brief rest period, the reorganized Canadians had returned to the front line along the Orne River on July 30.

The following day, First Canadian Army had officially taken command of both 11 Canadian Corps and 1 British Corps. For the Canadian parachutists, the short duration of their continued service with 1 Corps marked the first and ultimately last time during the war that they were to serve as part of First Canadian Army.[22]

For most of the ensuing three weeks, the Canadian battalion engaged in a static battle marked, as parachutist Sergeant Dan Hartigan later wrote, by "nasty patrol work and the gathering of information about the enemy . . . It was a war of nerves and punishment for both sides, just as it had been in the early days after the invasion. Now, though, in the heat and moisture of July and August, hordes of huge mosquitoes filled the Normandy countryside." Heavy sporadic rains and thunderstorms had turned the swampy coastal country in which the airborne division was deployed "into a swamp."

There was little movement. Men were killed or wounded while engaged in short, "wicked encounters" as the paratroops attempted to force the Germans out of fortified positions or blundered into undetected minefields. Shallow patrols into the heavily defended German lines required hours of creeping covertly through dense foliage and across mud-soaked farm fields. During these patrols, Hartigan was dogged by the horrifying feeling that at any moment, discovery could bring a rapid death.[23]

Being employed as regular infantry raised an internal organizational issue for the airborne division—a severe lack of supporting artillery. The entire division relied on the 75-millimetre pack howitzers of the 53rd (Worcestershire Yeomanry) Light Regiment, Royal Artillery—guns that could be loaded into gliders. To supplement this regiment, 1 British Corps had formed an ad hoc battery of twelve 95-millimetre Centaur self-propelled guns designated x Armoured Battery. This unit proved its worth by engaging in duels with German mortars during the latter part of June and throughout July. At the beginning of August, however, the corps withdrew the unit's personnel to reinforce regular artillery regiments depleted by combat losses.

Considering the battery's existence an "operational necessity," Crerar intervened and created a temporary Canadian unit. Thus, 1st Centaur Battery, Royal Canadian Army, was born on August 6 under command of Major D.W. Cooper. Seventeen British soldiers were retained—Captain E.J. Leapard as battery captain, fifteen Royal Artillery signals personnel, and a lone Royal Electrical and Mechanical Engineer Corps gun fitter. The rest of the battery was made up of gunners sent from the army's reinforcement pool.

The battery consisted of a headquarters section and three gun troops. Each troop had one Sherman tank fitted out for observation post duties and four Centaur MK4s. The Centaurs were heavily armed with a quick-firing 95-millimetre tank howitzer mounted on an outdated A24 Cavalier tank chassis. Extra firepower, as well as anti-aircraft protection, was provided by two 7.92 Besa machine guns and twin Vickers machine guns mounted next to the turret. The Centaur was also fitted with a smoke-bomb launcher and a rear smoke emitter. For personal arms, each crew had a Thompson submachine gun and a Sten submachine gun, as well as a variety of grenades. Being self-propelled, the Centaurs were relatively agile and thus well suited to supporting the lightly armed airborne troops.

On August 14, the Canadian gun crews were sufficiently familiar with their new roles and equipment to become operational. Their job, as officially stated, was to provide "maximum harassing fire on the enemy's administrative machinery" and "vigorous and immediate retaliatory fire." The battery went into action alongside 6th Airborne just as the division moved out of its static role on August 16.[24]

2

Press Forward

O N AUGUST 15, Lieutenant General Harry Crerar had instructed Lieutenant General John Crocker to switch 1 British Corps from a defensive posture to the offence. Crocker's front stretched from the village of St. Pierre-sur-Dives to the mouth of the Orne River, with 6th British Airborne Division holding the seaward flank, the 49th (West Riding) Infantry Division alongside, and the 51st (Highland) Infantry Division on the far right. Close behind the Highlanders was 7th British Armoured Division to give Crocker some much-needed armoured strength and mobility.

At the same time, the Royal Netherlands Brigade (Princess Irene's) and 1st Belgian Infantry Brigade came under 6th Airborne Division's command and were tucked protectively into its centre between Amfreville and Bréville.[1] This accorded with Twenty-First Army Group policy for these two brigades and also the 1st Czechoslovak Independent Armoured Brigade (not yet deployed) to be given "operational experience in quieter sections of the line in the hope that ultimately they would return to their own countries and form nuclei around which larger national forces might be organized." They were not to be employed in major combat operations.[2]

Even before 1 British Corps had come under First Canadian Army command on July 23, Crocker had raised Crerar's hackles. On July 4, 3rd Canadian Infantry Division had assaulted Carpiquet Airfield outside Caen with the Royal Winnipeg Rifles suffering heavy losses and being repulsed on the right flank, while the other units involved achieved only limited success. Since the June 6 landings, 3rd Division had been under Crocker's direct command. In a report to British Second Army's commander Lieutenant General Miles Dempsey, Crocker blamed the Carpiquet failure on Major General Rod Keller's "lack of leadership and control" and called for his firing. Dempsey took the complaint to Montgomery, stating that Keller "is not fit to command a division." Were Keller British rather than Canadian, Dempsey said, he would recommend his immediate removal. The three British generals, however, knew that only Crerar could authorize sacking a Canadian divisional commander.[3] And Crerar was unwilling to do so, largely because it was British officers calling for the sacking.

Crerar was first and foremost a Canadian nationalist. Unlike many Canadian senior officers, particularly Lieutenant General Guy Simonds, the fifty-five-year-old Crerar neither looked up to nor mimicked the British. A good number of Canadian officers had been born in Great Britain and were naturally inclined to adopt the mannerisms of their British colleagues. This was hardly surprising, as the Canadian army itself effectively mirrored that of Britain in virtually every aspect, from organization to equipment.

Simonds, for example, had been born in Bury St. Edmunds on April 23, 1903. His parents moved to Canada in 1911, settling in Victoria. Graduating from Royal Military College in 1925, Simonds entered the Canadian army and in 1936 returned to England to attend Staff College at Camberley, where he excelled. When war broke out and the first Canadians deployed to Britain, Simonds favourably impressed Montgomery, who took on the Canadian as a kind of protégé. With his pencil-thin moustache, black hair rising to a little wave at the temple, penetrating blue eyes, and tall and lean build, Simonds dressed and looked like a British officer from central casting. His sentences were clipped and directly to the point, in the manner of the best British generals and quite like Montgomery.

By comparison, Crerar had been born in Hamilton on April 28, 1888. Most of the city's population were Canadian born but of British stock. Crerar's father had emigrated from England, but his mother's roots were a mix of Irish and Pennsylvania Dutch. The family was prominent in Hamilton's upper class. After a private school education, he entered Royal Military College and graduated in 1909.[4] Commissioned into the artillery the following year, he served in the Great War and emerged from it as a Canadian Corps counter-battery staff officer. During the postwar years, his career thrived. Although he attended British Staff College and the Imperial Defence College, Crerar never adopted any British mannerisms. In 1940, he became Canada's Chief of the General Staff and was then appointed to command 1 Canadian Corps in Britain. Many British officers, Montgomery among them, found Crerar overly sensitive about Canadian independence, far too concerned about proper military protocol and dress, and excessively detail oriented. His penchant for long, intricate orders and reports particularly galled Montgomery, famous for brevity in all communications whether oral or written. Relatively short, a bit chunky, somewhat shy and introverted, Crerar did not radiate command presence. But he was tenacious in his pursuit of his own career advancement and in his defence of the Canadian army's reputation.

As a consequence, when British officers called for Keller's head, Crerar's instinct was to balk, despite his own reservations about both the man's competence and his possible drinking problem. Whether Crerar would have eventually removed Keller will never be known. On August 8, two twelve-plane formations of American bombers aiming to attack German positions in advance of the second phase of Operation Totalize bombed Canadian and Polish troops instead. The 3rd Canadian Infantry Division signals office took a direct hit that killed or wounded all inside. Standing nearby, Keller was critically wounded and his military service ended.

Crocker, meanwhile, had further soured his relationship with Crerar on the very day that he came under First Canadian Army command. Montgomery had decided 1 British Corps should seize heights overlooking Ouistreham to enable the Caen port facility to be opened, and Crerar had duly drafted a detailed operational and tactical directive to that effect. When he presented it to Crocker on July 23, the general replied that the operation was "not on." Freeing those heights from German observation, he said, accomplished nothing. There were many alternative points east of the Dives River that would serve the Germans equally well. Such an attack would likely result in five to six hundred British casualties, and Crocker "was not prepared, personally, to be responsible for carrying it out."

Furious, Crerar went to Montgomery and accused Crocker of rejecting the order "because of the fact that I am a Canadian." And the lack of "tact, nor desire to understand my views," Crerar said, demonstrated that Crocker was "temperamentally unsuited" to serve under Canadian command. He asked that Crocker be exchanged for another corps commander. Montgomery refused, scolded Crocker and told him to "quit bickering" and be "a loyal subordinate," but also cautioned Crerar not to interfere in how his corps commanders did their jobs.[5]

Crocker duly planned a more limited operation for August 8, but Montgomery subsequently stripped the corps of so much strength for other service that it was ultimately cancelled. The rift between Crocker and Crerar was never to heal. Thereafter, Crerar resisted giving I British Corps a major operational role. Instead, he generally assigned the lead role to II Canadian Corps, with Crocker's corps performing support. This was the primary reason why I British Corps had been stuck in a holding position, while II Canadian Corps had advanced from Caen to Falaise.

The other reason was the divisions that Crocker commanded. Sixth Airborne was, of course, a top-quality unit. But its very nature meant it lacked transport. Wherever it moved, the paratroops and the 4th Commando, Dutch, and Belgian brigades under its command did so mostly on foot. So speed was not feasible. While the two infantry divisions in the corps were as mobile as any others of their kind in the British army, the 51st (Highland) Infantry Division had faced sharp criticism for its performance in Normandy. So, too, had 7th Armoured Division. Both divisions had extensive combat experience, having served with Eighth Army in North Africa. Much had been expected of them in Normandy. Indeed, Montgomery had specifically included three famed Eighth Army divisions because he believed their experience would offset inadequacies likely to arise among the other entirely green divisions involved in the invasion and following campaign. Yet by mid-July, Montgomery had sent a confidential cable to Chief of the Imperial Staff General Sir Alan Brooke saying it was the "considered opinion [of] Crocker, Dempsey, and myself that 51st Division is at present not—NOT—battleworthy. It does not fight with determination and has failed in every operation it has been given to do. It cannot fight the Germans successfully." He sacked the divisional commander and gave the division to Major General Thomas "Tom" Rennie, who Montgomery was confident "would bring it up to its former fine state." As for 7th Armoured—the renowned "Desert Rats"—Montgomery and Dempsey concluded that its men had entered the campaign with a cocky attitude and then performed abominably. On August 4, its long-serving divisional commander was replaced by Major General Gerald Lloyd Verney. The new commander thought the division's problem was that its officers and men were "war weary" yet "swollen-headed . . . They greatly deserved the criticism they received."[6] Due to these command shakeups, by mid-August both divisions were still being whipped into shape, and their performance in the forthcoming advance could not be predicted.

CROCKER'S PLAN CALLED for 7th Armoured Division to advance on the town of Orbec, the Highlanders toward Lisieux, and the 49th (West Riding) Infantry Division on Pont l'Évêque. The latter town was also the aiming point for 6th Airborne Division. These objectives were but waypoints, however, with the Seine being the intended prize.[7] The country ahead of the airborne troops confined them to two roads. One hugged the coast and the other lay a short distance inland. Both ran through similar terrain that—as a later report on the Canadian Parachute Battalion in Normandy stated—consisted of "small undulating hills covered with scrub woods and thickly-hedged pasture land. The coastal road also passed through the obstacles of old beach defences of pillboxes and minefields. A series of river passages had to be carried before the final objective at the mouth of the Seine could be reached. Since these were near the sea, the rivers were wider and deeper than at crossing points farther inland, and were frequently tidal. The two main water barriers to overcome were the Dives and the Touques. The former lay in a broad marshy valley, and [its difficulty] as an obstacle was aggravated by the derelict Dives Canal. To the east, a formidable range of hills overlooked all movement across the valley. The Touques lay in a narrower valley with a flat marshy floor of watery meadows. A few minor streams ran into the sea between the Touques and the Risle. These, although not obstacles in themselves, ran through deep gorges which formed for the enemy excellent delaying positions." The total distance from the Orne to the Seine was about fifty-four miles.

For the 1 British Corps divisions to the right, the facing countryside was more suited to armoured operations, despite similar undulating ground punctuated with thick woods and "inevitable hedgerows." But there were also large areas of "open cultivated fields, pastures, and orchards." The woodlands were well scattered, and it was only at the Seine itself that a few thick forests were found.

While the forces facing 11 Canadian Corps as it emerged from the Falaise Gap operation were in what amounted to a general rout and so disorganized as to have no coherent command structure or identity, those facing 1 Corps retained some unity. They were under command of LXXXVI Corps. Holding from Troarn to the sea and largely facing the airborne troops was the 711th Infanterie-Division, then the 346th Infanterie-Division, and on the German far left the 272nd Infanterie-Division. Scattered among these three divisions were remnants of divisions shredded during the Normandy fighting. The Germans had little armour. What there was consisted of small battle groups with tanks and self-propelled guns drawn from elements of the 12th ss (Hitlerjugend) Panzer Division, 21st Panzer Division, and 1st ss Panzer Division. These armoured groups had concentrated on the left flank to hold the right side of the Falaise Gap open. As the gap was closed, they were expected to withdraw toward the Seine rather than seriously attempt to block the advance by 1 Corps.

Even without these armoured groups, however, the divisions arrayed before 1 Corps—despite being nowhere near full strength and suffering equipment and armour shortages—were "expected to be better able to put up a stiff resistance . . . as they had not been involved in severe fighting to the same extent" as those escaping through the gap.[8]

After some initial jockeying and localized actions to get the divisions positioned for the advance, Crocker attacked across the breadth of his front early on the morning of August 17. At once, it became clear that the corps advance was not to be executed with the dash and verve that had propelled General Patton's Third Army toward Paris. It was instead hobbled by two factors, both caused by 6th Airborne Division. First was the unavoidable problem that the division must advance by foot and so was slower than regular infantry using transport to close up on enemy resistance and engage it. As a result, Crocker's other divisions had to match pace with the airborne troops—even the 7th Armoured Division on the far-right flank. The second hobbling factor was the reluctance of the airborne division's Major General Richard Gale to take more casualties. A major rebuilding of the division would be required before it was again capable of airborne operations. Losing more of his veteran cadre would slow this rebuilding, so Gale ordered his brigadiers only "to advance if and when it is certain that the enemy is withdrawing."[9]

Operation Paddle, as the advance was code-named, started at 0300 hours. The 7th Armoured Division quickly got its badly understrength infantry brigade across the Dives, advancing on an easterly bearing toward Le Mesnil-Durand to tie in with 11 Canadian Corps. The 51st Highlanders faced a short delay while engineers threw two bridges across the river, but then its 153rd Brigade marched about five miles to Saint-Maclou without meeting significant resistance. The battalion covering the division's left flank, however, found the village of Moult defended by a mixed battle group of tanks, anti-tank guns, and 88-millimetre guns covering every line of approach. The 49th Division, meanwhile, advanced a battalion easily to Mezidon but was held up thereafter by blown bridges and road obstructions.[10]

As the British troops entered villages and hamlets only just abandoned by the Germans, they were met by citizens clamouring to assist them. Major Martin Lindsay, of 51st Division's 1st Battalion, Gordon Highlanders, noted that the French farmers "we passed came running out with garlands of flowers, milk and wine. They all tried to be very helpful with information about the Germans. They pointed out a farm with three soldiers in it, but *pas mechants*, they said, and we collected them on the way. Soon we were stopped by two dead horses blocking the lane, so, leaving two carriers to clear them away, I returned to give orders near the crossroads. Just as I had begun to do so an old Frenchman thrust himself upon us. There was a dead Mongolian German on his farm, he said, and was it permitted to bury him?"[11]

On the far left flank, the initial paratroop advance was carried out by the two British battalions in 3rd Brigade with the Canadian battalion remaining in reserve. But at 0800 hours, the Canadians were sent to clear a wood known as the Bois de Bures. Sweeping into the trees, the leading 'B' Company found the Germans had fled. Moving rapidly, the paratroops suddenly found themselves confronted by a maze of booby traps and mines. "They were S-mines or jumping mines," Company Sergeant Major John Kemp said. "There were three prongs that stuck out of the ground. It was in a casing. When you stepped on it, it was activated. When you took your foot off, it jumped up about three feet and exploded . . . It was full of ball bearing shot . . . and could kill or wound anyone within a radius of fifty yards." Six men were killed or wounded before the battalion emerged from the deadly wood.

The following day, the advance continued with the battalion crossing the Dives via a bridge erected by the 3rd Para Squadron, Royal Engineers. Darkness found the leading 'A' Company brushing up against the rear of German units offering virtually no resistance.[12] Heeding their divisional commander's caution, the paratroops contented themselves with maintaining contact—"driving his rearguards back, and mopping up isolated pockets of resistance as these were encountered."

This plan was partly foiled when 3rd Brigade was halted by a destroyed bridge over the canal paralleling the Dives River. Map consultations, however, showed four more bridges a short distance southward and each about four hundred yards distant from the next. The most northerly one was a railway bridge. The Canadians were ordered to seize these bridges and ascertain whether any were passable for infantry or vehicles. Zero hour for their attack was set for that evening at 2145 hours.

Forming up a little west of the village of Goustranville, 'C' Company led and by 2220 hours had seized the railway bridge. Although partially destroyed, it proved usable for infantry. The other bridges fell smoothly one after the other, with the final one taken by 'A' Company at 2350 hours. Along the way, the paratroops rooted two companies of about 150 Germans out of well-fortified positions without serious loss to themselves. 'A' Company named the most southerly bridge Canada Bridge.

SHORTLY AFTER MIDNIGHT, 9 Para Battalion crossed the canal beside the railway bridge, finding it easier to wade through four-foot-deep water than clamber across the damaged structure. They were soon driving back an enemy force estimated at about battalion strength. The following morning, August 19, the division's advance was taken over by 5th Para Brigade and the commando units, while 3rd Brigade maintained defensive positions around the bridges. Persistent enemy shelling caused several casualties and kept everybody on edge.[13]

To the left of 3rd Brigade, 1st Canadian Centaur Battery had provided heavy fire support for the 6th Air Landing Brigade since the advance's start on August 17. When this brigade forced a crossing of the Dives, the battery switched to supporting the 1st Belgian Brigade and then on August 21 the Royal Netherlands Brigade at Varaville.[14]

A major problem for the paratroops resulted from the fact that since landing in Normandy they had been engaged in largely static duty—fending off German counterattacks and mounting only limited advances of their own. Lack of activity and weeks of a tinned ration diet had taken a toll on fitness. 'B' Company's Captain Peter Griffin figured he had lost ten pounds before the advance began. By the time he and his men secured the bridges, Griffin noted that everybody had "sore feet [and] bad stomachs." By the end of one six-mile pursuit march, Griffin and his men were "on [their] knees."[15]

Such marches were, however, few. Over the ensuing days, 6th Airborne Division's average advance totalled two to three miles. The Canadian march on August 22 was typically both tedious and dangerous. As one report put it, "Their role as infantry [was] unpleasantly driven home to the parachute troops as they proceeded through pouring rain along a road that was being shelled heavily. No contact was made with the retreating enemy until the evening." Ordered to swing north and clear a resistance point on high ground at La Vallée Tantet, the Canadians came under fire from 81-millimetre mortars and self-propelled guns. Stymied, they dug in for the night. By dawn, the

Germans had melted away, and the Canadians returned to the main road to renew the advance. Their brigade was soon leapfrogged by 5th Brigade in what was to become a regular pattern, as units took their turn moving out to the sharp end.[16]

August 22 saw 1st Canadian Centaur Battery's guns firing on targets south of Deauville with the shoot directed by Major D.W. Cooper from a position on the top floor of one of the town's hotels. The pace of operations was wearing on the Centaurs, however, and five had been stranded alongside the road because of steering and brake failures. Two of the Shermans, meanwhile, had lost tracks to mines.[17]

BY THE TIME the paratroops had adapted to the routine of foot-slogging advances, 11 Canadian Corps was shaking clear of the "bottle" to join the push toward the Seine. Anticipating that the date for this was close at hand, Crerar had issued a general order on August 19 to both corps commanders. "When the liquidation of the enemy [inside the pocket] has been arranged," he wrote, 11 Canadian Corps "will then advance, with speed, along the general axis Trun—Vimoutiers—Orbec—Bernay—Elbeuf (or possibly Louviers). This advance will commence only on orders received from me."[18]

Crerar's emphasis that he was in control reflected not only his distrust of Crocker but also his dislike for Lieutenant General Guy Simonds. The roots of this mutual animosity stretched back to August 1942 and related directly to the army's first combat action in Europe— the disastrous Dieppe raid. As 1 Canadian Corps commander at the time, Crerar had played a pivotal role in having one of his divisions selected to carry out the raid. When poor weather led to the raid's cancellation, rather than accepting the outcome with relief, Crerar welcomed the proposal from Combined Operations to relaunch the raid under a different code name—swapping Rutter for Jubilee. Serving as Crerar's Brigadier General Staff, Simonds was furious. The subsequent tragedy, he believed, could have been entirely averted had Crerar refused to recommit his troops to a clearly badly planned operation. Although not above delving into palace conspiracies himself, Simonds also despised the way Crerar was constantly undercutting and cleverly backstabbing First Canadian Army's then commander, Lieutenant

General Andrew McNaughton. Simonds came to not only dislike Crerar but deeply distrust him.[19]

The relationship between the two officers worsened further when Simonds briefly came under Crerar's command in Italy. In October 1943, Crerar assumed command of 1 Canadian Corps as it deployed to Italy along with 5th Canadian Armoured Division in order to join 1st Canadian Infantry Division. The latter division had been serving in the Mediterranean Theatre since the July 10, 1943, invasion of Sicily. Simonds had commanded this division through the duration of Operation Husky and then for a short period after the Allies invaded the Italian mainland that September. A mild case of hepatitis and attendant jaundice had sidelined the then major general. Recovering about the same time that Crerar arrived in Italy, Simonds had been baffled to learn that rather than returning to the helm of his former division, he was to command 5th Armoured Division. Simonds considered the move a demotion and was only mollified when his mentor, General Bernard Montgomery, intervened to assure him that it was considered a prerequisite for corps command that a general first lead an armoured division. That Crerar had no such experience—in fact, no divisional command experience at all—was a thorn in Simonds's side, but he attributed the man's elevated rank to his having reached it before the Canadian army became engaged in divisional-level combat roles. Like his mentor, Simonds immediately donned the black tanker's beret and retained it after his brief tenure with the division ended on January 11, 1944—having been promoted to command 11 Canadian Corps in England.[20]

During the slightly less than two months that Simonds had been under Crerar's command in Italy, the two had engaged in an open, at times juvenile, feud. First there had been the caravan contretemps. When Crerar set eyes on the comfortable and efficiently designed command caravan that Simonds possessed, he immediately desired an equivalent model. As the caravan was custom-made, on December 2 Crerar dispatched an officer to measure it. Returning to his caravan to find the officer and an assistant skulking about inside with measuring tape and dirty boots, Simonds gave them fifteen minutes to clear off.

Crerar was incensed. "The least important aspect, which I will discuss first, is that this intolerant treatment of a junior officer dispatched to you on my initiative was, in effect, an indirect act, on your part, of personal discourtesy to me," he wrote in a sharply worded letter. "The much more important effect of this episode is that it tends to indicate that your nerves are over-stretched and that impulse, rather than considered judgement, may begin to affect your decisions."

Resorting also to correspondence rather than simply picking up a telephone, Simonds rejected the notion that he was under any mental strain. He also reiterated a series of disparaging comments that he accused Crerar of having made during their first meeting inside the now infamous caravan. "During the first evening's talk in my caravan you accused me of 'thinking of nothing but myself' and 'wanting to go home to bask in my newly won glory.' I thought the remarks . . . unjust and uncalled for . . . I can assure you quite honestly also, that you can rely upon my loyalty in carrying out your policies. I have worked for senior officers who I neither personally liked nor respected, but I have never had one complain of my loyalty, honesty or usefulness . . . Your letter reinforces the feeling that you are looking for an opportunity to 'take a crack' at me . . . If you cannot express full confidence in my judgement and ability to handle my command in battle, I shall have to ask to be relieved."[21]

This acrimonious letter exchange continued until Crerar escalated the matter by complaining to Montgomery and also summoning the Canadian army's chief psychiatric advisor, Dr. Fred Van Nostrand, from London to determine whether Simonds was mentally fit. Montgomery sent his Canadian liaison officer, Major Richard Malone, to tell Crerar to cease and desist. Arriving at Crerar's headquarters in the Sicilian seaside resort of Taormina, Malone conveyed Montgomery's message and then met covertly with the newly arrived doctor. The two men were old friends, and Van Nostrand was blunt about the reason he was there. When Malone and Van Nostrand joined Crerar for a private dinner, the corps commander insisted that Simonds was responding to his signals with insane replies and obviously suffering a nervous breakdown.

The next day, Malone offered Van Nostrand a lift in his plane to Simonds's headquarters on the Italian mainland. During that evening's dinner, Simonds was equally adamant that Crerar was "quite bonkers" and "sending insane signals all over the place." When Malone asked Van Nostrand what he was going to do now that both generals thought the other mad, the psychiatrist threw his hands in the air and said he was just going back to London as quickly as possible. It was time to flee the asylum.[22]

In the event, the curtain soon closed on the Italian follies. Montgomery was promoted to command British Second Army and prepare the Allies for the Normandy invasion. Simonds and Crerar soon followed—the latter replacing McNaughton as commander of First Canadian Army. The acrimonious relationships continued to prevail in England and then in Normandy. Stirred into the mix was Crerar's argumentative and distrustful relationship with Lieutenant General John Crocker.

Crerar's antipathy to both commanders was reflected in the extent of instructions and the language of his August 19th order. He admonished Simonds to begin the II Canadian Corps advance only on his order, except for "active reconnaissance in the direction indicated." During the Normandy Campaign, with the British–Canadian forces tightly controlled by Montgomery alone, Crerar had been little able to exert his authority over Simonds. Now he was making it clear who was in charge.

As for Crocker, Crerar was unhappy with I British Corps's progress to date and urged him to "press forward, seizing every favourable opportunity to do so." He was to continue along the axis running through Lisieux northeastward to Pont-Audemer beside the Risle River and then on to the Seine. The distance from the corps start line to Pont-Audemer was about forty-five miles. Crerar emphasized that Crocker must push the advance without looking beyond the resources of his corps for help. Crerar was indirectly telling Crocker that he was not to count on 2nd Tactical Air Force's Typhoon and Spitfire fighter-bombers to eliminate strongpoints. These aircraft were dedicated to harrying the retreating German main columns and supporting British Second Army in its more rapid advance to the Seine. Such support Crerar considered unneeded, as army intelligence predicted that the Germans in front of I Corps were only fighting a delaying action to cover their retreat to the Seine. Although the Germans would resist "with some determination" and could be expected to mount local counterattacks when opportunity arose, they were not going to fight Crocker's divisions to a stand. While Crerar's plan envisioned II Corps "right leading" the way to the Seine, I Corps was "not [to] hold back on that account." Where German garrisons in towns or other defensive positions appeared determined to hold, they were to be masked by "adequate forces" and "not be allowed to distract the main forces of I Brit[ish] Corps from their thrust along the axis given."[23]

ON AUGUST 21, II Canadian Corps struck out for the Seine. As 2nd Infantry Division had been in a holding position along the Dives since clearing the city of Falaise, Simonds advanced it first toward Vimoutiers and from there to Orbec.

The division moved along the main road from Falaise to Orbec with 5th Canadian Infantry Brigade leading, followed in turn by 6th Brigade and 4th Brigade. Despite the brief respite from combat while the gap was being closed, 2nd Division's infantry brigades were far from fighting fit. As was true for all the Canadian and British infantry battalions in Twenty-First Army Group, those in 2nd Division's brigades were at about half strength due to severe shortages in fresh reinforcements and soldiers returning to duty after recovering from wounds. Those soldiers still in the line were physically worn out, with many experiencing symptoms attributed to battle exhaustion. During the course of the Normandy Campaign from July through to late August, 2nd Division had evacuated more than a thousand battle exhaustion cases.[24] But there were still men in the line who suffered from listlessness, nightmares, depression, and extreme jumpiness—the malady's most common symptoms. At the end of the day, however, the infantrymen had no choice but to soldier on.

With the Germans in disarray and more interested in getting away than fighting, resistance was light. At about noon, Simonds ordered 4th Brigade to break from the column and move left to Livarot in order to free 7th British Armoured Division to direct its strength toward Lisieux.[25]

When 2nd Division's liaison officer visited the British division's headquarters to finalize details of this switchover, he was advised that the Germans facing the Canadian front consisted of small battle groups of 21st Panzer Division and 12th ss Panzer Division "fighting a rearguard action" to allow the main bodies of these divisions to escape across the Seine at Rouen. Lack of tanks and 88-millimetre guns limited the ability of these battle groups to offer effective resistance.[26]

In fact, the biggest obstacle 2nd Division faced was the continual fall of heavy, warm rain combined with deteriorating road conditions.[27] Out on point, 5th Brigade's Black Watch (Royal Highland Regiment) of Canada had three companies take a wrong turn. After wandering lost for a while, the troops were eventually set back on the proper course and renewed the lead.[28] Le Régiment de Maisonneuve (Maisies) and brigade headquarters followed the Black Watch from the start, while the Calgary Highlanders, in order to ease congestion, advanced via "a map maze of tracks and trails" that the division's 14th Canadian Hussars recce regiment had scouted the previous day. At noon, the Calgary regiment rejoined the main column. In a brief meeting, its intelligence officer, Lieutenant Stuart Moore, and that of the Black Watch agreed that both "were a little tired and unhappy because the maps had been anything but accurate and caused much worry." They soon discovered that the bridges across the Meulles River before Vimoutiers had been blown. While the rest of the brigade waited for engineers to arrive and jury-rig a bridge, the Black Watch waded across a ford and "were at once held up by a small party of enemy around the town with MGs."

When the other two battalions crossed on the bridge improvised from material left behind by the Germans, Brigadier W.J. "Bill" Megill ordered the Maisies to swing around the town's south flank to cut the enemy's line of retreat. At 2300 hours, the Black Watch reported the town cleared. One Black Watch company suffered a rough time in this short fight.[29] The regiment counted three men dead—Lieutenant Hugh Wilson Gall, twenty-year-old Sergeant William Owen Cartwright, and Corporal John Isherwood, as well as five other men wounded.[30]

Having been embroiled in a fixed fight for Vimoutiers, Megill was anxious to prevent the Germans from regrouping. So he ordered the Calgary Highlanders to get ready for a night advance. "We had curled up for the night . . . in this muddy field," Lieutenant Colonel Donald MacLauchlan recalled, "and Megill came up and said . . . we were to be sent up to pass through and take over."[31]

By 0200 hours of August 22, the battalion was on the march. "The night," Lieutenant Moore recorded in the Calgary Highlanders war diary, "was pitch black and only lightened up when Jerry dropped a few bombs in the distance and started fires. It must be a natural tendency to dislike night attacks because everyone seemed to feel a slight bit uneasy. We moved through Vimoutiers, through rubble, fire, and shell holes." Finding a passable route was no easy task and MacLauchlan put his support company commander, Captain Mark Tennant, well ahead to lead the way through the devastated town.[32] It was a duty Tennant was used to, so much so that he often boasted of being the only Calgary Highlander who "really knew how to read a map."[33]

Exiting Vimoutiers, the Calgaries entered a dense forest bordering both sides of the road. Everyone was edgy, "constantly on the alert." Moore expected that at any moment the Germans surely hidden in the woods would open fire. But "strange as it may seem," he wrote, the battalion walked through to the village of Le Boscarie, arriving there at 0530 hours "without having one enemy round fired at us." The village was quickly turned into a defensive position, while Captain Francis "Knobby" Clarke led 'B' Company toward a ridge that offered a commanding view into the valley of the Touques River, about two and a half miles to the east.[34]

The sun was rising, the earlier rain had lifted, and the day promised to be warm and fine as Clarke's men trudged wearily along the road to the ridge. There had been little sleep in the past thirty-six hours, and as they started climbing, the heat sapped what scant energy the men had left. The road climbed steeply and directly toward the ridge top. On the other side it bent first to the south and then east for a gentler descent into the valley where the Touques, a small stream, flowed from south to north. If the Calgaries had not been at war and so tired, the walk would have seemed pleasant, passing as it did through farmland, orchards, and small copses. Gaining the crest, the soldiers glimpsed through the trees, which were more prevalent on this side of the ridge, a bridge to the left that was about half a mile distant. They also saw German engineers preparing the bridge for demolition. Close by was a tank and an 88-millimetre gun.

Thirty-one-year-old Clarke had been wounded on July 20 and had only recently returned to the battalion—taking over command of 'B' Company when Captain Edgar "Wynn" Lasher was wounded on August 13. If ever there was a reluctant soldier, it was Clarke. War found him working in the Turner Valley oil industry, southwest of Calgary. Determined to do his duty, he sought to avoid army service by enlisting in the navy. Put on a waiting list, Clarke decided in the meantime to join the Highlanders just to get some militia training. After several weeks and with no word from the navy, he volunteered for the air force, only to be rejected because he was married and had three children. When the Calgaries offered to submit his name for officer selection, Clarke reluctantly accepted and was soon posted to the battalion overseas.

Determined to prevent the Germans from destroying the bridge, he split the company—which had lost so many men it numbered barely fifty—into two groups. While half would follow him in outflanking the Germans to the south, the others were to advance up the road and use their Bren guns to cover his group's advance. Nobody was to start shooting until the Germans detected them, but that happened in mere moments. Several machine guns and the 88-millimetre gun all opened up. The engineers, however, briefly withdrew from the bridge before returning with the tank trundling along in support.

By this time, Clarke and his section had waded the stream to take up a position above the bridge and out of sight of the Germans. The Calgaries on the road had taken cover and were rattling Bren gun rounds off the tank's armour. Ricocheting bullets scattered the engineers as Clarke's men closed in and hit the tank with a round from a PIAT anti-tank launcher. That ended the fight, the Germans suddenly giving up. 'B' Company rounded up two officers, fifty-four other ranks, several vehicles, and a battered Cadillac LaSalle converted oddly into an ad hoc pickup truck. 'B' Company did not have it all their way. One man, nineteen-year-old Private Norman Peddie, was dead and two others wounded. But the Calgaries had won a vital bridge.[35]

3

In Extremely High Fettle

O N AUGUST 22, despite Lieutenant General Harry Crerar's instruction three days earlier that 1 British Corps was to bypass
any strong German garrisons encountered, Lieutenant General John
Crocker allowed both 7th Armoured Division and 51st (Highland)
Infantry Division to get drawn into hard fighting for Lisieux. All across
the 1 Corps front, the focus that day was on winning bridgeheads
across the Touques River. Crocker, however, pointedly emphasized
the primary importance of "taking Lisieux," while Crerar had directed
him to only advance his main axis to Lisieux and then onward about
twenty miles to Pont-Audemer at the Risle River. Crocker, it seemed,
had overestimated Lisieux's importance.

The process whereby Crocker's troops were drawn into a fight for
Lisieux started simply enough in the morning with the 11th Hussars—
the corps's reconnaissance regiment—probing along roads to the
east and southeast of Lisieux and encountering roadblocks covered
by 711th Infanterie-Division troops armed with heavy machine guns
and Panzerfaust anti-tank weapons. The outgunned armoured cars
tried to dodge around the roadblocks by crossing the Orbiquet River
and gaining high ground east of Lisieux. Heavy fire from across the
river blocked this effort, and 7th Armoured Division's Major General
Gerald Lloyd Verney decided that Lisieux "was to require some hard
fighting before its capture."

By mid-afternoon, the division's 22nd Armoured Brigade had one regiment south of the town, another inside, and one west of the river. All three tank regiments were supported by an infantry battalion of the division's 131st Infantry Brigade. Now the 51st Highlanders joined the fray, attempting to encircle Lisieux from the west and north. As night fell, 7th Armoured Division handed the fight to the Highlanders, withdrew to the west, and managed to bridge the Touques in order to renew the corps advance.

At this point, Crocker could have masked and isolated the Germans in Lisieux in accordance with Crerar's instructions. Instead, he decided to have the Highlanders eliminate them. Meanwhile, the 49th (West Riding) Infantry Division, 7th Armoured Division, and 6th Airborne Division would continue to the Risle in the morning, with 6th Airborne Division also advancing to where this tributary spilled into the estuary of the Seine at the village of Berville-sur-Mer.

By the time the Highlanders took over the fight, Lisieux had been assigned a significantly more important role by First Canadian Army headquarters quartermaster staff. Currently, all the army's supplies were assembled into truckloads at Bayeux and then transported to the advancing troops. Bayeux was designated No. 1 Canadian Army Roadhead. Looking for a closer site, the quartermasters had now designated Lisieux on their staff maps as No. 3 Canadian Army Roadhead. By establishing an intermediary terminal where material could be amassed for transportation forward as the leading troops crossed the Seine, they hoped to relieve some of the supply issues the army increasingly faced.

Inadvertently, Crocker's decision to fight the garrison at Lisieux now bore some level of official sanction from army headquarters. Already badly understrength and exhausted by previous operations, the 51st Highlanders became entangled in a "severe" fight that intensified as they drove the Germans slowly back through the town for a short last-ditch stand on its eastern outskirts toward the end of August 24. Battle over, Crocker directed the division into reserve for two days of "much needed rest and reorganization."

No sooner was Lisieux cleared than engineers started transforming it into the planned supply centre. Bulldozers cleared building rubble from the streets, and bridges were replaced so that troops and supplies could move from west to east across the Touques and nearby Orbiquet Rivers. By end of the day on August 25, Lisieux was an operational hub that perhaps justified the casualties required to take it by storm.[1]

The condition of Major Martin Lindsay's 1st Gordon Highlanders mirrored the rest. Since August 8, Lindsay reported, the battalion had lost fifteen officers and about 150 other ranks. "Being understrength before we started [the Lisieux battle], we are now very short-handed indeed. In fact we have only one subaltern, Williams, left. The remnants of the four rifle companies are now amalgamated into one composite company. I have brought up the Pipe Band, the pioneers, and as many drivers and clerks as could be scraped together . . . to thicken us up."[2]

While the Highlanders deserved the break, their absence necessarily slowed the 1 British Corps's pace. The loss required the 49th and 7th Divisions to spread out across a wider front. This particularly challenged the armoured division, with its single weak infantry brigade composed of three battalions that were as worn and tired as any in the Highland division.

Consequently, as one report put it, when the rest of the corps moved north beyond Lisieux on the morning of August 23, "the Corps' plan [proved] somewhat ambitious." The 7th Armoured Division met unexpectedly stiff resistance on the corps's eastern flank. In its sector, 49th Division fared better—securing two crossings over the Touques at Le Bresuil-en-Auge and Ouilly-le-Vicomte. On the far left, 6th Airborne Division's 5th Brigade established a bridgehead over this river at Pont L'Évêque, but was unable to expand it farther because the Germans had dug in behind a paralleling raised railway bed. Southeast of the village of Touques, meanwhile, the 6th Air Landing Brigade also crossed the river.[3] Having on August 22 advanced fourteen miles—the first five happily loaded aboard trucks—1st Canadian Parachute Battalion and the other two 3rd Parachute Brigade battalions enjoyed a rest period. The Canadians were in the village of Gatien, from which they had at day's end driven off a German self-propelled gun that offered the only opposition encountered during their day's advance. After firing eight wildly inaccurate rounds, the SPG had slunk away into the gathering night.[4]

AUGUST 24 DAWNED with the corps expecting continued stiff resistance. But by midday, it began to look like LXXXVI Corps was abandoning the fight and conducting a general withdrawal behind the Seine. The 6th Airborne Division soon reported that the Germans had quit their strongpoint behind the railway at Pont L'Évêque, and all ground immediately across the Touques west of this village to the sea appeared clear of enemy. Before the end of the day, 6th Air Landing Brigade had patrols within one thousand yards of Honfleur, at the mouth of the Seine. To the right, 49th Division encountered almost no opposition that day. On the corps's right flank, 7th Armoured Division had established a broad front fourteen miles wide that stretched to the right from Lieurey to Brionne and was fifteen to twenty miles north of Lisieux. Brionne stood alongside the Risle River.

The plan for the morrow was to advance the entire corps across the Risle with its divisions converging on Pont-Audemer. Moving well ahead of the main body of the 49th Division on August 25, its recce regiment met resistance only as it closed on this town.[5] About the same time, 'B' Squadron of 7th Armoured Division's recce regiment, the 8th King's Royal Irish Hussars, also approached the town from the south. Travelling with the squadron was the FFI's Lieutenant Henri Belmont, who was hoping to join a strong force of resistance fighters reportedly mustered inside Pont-Audemer. The French officer rode with No. 2 and No. 5 Troops, which followed some rough tracks "to infiltrate [the town] unnoticed." The effort was foiled at 1100 hours by stiff resistance from Germans well dug in amid the "very thick" country. Directing artillery fire onto the German positions failed to break this "proper line," so the Hussars withdrew.

The squadron's No. 4 Troop, meanwhile, approached the town by the main road until blocked by a Tiger tank firing at a range of four hundred yards. Ahead, two "over bold" armoured cars of 49th Division's recce unit were brewed up by the Tiger's 88-millimetre gun. Told that Pont-Audemer was now within 49th Division's boundary, the Hussars happily left them to tackle the Tiger and shifted eastward toward Pont Authou. By 1300 hours, every turn the Hussars took brought them into an area that the 49th Division claimed was theirs, causing them to promptly demand that 'B' Squadron "get the hell out of it." This led the squadron's diarist to comment that "sometimes one wonders who one is fighting!"[6]

Across 1 British Corps's front, the situation was confusingly fluid. All three advancing divisions made steady progress, with most opposition coming from well-sited machine guns and anti-tank guns covering the roads. The 11th Hussars corps recce unit gained the most ground, managing to put a squadron over the Risle at Pont Authou. Another of its squadrons had also reached St. Philbert-sur-Boissey, about five miles northeast of Brionne. Following close behind the armoured cars, the regiments of 22nd Armoured Brigade reached a point just west of the river.

The 49th Division, meanwhile, was unable to muster sufficient strength to take Pont-Audemer, but expected to put in a strong attack the following morning. On the right flank, 6th Airborne's 5th Parachute Brigade also closed on the town. The paratroops had faced tougher resistance than the rest of the corps because as every river approached the coast it widened, providing a better defensive position for the Germans on the opposite bank. Consequently, most of 6th Airborne Division was only halfway between the Touques and the Risle by nightfall. Still, advancing along the coastal road, 6th Air Landing Brigade and 1st Belgian Infantry Brigade reached and secured Honfleur—the first 1 British Corps units to reach the Seine.[7]

By August 24, when 1st Canadian Centaur Battery crossed the Touques, its total armoured strength consisted of one Sherman, two Centaurs, and a Cromwell tank borrowed from the 49th (West Riding) Infantry Division's recce regiment. All the other Centaurs and Shermans had been disabled by breakdowns.[8]

Advancing in the division's centre, 1st Canadian Parachute Battalion and the two British battalions of 3rd Brigade had advanced during the morning of August 25 to Beuzeville, about six and a half miles south of the Seine. The Canadians marched hard from Saint-Gatien-des-Bois along a road running southeast to Saint-Benoît-d'Hébertot before swinging northeastward to approach Beuzeville—covering about seven miles in two hours. Arriving on its outskirts at 1000 hours, they found 8 Para Battalion and 9 Para Battalion locked in a fight. With 8 Para attacking from the south, and 9 Para the northwest, the Canadians stood down until the town was reported cleared in the late afternoon.[9] Having managed to repair a good number of its self-propelled guns, 1st Canadian Centaur Battery provided effective support to 3rd Brigade, with each operational gun firing sixty rounds.[10]

At 1900 hours, the Canadians skirted Beuzeville's west flank and, after leaving the main road, marched north along a series of tracks and footpaths that meandered through woods and across open fields by such a circuitous route that at nightfall they were still four miles short of their objective—a large farm called Maison Mauger. Instead of groping onward, the men were told to stand down for four hours.[11] Having encountered no Germans, the men relaxed. The weather was pleasant and the grass soft. As everyone stretched out for some well-deserved sleep, Sergeant Dan Hartigan heard a "little pop on the edge of a small wood, not more than two hundred feet away." It was such a "subdued 'pop,'" hardly any of the men noticed. So when the incoming hiss of a rifle grenade came, it was too late for anybody to dive for cover. The round, fired by a German straggler, detonated next to Sergeant Mosher Colin McPhee. The sergeant, who had seemingly proved himself immortal during the hard fighting that the battalion had seen since jumping into Normandy, was instantly killed by what his close friend Hartigan considered a "god-damned fluke."[12] McPhee was the last Canadian paratrooper to die in France.

Setting off in the pre-dawn light, the Canadians reached Maison Mauger at 0740 hours on August 26, encountering not a single German. August 26 marked the end of 6th Airborne Division's operations. By nightfall, its formations were stretched along the Risle from Pont-Audemer to its junction with the Seine at Berville-sur-Mer and then along the Seine itself to Honfleur.[13] Since beginning the advance to the Seine, the division had cleared about four hundred square miles of territory and captured more than a thousand Germans. The Canadians counted fourteen killed and twenty-four wounded in the effort. Over the past eighty-one days of fighting in Normandy, however, the battalion had suffered heavily. Of 547 men who had jumped into Normandy, only 197 were still standing. They had entered combat with no previous battlefield experience and had been hardened into seasoned and reliable veterans who would form the backbone of the battalion's rebuilding and preparation for a return to airborne operations. "Don't think the men in our battalion aren't the best in the world," 'B' Company's Captain Peter Griffin wrote without a shade of humility.

For his part, 6th Airborne Division's Major General Richard Gale wrote to Lieutenant General Harry Crerar that it "was a great day for us when the Canadian government deemed it fit to place 1st Canadian Parachute Battalion under my command. You know how magnificently that Battalion has done." He added that it was also a great day for the division when it came under First Canadian Army command.

In a special order of the day on August 26, Gale thanked his troops for their service. "I congratulate you on your greatest achievements, on your stamina, on your skill and your grim determination. The motto of the 6th Airborne Division is 'Go To It' . . . You have gone to it and right splendidly, you have done it."[14]

August 26 also marked the last day of 1st Canadian Centaur Battery's active operations. First, it carried the Dutch Princess Irene Brigade on its guns through to their objective and then provided fire support for the 49th Division's recce regiment and a section of Belgian armoured cars clearing Pont-Audemer. As the Airborne Division stood down, so did the battery. On August 29, orders were received disbanding the unit effective the next day. By September 2, all its personnel had been reassigned and the battery ceased to exist. First Canadian Army's artillery commander, Brigadier H.O. Brownfield, felt that the battery "performed a very useful purpose, and . . . was able to keep up with the advance of 6 Airborne Div[ision] and give useful fire support."[15]

The paratroops, meanwhile, were in the midst of returning to England. By September 4, 1st Canadian Parachute Battalion reached the Normandy beaches to take a ship across the channel. Two days later, the unit sailed.[16]

ON AUGUST 23, as 1 British Corps was clearing Lisieux and gaining the Risle, Lieutenant General Guy Simonds started 11 Canadian Corps on a pursuit to the Seine. This entailed a rapid expansion beyond the previous day's eastward thrust by 2nd Infantry Division, whose 5th Infantry Brigade had managed to wrest control of Vimoutiers from the Germans in a stiff fight and then chase them to the Meulles River. The division now advanced toward Orbec. In the corps centre, Major General Dan Spry's 3rd Infantry Division aimed to pass through Orbec and on to Elbeuf—on the southern bank of the Seine near Rouen. Forming on 3rd Division's right, 4th Armoured Division was bound for the Seine at Pont de l'Arche via an axis running through Broglie to Bernay.[17]

Less than forty-eight hours earlier, 4th Armoured Division had got a new commander when Simonds unceremoniously sacked Major General George Kitching, who had led it through Normandy. Simonds blamed Kitching for the division's failure to more quickly close the Falaise Gap. Instead of ruthlessly sealing the gap whatever the costs, Kitching, Simonds believed, had allowed his subordinates to proceed with undue caution, in order to avoid heavier casualties. Some divisional officers thought Kitching was the scapegoat for an overall failure of command leadership running up past Simonds to Montgomery. Their opinion was based on Montgomery's August 14 decision to keep British Second Army's divisions trailing the retreating Germans through the pocket instead of sending one to reinforce the badly worn First Canadian Army. The addition of a single British division would have led to an earlier closing of the gap. It was a critical oversight on Montgomery's part, but one likely influenced by the fact that neither Simonds nor Crerar had called for reinforcement. Whatever the cause, an opportunity was lost.[18]

Captain Ernest Sirluck, an Argyll and Sutherland Highlander posted to divisional headquarters as its intelligence officer, had mixed feelings about Kitching's firing. He realized the writing had been on the wall when Kitching phoned him at 0300 hours on August 21 inquiring where the leading elements of his division were. Kitching's "voice," Sirluck said later, "went way down. I mean, he was obviously very depressed, and [he] phoned again at about four and asked whether we had [made it] to such-and-such place. And I had to tell him that at last report we had not. And he wanted to know when the last report was. And I said I had been in touch about ten minutes earlier." There was no hope that the units were more advanced. Shortly after dawn, Simonds told Kitching he was out and 7th Infantry Brigade's Major General Harry Foster was in.

Thinking it over afterwards, Sirluck had to agree that "Kitching was not ruthless enough . . . But, if you ask yourself, 'Had a more ruthless man been in Kitching's position, would he have got more out of the troops?' I don't think the answer is as clear as it might be." Sirluck believed that, with Falaise, Chambois, and St. Lambert-sur-Dives taken and surrounded by the carnage of seemingly thousands of dead Germans and hordes of prisoners, the division's troops had considered the battle won. "The fact that some Germans were escaping seemed to be less significant than that they should themselves remain alive."

Sirluck had been less impressed by Montgomery's public-schoolboy references to "corking the bottle" and other such metaphors coming down from on high. He particularly disliked being wished "good hunting" when what was being discussed was men killing and being killed. None of this struck Sirluck as reflecting a Canadian attitude. And there was the simple fact that the division was badly beaten up, its men reeling with exhaustion and offered no respite.

He also admitted that the division's inexperience handicapped its performance. "We were not as yet a seasoned formation. We sure as hell did not know much about keeping good communications contact, either at the infantry level—certainly not at the tank level—or even at the formation level. There is enough blame to go around . . . Was Kitching a bad commander? No. If he . . . hadn't been in such a key position with so little experience with such a green division he might have done better. But did he do well enough? No. No, he didn't."[19]

Kitching's forty-four-year-old replacement, having just led 7th Brigade through the campaign, had performed admirably and was well regarded by subordinates and superiors. Foster and Kitching had each been tagged for promotion to brigade-level command in a January 14, 1943, I Canadian Corps report. Both were permanent force officers with no experience in commanding armoured formations before being given 4th Division.

The two were good friends, and Foster hated being promoted at Kitching's expense. What Foster quickly realized was that, whatever Kitching's failings might be, he had built a superb headquarters staff. This was not surprising, for Kitching had served in several staff postings and performed so well in those capacities that when Simonds was tipped for II Corps command, he had insisted on bringing Kitching along as his general staff officer. Foster had no intention of fiddling with what Kitching had built. Whereas Kitching kept meticulous paperwork—somewhat in Crerar's manner—Foster confessed to hating "paperwork and administration. I'm not worth a shit at it. It's up to you to run [the headquarters]," he told Lieutenant Colonel J.W. Proctor, the division's assistant adjutant and quartermaster general. "I won't interfere. I'll keep you in the picture, but you run it. Understood?" Foster would see to the fighting, while his staff made sure the tools were at hand.

As Foster had no armoured command experience, Simonds urged him to lean on twenty-six-year-old and newly promoted 4th Canadian Armoured Brigade's Brigadier Robert Moncel. He was considered one of the Canadian Army's armoured corps's rising stars. It had been Kitching who, again showing astute judgment, had convinced Simonds to promote Moncel from a corps staff job to brigade command after Brigadier Leslie Booth was killed on August 14. The division's 10th Infantry Brigade was under the competent command of Brigadier Jim Jefferson, who had led the Loyal Edmonton Regiment in Italy through Sicily and the street battle in Ortona. Jefferson had taken command of the brigade before its deployment to Normandy.

Although the division's infantry battalions were badly depleted and worn down, the armoured regiments were far worse off. The British Columbia Regiment had faced almost complete destruction near Point 140 on August 9, when it lost 47 tanks and 112 crew. The other two regiments—Governor General's Horse Guards and Canadian Grenadier Guards—had emerged from the gap closure reduced to little more than single-squadron strength rather than the normal three.

Quickly reorganizing, Foster was ready to go by 1800 hours on August 22. While the Canadian advance centred on 2nd and 3rd Infantry Divisions staying alongside 1 British Corps, 4th Armoured Division would be out on the far-right flank. Should the infantry divisions meet stiff opposition, Foster would sweep in "to dislodge the enemy." Seeking maximum mobility, Foster had his tank regiments lead.[20] Each armoured regiment would advance with one company of the Lake Superior Regiment (Motor) alongside.[21] This was the division's single infantry battalion equipped with half-tracked armoured personnel carriers and Bren carriers, which enabled it to easily match the pace of tanks. Although nominally attached to divisional headquarters, the Superiors normally worked with the armour, with one company attached to each tank regiment.

ACROSS THE ENTIRE Canadian front, Simonds had instructed that the armoured cars of the 12th Manitoba Dragoons, the recce regiment directly under corps headquarters command, be well out in front. Lieutenant Colonel James Alan "Jim" Roberts, the Dragoon commander, was not surprised by the breadth of action he was to undertake. Roberts believed Simonds to be "one of the very few Canadian senior officers who understood the role and proper employment of an armoured car regiment." He was excited to learn the regiment was to exploit out of Vimoutiers "and proceed at fullest possible speed to the . . . Seine . . . We were ordered to bypass defensive positions taken up by the German rearguard and not to bother with prisoners, simply send them marching to the rear after disarming. Speed was of the essence in order to take advantage of the demoralized condition of the German forces . . . I accepted these orders and our task with satisfaction. For the first time since D-Day there was an opportunity to operate as our cavalry predecessors had once done."

Contacting his squadron commanders by wireless, Roberts arranged a morning meeting at Vimoutiers for what he figured would be "the beginning of the greatest days of 12th Manitoba Dragoons." With command armoured cars lined up along a roadside on the town's outskirts, Roberts sat on a large rock and held a hurried Orders Group. As the crow flies, Elbeuf was only thirty-seven miles away. But it was much farther by the winding roads or even available cross-country routes. "I passed on to the squadron commanders the corps instructions to cover a wide front and to report any enemy pockets of resistance but to bypass them and keep up the speed. We discussed the anticipated difficulties of shallow river crossings and I urged them to use their initiative and the steel trackways that each troop carried strapped on the side of one of the armoured cars." That the rivers would be hard to cross and all bridges likely blown was a given just to be overcome. "A combination of speed and initiative should do the trick. A small convoy of lorries would follow the fighting squadrons on the centre line to keep ammunition and supplies nearby."

As his squadron commanders saddled up and roared away in their armoured chargers, Roberts walked behind a large tree to urinate in private and immediately "found I shared [it] with a smart-looking German officer, sitting on the ground with an automatic pistol in his hand. I instinctively reached for my own pistol but dropped my hand when I realized that my tree-sharing companion was dead, shot by his own automatic. It seemed to signify what must have been the frustration and despair of the German army, and particularly of intelligent officers, at the turn of events now taking place and the obvious understanding that the war was turning against them."22

The Dragoons considered themselves more than capable of the assigned task. Until now, they had played only a limited combat role because there had been no room in the tight confines of the Normandy battleground for far-flung operations. As often as not, they had ended up fighting as infantry in short, sharp actions where casualties had been light. Those losses had been made up a few days earlier by the arrival of fifteen officers and sixty-five other ranks. Most of these were returning members of the regiment, which meant "all vacancies [were filled] with the best of operators and seasoned veterans. In a nutshell," as one regimental report put it, the Dragoons were "battle worthy before they started their own task of recce. Equipment was almost complete and in perfect shape . . . The regiment . . . was in extremely high fettle . . . The two months of infantry training had taught them the other side of the picture, they had learned when to duck and when not to. They had also learned that one gets less casualties by inflicting casualties."

Just before he set off, Roberts received more detailed orders from the 3rd Infantry Division commander. Just thirty-one, Dan Spry was the youngest general in all the western Allied forces. He had taken command on August 18 after Major General Rod Keller's critical wounding. Tall, and spare almost to the point of gauntness, Spry was an avid follower of the Boy Scout movement. Friends and detractors both believed the man modelled his behaviour on Boy Scout values. Although he had not seen action in Normandy, Spry had faced combat in Sicily with the Royal Canadian Regiment and was in command of that battalion when it crossed over to mainland Italy. Promoted to brigadier on December 18, 1943, he led 1st Infantry Brigade through most of the fight for Ortona. On July 13, 1944, he arrived in Britain to command 12th Infantry Brigade. His job was to regroup within it several Canadian units serving in Italy but due to be transferred to the northwest Europe front. It was from there that Crerar had plucked him to take over 3rd Division.[23] The advance to the Seine would be his proving ground. Like Simonds, Spry wanted Roberts to be bold—get to the Seine at Rouen quickly and win his division a bridge. Then the Dragoons would press onward to the Somme near Abbeville and get a bridge there as well. This would position the Dragoons to cut off the line of escape for the large German garrisons at Boulogne and Calais and enable the following 3rd Division to "destroy [these] garrisons."

Spry's division would follow the armoured cars in tried and true British–Canadian fashion, with one brigade held in reserve while the other two leapfrogged each other forward. His advance would be made "at the greatest possible speed," with brigades "being lifted on any and every available means of transport." And always the Dragoons would be charging forward well to the front.[24]

Having first to cross the Touques, the charge's start was less than glorious. Finding the armoured car winches insufficiently powerful to drag the heavy Staghounds through the soft riverbed, the Dragoons resorted to rounding up stray German horses. These, along with every available Dragoon pulling for all his worth, managed to lug the vehicles across the river. From there they dashed to Le Sap. 'D' Squadron was already there, having returned, as promised, to the old woman who had pledged to oversee the town's defence the previous day. The Dragoons pushed forward on a line extending across to Monnai. "There was little opposition . . . only scattered rifle fire . . . quickly dealt with by a blast from our machineguns," Roberts later wrote. "We did, however, pick up several odd-looking types in bedraggled French farm clothing who turned out to be American fighter pilots, shot down in previous weeks." Although happy to be liberated, the pilots refused transport to the rear because they wanted to have dinner one last time with the farmers who had risked their families' lives hiding them.[25]

Hoping to barrel straight up Route Nationale 138 to Bernay, the Dragoons were quickly brought to a sharp halt when Major Gerry Price's 'D' Squadron came under fire from an 88-millimetre gun hidden in a thick wood alongside the road. Well out front of the rest of the squadron, Lieutenant Mike Davis's Staghound was disabled by the first round. The five-man crew bailed out just before the German gunners punched several more rounds through the car. Davis was wounded in the back. With their light armour and only a 37-millimetre gun for main armament, the Staghounds were severely outgunned by the 88 and unable to manoeuvre around it.[26] 'D' Squadron was effectively blocked and Roberts—whose headquarters section had been in trail behind—sought to keep the advance going by radioing the squadrons on either flank to keep pushing forward. He and 'D' Squadron would catch up when able.

Roberts called for help, which resulted in the arrival of the British Columbia Regiment's 'C' Squadron from 4th Armoured Division. Equally unable to manoeuvre to take on the gun, the BCR Shermans tried to overwhelm it with a head-on charge. Within minutes, five Shermans were knocked out and 'C' Squadron withdrew. When 'B' Squadron tried the same blunt tactic, another two tanks were put out of action by the skilful fire of the 88-millimetre gun crew. Having had two men killed and seven wounded, the BCR tankers backed off. Already well below normal squadron strength, 'C' Squadron had so few tanks remaining that these were used to bulk up the regiment's other two squadrons.[27]

When it became clear that only infantry could eliminate the gun, the Algonquin Regiment was ordered to reinforce the tankers. It was dusk by the time the regiment's 'D' Company teed up an attack with artillery and mortars laying down covering fire.[28] By the time the company reached the wood, the German gunners had withdrawn—somehow taking the gun with them.[29]

Moving on a short distance, the Dragoon's 'D' Squadron and Roberts's headquarters section settled in for the night. For the rest of the regiment, the anticipated charge had also been frustrated. On the right, 'A' Squadron's No. 3 Troop had led. As Lieutenant Thomas "Tommy" Taylor's Staghound rumbled into the village of Montreuil

L'Argille, the troop commander spotted some infantry standing beside a German staff car. Taylor opened fire with both the main gun and the Staghound's .30-calibre machine guns. Having scattered the infantry and shredded the car, Taylor saw that the troop's much lighter and nimbler scout car was under fire from an 88-millimetre gun. Rushing to its aid, Taylor "stopped and was only stationary about one minute" when the German gun slammed a round into his Staghound. The armoured car burst into flames and only the co-driver managed to escape—everybody else was killed. In his day's end entry, the regiment's war diarist declared Taylor's death "a great loss. He was an able troop leader doing an outstanding job. He was a fine man and will be missed by his men and his brother officers a great deal." Taylor was twenty-nine and left a wife in Winnipeg.

On the left flank, meanwhile, 'B' Squadron had been stymied by a blown bridge and fire from an anti-tank gun hidden on the other side of a stream. Learning of the problems his other squadrons had encountered, Roberts called for a stop. With an obvious enemy line facing each squadron, he considered "our job . . . completed" for the night. It was time for the infantry and tanks to clear the way. The regiment's diarist considered the "move today . . . most successful . . . but not followed up properly or quickly enough, making it possible for the Hun to get further away than ever. Orders were given at odd times through the night and the general plan is 'A' Squadron on the right as yesterday and the centre line covered by 'B' Squadron. 'C' and 'D' Squadrons will be in reserve. Possibly tomorrow will take us beyond Bernay and towards the Seine River."[30]

Shortly before nightfall, 4th Armoured Division's motorized infantry—the Lake Superior Regiment—and tanks of the Governor General's Foot Guards arrived. At the cost of two tanks knocked out, the German blocking position was soon eliminated.[31] The 12th Manitoba Dragoons' war diarist was little impressed by the 4th Division effort. "Their late arrival on the scene made the job easy for their patrols as the enemy had, like the Arab, silently folded his tent and faded into the night." At least, he concluded, the way was now clear for the Dragoons to renew the charge in the morning.[32]

4

On to the Seine

THE 12TH MANITOBA Dragoons started moving at dawn on August 24, and the "advance . . . was very fast and uneventful." The Germans had used the night to break contact and withdraw "across the Seine River at speed and leaving only an occasional party to delay us," wrote the regiment's war diarist.

Although the Dragoons had hoped to keep racing along, Lieutenant Colonel Jim Roberts soon realized he and his staff had made an administrative blunder. Through July and August, the regiment's armoured cars had never fired their entire ammunition allotment in a single day despite some relatively heavy fighting in a quasi-infantry role. This led the administration to assume that when back in reconnaissance mode, the regiment would need even less ammunition. To free the squadrons for a full-tilt run, they hence decided to "dump" most of the ammunition that would normally be carried close behind by support trucks. The trucks were returned to the rear echelon area with the understanding that some would infrequently shuttle ammunition forward as needed. Now, however, they realized the rear echelon was so far behind that the trucks were unable to catch up during a single day. Meanwhile, the scout troops of each squadron were burning through their allotted machine-gun ammunition, and even the Staghounds were firing about twenty rounds per day of anti-tank shells. Solving the problem required establishing waypoints between the slow-moving rear echelon and the increasingly distant squadrons, which still did not entirely rectify the shortages. "The results of these errors of judgement," one Dragoon report concluded, "although remedied before causing ill effects of operational efficiency, did cause a great deal of consternation and worry."[1]

Roberts and his headquarters section were also left far behind his fast and far-ranging squadrons. After spending much of the day jockeying around the slower moving trucks carrying infantry regiments toward Bernay, Roberts finally managed to shake free and soon arrived at the Château de Menneval. The Dragoons had identified this château a couple of miles northeast of Bernay as ideal for an overnight headquarters. As the armoured cars rolled into the courtyard, about a dozen Germans burst through the front door. They were quickly rounded up. "The residents were very put out to think that we would point our guns at these men," the diarist noted. "We did not receive a warm reception from these people at all and they gave us the impression that they were definitely pro-German. As further proof of our beliefs, they shook hands and waved as we sent the prisoners back."[2]

For Captain Robert Spencer of the division's 15th Field Regiment, August 24 was a relief. The road the artillerymen had travelled the previous day had been a charnel house and he had watched with horror as his trucks and gun tractors had crept past teams of engineers, who "with rags tied around their faces . . . drag[ged] the rotting horses out of the way. Bulldozers attacked the broken, battered, burned-out rubble that was once matériel of war, and cleared a narrow track through which . . . 4th Division could pass. All morning the column inched slowly forward. As the sun grew warm the smell of smouldering vehicles and decaying flesh, both horse and human, became unbearable. The sight of dead enemy is an easy one for troops hardened to battle, but there is something extremely distasteful in the sight of dead horses lying with their bloated bellies upturned by the side of the road."

So narrow was the road that a bulldozer had preceded the convoy, carving a path through the destruction. Back in the Falaise Pocket the slaughter had been the work of both army and air force. "Here, however, the treatment meted out to the fleeing remnants was the work of the air force alone. Tightly packed columns of lorries, staff cars, tanks, guns, and carts had been caught in the deadly rain of destruction that dropped from the skies. It is not difficult to imagine the scene: one vehicle on fire, and blocking the road; terrified horses screaming and desperate men shouting as vehicle after vehicle lumbered to a halt; then the planes swooping low in the sunlight, raking the column with machine-gun and cannon fire. Some men would escape but not a vehicle could get out of that tangled burning mass of shapeless debris. The Battle of the Gap destroyed the German army in Normandy, but the destruction wrought on these narrow roads ended forever any hope the beaten enemy may have held of making a stand on the banks of the Seine with the salvaged remnants of men and equipment."[3]

On August 24, Spencer's artillery regiment joined a flying column formed around 'B' Company of the motorized Lake Superior Regiment and named Keane Force after its commander, Lieutenant Colonel Robert Keane. The British Columbia Regiment provided the column's armoured punch.[4] Following close behind were elements of the Argyll and Sutherland Highlanders, engineers, a 5th Anti-Tank Regiment battery, and the 15th Field Regiment. Keane Force was created to avoid the advance being blocked as it had been the day before. If the Germans offered resistance that "could not be brushed aside by the tanks and the Lake Superiors, then the Argylls would be available to add the necessary punch," with the Governor General's Foot Guards at the column's rear able to break out across country to flank the opposition and hit it from behind.[5]

Tucked into the column's centre, 15th Field Regiment's Captain Spencer had grimly noted the two knocked-out Foot Guards Shermans as Keane Force rolled past the previous day's blocking position and headed for Broglie. Before them was a fine, level highway along which the column moved quickly.[6] Unable or unwilling to offer battle, the Germans had left behind "all manner of delaying devices, mines, booby traps, demolitions and felled trees," wrote the Superior's historian. "None offered any serious problems and were quickly cleared away by engineers. At Broglie . . . the column was held up while No. 3 Troop of the 8th Field Company took over, and bulldozers . . . cleared the road towards Bernay."[7]

It was noon when 15th Field Regiment ground through Broglie, and by mid-afternoon the gunners had entered Bernay. "The reception which the troops had been receiving all along the route was outdone by the people of Bernay, who lined the road and offered flowers, cider, wine and calvados to the grinning soldiers, who were not accustomed to the new role of hero-liberators. The town was delirious with joy for the Germans had left there only that morning, and liberty and freedom was a new cup on their lips. FFI fighters were everywhere, proudly sporting the weapons they had so long concealed. Already traitors were being rounded up and marched through the streets, and a number of women who had associated with the Germans now appeared with cropped hair."[8]

After watching long snaking convoys carrying 4th Armoured Division's 10th Infantry Brigade through the town, the brigade's historian was moved to ask, "Will Bernay ever be forgotten? Bernay where the people stood from morning till night, at times in the pouring rain, and at times in the August sun. Bernay where they never tired of waving, of throwing flowers or fruit, of giving their best wines and spirits to some halted column. Bernay where the local schoolmistress had her children lined along the main street singing in unison and in English, 'Thank you for liberating us.' It was the Brigade's first large town, and many a hardened lad from Caen and Falaise felt his eyes fill as he witnessed the joys, the smiles, the tears of wild gratitude and triumph all around him. These were the days of tremendous confidence and a realization that maybe it was worthwhile, and that those boys left along the hedges, in the grain fields, in the casualty posts of Normandy might not have fallen in vain. The never failing hand, the smiles of these people along the road, in cottage, hamlet or town, flooded us with emotion for we knew we had kept faith with them and had come back as those men at Dunkirk promised long ago."[9]

Keane and the other commanders chivvied their men out of Bernay. All the vehicles had been decorated with little French flags pressed upon them by the civilians. Once outside the town, these "were hastily removed and the column assumed its former appearance of a team whose business was to fight rather than to parade before admiring audiences."

The column soon reached Serquigny, about six miles east and eighteen miles short of the Seine, to find the Risle River bridges all blown. While the Lake Superior infantrymen were able to "pick their way across the little stream on the rubble," the vehicles and tanks could not follow. Keane ordered the column halted for the night while the engineers started bridging work.[10] Fortuitously for the Foot Guards, the column's tail stopped inside Bernay. "To unsuspecting Guardsmen, the power of calvados to wreak havoc on mind and body was a revelation," the Foot Guards historian ruefully noted with regard to the partying that ensued.[11]

Out in the middle of nowhere, the 15th Field Regiment halted on the road. "The evening meal was prepared and word was passed around that the night would be spent by the roadside. However, just as everyone was preparing to bed down, orders were received to concentrate off the road in a large wheatfield." No sooner was this move completed than new orders directed the regiment to a different concentration point. A flurry of signals passed up and down the command chain, with the regiment's recce parties finally loudly declaring to higher command that it would be "impossible to get the guns across the bad roads, tracks, and fields before first light." By that time, Keane Force would once again be moving, so the regiment might as well sit tight and get some needed sleep.[12] Somewhat grudgingly, staff at divisional headquarters—who had taken it upon themselves to start ordering elements of Keane Force to be distributed this way and that across the countryside in some misguided attempt to ensure that each unit was safely positioned in concentrated clusters rather than straggling along the road—acquiesced.

The confusion of movement orders, however, caused a number of vehicles and tanks to blunder around in the dark. As a result, the Superiors suffered a needless tragedy when a vehicle ran over and killed twenty-year-old Private William Thomas Latanville and Private Charles Edward Tait as the two men were sleeping.[13]

IN ITS ADVANCE on the corps's right flank, 4th Armoured Division had cleared the highest terrain features along the forward line. These lay to the east of Broglie. 11 Canadian Corps commander Lieutenant General Guy Simonds had half expected the Germans to stand on this ground and had positioned Keane Force so it could strike while 3rd Canadian Infantry Division turned sharply right to assist. But the Germans offered little resistance, so 3rd Division continued straight into Orbec, where 8th Infantry Brigade remained to ensure that the community and area were secured. Civilians in Orbec—no less elated than those in Bernay—reported that the Germans had fled the town at about 0100 hours that morning. The division's 9th Brigade, with 2nd Armoured Brigade's Fort Garry Horse regiment in support, led the way out of Orbec, followed by 7th Infantry Brigade and Major General Dan Spry's divisional headquarters. The advance carried the division through Thiboutière.[14]

Despite sporadic reports of German concentrations near the road, no resistance was met. The biggest problem was the ever-worsening condition of the road as more vehicles passed along it. Due to heavy rain the previous night, the trucks, Bren carriers, and tanks wallowed through deepening mud.[15]

Throughout the day, 3rd Division and 2nd Division kept crossing paths, with the latter generally showing up first. At Orbec, 3rd Division had found that the town had already been occupied by 6th Infantry Brigade, which was more than happy to hand securing it off to 3rd Division's 8th Infantry Brigade. The same proved true at Thiboutière, which 4th Infantry Brigade had passed through earlier that morning. The reason for these surprise encounters was that 2nd Division had started moving sooner than the other two divisions.[16]

At 1030 hours, both 5th and 6th Infantry Brigades headed north-westward from Orbec toward St-Germain-la-Campagne. Securing the village was assigned to 6th Brigade's Les Fusiliers Mont-Royal. All the Canadian infantry battalions were badly short of men, but the situation was far worse for the French-Canadian units. Instead of the mandated 850 men, the Fusiliers numbered fewer than 150. To create a semblance of a fighting force, Lieutenant Colonel J.G. "Guy" Gauvreau had allotted fifty men each to form two companies—'A' Company under Major Armand Brochu and 'D' Company led by Major Jacques "Jimmy" Dextraze. The surplus men were deployed to the support company and Gauvreau's headquarters. The support company's Bren carriers were loaded with the battalion's 3-inch mortars, extra ammunition, medical supplies, and stretchers. The Fusiliers had received no rations, so nobody had eaten in more than twenty-four hours.

According to plan, the Fusiliers were to meet a squadron of the division's 14th Canadian Hussars recce regiment so the infantry companies could ride on their armoured cars to St-Germain. The advance was to have begun before dawn, but the armoured cars did not show up until just before 0530 hours. Their delayed arrival was the result of the Hussars having never operated at night and the squadron leader's consequent reluctance to drive along roads in the dark and potentially be blown up by undetectable mines. When the squadron leader cautioned Dextraze that the night advance was "too dangerous," it was abandoned. He rejected loading the Fusiliers up for the same reason.

Instead, two sections of infantry walked out of Orbec ahead of the armoured cars at dawn—eyes scanning the road surface for signs of buried mines. As it was daylight and the small column moved so slowly, slipping unobserved past the numerous farmhouses—each of which contained a small garrison of Germans—proved impossible. That meant each had to be cleared, costing the Fusiliers "delay, casualties, and considerable uncertainty." Hope of reaching St-Germain quickly dissolved when a large castle on the western corner of a crossroads proved to be held in force. For fifteen minutes, the Fusiliers fruitlessly hammered away at the defences with their rifles and Bren guns. While the infantry was so engaged, the support company hauled up one of its 6-pounder anti-tank guns with rope lines. Stopping fifty yards from the castle's heavy gate, the Fusiliers fired two rounds of high-explosive shells that shattered the gate. A heavy volley of armour-piercing shot then knocked down sections of the castle's surrounding walls and chunks of the building itself. Throughout this siege, the Staghounds were also throwing out heavy fire with their light guns. Resistance from the castle soon ceased and the advance continued.

But it stalled shortly after, when an 88-millimetre self-propelled gun started firing both its main gun and machine guns from high ground overlooking the road. When the Fusiliers deployed their PIAT gunners to flank the SPG, it withdrew to the next bend in the road and the time-consuming outflanking process had to be repeated. One PIAT team managed to get within forty yards of the SPG and loosed off a round that hit a tree, knocked it down, and blocked the team's angle of fire. The inadvertent tree cutting, however, spooked the SPG crew into retreating with ten to fifteen infantrymen—who had been providing a covering screen—running after it. But the retreat was short-lived, the SPG backing into the cover of a farmyard, where only the turret was exposed above a protective brick wall with its flanks guarded by the infantry.

After two hours of fruitlessly trying to close on and engage the spg with piats, Dextraze—whose company led the advance—pulled his men back three hundred yards and called artillery fire down on the farm. After a ten-minute bombardment, one of the Staghounds rolled forward and started shooting at the spg. Dextraze expected the car to fire two rounds and then nimbly relocate. Instead, the armoured car stayed in one spot for a five-round salvo. Before a sixth round could be fired, the spg's 88-millimetre gun spat a round that knocked the Staghound out. Dextraze's infantry opened fire and the Fusiliers deployed their 2- and 3-inch mortars for seven minutes of intense fire. As the smoke from the mortaring cleared, Dextraze led the Fusiliers in an attack, only to discover the spg and German infantry had again withdrawn.

Determined to keep advancing, Dextraze moved a section of his most experienced men out front. Maintaining a twenty-yard separation between each man to deny a clustered target, they were within a quarter mile of St-Germain when they were fired on from houses to the left. Another clearing operation began. Once this was done, Dextraze ordered his men to enter the town through back gardens and orchards without bothering to regroup into assigned sections. This hurried effort was blocked by three German light armoured cars and a handful of infantry. Dextraze tried shifting his advance into another orchard, but the armoured cars easily relocated to blunt the attempt. Acknowledging that the Fusiliers were too weak to win this fight, Dextraze urgently requested help from the Calgary Highlanders of 5th Brigade, who were coming toward the town from the right.[17]

The Calgaries approached via the main road leading directly from Orbec to St-Germain, with Le Régiment de Maisonneuve marching cross-country to their right. Captain Dalt Heyland's 'C' Company was on point with 'D,' 'B,' and 'A' Companies trailing in that order. The Black Watch followed with a squadron of 14th Canadian Hussars armoured cars bringing up the rear. As the brigade had been passing through Orbec, the town had been struck by a salvo of German artillery fire, so the Calgaries and Maisies were alert to trouble. They were also entering ideal ambush country, the road rising steeply and passing through a heavily wooded series of hills. The men moved through this dangerous ground without incident. Beyond lay a plateau of open farmland with stout farmhouses bordering the road and St-Germain standing at a crossroads. It was a typical Norman village dominated by a church on the main street and facing the central square, which was surrounded by solid brick houses backed by high-walled courtyards.[18]

No villagers poured out to greet the Calgaries, and the sounds of gunfire from the flank where the Fusiliers were engaged warned that a fight might be pending. The jeeps and trucks carrying Lieutenant Colonel Donald MacLauchlan's command group had just pulled into the square and the infantry companies were beginning to search the houses, when an anti-tank gun opened fire from a side street. The loud grinding of tracked vehicles came from the same direction. The Calgaries quickly found cover amid the buildings around the square and deployed their PIAT guns. Sensing which street the vehicles were approaching by, the artillery officer with the regiment—Captain Walter Newman—ran around the left side of the church with a couple of PIAT men trailing. This positioned them perfectly to fire on what proved to be two German half-tracks. Direct hits set the half-tracks burning and detonated large loads of mines and demolition equipment on board. A series of intense explosions rocked the village. When the smoke cleared, one dead German was found and others were seen running away. As silence descended, the unmistakable sound of German tanks moving nearby could be heard. When MacLauchlan contacted Brigadier Bill Megill for orders, he was told to establish defensive positions in the village and sit tight.[19]

The Fusiliers, meanwhile, had no intention of hanging back. There were still Germans in the village, and Dextraze called down another ten-minute artillery concentration. Then, with both companies of Fusiliers on the left of the road and a company of Calgaries to its right, the advance "became like cutting butter," Dextraze said later, as the two units sliced out from the centre of the village to the northern side. At 2000 hours, St-Germain was declared clear. The exhausted Fusiliers settled in for the night. Dextraze was satisfied with their showing. Despite their low numbers and the fact that all the platoon lieutenants were newly arrived from Canada and lacked combat experience, the sections had carried out efficient fire-and-manoeuvre tactics in difficult fighting terrain.[20]

There was to be no rest for the Calgaries. Brigadier Megill ordered his brigade to get moving. The Calgaries marched rapidly north to

Bournainville-Faverolles, about six miles distant, after which the Maisies were to continue a couple of miles farther to Duranville. As the Calgaries started out, Megill sent a sharply worded reminder that half-tracks were not tanks and should not be reported as such. MacLauchlan and his intelligence officer insisted that they had heard tanks. This assertion was borne out when some of Major General Dan Spry's staff discovered an abandoned broken-down Panther tank in roughly the spot where the Calgaries had reported hearing one.

The Germans once again melted away, and the advance proceeded "without a single shot being fired," Calgary Highlanders intelligence officer Lieutenant Stuart Moore noted. At Bournainville, the regiment was "greeted by a grand representation of the French people . . . and were showered with flowers and food and drink."[21]

By nightfall, 2nd Division had closed up on the Risle. Meanwhile, to keep from tripping over 2nd Division, 3rd Division had swung sharply rightward and headed east to pass north of Bernay. The division's 9th Brigade ended its advance at the village of St. Vincent-du-Boulai, eight miles northeast of Thiboutière. All of 11 Canadian Corps was well positioned to cross the Risle in the morning on bridges the engineers were now building. On the morrow, Simonds hoped to gain the Seine.[22]

DESPITE STALWART EFFORTS, 4th Canadian Armoured Division's 8th Field Squadron had found it all but impossible to erect a bridge across the Risle at Serquigny during the night of August 24–25. Because of damage to the area inflicted by both German demolitions and Allied aerial bombardments, the squadron's Captain M. Turner said "the whole thing presented a rather formidable obstacle."[23]

Between August 17 and 24, U.S. Marauders had repeatedly bombed about ten bridges over the Risle, while seven bridges crossing the Meuse had been struck by the much larger B-17 Flying Fortresses. There had also been attacks by RAF and RCAF Halifaxes and Lancasters on railway centres from the coast to near Paris. In all, 3,800 tons of bombs had been dropped, and rocket-armed fighter-bombers had struck at the bridges with hundreds of projectiles.[24]

Although the damage had hindered the German retreat, the destruction of bridges and riverbanks along the Risle now hampered the Canadian advance. Protected by a Staghound troop of 12th Manitoba

Dragoons, Turner started seeking a bridging site that could be quickly put into operation. Finally, four miles north of Serquigny, he happened upon a bridge at Fontaine that the Allied bombers had missed and the Germans had done a hasty "and very poor job of blowing." The bridge proved sufficiently sound to allow even the heavy Staghounds to gingerly cross it. That was good enough for Turner. When his report reached the division's chief engineer, Lieutenant Colonel J.R.B. Jones, it provided welcome relief. Although Fontaine was off the projected line of 4th Armoured Division's advance, Jones decided it "was the only place to get across." He ordered 8th Field Squadron's No. 1 Troop to ready the bridge for heavy traffic.

Working feverishly through the early-morning hours of August 25, the engineers managed to install a fifty-foot-long Bailey bridge on "top of the weakened existing bridge." At 0800 hours, they declared the bridge fully operational, and it was soon handling fifteen hundred vehicles per hour.[25]

Bridging the Risle in front of both 2nd and 3rd Infantry Divisions had proven equally complicated because of the extent of destruction. Although it meant having the two divisions again tripping over each other, the engineers from both decided the only recourse was to build two bridges almost side by side at Brionne. Each division was to have its exclusive bridge.[26]

Even before the bridge at Fontaine had officially opened, 'C' Squadron of the 12th Manitoba Dragoons slipped across it at 0745 hours in a deliberate attempt to get well ahead of 4th Armoured Division's main column. The recce troops believed the division's main body kept following too closely, leading to delays.[27] 'B' Squadron also ducked across just before the main column reached the bridge.[28]

As Keane Force led the division across, the Lake Superior Regiment's Lieutenant Colonel Robert Keane ordered that the speed of advance be much faster than on the previous day. "It was far too easy," he said, "to accept the little delays, and to fall into the little habits of procrastination." Keane's sights were fixed on Louviers beside the Seine River.[29] With the bit between its teeth, Keane Force lunged forward so quickly, with 4th Armoured Brigade racing along behind, that Brigadier Robert Moncel had trouble maintaining wireless contact with Major General Harry Foster's divisional headquarters.[30]

Encountering good roads and no German resistance, Keane urged his men to pick up the pace even more. Six miles out from the Risle, the force brushed up against a couple of patrols from 2nd Armored Division of First U.S. Army's xixth Corps at the major junction of Le Neubourg.[31] The Allied front was narrowing so dramatically this close to the Seine that patrols from 7th British Armoured Division advancing on the left flank of 1 British Corps also showed up. A short time earlier, 'C' Squadron had further detected unidentified patrols on its right flank. Creeping closer, they discovered that the patrols were American. Both sides were surprised to meet the other. The Americans told the Dragoons they had been headed for Saguenay to win the bridges there. When the Dragoons reported they were bound for Louviers and the Seine, the Americans said they had already won that ground.[32]

Abandoning the route to Louviers, the Dragoons turned westward toward Elbeuf—the objective for 3rd Canadian Infantry Division. With both 'C' and 'B' Squadrons operating practically side by side, they easily outflanked the few German outposts encountered, and with their line of retreat cut, these troops generally surrendered. The Dragoons ended their day by sending patrols into Elbeuf and triumphantly reporting back to Lieutenant General Simonds that "the southern bank of the Seine was in our hands."[33]

Keane Force, meanwhile, had found its roads "more and more congested with the vehicles of an American division which had reached the same area the preceding day." By the time it advanced another seven miles from Le Neubourg to the village of Crassville, "the congestion had become such that further progress was impossible. It was clear that both armies were making for the same destination. With all the problems of confusion and, perhaps, national jealousies, that would result from indiscriminate mixing, it was decided, once it was clear that the Americans were going to cross at Louviers, that the Canadian axis of advance should be altered." Accordingly, 4th Armoured Division would move northward toward Pont de l'Arche. But the roads were still so jammed that the Canadian division ended gridlocked in traffic. Keane Force and the rest of the division received orders to stand down and take a well-earned rest. "There was a great deal of shaking of hands, of slapping of backs, of exchanging mutual congratulations," the Lake

Superior historian reported. "But there were little signs of jealousy too, as the Americans looked hard at their tasteless κ rations and then at the bread and the more appetizing food served the Canadians. Perhaps it was just as well that this brief and healthy encounter did not last too long."[34]

TO THE CANADIANS on the sharp end, the appearance of Americans across their line of advance had been entirely unexpected. The Dragoons declared it yet another example of "the lack of information that is passed between higher formations."[35] In fact, this development had been fully anticipated by General Bernard Montgomery back on August 20 and actually conformed with the Allied plan of advance to the Seine. With both the American Twelfth Army Group and now— with the elimination of the Germans within the Falaise Pocket—all of British Twenty-First Army Group able to advance, Montgomery had declared that the Americans would already be so far forward that its divisions on the left flank would "have driven northwest to Louviers, and Elbeuf, and beyond" before the British and Canadian divisions arrived. Montgomery had envisioned the Americans pushing their left flank westward as far as Bourgtheroulde and even sending "light forces . . . towards the mouth of the Seine." This would result in the Germans currently being driven by the British and Canadian forces toward the river finding their "lines of withdrawal across the Seine in Allied hands and [their] situation [would] then be very awkward."

The Americans had not, however, fully completed this ambition, the leftward 2nd Armored Division and 28th Infantry Divisions having reached only Elbeuf by August 25. Between Elbeuf and Bourgtheroulde was a stretch of five miles of river frontage that remained open to the retreating Germans.[36] This was largely due to a change of plan agreed to during an afternoon conference on the 25th where British Second Army's General Miles Dempsey, First U.S. Army's Lieutenant General Courtenay H. Hodges, and Major General Charles H. Corlett— commanding xix U.S. Corps—met to sort out the traffic jam around Louviers. As soon as the meeting adjourned and unable to establish contact with either Lieutenant Generals Guy Simonds or Harry Crerar, Corlett passed a short note to Major General Harry Foster at 4th Armoured Division seeking Canadian assistance in taking over his current area of operations. "We are near each other and have a problem of mutual interest," Corlett wrote.

Dempsey, he advised, had insisted that his xxx British Corps required exclusive use of the Le Neubourg–Louviers road between 0700 and 1000 hours on August 26. Thereafter, the road would open to Corlett for his corps to move south and exit the Canadian–British operational area. "I would like very much to move south as quickly as I can consistent with the turning over of the area in which we are now located. I have a very tight schedule for other road crossings to the south. The British 2nd Army wants to get east and my Corps wants to get south to the vicinity of Nantes Cassicourt where we are to make a crossing. At the same time it is presumed that you will desire to go east.

"Outside of the combat elements of the 2nd Armored Division and a Regimental Combat Team and some Corps artillery, most of my troops are already south of the Le Neubourg-Louviers road. We must get entirely south of that road within 21 hours after 10 a.m. tomorrow morning.

"We hope to secure the town of Elbeuf tonight and be able to turn it over to some element of your corps. We have not gone east of Elbeuf or north of Louviers. The Boche have two pontoon bridges (reported by the Air Corps) in the bend of the river south of Rouen. There may be a good many Germans over in that area and I presume that you will want to get at them.

"Will you please do all you can to effect a transfer of our responsibilities in your area and in the area of your corps so that we may meet our schedule. If you can get in touch with your corps commander I would very much appreciate your explaining the situation to him."[37]

Foster hurried Corlett's request up the Canadian command chain, and at 1900 hours that evening, Lieutenant General Harry Crerar issued written orders to his II Canadian Corps divisional commanders. Much emphasis was placed on seizing Seine crossings by *coup de main* with both 4th Armoured Division and 3rd Infantry Division instructed to immediately do so. Foster's 4th Division would establish two bridgeheads by sudden surprise attacks—one at Pont de l'Arche and another about two miles to the west at Criquebeuf-sur-Seine. The 3rd Division was to do the same at Elbeuf by capturing the railway bridge there and also erecting a nearby bridge. The task for 2nd Division was twofold.

First it must "clear the meander" of the Seine at Rouen that lay between the villages of La Bouille and Orival. By *coup de main*, it would then seize bridgeheads by first crossing the Seine via a railway bridge on the eastward leg of the meander and secondly by capturing a couple of bridges that crossed in its centre directly into Rouen.[38]

As the Seine nears the coast, it follows a course that snakes in a series of long loops around chalk bluffs that create several narrow isthmus-like features. The "meander" that 2nd Division was to clear was such an isthmus—three miles wide at its La Bouille–Orival base, bulging to about five miles wide in the middle, and then returning to the three-mile width at the tip where Rouen lay. Most of the city was on the opposite side of the river. The ground inside the meander was heavily forested and known as Forêt de la Londe.[39]

Crerar's orders promised to heavily tax the engineering resources of 11 Canadian Corps. Recognizing this, Simonds set priorities for each division's bridgehead operations, with 4th Armoured Division being first in line, followed by 3rd Infantry Division and lastly 2nd Infantry Division. The first two divisions were to cross the Seine where the river's erratic course created a reverse isthmus immediately east of the one encompassing Forêt de la Londe and had the town of Tourville-la-Rivière at its base. This isthmus thrust out on a westward line, and the distance between Tourville and Elbeuf was about eight miles. Once across the river, the two divisions would pass to the east of Rouen and advance toward the Somme.

"It is clear," Crerar emphasized, "that the enemy no longer has the troops to hold any strong positions—or to hold any positions for any length of time—if it is aggressively outflanked or attacked. Speed of action and forcible tactics are, therefore, urgently required from commanders at every level . . . We must drive ahead with utmost energy. Any tendency to be slow or 'sticky' on the part of subordinate commanders should be quickly and positively eliminated."[40]

All First Canadian Army high-level commanders saw the problem before them not so much as troops confronting a determined enemy but rather as a challenge to be solved by the 11 Corps engineers. The task of getting the corps across the Seine rapidly and at a number of fairly broadly dispersed points would rest on their shoulders.

5

Strenuous Efforts by All

A T 1630 HOURS on August 25, 2nd Canadian Infantry Division's 5th Brigade prepared to cross the Risle River. An hour earlier, the division's 6th Brigade had uneventfully crossed at Brionne, and Brigadier Bill Megill's brigade was to follow it. The Black Watch would lead, advancing about twelve miles from the Risle to Bourgtheroulde. This would bring the battalion to within six miles of the Seine and close to the Forêt de la Londe meander next to Rouen. The Calgary Highlanders would then pass through and lead the way into the forest.

Having received his orders, Calgary Highlanders commander Lieutenant Colonel Don MacLauchlan ordered the battalion to gather in a truck park at St. Cyr. There would be no need this time for marching. News soon arrived, however, that 6th Brigade was not advancing as quickly as anticipated. The move was pushed back to 1830 hours and then to whenever the brigade decided the road was clear. At 2330 hours, the Calgaries were still crowded around their trucks when several German planes droned overhead and dropped many flares. Lieutenant Stuart Moore thought it "struck queer to see one complete area ringed by bright lights." That area included the Calgaries truck park.

At the same time, orders came for MacLauchlan to meet Megill at the Risle crossing. He and Moore set off in a Bren carrier and were well away when the two men saw over their shoulders the "horrible sight" of the Calgaries area being bombed by the Luftwaffe. Continuing on to meet Megill, MacLauchlan and Moore repeatedly tried unsuccessfully to establish wireless communication with their battalion. Both officers experienced "a very definite feeling of anxiety . . . and yet nothing could be done at the time."[1]

Back at the truck park, Captain Mark Tennant had stared up at the flares illuminating the area and saw several Stuka bombers diving down with their sirens screaming. "You could have struck a match on their noses, they came so close to the ground. As they pulled up, down came their bombs." Mortar platoon Private Rob Roy McGregor tried to take cover under the platoon's carriers but was unable to do so, as the ground was already jammed with men. As each bomb whistled down he was sure it was going to land right on top of him. Most struck Tennant's 'D' Company and the support company. Several bombs also fell into Le Régiment de Maisonneuve's area, wounding fifteen men and killing a platoon commander.[2] Bombs also struck around No. 18 Field Ambulance's position, destroying the unit's signal truck and wounding five men. The unit's war diarist thought they had got off lucky, until 0515 hours the next morning when a delayed-action blockbuster bomb exploded in their midst. Rocks thrown out of the resulting forty- by twenty-five-foot crater struck several men and shattered the windows in nearby houses. The blast also set one ambulance on fire, shrapnel felled a number of nearby four-inch trees as cleanly as a chainsaw, and several buildings collapsed.[3]

The Calgaries suffered the worst mauling, with most of their 120 casualties for August 26 resulting from the aerial attack.[4] Sixteen men died that day, and two were officers killed in a later skirmish.[5] It was the second-worst day for casualties that the regiment had suffered since landing in Normandy.[6]

War left no time for licking wounds. At 0800 hours, the Calgaries moved out as part of a long column led by the Staghounds of 14th Canadian Hussars. Following behind, Moore observed a snaking line of "tanks, artillery, engineers, press and everything but the Cabinet itself." The Calgaries were bunched up behind and supported by a squadron of the Sherbrooke Fusiliers tanks. Then, after travelling just a short distance forward, the sharp ripping of an MG-42 machine gun was heard, and suddenly "there were only tanks and recce to our front."[7]

WELL AHEAD OF this main column was the battle group formed around 5th Brigade's Black Watch, which had crossed the Risle at Brionne and headed toward Bourgtheroulde at 0415 hours. This advance had originally been scheduled to start the previous day at 1730 hours, but a series of delays pushed it back to the pre-dawn hours of August 26.[8] Some of the delay was due to Brigadier Megill giving Black Watch Lieutenant Colonel Frank Mitchell two options for advancing his infantry. Mitchell was left to decide whether to go on the march or move forward with the battalion loaded into troop-carrying vehicles. Given that Megill envisioned the battle group pushing through to Bourgtheroulde and on to the Seine in one day, Mitchell decided to forgo caution for the speed provided by the trucks.[9]

Megill and Mitchell held each other in mutual disregard. The brigadier had tried to prevent Mitchell from being given command of the Black Watch after the battalion was slaughtered at Verrières Ridge, with most of its officers killed, wounded, or taken prisoner. Megill thought Mitchell incompetent, but had been unable to stop his promotion, largely because of the officer's deep ties to the regiment. For his part, Mitchell blamed Megill personally for the disaster that had cost the Black Watch so many casualties.[10]

Before the advance could begin, the Black Watch had to await the arrival of a transport platoon of thin-skinned, three-ton lorries summoned from the Royal Canadian Army Service Corps's 4th Brigade Company. This platoon was commanded by Captain Rolland Durand, who thought it "must have been believed at all levels that the enemy had been cleared from the area because it was not customary to drive the infantry into battle."[11]

Neither Mitchell nor Megill actually had a clue what the situation before them was. All Mitchell knew was that the distance from the Risle start point to Bourgtheroulde was seven miles and it was then four more miles to the Seine. There was no way his infantry could march that distance and reach the river in time to carry out Megill's expectation of establishing a bridgehead on the other bank. So Mitchell gambled on resistance being light. He also hoped that the sheer audacity and rapidity of a motorized column advance would catch any Germans unprepared for a fight.

Supporting the Black Watch was 'C' Squadron of the Sherbrooke Fusiliers, one engineer platoon, and a detachment from No. 18 Field Ambulance. Mitchell had his carrier platoon leading with the Sherbrookes rumbling along behind. Then followed the Black Watch's four companies in their vulnerable trucks, with 'A' Company leading. To enable each company to fight independently, Mitchell had assigned it a mortar team, an anti-tank gun crew, and some pioneers from the support company. Mitchell travelled with his leading company.

Within minutes of setting off, the column drew spatters of rifle fire from nearby woods that was directed at the trucks and men aboard. The fire was too light to slow the column and no attempt was made to engage the German snipers. When the column was still about four and a half miles short of Bourgtheroulde, however, a stronger and more organized force ambushed its centre with heavy fire that prompted the men in the second company in line to dismount and engage them from the roadside. Hoping to set trucks ablaze, the Germans started chucking phosphorous grenades. The tanks and trucks ahead of the ambush, meanwhile, were making so much racket nobody in that group heard the gunfire behind. As a result, the front of the column carried on obliviously into the town.

As Mitchell's jeep drove in, he received wireless orders from Megill to curl up inside Bourgtheroulde and establish a firm base there. Mitchell radioed the news to his company commanders, but only the first three in line responded. None of them told Mitchell what was going on behind him. Pulling to a halt, Mitchell finally looked back and saw only the second company's headquarters section drive up. It was 0540 hours and getting light. Mitchell got what infantry he had unloaded and established a perimeter around the trucks, carriers, and tanks in a field on the northeast corner of the town's main square.

Suddenly, a 75-millimetre anti-tank gun opened fire on a line that enabled it to engage the trailing column as it arrived.[12] The gun's first shot seemed like a signal, for German infantry erupted into action throughout Bourgtheroulde. Yet the German response was chaotic, and the Black Watch's intelligence officer, Lieutenant W.J. Shea, believed the column's arrival in the town had surprised the enemy.[13] A confused melee followed, "in which every man carried on his own private war, firing in any direction he heard shots coming, taking his own prisoners and not knowing in the confusion where to send them," Mitchell later said. "The enemy fired from the buildings and streets . . . During the first quarter hour nine prisoners, including one officer, were taken and many more were brought in later."

Mitchell figured the force with him was getting organized and he was now in wireless contact with the rest of the column, which was approaching.[14] He and Shea discussed whether they should withdraw or bring the rest forward. Mitchell decided to bring the others in, and soon the rear companies "began running the gauntlet of the gun through the centre of the square. About every seventh or eighth vehicle the gun would fire," Shea reported, "and often would catch a vehicle. Considerable casualties were suffered." German snipers fired from the windows of buildings surrounding the square. As the trucks raced through the square itself, they were also bombarded by phosphorous grenades. The anti-tank gun's fire was unrelentingly steady. When it came the engineers' turn to run the gauntlet, their trucks attracted particularly heavy fire and many men were killed or wounded. Mitchell stood on the road behind 'A' Company's position, directing each truck to where it could offload the men right where they were to set up. Shea remarked that Mitchell did this despite incoming machine-gun fire and the fall of mortar rounds and artillery shells all around him. Mitchell sent 'C' Company to the right flank and 'B' and 'D' Companies to the left. These companies then started working back toward where 'A' Company with the tanks and carriers were holding in the field by the square. This move seemed to confuse the Germans even further. From the weight of fire the enemy was throwing out, Shea thought the Germans had been caught with all their heavy weapons pointing in the direction opposite the advance line being taken by the three companies.[15]

Rather than having his drivers become spectators once their trucks were unloaded, Captain Durand sorted them into fighting sections that worked alongside the Black Watch infantrymen. Each section was led by a corporal. Durand had never been in combat before. "But, believe me, you learn fast," he said later. The captain juggled two tasks: keeping in touch with his fighting driver sections and monitoring the damage his trucks were suffering. He did so by racing from position to position in his jeep with his batman at the wheel. It was, he said, "my job to keep myself informed of the state of my transport so that, when the order came to get the hell out of there, we could go. When they gave us the 'all-clear,' it didn't take us very long to get out of the place . . . There was some damage to the vehicles from enemy fire—several tires that had to be replaced and they had to be replaced under fire . . . I recall my batman having to change a tire on my jeep while I held the damned jeep on my back." Durand's actions that day earned a Military Cross.[16]

In the midst of the fighting, a German supply truck drove into town on the same road the Canadian advance had travelled. It was quickly shot up. Then a motorcycle with a corporal driving and an officer in the sidecar came in from the same direction, and the two men were killed by gunfire. A quick search of the officer yielded a map showing the location of a nearby German battalion headquarters and a number of mortar positions around Bourgtheroulde. The medium artillery regiment forward observation officer (FOO) with Mitchell's headquarters quickly called in the coordinates of twelve German guns, and these were drenched with shellfire. Prisoners subsequently reported that the accurate fire had forced each mortar team to relocate four times, and they were never able to escape from the shelling long enough to bring their mortars back into action.

Inside Bourgtheroulde, the situation remained fluid. In the afternoon, a force of fifty Germans struck 'C' Company from the northwest, but the Sherbrooke Fusiliers brought fire on them from behind. The panicked Germans ran into a platoon of 'C' Company and were cut to pieces, with only one Canadian being wounded. 'A' Company, meanwhile, fended off a series of counterattacks that Shea considered "of the nuisance variety." Throughout the day, however, the Germans were able to heavily engage the Canadians with 88-millimetre and mortar fire that concentrated on the main square and its telltale church spire.

By evening, the Black Watch had managed to clear the houses throughout the town, and the Germans had slunk away.[17] The fight cost the Black Watch dearly—about one hundred casualties, of which thirteen were fatal.[18] Approximately one hundred prisoners had been taken, but a number of these who had been lined up against the brick wall of a building near Mitchell's headquarters were killed by German artillery fire.[19]

Battle won, Mitchell thought the "boldness of the move was justified by the surprise achieved. The enemy had reasonably good defences in the fields occupied by 'A' Company, but was not set up there when the battalion entered the town. He also had sitting along the road many mines, which according to civilian reports, were to have been laid against an attack expected on the night 27–28 August. In other words, had the advance been delayed, casualties from the mines and from the completion of other enemy defences would have been considerably greater. On the other hand advancing further to the . . . Seine would have been unwise as the battalion would have been very much out of touch and beyond artillery support and because the other units in the Division to our rear were still engaging the enemy."[20]

THE BLACK WATCH ended August 26 with just 176 officers and men still fit for combat. This, however, was little different from the strengths reported by the other 2nd Division's infantry battalions for that day. In 5th Brigade, the Calgary Highlanders counted 205 men and Le Régiment de Maisonneuve 246. The entire brigade fielded just 627 infantrymen instead of what should have been about 2,550. It was the same with the other brigades—4th Brigade reported total strength for its three battalions was 639, and 6th Brigade's was 746. While there would be some reinforcements sent forward, there was no chance of bringing the regiments anywhere close to full fighting strength.[21]

In fact, the shortage of front-line personnel within II Canadian Corps—most particularly among infantrymen—was approaching crisis level. By the end of August, it was apparent that Canadian, British, and American reinforcement plans drafted prior to the invasion had been "grossly miscalculated." It turned out that the Canadian planners charged with determining "rates of wastage" had drawn on data provided by the British War Office because it had more experience in combat operations. The rates provided, however, were based on North Africa, where the battlefield sprawled over a vast geography and intense fighting was never as prolonged as it had been in Normandy

92 / THE CINDERELLA CAMPAIGN

and might continue to be throughout the northwest Europe campaign. The War Office had predicted that during "intense" fighting, infantry battalions would see losses of 48 per cent, armoured regiments 15 per cent, and artillery regiments 14 per cent. During normal operations, these loss levels would drop to 34, 11, and 16 per cent, respectively.[22]

As the fighting in Normandy progressed through July, the Canadian planners had realized that infantry losses were greatly outstripping these predictions, while armoured and artillery casualties were generally somewhat less than forecast. Accordingly, they increased the infantry component to 63 per cent of whole-force casualties. On July 14, however, First Canadian Army's Acting Chief of Staff Colonel George Beament had advised Canadian Military Headquarters' Chief of Staff Lieutenant General P.J. Montague by letter that this figure was still too low. Up to this point, it had been generally accepted that provisions for all reinforcement requirements were easily met by the influx of appropriately trained men from Canada. The only exception was infantry for the French-Canadian units. To make up the shortfall here, all French-Canadian personnel were to be shifted from English-speaking units. If that and the influx of French-speaking soldiers from Canada proved insufficient, the planners reluctantly forecasted the need to disband one or more of the French-Canadian battalions to bring the others up to strength.

Overall, Beament wrote, between June 6 and July 10, infantry losses had been 78.6 per cent of total casualties. "Even non-battle casualties . . . were higher among infantrymen, due to the more dangerous conditions under which they lived." To try to relieve the situation, First Canadian Army had already scoured its ranks of rear-area personnel and sent several hundred men who had qualified as infantry specialists before being assigned to duties such as drivers, cooks, and clerks. But this was no more than a stopgap measure.[23]

When First Canadian Army advanced toward the Seine, senior staff responsible for managing the flow of reinforcements had counted on a break due to fewer casualties. Instead, they were shaken by the "heavy opposition" encountered and resultant numbers of killed and wounded infantrymen. Both Crerar and Simonds had sent repeated messages to Canadian Military Headquarters in London voicing concerns and calling for more infantry reinforcements to be delivered at a faster rate from the reinforcement pools in England. The Chief of General Staff, Lieutenant General Ken Stuart, cabled Crerar on August 26 to reassure him that everyone at CMHQ was aware of the "vital importance" of the next three weeks of operations and would send all available infantry-men forward as quickly as possible. The previous system of gathering men together for a weekly draft sent to the Normandy beaches and then up to the advancing army was to be immediately abandoned. Instead, as soon as one hundred infantrymen were assembled, they would be sent to the front. CMHQ, he said, was "playing ball" and guaranteed to fill any manpower request within forty-eight hours.

Stuart was, in fact, playing a delicate balancing act. On the one hand, he must strive to meet Crerar's demands and set the First Canadian Army commander's mind at ease. At the same time, however, he had to answer to the government and to the Army's Chief of the General Staff, Lieutenant General John Carl Murchie, in Ottawa. Stuart knew that Ottawa, particularly Prime Minister William Lyon Mackenzie King, sought assurance that any manpower shortages could be addressed without conscripting soldiers—who were enlisted and trained for home defence under the *National Mobilization Resources Act*—for service overseas. King had made clear many times that such conscription was only to be a last resort.

Consequently, hours before Stuart cabled Crerar, he sent a lengthy signal to Murchie assuring him that all was under control. "We will have the infantry reinforcement situation in a satisfactory condition in from three weeks to one month's time," he said. Although Stuart was unable to currently keep the infantry units at full strength and count-ed the twenty-one such battalions in First Canadian Army as short three thousand men, he expected that by combining other units and the reinforcement pools he could provide two thousand infantrymen "within the next six days."

Stuart asked Murchie to permit transferring infantry tradesmen who were surplus to general infantry duties without cutting the extra trades pay they received. The current policy, that such pay must be lost if a man was reduced to a general infantryman, Stuart declared "ridiculous . . . I consider we would be breaking faith with them if we cut their trades pay." He wanted free discretion to assign such men as required.

"The present situation is not a manpower problem in the true sense," Stuart emphasized. "We have the men. It is not a problem of general supply. It is a problem of detailed distribution." The British War Office wastage-rate predictions had been badly flawed. This left the infantry reinforcement numbers too low and those for "practically all other arms . . . too high." A period of adjustment was under way, and Stuart anticipated that in three weeks to a month the crisis would pass. The only way to bridge the problem in the meantime was to send infantry tradesmen to the battalions without cutting their pay. When the crisis was past, these men could gradually return to their previous positions.

After some temporizing from Ottawa, Stuart's proposal was accepted. But implementation of the process of transferring infantry trades personnel to the rifle battalions was slow and overly bureaucratized. Consequently, it was to be many more weeks than Stuart had promised Crerar before he started receiving significant reinforcements from this source. The infantry battalions would continue to march into battle woefully understrength.[24]

Having met stiff resistance at Bourgtheroulde and now preparing to push into the dense Forêt de la Londe, 2nd Infantry Division was— in the words of one army report—"not up to full battle efficiency." Expectation was growing that the forest would be strongly defended and clearing it "was bound to tax to the limit the depleted resources of the rifle companies, which must be considered at this time as averaging less than half strength."[25]

UNLIKE 2ND INFANTRY Division, on August 26 II Canadian Corps's other two divisions met no significant German resistance. Consequently, the deficiencies of their similarly reduced infantry battalions were less noted. Instead, what these divisions noticeably lacked was sufficient bridging materials for the engineers. As each closed on the Seine, First Canadian Army's engineers were still bringing equipment up to the newly created supply depot at Lisieux. Once there, they began scrambling to meet the demands by the engineers at corps and divisional level for bridging equipment, ferries, and stormboats.

The Lisieux dump could only meet a fraction of the orders. Everything else was still held in a depot west of the Orne River. By mid-morning, a long column of trucks departed this distant depot and finally, at 1100 hours, delivered more than seven hundred tons of ferry and bridge equipment to 11 Canadian Corps. Another four hundred tons of pontoon equipment was reported as still en route.

The actual river crossings were to be built by divisional engineers. With most of the necessary equipment still far to the rear, even getting infantry across to establish bridgeheads before the day was out proved "a severe test upon their efficiency and resourcefulness." Still, the engineers were confident the job could be done. "Late in the afternoon," wrote the war diarist at 3rd Division's Royal Canadian Engineer Headquarters, "it became apparent that a crossing of the . . . Seine was going to be done tonight . . . Very little time was available to tie up details with the infantry . . . but as very little, if any, opposition was expected it was not considered very serious. Work on building the rafts and operating storm boats, assault boats, etc. was issued to the [engineer] companies late that night and after strenuous efforts by all concerned the equipment was got up to the sites."[26]

By the time this equipment arrived, efforts to effect an orderly crossing had been abandoned. Instead, as the official historians for the Canadian engineers later wrote, "it was more of a scramble crossing," with much disorganization. Having never before undertaken the crossing of a major river in combat conditions, the engineers of both divisions learned on the job.[27]

With no engineers in sight, 4th Armoured Division's Lincoln and Welland Regiment found its own way across. In the mid-afternoon, the Lincs had marched on foot into Criquebeuf-sur-Seine. No sooner were 'A' and 'B' Companies with two platoons of 'C' Company established along the river's edge and the village fully secured than German artillery opened up with heavy shelling. Across the river, the shoreline was dominated by heights that gently sloped down to the water's edge. From the higher ground, artillery observers could provide accurate gun direction. The Lincs lashed back, however, with a rapid counter-fire utilizing their 3-inch mortars and a battery of 20-millimetre Oerlikon anti-aircraft guns that had come forward to support them.

Lieutenant Colonel Bill Cromb badly desired a foothold across the river before the Germans decided to establish a defensive line along its northern bank. Fearing the engineers would arrive too late, he ordered the scout platoon to cross using a small boat they had found. Lacking paddles, the scouts launched at 1700 hours and used their shovels to propel the boat across the five-hundred-foot-wide river. The scouts soon returned news that the Germans had not yet established any defensive positions in the small hamlet of Freneuse, directly across from Criquebeuf. Knowing that situation could not last long, Cromb took "the daring step," as one regimental historian put it, of sending Major C.K. Crummer's 'D' Company across to occupy the hamlet. As the only means for crossing remained the small boat, the leading platoon, commanded by Lieutenant H.C. Paillefer, was divided into two groups. Resorting again to shovels, one group paddled across. The boat then returned and the second group crossed. By 1930 hours, this platoon was firmly in place. Shortly after dark, the rest of the company crossed by the same means.

At midnight, while Crummer's men were still getting in place, a German patrol entered the hamlet, surprising the platoon, and captured Paillefer and one other man before being driven off. Despite this setback, the battalion's war diarist was able to legitimately claim that the Lincs had denied the Germans the opportunity to establish a defensive line along this section of the Seine. Had they been able to form the line, 4th Division would have been forced to break it with an undoubtedly costly frontal assault. The Lincs also had the distinction of being the first Canadian soldiers across the Seine.[28]

Not long after 'D' Company's crossing, 4th Division's Nos. 8 and 9 Field Squadrons reached Criquebeuf and worked through the night to find a suitable ferry operation site. The engineers were running late—Major General Harry Foster having planned for 10th Infantry Brigade to be ferried across the river just after midnight, with the Algonquin Regiment passing through the Lincoln and Welland positions and the Argyll and Sutherland Highlanders following. Although the Lincs had advanced the plan with their spontaneous establishment of a narrow bridgehead, dawn found the engineers still awaiting stormboats. Under heavy mortar and shellfire that inflicted eight casualties, No. 9 Field Squadron managed to construct and deploy a raft.[29]

The 20th Field Company—a corps engineer unit—arrived at 0800 hours and started constructing two rafts. At 0910 hours, the company launched its first raft with an unarmoured D-4 bulldozer from No. 6 Field Park Squadron aboard to construct a causeway on the opposite bank. This close to the sea, the Seine was gently tidal, ebbing or flowing between three and four feet per cycle, with a one-knot current at high tide. Upon reaching the opposite shore, Sapper Clifford Henry William Marchment got to work with the bulldozer. At 0945 hours, however, German mortar fire struck the work site, and the thirty-five-year-old Marchment was killed. Sapper Noble John Hore manned the bulldozer and finished the work under fire—an action later recognized by the French Croix de Guerre. By 1000 hours, the engineers had two rafts afloat, with one crossing the river every three minutes and able to carry a single vehicle or one infantry platoon per trip.

As the Algonquin Regiment made this crossing, it came under fire from 88-millimetre guns and mortars, but suffered no casualties. The Algonquin objective was Sotteville-sous-le-Val and Point 88, a prominent hill beyond. Sotteville was less than a mile from the river and Point 88 a mile farther on. To the right of the Algonquins, the Arygll and Sutherland Highlanders were to take Igoville, a village about five hundred yards to the right of Sotteville and another height of ground—Point 95.

The Argylls ran into a storm of fire advancing from the riverbank toward a nearby railway embankment. Gaining the railway, soldiers huddled in its lee to escape the fire, and Lieutenant Colonel Dave Stewart ordered them to sit tight. The Argylls were so few in number that 'B' and 'C' Companies had been combined for the operation under command of Major A.C. Logie. This company and 'A' Company had led the attack, and both were pinned behind the railway embankment.[30]

To the left, the Algonquins had also left the river to cross open fields to gain the railway embankment, which lay about equidistant from the Seine and Sotteville. Tunnels through the embankment enabled roads from the river to reach the town. Harried by shellfire, the Algonquins easily gained the embankment and paused to reorganize. Captain Jack Forbes, a 15th Field Regiment FOO, called down covering fire as 'D' Company launched itself in a mad dash toward the town. The dash was made by two platoons commanded respectively by Lieutenant Pat

Richardson and Lieutenant Doug MacDonald, while Lieutenant G.E. Mageau's platoon provided covering fire. Raked the entire distance by machine-gun fire, the two platoons gained the town's outskirts at a cost of six casualties. When Mageau tried to bring his platoon forward, he was wounded, and Private Stuart Aubrey Burnett was killed while single-handedly eliminating a machine-gun position.

Sotteville fell quickly, and 'B' Company led off toward Point 88. 'A' Company, meanwhile, had been ordered to slip right and gain a foothold in Igoville. Using the road underpasses as a guide, the company commander miscounted and stopped prematurely in the eastern outskirts of Sotteville. Algonquin Major George Cassidy decided this was a fortunate error when it became apparent that the Argylls were conducting a full-scale battalion fight for Igoville.

The moment 'B' Company stepped out of Sotteville, it was abruptly halted by fire from a German self-propelled gun firing at near point-blank range. Both the SPG and two armoured half-tracks loaded with infantry seemed intent on overrunning 'B' Company and forcing their way into the town beyond. Corporal William John Lynnsay "Pee-wee" Lafontaine and his PIAT teammate, Lance Corporal A.C. Brightman, were able to knock out the SPG as it tried to rumble past. With the loss of the SPG, the German half-tracks withdrew. But the Algonquins could make no further progress and fell back to Sotteville. Later in the day, Lafontaine was killed.[31]

At Igoville, the Argylls were locked in a bitter, confused fight when the battalion's headquarters party in Bren carriers and a half-track inexplicably passed directly across the front of the leading two companies and into the midst of the Germans. Gunfire erupted, and the Argylls watched in dismay as many of the headquarters personnel were shot down and the vehicles burst into flames. Three men were killed. Fifteen were taken prisoner, some being badly wounded. Only two dispatch riders managed to escape on their motorcycles. Having joined the leading companies, Lieutenant Colonel Dave Stewart could only watch helplessly as his headquarters personnel were lost. Hard fighting continued through the day, but by nightfall, the Argylls held Igoville.[32] Including the headquarter losses, the battalion had suffered seventy-five casualties.[33]

WHILE 4TH ARMOURED Division had been preparing to cross at Criquebeuf, 3rd Infantry Division's engineers had deployed downstream at Elbeuf. The 6th Field Company arrived first, but was forced to await the promised stormboats. Constructed of plywood, they each weighed about nine hundred pounds, were six and a half feet wide and twenty feet long, and could carry a jeep, a 6-pounder anti-tank gun, or twelve to sixteen soldiers, depending on equipment loads. Each boat was powered by a fifty-horsepower Evinrude outboard motor.[34]

Fearing the boats would not arrive in time to facilitate a night crossing, 7th Infantry Brigade's Regina Rifle Regiment commander, Lieutenant Colonel Foster Matheson, summoned scout platoon leader Lieutenant Lorenzo Bergeron just before midnight. Matheson ordered Bergeron to cross the Seine in a small boat, with two FFI resistance fighters providing local guidance. Bergeron was to discreetly determine the German strength on the opposite bank and within St. Aubin, a village directly across from the Reginas. Taking a wireless set, Bergeron and the FFI men paddled quietly into the darkness.

At 0300 hours, Bergeron reported that the banks of the river were undefended, yet he could hear intermittent machine-gun and rifle fire inside the village. Bergeron also thought he heard tank engines in the distance.[35]

Puzzled about the cause of gunfire in St. Aubin, Matheson felt helpless to decide the next move. By the time the trucks bearing stormboats turned up at 0430 hours, the first glimmer of dawn tinted the eastern skyline. Then the engineers unloading the boats reported with dismay that all the outboard motors were still packed in factory crates and had obviously never been serviced. When the crates were opened, the motors proved to be covered in protective grease that had to be meticulously cleaned off before servicing could even begin. Consequently, it was 0830 hours before the boats were declared ready.[36]

By this time, Bergeron had radioed Matheson the welcome news that the village was undefended, and the gunfire had come from FFI men armed with German weapons. He expected the crossing could be made without serious opposition. Matheson, however, took no chances. He had the battalion's carrier platoon line up alongside the river, ready to provide covering fire with its machine guns. Artillery FOOs were also assigned to each rifle company to provide fire support if any resistance was met. At 0900 hours, 'C' Company led off with about thirty men in each stormboat. The crossing was unopposed and proceeded quickly, with 'D' Company following, then Matheson's headquarters, then 'B' Company, and finally 'A' Company. As the men piled out of the boats, they were greeted by cheering civilians and FFI fighters, who turned over twenty-eight "ragged, bedraggled stragglers from Hitler's 'Master Race,'" reported the Reginas' war diarist.[37]

The Canadian Scottish Regiment, meanwhile, was to have crossed in concert with the Reginas and under cover of darkness. This plan was thwarted by the late arrival of its stormboats. Hoping to still cross while it was dark, the Can Scots' 'A' and 'B' Companies marched to a huge stone and concrete bridge. Unable to judge the bridge's condition in the gloom, the leading men got about two-thirds of the way across before discovering that the span ahead had been demolished. It was, the regiment's historian wrote, "impossible to go farther as there were not even twisted girders and cables the men could use to crawl across. So back they came, their hob-nailed boots ringing loudly through an otherwise quiet night." The Can Scots could only await the stormboats. Crossing about an hour after the Reginas, the Can Scots were also greeted by cheering civilians. While the battalion had been waiting on the engineers, men had rounded up a number of small boats found along the banks. These were used to accelerate the crossing.[38]

The brigade plan called for the Reginas and Can Scots to advance up the length of the peninsula to the village of Tourville—about five miles distant—with the Royal Winnipeg Rifles following in reserve. All went well until the Reginas on the left were closing on Tourville at about 1700 hours and 'C' Company came under intense fire from the town. Finding the ground between the company and the town too open to cross in a frontal assault, Matheson ordered a stand down.[39]

To the Reginas' right, the Can Scots also met resistance, and 'B' Company with the battalion headquarters trailing became separated from the rest of the battalion. Advancing alone toward the battalion objective of the railway junction beside Tourville, the company became entangled in an isolated battle that raged for two hours, with the Germans using the high ground behind Tourville to bring artillery, mortar, and machine-gun fire to bear on Major P.F. Ramsay's platoons. Unable to call for artillery support and having nothing heavier than the company's 2-inch mortars to fire back, 'B' Company broke into loose formation and its platoon leaders directed their men to use fire and manoeuvre to continue the advance. In this manner the company managed to seize a wooded knoll southwest of Tourville that commanded the ground leading into the peninsula and prevented any German advance beyond the town. The company suffered about fifteen casualties, among them No. 12 Platoon's Lieutenant Edward Gustav Schwandt—a twenty-seven-year-old former schoolteacher from Strasbourg, Saskatchewan—who was killed.[40] The German force that 'B' Company had engaged was estimated to number about three hundred and its casualties were thought to have run to about thirty killed or wounded.[41] By seizing the knoll, 'B' Company held a firm base that the brigade could use to renew the advance the following day.

As August 27 closed, Lieutenant General Guy Simonds held a meeting to discuss plans for the next day's operations. Simonds noted that 3rd Division's engineers were further advanced in their bridging efforts than 4th Division's and should have a Class 40 Bailey bridge ready by 0600 hours. In light of this, he decided to send 4th Division's 4th Canadian Armoured Brigade to Elbeuf, with its tanks having priority use of the bridge there. The division's 10th Infantry Brigade would meanwhile continue ferrying across the Seine at Criquebeuf to consolidate the hold on Sotteville and Igoville. Once 4th Division's armour and infantry reunited, the advance would begin anew on August 29. For its part, 3rd Division's 7th Brigade would continue clearing the high ground behind Tourville.[42] As for 2nd Division, its focus was squarely on winning the great meander before Rouen that contained Forêt de la Londe.

6

The Quickest Way to Win

S THE CANADIANS closed on the Seine, the Germans realized they were running out of time to conduct an orderly extraction of their remaining forces south of the river. During the period of August 21–25, the main withdrawal on either side of Rouen had gone smoothly due to an efficient ferrying system. Generalleutnant Bodo Zimmerman at Oberbefehlshaber West [OB West] later summarized the ebb and flow of operations here, claiming a surprising level of success in getting personnel across despite an increasingly chaotic situation. This, he wrote, "was accomplished at the expense of losing the bulk of our matériel, in an almost inextricable confusion of units, and with tremendous losses. The fighter-bombers attacked incessantly, Rouen itself underwent severe carpet-bombing, and several enemy tanks advanced as far as the Seine bends and fired into the columns and the elements crossing the river. An enormous traffic jam resulted, especially near Elbeuf, where some two thousand massed vehicles fell prey to the air attacks. Nevertheless, about 20 per cent to 30 per cent of the units and matériel, including staffs, managed to get across the Seine."

But on August 25, the loops south of Rouen were also clogged with seemingly stranded transport. Two major ferries—both near the coast at Quillebeuf and Caudebec-en-Caux—had been sunk by fighter-bombers. Efforts to construct a floating bridge at Rouen were abandoned when three boats pivotal to its completion were destroyed.

Desperate to save the masses of vehicles, Fifth Panzer Army head-quarters realized that the defending 331st Infanterie-Division could not alone hold back the attacking Canadians.[1] The division ably commanded by Colonel Walter Steinmüller had not been caught in the Falaise Pocket's collapse but had still lost one of three grenadier regiments during the retreat to the Seine. This left the division too weak to cover the crossings at Rouen and Duclair within the two great loops north and east of Bourgtheroulde.

To beef up the division's strength, on the afternoon of August 25 a battle group hastily organized the day before and under command of 116th Panzer Division's Generalleutnant Graf Gerhard von Schwerin brought all available armour together. Von Schwerin then split the group into two formations—one composed of 2nd and 9th ss Panzer Divisions, the other of 21st and 116th Panzer Divisions. Each was to operate within one of the loops by establishing blocking lines across their entrants.[2]

On August 27, however, with the Germans losing ever-more ground south of the Seine, Fifth Panzer Army became desperate to save as much armour as possible and began pulling away the tanks. Although estimates remained fluid, the Germans predicted it would take about three days to get all the armour and most of the vehicles across the river. Over the course of the day, a compromise decision was taken whereby 2nd ss Panzer Division's tanks and elite infantry were to remain in support of 331st Infanterie-Division, while the rest of the armour departed. The hope was to still pull 2nd ss Panzer Division out sometime on August 28.[3]

A confused flurry of instructions to the units still on the wrong side of the Seine ensued that finally resulted in a significantly stronger panzer force than just those of 2nd ss Panzer Division left to support 331st Infanterie-Division.[4]

The German focus around Rouen was now entirely set on delaying the Canadians—particularly 2nd Infantry Division—in overrunning the two loops and gaining the riverbank before they were able to withdraw the majority of vehicles and soldiers there. Clearly, time was running out. Upstream, the British and American formations were "surging across the Seine in many places." The German situation was becoming untenable. If there was to be any semblance of an orderly withdrawal to the Somme, the time for it was now. The speed of the advance upstream showed that the Allies still hoped to envelope Army Group B in the general area of Amiens and Arras. For the Germans across from Rouen, a hasty escape was "imperative," and yet Fifth Panzer Army kept insisting that no armour be left behind.

Rescuing the armour and transport, however, was almost impossible. Although Allied air attacks had successfully destroyed most bridges, the Germans had launched about sixty ferry operations between Elbeuf and Vieux-Port. These ferries worked miracles in getting manpower across the Seine. But with no anti-aircraft batteries to guard the ferries, whenever the slower process of loading and moving vehicles across the river began, the operation suffered what I SS Panzer Corps Oberstgruppenführer Joseph "Sepp" Dietrich described as "terrific" losses. The debacle at the Seine, in his opinion, matched that of the Falaise Pocket "from the standpoint of equipment abandoned by the Wehrmacht in its headlong flight."[5]

Recognizing how vulnerable the ferries were to air attack, Dietrich had issued orders demanding that anti-aircraft batteries be deployed in sufficient mass to maintain "a defensive barrage at the crossing points." When he arrived in the Rouen area on about August 27, Dietrich found no Luftwaffe Flak troops protecting the crossings. They appeared to have fled, taking their guns with them. This meant, Dietrich later reported, that for "the last three days of the crossing operations there was no Flak protection . . . at all."

For two infantry divisions, this forced complete abandonment of all heavy equipment. In a desperate bid, 272nd Infanterie-Division attempted to swim its horses across the river, losing 1,500 to the current. Gaining the other side, the division counted only 300 men fighting fit. Although the 346th Infanterie-Division managed to cross the Seine without losing a man in the effort, a third (600) of its horse transport drowned. Having lost 150 to 200 men in combat within Forêt de Brotonne, the division was judged barely fighting capable.[6]

The 331st Infanterie-Division remained south of the Seine within the two loops at Rouen, preparing to fight the Canadians to the last. Behind it, despite relentless aerial bombardments, the steadily

diminishing ferry fleet continued bearing men and occasional transport to safety.

Even at this late date, Hitler continued to call for a stand behind
the Seine, but Generalfeldmarschall Walter Model, Oberbefehlshaber
West (OB West), understood this hope was futile. Stocky, constantly
moving, often up front with his troops, Model had proven competent
in a wide variety of commands, including the fighting in Kursk and
the approaches of Warsaw. Now he was attempting to salvage the disastrous situation in the west. It was a job Model sensed was impossible.
On August 29, as the last remnants of troops trickled across the Seine,
Model delivered a disastrously bad news report to Hitler. Those panzer
and panzer grenadier divisions that had fought in Normandy now
fielded no more than five to ten tanks apiece. Of eleven mechanized
divisions, he would be lucky to form eleven battle groups, each of
no more than regimental strength. From sixteen infantry divisions
evacuated across the Seine, there were enough men to cobble together
only four full-sized divisions. And he had little equipment, supplies, or
weapons with which to equip them. The infantry, he said, "have only
a few heavy weapons and for the most part are equipped with nothing
more than small arms . . . The supply of replacements in men and
material is utterly inadequate . . . There is no reserve whatever of assault
guns and other heavy anti-tank equipment." A stand behind the Seine
to enable preparation of a strong defensive line at the Somme and the
Marne was unthinkable. Paris was lost, the British and Canadians had
bridgeheads now across the Seine, and the Americans were advancing
to the east and northeast of the French capital.

Model returned to a warning he had given Hitler on August 24,
that the situation in France could only be saved with reinforcement
by "at least thirty to thirty-five infantry divisions . . . and twelve panzer
divisions." Yet even as Model spelled out the hard facts, he was by no
means counselling defeatism—Model styled himself as "the Führer's
fireman." But neither was he a toady. Model never sugar-coated the
grim realities of situations, often insisting that his reports be passed
unopened to Hitler.

So even as he accepted that the bridgehead south of Rouen was
doomed, Model told Hitler that it "will be withdrawn only when the

advantages of holding it are outweighed by disadvantages." Model had ordered the 331st Infanterie-Division with 2nd ss Panzer to hang on inside the two loops until he instructed otherwise. And he had done so without consulting Hitler. This allowed Model to pursue a localized strategy that could achieve only temporary results without having to argue its merits with either Hitler or the staff minions of Oberkommando der Wehrmacht (Supreme Command of the Armed Forces), whom he considered quite out of touch with reality.[7]

IF HITLER AND the German high command were little able to grasp or seriously influence the military situation developing in France at the end of August, the Allied high command was grappling indecisively with the meaning and consequences of its sudden successes. Eisenhower, Montgomery, Bradley, and Patton each sensed that a 1944 victory was at hand and were prepared to take risks to achieve one. While focused on the same goal, the path to this victory was anything but clear and was cause for growing acrimonious debate.

What all these generals did agree on was that the Allies lacked the logistical supply chain necessary to enable their entire military might to keep thundering forward as one overwhelming juggernaut. Not only did the Allies have to feed and supply their huge armies via a route that still extended back to the Normandy beaches, but now—since the original plan not to liberate Paris immediately had been outpaced by events within the city—they were responsible for feeding that large civilian population, too. By the last days of August, it was abundantly clear that the number of trucks available for supplying the advancing columns of troops and providing humanitarian aid to the French was hugely insufficient. Something was going to have to give.[8]

With typical "can do" determination, on August 23, American transportation officers had established the "Red Ball Express." Two one-way routes from St. Lô to the southwest of Paris were set aside exclusively for the use of designated convoys that ran round the clock. The convoys were composed initially of 67 truck companies, each fielding an average of 48 trucks. On the first day, 500 tons of supplies were delivered. A grand scheme called for 100,000 tons to be advanced by September 1. Of this, only 25,000 tons could be moved by rail—the tracks, locomotives, and rolling stock just slowly being brought back on line after largely being bombed out of action by the Allies during the Normandy invasion. By August 27, the Red Ball counted 132 companies totalling 5,958 trucks drafted from all over the U.S. armies. But the round trip was 700 miles and took five days for each truck to complete at an average speed of 20 miles per hour. So only 1,200 trucks a day reached the delivery point with an average of 7,000 tons of supply. The effort was gargantuan, but it could not meet the insatiable needs of the American armies. Confounding the problem was that the trucks themselves consumed vast quantities of fuel. Total American Army daily consumption requirements were estimated at 800,000 gallons. Red Ball swallowed 300,000 gallons of this.[9]

In the British–Canadian sector, the supply situation was serious but not quite approaching the crisis level the Americans faced. Lines of communication from Bayeux and other major supply depots back in Normandy were shorter. At the same time, the advancing forces were not covering such great distances, and on some days consumption did not reach daily maximums. With 1 British Corps having reached the Seine, the decision was taken to ground it for several days and shift its allotments to British Second Army in order to help fuel its advance. Even then, it was found necessary to also ground two of Second Army's eight divisions in order to shift the transport from these and help enable the advance of the others.[10] First Canadian Army also faced reduced fuel, ammunition, and food supply. The grounding of 1 British Corps and this perceived miserliness of supply to the rest of First Canadian Army germinated the seed of discontent that led many in its ranks—particularly among the quartermaster officers—to describe themselves as the Cinderella Army. Like the fairy-tale heroine, First Canadian Army was seen to be given the grimy, miserable, and yet necessary work, while its British and American cousins headed for glory with a bountiful supply of all that was required for the task. The moniker would stick, becoming something of a badge of pride that the Canadians carried through to war's end.

Montgomery, of course, had no time for such petty complaint. He had predicted this logistical problem in early July, and it was one that invasion planners had also sought to address well before the June 6 landings. Relying on the Mulberry artificial harbours and landing supplies directly onto the beaches was recognized as insufficient for the growing Allied needs. For this reason, Cherbourg in Brittany had been designated as a major early American objective. When a summer gale on June 19 badly damaged the Mulberry in the American sector, it was abandoned, and the need for port facilities was only amplified. Yet in late August, Cherbourg remained the only major port on the western coast of France in Allied hands. Extensive German demolition of its port facilities, however, limited offloading capacity to only 12,900 tons a day, rather than the expected 20,000 tons.[11] Marseilles on the Riviera was not scheduled to open to major supply deliveries until late September, and even then its capacity was primarily earmarked for Seventh U.S. Army consumption.[12]

Allied pre-invasion plans had foreseen that as the Americans broke out of Normandy to advance toward the Rhine, in addition to Cherbourg they would capture the other Breton ports of Brest, St. Malo, Quiberon Bay, and Nantes. Shortly thereafter, Twenty-First Army Group would open Rouen and Le Havre. The Canadian and British forces were then to open the channel ports, such as Dunkirk, Dieppe, Boulogne, Calais, and as soon as possible the much larger port of Antwerp. The channel ports were to exclusively serve Twenty-First Army Group's needs, while the Breton ports supplied the Americans. By the end of August, however, this plan was in tatters. Although the Americans captured St. Malo, the Germans had rendered its harbour facilities useless. Twenty-First Army Group had yet to open any ports in its sector.

The pressing need for ports weighed heavily on both Montgomery and Eisenhower. In conversation with and memos to Montgomery, Eisenhower emphasized this repeatedly as the two generals debated how the Allies should advance beyond the Seine. "We are promised greatly accelerated shipments of American divisions directly from the United States," Eisenhower told Montgomery, "and it is mandatory that we capture and prepare ports and communications to receive them. This has an importance second only to the destruction of the remaining forces on our front."

Accordingly, even as the main American force thrust eastward from the Seine, fifty thousand U.S. troops brought Brest under siege three hundred miles west of the front lines. The Germans had transformed Brest into a major naval base, and American planners considered its capture—particularly the submarine pens—critical to their ability to open the other Breton ports. Expecting the German garrison would destroy all port facilities before allowing Brest to fall, the Americans planned to construct a major port complex virtually from scratch at Quiberon Bay to the south. Again, the continued existence of Brest as a German naval port threatened the sea lanes around the bay and the tip of Brittany. Once Brest fell, the Americans predicted that the German garrisons holding the other Breton ports would surrender, and these would soon be brought on line to receive the divisions that were key to Eisenhower's plans for the advance to the Rhine and into Germany.[13]

MONTGOMERY AND EISENHOWER fully agreed on the need for the ports, and both continued to believe victory over Germany in 1944 remained feasible. However, they disagreed entirely on how that victory should be won.

Eisenhower still stuck to the pre-invasion strategy. This called for the advance of Twenty-First Army Group and Twelfth Army Group to diverge, with the British and Canadians operating northeastward to secure successive bases along the coast and likely establish a final base at Antwerp before turning to enter Germany north of the Ardennes. Twenty-First Army Group's primary mission during the coastal-advance phase was to destroy the Germans between the Seine and Pas de Calais and gain control of that area. Eisenhower planned to drop the entire Allied airborne command behind the German line of retreat to facilitate this destruction.

Twelfth Army Group, under command of Lieutenant General Omar Bradley, meanwhile, would pursue one of two options. If German strength in the Pas de Calais proved stronger than expected, it would strike northeastward to assist Twenty-First Army Group. More likely, however, it would move eastward to pass south of the Ardennes and break into the Saar region of Germany.

During the Normandy Campaign, both army groups had operated under Montgomery's command, with Eisenhower overseeing overall naval, air, and army operations. Now, with the two armies likely parting ways, Eisenhower was to supersede Montgomery, who reverted to command only Twenty-First Army Group in the same manner as Bradley commanded Twelfth Army Group.

Montgomery opposed both Eisenhower's strategy and the command structure change. As early as August 18, Montgomery had stated his opposition in a telegram to Chief of the Imperial General Staff General Sir Alan Brooke. Instead of diverging, the two army groups should be kept together "as a solid mass" of forty divisions, "which would be so strong that it need fear nothing. The force should move northwards" with Twenty-First Army Group on the western flank clearing the channel coast, Pas de Calais, western Flanders, and then securing Antwerp. Twelfth Army Group, meanwhile, would advance north of the Ardennes and adjacent to Twenty-First Army Group to seize Brussels, Aachen, and Cologne. In this way, the Americans would be cutting the retreating German lines of communication and supporting Twenty-First Army Group's destruction effort, which he declared the primary Allied purpose. Additionally, the taking of Belgian soil would facilitate establishing bases for Allied air forces to operate strongly against Germany and overrun the v-1 launching sites that had been ranging in on England with deadly effect since June 13, 1944. Montgomery said he had discussed this plan with Bradley and had his agreement, but had not yet raised the idea with Eisenhower. He first wanted Brooke's blessing.

Montgomery had discussed this plan with Bradley the previous day. Inclined as he was to believe in his infallibility, Montgomery often misinterpreted how others saw things. In fact, Bradley—in conjunction with Third U.S. Army commander General George Patton—wanted the Americans to thrust straight through the centre of France into the Saar region of Germany and then to the Rhine at Frankfurt. Both the First and Third Armies would be required for this effort, so there would be little or no cohesion between the American and British–Canadian forces.

On August 19, Bradley set out this plan for Montgomery, emphasizing the point that it adhered with what Eisenhower envisioned. Montgomery continued to advance his idea, which he fleshed out in detail on August 22. "The quickest way to win the war is for the great mass of the Allied armies to advance northwards," he told Vice-Chief of the Imperial General Staff Lieutenant General Sir Archibald Nyes during a meeting. There must be one great, cohesive force that could "do the job quickly." And there must be just one commander for this land operation. "This is a *whole time* job for one man," he emphasized. It was one man—himself—who had won the "great victory in N.W. France. Only in this way will future victories be won. If staff control of operations is allowed to creep in, then quick success becomes endangered. To change the system of command now, after having won a great victory, would be to prolong the war."

Eisenhower was having none of this. The following day, he visited Montgomery's headquarters. "After a long and weary discussion," Montgomery reported to Brooke, "he agreed [that] on our left flank we must clear the channel coast and establish a powerful Air Force in Belgium and invade Ruhr. He also considers it necessary to invade Saar and would like to split the force . . . The problem of command and control was then discussed. It seems public opinion in America demands Bradley shall hold his command directly under Ike and shall not be . . . subordinated to me."14

Even if Montgomery's plan was the best militarily—something Eisenhower was unwilling to concede—the supreme commander made it clear that political expediency forced him to follow the broad-front strategy. Grounding Patton's Third Army to give Montgomery all the resources was, he said, something that the "American public would never stand for . . . and public opinion wins war."

Montgomery dryly replied, "Victories win wars. Give people victory and they won't care who won it."

Undoubtedly true for the people of Britain and the Commonwealth nations, this was not so for the Americans. Patton's dramatic breakout and subsequent "end run" that carried his army to Paris had captured the imagination of the American soldiers in Europe and the people back home. It was akin to a stunning football game win wherein Patton was "carrying the ball" to eternal glory. Eisenhower believed that if he snatched the ball from Patton, like some misguided referee invoking a technical rule breach, he would be pilloried by those Americans he commanded, the American press hovering close at hand, and public opinion at home. All that could lead to major problems for SHAEF and even President Franklin D. Roosevelt's administration.

Eisenhower, however, conceded that his priority was to "secure the channel ports and Antwerp as soon as possible, and this could be achieved only if he were to give some measure of priority to Montgomery." He promised the full support of First U.S. Army in this endeavour. But Patton's army would continue its easterly advance, and as soon as Montgomery cleared the v-1 launching sites in the Pas de Calais and seized Antwerp, he would give Patton the resources necessary to strike out in force and link up with Sixth Army Group in the Vosges region.[15]

Montgomery realized he must be content with this compromise. But he misread the degree to which Eisenhower was willing to have Twelfth Army Group support his cause. Montgomery assumed Twelfth Army Group would provide all the support required to win the ports and clear Pas de Calais. To some extent, Eisenhower confirmed this in a letter on August 24, where he stated that Bradley would provide Montgomery with "every effort toward speeding up the deployment of his forces in that direction. The faster we do it the more certain will be our success and the earlier will come our opportunity to advance eastward from the Paris area." The primary requirement was "speed in execution."

In a signal to Brooke on August 24, Montgomery reported that Eisenhower intended to take overall command of land forces in Europe on September 1, and that after the Pas de Calais and Belgian airfields were secured, he was going to "split the force and to move the American portion eastwards . . . into Germany via the Saar. I do not myself agree with what he proposes to do and have said so quite plainly." But he saw no further argument as likely to succeed. "The great point is that I have been given power to coordinate and control movement of left wing northward towards Antwerp and Belgium."

Eisenhower's letter, however, was open to differing interpretations. Bradley saw it as stating that "for the moment" he was to put primary emphasis on thrusting forward to the left in support of Montgomery. But he also felt authorized to immediately send Patton eastward. He told Patton to be prepared "to continue the advance rapidly in order to seize crossings of the Rhine . . . from Mannheim to Koblenz." At the same time, Patton was to clear Brittany.[16]

Montgomery, meanwhile, issued a new directive to Twenty-First Army Group on August 26. Although the Germans still held in some places south of the Seine, he said, they were badly overextended, disorganized, and "in no fit condition to stand and fight us. This, then, is our opportunity to achieve our further objects quickly, and to deal the enemy further heavy blows which will cripple his power to continue in the war." Immediate tasks for the army group were to destroy the Germans still within northeastern France and Belgium, win the Pas de Calais and Belgian airfields, and "secure Antwerp as a base." Once these tasks were complete, the advance eastward to the Ruhr would begin. "Speed of action and of movement is now vital. I cannot emphasise this too strongly; what we have to do must be done quickly. Every officer and man must understand that by a stupendous effort now we shall not only hasten the end of the war; we shall also bring quick relief to our families and friends in England by over-running the flying bomb launching sites in the Pas de Calais."

First Canadian Army, having crossed the Seine, was to operate northwards to secure Dieppe and then proceed quickly with the destruction of the Germans in the coastal belt up to the Belgian city of Bruges. This task fell primarily to II Canadian Corps, with I British Corps to turn westward into the Le Havre peninsula to destroy the German garrison there and secure the port city. No more forces were to be dedicated to the Le Havre operation than were necessary to get the job done. "The main business lies to the north, and in the Pas de Calais," Montgomery wrote. Antwerp, of course, was the "main business," and with it the necessity of securing the fifty-mile-long Scheldt Estuary that linked the city to the sea. As the Canadian army moved northward, its main weight was to be concentrated on the right flank, "dealing with enemy resistance by outflanking movements, and 'right hooks.'"

Montgomery believed that I British Corps did not require much strength to capture Le Havre. Already 6th Airborne Division was standing down and preparing for withdrawal to England. Now he transferred 7th Armoured Division to British Second Army "at once."

This left 1 British Corps with just two divisions and the Dutch, Czech, and British Commando units.

Montgomery's transfer of 7th Armoured Division to Second Army was intended to give it great mobility. This "armoured strength" was to be deployed well forward of the following infantry divisions, with the army's "passage northward" to "be swift and relentless. By this means it will cut across the communications of the enemy forces in the coastal belt, and will thus facilitate the operations of Canadian Army. Immediately the Seine is bridged, a strong armoured force will be pushed quickly ahead to seize Amiens; this thrust will be the spearhead of the army movement."

Right of Second Army, Twelfth Army Group was to operate on the right flank, with orders to "thrust forward on its left, its principal offensive mission being, for the present, to support [Twenty-First Army Group]." The American thrust would specifically be carried out by First U.S. Army.

Montgomery emphasized again that the tactics he sought entailed strong armoured and mobile columns bypassing enemy resistance pockets "to push boldly ahead, creating alarm and despondency in the enemy rear areas." The bypassed elements would be cleaned up by following infantry columns. "I rely on commanders of every rank and grade to 'drive' ahead with the utmost energy; any tendency to be 'sticky' or cautious must be stamped on ruthlessly."[17]

[7]

A Great Spot to Be Ambushed

O N THE DAY Montgomery issued his directive, First Canadian
Army was already becoming entangled in a "sticky" fight for the
Forêt de la Londe meander of the Seine. But this was not the only place
where Germans offered a stiff fight. All across First Canadian Army's
front, opposition had proved greater than anything encountered by
the American or British forces. Although the British Second Army's
xxx Corps had met sharp resistance crossing the Seine at Vernon on
August 25–26, it was still less than what II Canadian Corps and I British
Corps had faced. The reason was that the German army retreating from
Normandy was largely escaping across the Seine between Elbeuf and
Vieux-Port, where the river followed six long oxbow-shaped meanders.
All these meanders were in the Canadian operational area. The best and
most active ferry sites were those in the two meanders closest to Rouen.[1]

The 331st Infanterie-Division was assigned to prevent the approaching Canadians from shutting down these ferry sites. It was a task that
stretched the division thin, so the less important western loop south of
Duclair was defended only by the division's 557th Grenadier Regiment,
with a fusilier battalion (troops specialized in reconnaissance or defensive roles and equipped with more heavy weapons than were regular
infantry battalions) in support. Also in place here was a light artillery
battalion and a handful of tanks cobbled together from the 9th ss, 10th
ss, and 21st Panzer Divisions.

Most of the division was deployed in the eastern loop dominated by Forêt de la Londe. Here, the 559th Grenadier Regiment had under command a light artillery battalion reinforced by one heavy artillery battery. More important was the support of a battle group of 6th Fallschirmjäger Division and 1053rd Regimental Group from 85th Infanterie-Division. Armoured strength was provided by elements of 116th Panzer Division and 2nd ss Panzer Division. The tanks of 116th Panzer, however, were to be ferried across the Seine on the night of August 27–28, leaving just 2nd ss Panzer Division to support the infantry against the forthcoming attack by 2nd Canadian Infantry Division. On the river's north shore, between the two loops, was another regimental group (primarily infantry) drawn from 344th Infanterie-Division. Most of 331st Infanterie-Division's artillery was also deployed north of the river within range of the ground inside both meanders.[2]

Early on the morning of August 27, 2nd Canadian Infantry Division entered a landscape ideally suited for defence. As one Canadian report stated, the Germans "had chosen a good place in which to make a stand. Except on the extreme German right, which was open level ground protected by fire from north of the Seine, the isthmus consisted of heavily wooded, hilly ground with a maze of tracks approaching it through the forest. Along the railway line running north from Port du Gravier the enemy found good cover, high ground, good observation and excellent fields of fire. In well-prepared positions were the most determined troops, including men from paratroop and ss units, with orders to hold at all costs. The enemy strength was estimated at two battalions."[3] The forest was largely uninhabited, many tracks developed purely to enable foresters to cut timber blocks. As the forest closed on the river, the ground also rose to heights of as much as twelve hundred feet—providing yet more observation points for German artillery spotters and defensive strongpoints.

The woods were dense—mixed stands of birch, beech, chestnut, and pine with the odd remnant of the oak forests that had once stretched along the Seine from Paris almost to its mouth. That forest had been decimated by indiscriminate cutting in the Middle Ages. Since the war, the present-day forest had not been well managed, allowing a thick understorey of bracken and broom to develop that hampered easy movement.

Although Canadian intelligence staff had earlier forecasted that Forêt de la Londe would be heavily defended, by August 27 their minds had changed. Civilian reports two days earlier of the forest containing a "large concentration of tanks" were discredited. The morning intelligence summary issued on the 27th by II Canadian Corps described the German forces as "nothing more than local rearguards."[4] This led 2nd Division's Major General Charles Foulkes to understand that the "Boche has pulled out and little opposition can be expected."[5] In the Normandy campaign, the forty-one-year-old Foulkes had proven a lackluster divisional commander, especially during the debacle of Verrières Ridge, where the division suffered massive casualties to no purpose. Seen by many subordinates and some peers as a leader apt to shamelessly toady up to his superiors, Foulkes was unlikely to question orders or intelligence assessments from above. He was equally unlikely to bring imagination to an operation. Heavy-set and grim of nature, Foulkes little inspired a division plagued by bad luck and shaky morale.

At 2050 hours, a patrol into the forest by the division's 14th Canadian Hussars recce regiment's 'C' Squadron came under heavy machine-gun and mortar fire from infantry covering a railway bridge who were also supported by a tank or self-propelled gun. Thirty-year-old Lieutenant Edward Boothroyd was killed, his comrades unable to recover the body in their haste to escape the deadly fire.[6] Despite this incident, divisional staff did not revise its potential resistance assessment.

Given the haste being urged from on high, no further reconnaissance was undertaken. This left divisional staff unable to develop either an appreciation of opposition or means to work out a detailed attack plan. Instead, what passed for a final plan was that 4th Brigade would advance on the right through Elbeuf with the Royal Hamilton Light Infantry leading, the Essex Scottish Regiment following, and the Royal Regiment of Canada being kept in reserve. The two battalions leading would seize high ground overlooking the Seine north of the hamlet of Port du Gravier. The Royal Regiment would then pass through to a point just south of Grand Essart.[7] To some extent, this advance sought to avoid the densest forest. On the left, however,

6th Brigade was to penetrate directly through its heart, with South Saskatchewan Regiment punching through to the village of La Bouille on the Seine and the hamlet of Le Buisson, a little to the southeast and astride a road slightly south of the river. The Queen's Own Cameron Highlanders would then push along this road to Moulineaux and La Chenaie, while Les Fusiliers Mont-Royal carried out a wide hook on the eastern flank of the forest—almost directly alongside the battalions of 4th Brigade—to approach La Chenaie from the south.[8]

Even as this plan was cobbled into place, a complication facing the staffs from division down through brigades to the battalions was the woeful state of available maps. Usually, this lack was made good by aerial photography of terrain being compared to the maps and those duly corrected. But no such photography was immediately available, and what little came in during the ensuing days was too limited in scope to be of much value.[9] The map problem had major implications for the artillery forward observation officers of 4th Field Regiment supporting the division. As the FOOs entered the woods, they found it almost impossible to pinpoint enemy positions or even to situate their actual location. So dense were the woods, meanwhile, that the FOOs had to abandon their Bren carriers and go forward with the infantry on foot—the small teams carrying their radio sets and other equipment into a landscape that left them most often effectively blind.[10]

INADEQUATE MAPS, REBUFFED recce regiments, and artillery officers mulling over how they were possibly to deliver accurate fire-support missions aside, in the early-morning hours of August 27, the two brigades marched toward battle. Their battalions, one army report later noted, advanced "into action after a week of continuous and strenuous pursuit which had followed a month of very hard fighting. Units entered the forest either considerably under strength or carrying relatively new reinforcements who were as yet inexperienced in battle."[11]

It was still dark when the Royal Hamilton Light Infantry (Rileys) formed on a hill near Elbeuf. They immediately discovered that these heights were overlooked by even higher ground, from which concealed Germans let loose with steady sniper, machine-gun, and mortar fire that inflicted about twenty casualties before the Rileys even began their advance. 'D' Company's commander, Major A.J. O'Donohoe, was wounded, as was the battalion's medical officer—the latter struck by shrapnel.[12] A number of trucks, carriers, and jeeps were left burning or wrecked as the battalion descended the hill to gain the road bordering the Seine that led to Port du Gravier. Groping through the darkness, trying to match terrain to maps, the leading company's commander took a road that forked to the left from the one hugging the river. This road entered a valley bordered by one spur of a railway network, consisting of multiple lines that cut through the forest via a confusing route, whereby tracks passed over roads on overpasses or tunnelled under points of high ground. With the dubious maps at hand, the Canadians were hard pressed to situate themselves in relation to these tracks. After advancing about five hundred yards north along this narrow road, the Rileys came to a roadblock. Such intense machine-gun and mortar fire lashed out from it that the Rileys were forced to withdraw back to their starting point on the German-shelled high ground.[13]

Realizing the Rileys were no longer ahead of his battalion, Lieutenant Colonel Peter Bennett ordered his Essex Scottish to lead the way along the river road. The battalion quickly arrayed in "advance to contact" formation with 'B' Company out front. Accordingly, two of 'B' Company's platoons moved in single file on alternate sides of the road, with Major Haughton "Hut" Laird's headquarters section and the third platoon following. A section of six or seven men from each platoon was well out on point, walking steadily at a pace of about three miles per hour while warily eyeing the ground ahead for the first inkling of an ambush. Oissel, the brigade objective, was about two miles ahead.[14]

Right of the Essex, the Seine hugged the road with only a narrow patch of open ground between. To the left, a high ridge loomed, thick vegetation clinging to parts of its mostly sheer white chalk face. The ridge's summit was thickly wooded. Well back in the Essex column, Major Doug W. McIntyre, commanding the support company, thought they had entered "a great spot to be ambushed just like in the old Hollywood westerns."[15]

No sooner did the thought enter his mind than someone on the forested ridge shouted loudly in English, "Halt." Major Laird immediately ordered his men to take cover in the narrow, open ground between road and river that fell away steeply to the water. German machine-gun and mortar teams on the ridge lashed 'B' Company with fire while some infantry started chucking down grenades.

'A' Company was just emerging from Port du Gravier when the same burst of fire struck it. Captain Tom Stewart and his men took cover on the left side of the road, where some scraggly trees and brush provided some concealment.

Both Stewart and Laird grabbed their wireless handsets and told Bennett the river road was clearly "covered by fixed, probably ranged-in fire," and the Germans ahead and to the side of them were sure as hell not "some 'hit and run' rearguard." They had expertly drawn both the Rileys before them and now the Essex into well-prepared traps.

Back almost at the tail of the Essex column, McIntyre realized the entire battalion was in grave danger. 'C' and 'D' Companies, with his support company's Bren carriers and jeeps bringing up the rear, were still approaching the village when they were all "hose-piped" by light and medium mortar fire that struck along a thousand-yard line. McIntyre was in a jeep's passenger seat just short of the demolished rail bridge that had crossed the Seine from the village when mortar rounds started methodically thumping along the middle of the road toward him. The Germans, he realized, were intent on destroying his company's vehicles. If they reduced enough jeeps and Bren carriers to burning wrecks in the road, the Essex infantry would have a hard time retreating. They could effectively be trapped in place and slaughtered at leisure.

There was nothing he could do about that, though. All McIntyre had time for was to shout: "Dismount, forget your gear, just small arms and radios . . . take cover along the cliffs on the left." Most men responded immediately, but a few hesitated as the mortar bombs closed in. McIntyre and his signaller, Corporal "Chief" Thompson, bailed out of the jeep and hunkered behind a wall beside the road. But McIntyre's driver and batman, twenty-year-old Private Harold R. Kalbfleisch, failed to respond quickly enough. A mortar round "detonated on the thin steel floor in the back of the jeep thus contributing to the force of the fragmentation." The German-Canadian from Kitchener, Ontario, died instantly. The jeep directly behind McIntyre's suffered a near miss and shrapnel from the exploding round seriously wounded the pioneer platoon's commander, Lieutenant Angus McCrimmon, and another man. Luckily, the German mortar fire missed all several dozen other vehicles in the column. The road to the rear remained open.

McIntyre discovered that the chalk cliff was pocked with caves of varying depths. While Corporal Thompson set up the support company headquarters in a cave opposite his burning jeep, McIntyre evacuated wounded to the Regimental Aid Post (RAP). The Essex medical officer, Captain Cliff Richardson, had already set this up in a spacious cave several hundred yards short of the village. As McIntyre and some stretcher-bearers carried wounded to the RAP, he came across a friend, Sergeant Walter Buszowski of 'D' Company. The sergeant had a chunk of shrapnel in one eye, a wound that proved fatal. Richardson, meanwhile, was driving back and forth on the road rescuing the wounded, despite being under constant fire. Some he managed to pick up, others bled to death alone in the dark. For his actions, Richardson would be awarded a Military Cross.[16]

Closer to the village than the RAP, McIntyre found that Bennett had established battalion headquarters in the courtyard of one of the ruined houses at the intersection where the road that the Rileys had gone astray on forked away from the river. The rail embankment here provided some protection from the fire coming off the ridge. As dawn broke, the Essex could see that the cliffs overlooking Port du Gravier were dotted with caves from which German machine guns enjoyed excellent firing positions, while the thick woods along the ridgeline made it easy for them to move about undetected. Not the case for the Canadians. Just moving to and from battalion headquarters, Lieutenant T. Tucker wrote in the Essex war diary, required "running a gauntlet of fire for some 200 yards and then swinging quickly into the courtyard." Such was the danger of that gauntlet that the battalion's second-in-command, Major Tom Brown, was wounded in the head by mortar shrapnel while running it.[17]

With the forward Essex Scottish companies pinned in place and the Rileys licking their wounds, Brigadier J.E. "Eddy" Ganong decided striking the Germans frontally with another attack was doomed to fail.

Instead, he brought the Royal Regiment out of reserve and instructed it to advance about two thousand yards northwest in a wide flanking manoeuvre through the woods and then cross the road from Port du Gravier to Moulineaux. Once across the road, the battalion would turn about and fall from behind upon the Germans blocking the river road.[18]

By 1130 hours, the day had turned exceedingly hot, the sun blazing down from a cloudless sky. Sweating heavily under their equipment, the Royals entered the woods and were soon wandering half lost through a maze of intersecting trails. Progress was excruciatingly slow. At one point, several mortar rounds fell. Several men from 'C' Company were wounded, including Major A. MacMillan, who was struck in the face by shrapnel.[19] Because of the dense tree canopy, Captain George Blackburn, a 4th Field Artillery Regiment FOO moving with the Royals, later wrote that the Canadians came "to dread the arrival of German shells and mortar bombs anywhere near them in the forest, for they detonate in the trees overhead with horrible, resounding airbursts that shower the forest floor with branches and steel shards that can maim and kill."[20]

At 1500 hours, the leading troops blundered into a company of Les Fusiliers Mont-Royal from 6th Brigade. According to the divisional plan, the Fusiliers had conducted a sweep eastward away from their own brigade's main line of advance on the western flank of the forest, turned sharply left at Le Buquet, and then pushed north into the forest.

By the time the Royals appeared, the Fusiliers had nearly finished readying an attack across the Port du Gravier–Moulineaux road, supported by an artillery barrage. The company commander leading the attack warned that if the Royals continued on their current path, they would be caught in the shelling. 'C' Company quickly pulled back, while the other three companies moved into the woods well behind the Fusiliers. Major T.F. Whitley, temporarily commanding the Royals, reported the situation to Ganong.[21]

The 4th Brigade commander quickly relayed this information to 2nd Division, and Major General Foulkes placed the Fusiliers under Ganong's command, informing 6th Brigade's newly appointed Brigadier Fred Clift of this decision at 1519 hours. Foulkes reaffirmed this order with a signal to Ganong at 1616 hours. As the Royals had an entire battalion in place compared to a single company of Fusiliers, Ganong decided to switch the artillery support to them for an attack across the wood. No sooner had Whitley summoned his company commanders to brief them on this plan, however, than Ganong cancelled the attack entirely.

At this point, Ganong's control of 4th Brigade's operations became inexplicably confused—perhaps a result of his headquarters being situated in an orchard a mile and half southwest of Bourgtheroulde and over six miles from Port du Gravier, which left him badly separated from his command.[22] He ordered the Royals to advance northward by trails through the forest to meet up with the Essex Scottish.[23] The Essex, at this time, were trying to advance 'C' and 'D' Companies out from the rear of their embattled column on a line just a short distance west of Port du Gravier in an attempt to link up with the Royals, who they thought were immediately on their left, rather than almost two miles away. Finding the steep ground and dense woods impossible to penetrate, the Essex attack quickly ran out of steam. They remained stuck on the road.[24]

Guided by a member of the French resistance, the Royals, meanwhile, moved northward at 1830 hours on a course taking them ever deeper into the forest and away from the Essex. After two hours, without incident, they reached a crude railway landing that matched the map reference Ganong had provided for where the Essex were to join them. All they found was a "depleted company of [Fusiliers Mont-Royal] . . . on high ground to the south and west of the station." When the lead company of Royals started across the tracks, it was immediately driven back by machine-gun fire without being able to determine the probable strength of the defending Germans. "The exhausted and hungry" Royals were then ordered to stand down until first light.

As evening closed in, Ganong reported to Foulkes that his attack "this afternoon bogged down entirely in thick wood." He had ordered the Royals and Essex Scottish to return southward. Once the brigadier ascertained where the Essex actually were, he intended to have them attack to the west of Port du Gravier and clear the cliffs overlooking the river road. Les Fusiliers Mont-Royal would also attack from where the Royals had first met up with them. He promised to let Foulkes know the locations of the two missing companies of Essex Scottish and the Royal Hamilton Light Infantry "as soon as I get them."

Shortly after midnight, Foulkes gave Ganong new instructions. The Royals and Essex Scottish were now to try outflanking the enemy on the cliffs overlooking the river road. Soon thereafter, however, Foulkes returned the Fusiliers to 6th Brigade command. When it was learned that the Royals were still in place at the rail-stop siding, they were ordered to advance from there to seize the high ground on the other side of the tracks and gain the road running from Port du Gravier to Moulineaux. Foulkes ordered this movement started right away, particularly an advance by one company to seize a low hill standing between the Royals and the road.[25]

Soon designated Chalk Pits Hill because of three large quarry holes in its side, this hill stood about as high as the cliffs overlooking the river road where the Essex Scottish were still pinned down. Dense woods on its slopes and summit provided the Germans with perfect concealment. In addition to Chalk Pits Hill, the Royals were to seize another, higher feature to its right. Code-named Maisie, this was the heavily forested hill overlooking Port du Gravier and lying between the road running from that village to Moulineux and the railway tracks to the southwest. Major Whitley had just completed briefing 'C' Company when, unexpectedly, the quartermasters showed up with rations and water. "As the men had, generally speaking, been without water for about 18 hours and without food, except for odd scraps which they had carried with them for a longer period, [Whitley] took it upon himself to allow the troops to eat and fill their water-bottles before starting the move," recorded the war diarist. The attack would now take place after first light on August 28.[26]

WHILE 4TH BRIGADE had been brought to a standstill on the eastern flank of the forest, the South Saskatchewan Regiment had fared better in leading 6th Brigade's advance to the west. On the road from Bourgtheroulde to Le Buisson, the main force of 'A,' 'B,' and 'D' Companies met only light resistance from scattered machine-gun positions and snipers, which were quickly silenced. 'C' Company, meanwhile, had conducted a wide leftward sweep through the woods and then hooked via a road that ran due eastward to join the main force as it entered Le Buisson. During this sweep, 'C' Company took eleven German stragglers prisoner. The four companies then moved without meeting any resistance into the high, thickly wooded ground that overlooked La Bouille from the south. La Bouille stood alongside the Seine, and these heights were the battalion's objective for August 27.[27] It was 1720 hours.

Having trailed along behind the Sasks, the Queen's Own Cameron Highlanders headed eastward parallel to the Seine toward high ground dominating the riverside village of Moulineaux.[28] Ostensibly, two combined companies under command of Major Don Gillespie led the advance, but this force numbered just forty men.[29] Given the scant resistance that the Sasks had met, Camerons intelligence officer Captain Bruce Marshall understood the "move was made on the assumption that it would be a non-tactical move and that no or very few enemy would be encountered."[30] About fifteen hundred yards short of their objective, however, the small force was drenched by heavy mortar, artillery, and machine-gun fire.[31]

When the rest of the battalion rushed forward, the advance was renewed, only to be brought up short by the appearance of German tanks and self-propelled guns. "What had been a march to contact," Marshall later wrote, "became a regular slugging match as enemy rearguards protected their lines of retreat over [the] Seine furiously and fanatically."[32]

At 1800 hours, when the first contact with tanks was reported, the Shermans of 'A' Squadron Sherbrooke Fusiliers rumbled into the forest to support the infantry. Major Sydney Radley-Walters, who commanded the tanks, was soon frustrated beyond measure by the seeming inability of the Camerons' infantrymen to work with his squadron. "The infantry-tank cooperation was dreadful . . . Our communications were poor; our artillery support was terrible; and we had very heavy casualties." The German tanks holed up in the forest, he believed, were cut off from any avenue of escape and with "lots of ammunition and sufficient food to hold out . . . they intended just to stay there. We were beating our heads against a brick wall and every time we moved, we took casualties. They put mines on the roads and the roads were very narrow. We were just going through forestry roads. Consequently in some places we couldn't traverse our tank guns from right to left they were so close, and a number of our tanks were lost on mines."[33]

Mostly, the Sherbrookes and Camerons operated ignorant of the whereabouts of the other. At nightfall, the tanks withdrew. The Camerons, meanwhile, dug in with the companies circled. Pinpointed by the Germans, the troops were subjected to near continuous heavy mortaring, shelling, and machine-gun fire with occasional showers of rifle grenades added to the mix.[34]

Just after midnight, Brigadier Fred Clift summoned his battalion commanders. Clift had just been promoted to 6th Brigade command, replacing Brigadier Hugh Young, who on August 23 had been promoted to major general and appointed the Canadian Army's Quartermaster General back in Canada.[35] Having commanded the South Saskatchewan Regiment, Clift was well familiar with the strengths and weaknesses of his battalions. The Camerons, Clift said, would stay in place. With daylight, they would be positioned to look down upon and harass a ferry operating out of La Vacherie—a hamlet on the river directly north of Moulineaux. The South Saskatchewan Regiment and Les Fusiliers Mont-Royal, meanwhile, would advance eastward in the hope of linking up with the 4th Canadian Infantry Brigade coming toward them from the east. Clift chose the Sasks to lead the advance, with the Fusiliers following. August 28 promised to be a hard day for 2nd Division.[36]

THE PLAN FOR Les Fusiliers Mont-Royal to withdraw from west of Port du Gravier, cross the railway line, and hook east to come up alongside the South Saskatchewan Regiment proved impossible. As soon as the move began, the Fusiliers came straight into the gunsights of Germans in strength holding the ground before them. Withering machine-gun and mortar fire broke the battalion into two sub-units and pinned each in place. While each was within a short distance of the other, neither could cross the intervening ground. Rendered immobile, the Fusiliers dug in and hoped to somehow be reinforced.[37]

Unaware of the Fusiliers' predicament, the South Saskatchewan Regiment had kicked off its advance at 0300 hours. 'C' Company led, followed in turn by 'D,' 'A,' and 'B' Companies. Their objective was Chalk Pits Hill, which would put them about a mile north of Port du Gravier and able to threaten the escape route for the Germans bedevilling 4th Infantry Brigade.[38]

Shortly before daylight, Major Sydney Radley-Walters and 'A' Squadron of the Sherbrooke Fusiliers were catching up to the Sasks' tail. Again, the narrow road flanked by thick woods made it impossible to manoeuvre and the tanks were confined to single file. In the lead, Radley-Walters was in a foul mood. The day was playing out as badly as the one before. Infantry-tank cooperation "dreadful," communications useless, artillery support "terrible." Suddenly, a demolition charge exploded under his tank, and the Sherman started to burn. He narrowly escaped with minor facial and hand burns.[39] That was it for the Sherbrookes. 'A' Squadron withdrew to Moulineaux and set up alongside the Camerons. With a good view from the heights across the river, the tankers, as their war diarist recorded, "enjoyed some . . . good shoots . . . onto Hun positions in the low ground below." Catching some Germans in the open, they "caused considerable havoc."[40]

Also at Moulineaux were Nos. 8 and 9 Platoons of the Toronto Scottish (MG) Regiment and its heavy mortar company. The two platoons were equipped with Vickers medium machine guns. With its machine guns and 4.2-inch mortars, the Toronto Scottish provided heavy weapon support for 2nd Division and were parsed out as required to support the infantry brigades. Here, their heavier weapons could easily range across the river. There was also a short stretch of open ground between the river and Moulineaux, with the small hamlet of La Vacherie close by the water. Seeing a long line of marching troops emerge from La Vacherie and make for the woods, the Toronto machine-gun teams laced into them at a range of three thousand yards. The Germans scattered, running full tilt for the cover of the woods on the ridge's lower slope. Neither the machine guns nor the mortars could gain an angle of fire on the Germans once they reached the woods below their position.[41] They were also too close for either artillery or the Typhoon fighter-bombers circling overhead in the brilliantly blue sky to engage them without risking a friendly-fire incident. At the same time, the German infantry were also stuck—unable to either withdraw or bull up the steep slope without exposing themselves to the guns of the soldiers at the summit. A standoff ensued, with the tankers and Toronto Scottish shifting their attention back to firing at targets across the river. The Germans lashed back with artillery from the other side of the Seine and self-propelled guns blasted away from the protective cover of La Vacherie. Both sides as a result suffered heavy casualties.[42]

Meanwhile, the South Saskatchewan Regiment's advance had continued to go well into the early morning. Approaching the railway tracks from the north, Captain Vic Schubert and 'C' Company were only about five hundred yards short of Chalk Pits Hill and had yet to meet any opposition. He commanded just thirty-five men, about the same number as in the regiment's other companies. The entire battalion counted in at only slightly more than 150 men. About half of 'C' Company had crossed the tracks when a sniper and machine gun simultaneously opened fire from woods to their left. Schubert quickly established a company headquarters under the span of an overhead railway bridge and sent a section of men to eliminate the sniper, but the German had the ground before him so well covered that the section was forced back. Deciding to tackle things himself, Schubert took one platoon and several scouts from the battalion's headquarters company and approached the sniper and machine gun position from the left.

No sooner had Schubert and his men moved into the dense woods than the sounds of heavy fire came from that direction. Lieutenant John Jesson, commanding the rest of the company back at the bridge, figured Schubert had walked into an ambush. But there was nothing he could do about it, for heavy small-arms fire had driven his men to ground.

As soon as he learned of 'C' Company's predicament, Major Francis Bernard Courtney—who had assumed command upon Fred Clift's promotion to brigadier—ordered Jesson to extract his men. Hugging low ground, Jesson and the small group broke contact with the Germans they were escaping, but immediately came under accurate mortar fire that killed an entire section and part of the company headquarters. Jesson was among those killed. Another round killed the company's remaining officer, Lieutenant Robert Climie Cree. Company Sergeant

Major J.A. Smith took over. He and twelve men reached the lines of 'D' Company. Organizing Smith's men as a platoon, Courtney assigned them to 'A' Company. There was still no sign of Schubert and his lost platoon. They were written off as either dead or taken prisoner.*

At 1315 hours, Courtney withdrew the battalion to a position about a mile west of Moulineaux to reorganize and be fed a hot meal. While the troops rested, Courtney and his intelligence officer, Captain Neville Hughes Hadley, attended a brigade Orders Group. With the Fusiliers still immobilized, and the Camerons too weak to do more than harass the Germans from their positions at Moulineaux, Clift could only call on the South Saskatchewan Regiment to again try reaching Chalk Pits Hill. This time, they would be supported by a thirty-minute artillery barrage set to begin at 2000 hours.[43]

---

* Ambushed by the Germans, Schubert and his platoon were forced to surrender. Several days later, however, they were freed when a British armoured regiment overtook the retreating Germans guarding them.

[8]

A Nightmare

O N FORÊT DE la Londe's right flank, 2nd Division's 4th Infantry
Brigade had also attempted to seize Chalk Pits Hill and the higher ground to its east code-named Maisie. Delayed by Royal Regiment
of Canada's commander Major T.F. Whitley's decision to first feed the
men, the one-company attack went in after dawn, losing any advantage
darkness might have given. 'C' Company's objective was Chalk Pits
Hill, and Captain R.W. Rich planned to take it by sending two platoons
forward in a pincer movement—one swinging to the left and up a
spur, while the other went right and used the cover provided by what
appeared to be low scrub. His third platoon would provide covering
fire. As soon as the attack started, 'C' Company came under intense
fire from the Germans on the heights ahead. Casualties were severe,
and the attack collapsed. Rich, his signaller, and one infantryman
fell wounded beside the road. As they lay there, a German officer and
five men walked openly through the brush to their position, calmly
searched the three men's pockets, took whatever they fancied, and
then slipped quietly away even as fighting raged nearby.

Having ordered 'C' Company back, Whitley decided a battal-
ion-scale attack with artillery support was required. Both Chalk Pits
Hill and Maisie were to be shelled heavily and then, as the artillery
and mortars ceased firing, 'A' Company would advance on the right
through the low scrub to the second railway, before turning northward

and meeting up with 'B' Company in front of Chalk Pits Hill. The two would then assault the hill together. 'D' Company would come up into 'A' Company's start position and hold in reserve. 'C' Company was deemed too cut up to participate.

The moment the artillery and mortar fire lifted, at 1130 hours, the two companies advanced. 'B' Company moved through an underpass at the first set of tracks and entered a small wood. Beyond the wood, a stretch of open ground led to the base of Chalk Pits Hill. Emerging from the cover of the trees, 'B' Company was struck by heavy mortar fire. Captain J.G. Plante and several men were wounded. Those who were not dragged casualties back to the wood.[1] Whitley considered sending 'C' Company to reinforce the beleaguered company, but that would only have added another twenty fit men. So he decided instead to extricate 'B' Company by having the battalion's 3-inch mortars fire a covering smokescreen. That idea was quickly abandoned when the ground requiring obscuring proved too great for the available mortars to cover.[2]

To the left, 'A' Company had attacked with No. 7 Platoon leading and proceeded via an underpass past the first railway track. It then broke right, while the following No. 9 Platoon headed left. Captain H.W. "Hank" Caldwell immediately lost sight of both platoons, as they were swallowed by what proved to be a dense ten-foot-high thicket rather than the expected low scrub. After advancing five hundred yards, Caldwell halted his company headquarters section and sent two scouts to try to find his missing platoons. No. 9 Platoon was finally located sitting back with 'D' Company in reserve.

Watching from some high ground near 'D' Company, Whitley spotted No. 7 Platoon at its preliminary objective of the second railroad's underpass. He ordered 'D' Company to advance behind No. 9 Platoon to where the road crossed the second railroad via another overpass about three hundred yards south of No. 7 Platoon's position. Caldwell joined this force, which soon reached the overpass. Out front, No. 9 Platoon took cover in a small copse about fifteen yards short of the railroad track. When Caldwell radioed his position to Whitley, he was told to stay put until told otherwise. It was now about 1300 hours. 'D' Company was strung out in single file behind Caldwell and No. 9

Platoon, all the men hunkering down in underbrush. Caldwell's scouts probed forward and returned with news that beyond No. 9 Platoon's position, the ground fell away into a clearing before rising sharply for about sixty yards of open ground fronted by thick, unbroken forest for as far as one could see. There was also a large chalk pit gouged out of the slope directly ahead of No. 9 Platoon's position. When Caldwell told Whitley what the scouts had seen, the frontal attack was scrapped.

Lieutenant Philip Gordon Carter and No. 7 Platoon, meanwhile, ventured through the underpass, only to have the leading section struck by withering small-arms fire. The twenty-seven-year-old officer was shot dead and several men fell wounded. Although previously undetected, the platoon now drew a storm of fire that inflicted more casualties. Crawling on his stomach through the gunfire, Caldwell reached the platoon. Only six or seven men were unhurt. He ordered these to withdraw, taking their casualties with them. Crawling back to No. 9 Platoon and his wireless set, Caldwell sought instructions from Whitley, but learned he had gone off to brigade for an Orders Group (O Group). So far, and much to Caldwell's amazement, the Germans seemed unaware of No. 9 Platoon and 'D' Company's presence. Normally, he would have had the men dig in. But knowing the sounds of shovels would betray them, Caldwell instead had the men just lie down where they were and keep quiet. At 2130 hours, Whitley contacted Caldwell and asked him to send back guides. The brigade plan was to send the Royal Hamilton Light Infantry (Rileys) at first light through to Caldwell's position.[3]

TO THE RIGHT of the Royals, the Essex Scottish Regiment had again attempted to punch forward left of Port du Gravier to outflank the high ground overlooking the village. A lavish artillery barrage and the machine guns of a Toronto Scottish Regiment platoon hammered the heights and ground east of it.[4] Then, at 1330 hours, 'C' and 'D' Companies attacked—moving through the railway underpass in the north part of the village and emerging on the east side of the road running to Moulineaux. Immediately, the men came under heavy machine-gun, light mortar, and rifle grenade fire. Again, poor maps had failed to indicate the true nature of the ground. To reach the base of the heights, both companies must cross the raised railway track and descend its steep embankment on the other side. Then they had to cross a narrow, mostly open valley to begin climbing the heights. Both 'C' Company's Major Tim McCoy and Major Telford Steele of 'D' Company had seen stiff fighting in the Normandy Campaign. Steele had earned a Military Cross at Tilly-la-Campagne. Neither man was under any illusions that this fight was likely winnable.

To get to the bottom of the railway embankment, the lead platoons literally slid on their butts to the valley floor. And here they were trapped, unable to advance in the face of blistering fire. Frantically digging in, the two companies could only go to ground. McCoy was wounded in the shoulder but refused to be evacuated.[5] Although already wounded and having lost his revolver, Lieutenant George Jones led his 'C' Company platoon down the embankment, only to be killed upon reaching the bottom. Any attempt to renew the advance met intense fire, while—as long as they stayed put—the Germans seemed content to merely harry the Canadians with occasional sniper and mortar fire. Plans were made to withdraw once night fell.[6]

By the time the Essex Scottish attack was stopped cold, the regiment's commander, Lieutenant Colonel Peter Bennett, was completing the six-mile journey back to 4th Brigade headquarters in the orchard southwest of Bourgtheroulde for an O Group. At 1600 hours, Major General Charles Foulkes and Brigadier Eddy Ganong presented a new plan to Bennett, Major Whitley of the Royals, and the Royal Hamilton Light Infantry's Lieutenant Colonel Graham Maclachlan.

In the late morning of August 28, Foulkes had briefly considered abandoning 2nd Division's efforts in the forest and moving instead through 3rd Division's bridgehead across the Seine at nearby Elbeuf. From there, he could advance on Rouen from the east. But his orders from 11 Corps were to press on through the forest to cross directly into Rouen as quickly as possible.[7] And Foulkes was not one to confront his superiors or question orders—not even when the reality at the front suggested no likelihood of success.

Instead, Foulkes ordered the Rileys to pass through 'A' and 'D' Companies of the Royals in a night attack by swinging southeast onto the heights of Maisie, which overlooked the stalemated Essex

Scottish at Port du Gravier. Both Maclachlan and Whitley vehemently opposed the idea, arguing that "this task was beyond the powers of a battalion composed largely of reinforcement personnel with little training." They tried to convince Foulkes and Ganong that "the enemy was actually stronger than intelligence reports had indicated, and that the ground was immensely favourable for defence." Moreover, although the proposed line of advance might look feasible on the map, to reach Maisie that way required passing "up a draw on both sides of which enemy machineguns" had been detected by the Royals. Foulkes was unmoved. The Rileys must go forward as soon as possible, establish themselves on the summit of Maisie that night, and then at first light drive the Germans from it.[8]

As the o Group ended, Maclachlan—who had been wounded on August 12 but returned to duty the following day because the Rileys were so shorthanded—fell physically ill and was rushed to hospital. Taking temporary command, Major Jack Halladay hurried to brigade headquarters to receive the battalion's orders. He then returned to where the Rileys were stationed behind Les Fusiliers Mont-Royal's lines. It was 2000 hours when Halladay briefed his officers. As the briefing concluded, the Rileys' second-in-command, Major Hugh Arrell, arrived from rear echelon to assume command. He and a small number of junior officers and non-commissioned officers had been designated Left Out of Battle. This standard practice provided a core of veterans around which a battalion could rebuild should it be cut to pieces in combat.

All this command reshuffling ate up time, so it was 2330 hours before the Rileys advanced. A heavy drizzle was falling as the companies marched in line along a narrow road and then onto an even narrower track. 'D' Company led, followed in turn by 'A' Company, 'B' Company, and lastly 'C' Company. On the maps, the road and track to be followed had looked clear and simple, but each proved to intersect with other unmarked tracks. In the darkness and dense forest, the Rileys found it difficult to navigate. Wrong turns were taken, men had to be turned around and marched back onto course. The guides sent by the Royals to help bring the Rileys forward were as confused as anyone. Consequently, first light found the Rileys only crossing the first railway—still short of where 'A' and 'D' Companies of the Royals were hidden next to the second railway.

Caught by daylight in the relatively open ground between railways, the Rileys came under machine-gun and mortar fire from Maisie. Spotting four machine guns to the right in woods fronting the second set of tracks, Arrell decided these must be silenced before the main attack could go in. Grabbing the handset of the No. 22 wireless the battalion signaller was carrying, Arrell provided coordinates for a heavy cloak of smoke shells to be fired onto his planned line of attack. He then sent 'D' Company to approach the guns from the right and 'A' Company the left.[9]

Dashing though the now pouring rain and thick smoke, 'D' Company under Captain Dunc Kennedy had almost reached the enemy gun positions when they were ambushed by more machine-gunners to their right. Calling for more smoke to mask his men from this threat, Kennedy ordered a withdrawal. The men went back, carrying their wounded. Captain Bill Parker's 'A' Company, meanwhile, also closed on the targeted German positions. With one platoon apparently safely across the tracks and running toward the woods, Parker followed with a second platoon. Suddenly, the woods ahead came alive with Germans firing Spandau machine guns and Schmeisser submachine guns. Clearly, they had held fire until most of the company was exposed in the open. 'A' Company took heavy casualties before it was able to fall back to cover behind the railway track. Parker suffered a head wound. Captain Harry Tolchard was spotted lying seriously wounded on the tracks. When two stretcher-bearers tried to reach him, one was killed and the other wounded by a burst of fire. Rescuing Tolchard proved impossible.

Unable to even start the attack, Arrell ordered the Rileys to hold in place. Then, at 1400 hours, orders arrived to withdraw. The men broke away and fell back to their previous position behind the Royals. The battalion counted six officers wounded, with eight other ranks killed, twenty-five wounded, and eight missing. The next day, August 30, Lieutenant H.A. Oliver—having been wounded in the thigh—and two men from 'A' Company were brought in. The three had managed to sneak back through the forest to the Canadian lines. They reported that

Tolchard was still lying helplessly on the railway tracks. Sergeants Ernie Knott and D.G. Dolman with one of the men serving as a guide headed out to find the officer. Three and a half hours later they returned, having rescued Tolchard and taken him to a field hospital. Four of the battalion's men were still missing and presumed taken prisoner.[10]

AS MAJOR ARRELL had been briefing the Rileys for their attack at 2000 hours on August 28, the South Saskatchewan Regiment had headed again toward Chalk Pits Hill from the west. This time, the plan was for the regiment to advance along the road from Moulineaux to Port du Gravier and then along the railway tracks, entering the forest from the north to gain the hill. Their intermediate objective was a Y-shaped junction where the Moulineaux–Port du Gravier road was joined by a road from the northeast.[11] This line of advance would take the regiment along the escarpment overlooking the Seine to the Y-junction next to which stood the ruins of the Château de Robert le Diable, a medieval castle deriving its name from the likely mythical Norman knight Robert the Devil.

The South Saskatchewan Regiment attack was supported by an artillery barrage that began at 2000 hours and lasted for thirty minutes. Running a bit late, however, the infantry lost the barrage's full advantage, as the Germans were able to emerge from their slit trenches and dash to their machine guns and mortars. 'A' and 'D' Companies led the advance and soon closed on the castle. Chalk Pits Hill lay another mile distant.

Major Ernest Thomas—"June" to his friends—commanded 'D' Company. He was also the regiment's second-in-command, but there were so few officers that he stayed with the company rather than going into Left Out of Battle status back at rear echelon. The Sasks were too weak to leave any men out of action. Thomas had cut his combat teeth as an officer in the Seaforth Highlanders of Canada in Italy. He was one of a number of officers brought in from that theatre to provide experienced leadership to 2nd Division. As 'D' Company approached the Y-junction, the German mortars and machine guns started firing. Thomas led his men straight at them, while 'A' Company provided covering fire from a position beside the castle.

Farther back, battalion commander Major Francis Bernard Courtney and his headquarters were coming up fast in a Bren carrier, when a mortar round almost hit the vehicle. Shrapnel damaged the No. 22 wireless and wounded signaller Lance-Corporal R.L. Dalziel. Courtney managed to get word back to 6th Brigade headquarters that he was no longer able to communicate with the supporting artillery field regiment. A replacement set was sent forward. By the time Courtney took possession of the set and started moving again, 'D' Company reported that it had cleaned out the machine-gun positions and eliminated several snipers. The advance toward Chalk Pits Hill was renewed at 2230 hours, with 'A' and 'C' Companies leading and 'D' Company in trail.

Courtney tucked his carrier behind 'D' Company. The battalion commander and driver Private R. Curtis were in the front, Lieutenant D.F. Fairgrieve was in the back manning the No. 22 set, and Private T.R. McLean was beside him with the No. 18 set. Walking on each side and ahead of the carrier were the company headquarters' scouts. Just as the carrier came abreast of the castle, it drove over a German Teller mine. Shaped like a covered cooking pan about two and a half inches deep and fifteen inches across, the mine was loaded with high explosive that detonated when its plunger-style trigger buried just under the road surface was depressed by the tires or tracks of a vehicle. The powerful mine ripped a hole in the floor directly under Courtney and overturned the carrier. Courtney died instantly. Walking beside the carrier next to where Courtney had been seated, intelligence officer Captain Neville Hughes Hadley was also killed, his body thrown into brush on the left side of the road. The other three men in the carrier were flung clear. Fairgrieve suffered phosphorous burns to his head and was in shock. The other two men were also in shock and McLean had cuts on his face.

When he learned what had happened, Thomas rushed back to the battalion headquarters and assumed command. The advance slowly continued in the face of constant machine-gun, mortar, and rifle-grenade fire. At 0005 hours on August 29, 'D' Company moved to the front and tried breaking through a staunch German line but was driven back. Then 'B' Company attempted to work around the enemy position to the right, but was stopped cold in front of more enemy positions at 0230 hours. At 0303 hours, all three companies reported being pinned down. As dawn broke, the Germans counterattacked. Although, as the Sasks' war diarist wrote, the battalion "fought hard using all weapons, including hand grenades when the enemy got close enough, they were forced to withdraw" to the Y-junction. Here they dug in, with 'A' Squadron of the Sherbrooke Fusiliers coming up to support them.

Brigadier Fred Clift soon arrived and announced that he planned to pass the Queen's Own Cameron Highlanders through to renew the attack. He, Thomas, and several other officers then visited the Sasks' company positions. Clift ordered 'D' Company to send a section to establish an outpost on some high ground overlooking the road. Having checked 'B' Company's position, Clift and Thomas were walking back to battalion headquarters when a sniper round hit the brigadier in the leg and broke it above the ankle. Seeing Clift fall, Sherbrooke Major Sydney Radley-Walters backed his tank in to block the sniper's line of fire. While Radley-Walters bandaged Clift's leg, Thomas fetched a jeep and stretcher. Clift was evacuated.

The section of 'D' Company—actually nineteen men and about half of its entire strength—started out toward the high ground. "The men never got that far," the war diarist recorded, "as they came under heavy small-arms fire and the Germans then threw in a counterattack on 'D' Company's front which drove the section back to its original position." With support from the tanks, the counterattack was repelled. Shortly thereafter word came that the planned attack by the Camerons was postponed.[12] Their commander, Lieutenant Colonel A.S. Gregory, had been wounded at 1400 hours by mortar shrapnel.[13] Major E.P. Thompson took over the Camerons, and Les Fusiliers Mont-Royal commander Lieutenant Colonel Guy Gauvreau assumed brigade command.

In order to prepare for their attack, the Camerons had withdrawn from positions immediately west of Moulineaux—turning these over to the Calgary Highlanders from 5th Brigade. For the Calgaries the new position was, as their diarist wrote, "a nightmare." They spent the day pounded by artillery and raked by small-arms fire. There was great relief when news arrived that they were to withdraw and turn the area over to Les Fusiliers Mont-Royal. When they pulled out that evening, the Calgaries counted forty-three other ranks and three officers as casualties for the day.[14]

THE ONLY GOOD news in the Forêt de la Londe fight on August 29 came on the Essex Scottish front at Port du Gravier, where scouts reported the Germans appeared to have broken contact. 'A' and 'B' Companies cautiously moved across the railroad and then about eight hundred yards up the river road leading to Oissel without meeting opposition. Ahead, however, a network of caves along the face of the escarpment that overlooked the road was found to conceal German positions. The Essex Scottish subjected these to fire with their machine guns and a 6-pounder anti-tank gun. At times, a targeted cave proved to be occupied by civilians rather than Germans. Most of the civilians managed to escape to safety through the Essex lines.[15]

Even though the Germans appeared to be somewhat loosening their grip on the forest, it was abundantly clear that 2nd Division was spent. On the afternoon of August 29, Foulkes cancelled the proposed attack by the Camerons and ordered both the 4th and 6th Brigades to consolidate their positions. That evening, however, the South Saskatchewan Regiment again met misfortune when it received a signal to withdraw from its positions near the castle. Major June Thomas was at the time attending an o Group at brigade headquarters, the order went unquestioned, and the companies pulled back to a quarry near Moulineaux. But the order was bogus, the work of German signallers who had broken into the brigade's wireless net. Thomas hurriedly returned to the battalion and reorganized its diminished ranks into two companies. Then, at 2115 hours, with tanks and artillery firing in support, the Sasks advanced, met only slight resistance, and regained their former positions by the castle.

By dawn on August 30, fighting in the forest had ended, although the Germans continued to throw sporadic artillery and mortar fire into the woods from across the Seine. The Sasks moved their headquarters into the castle, whose walls varied from two to four feet thick and provided good protection. Deep tunnels were found under the castle that proved too long to fully explore. Several patrols were sent out to the hamlets on the low ground by the river and returned with about eighty prisoners. Some of these reported that the force engaging the Sasks during the past couple of days had numbered about 250 men. After breaking off the battle at midnight on August 29–30, most had escaped across the river. Those taken prisoner had been left stranded when the ferrying operation ceased.

When the fighting stopped, the regiment's infantry companies had been reduced to just sixty men and four officers. To strengthen the companies, the carrier platoon was sent forward from headquarters and its twenty men divided up in an ad hoc manner. This left 'A' Company with a strength of twenty-three men under one officer, 'B' Company with twenty-one men and a single officer, nine men of 'C' Company under Company Sergeant Major J.A. Smith's command, and 'D' Company at twelve men commanded by Lieutenant Fraser Lee.[16]

The South Saskatchewan Regiment had the heaviest casualties of all the regiments engaged in the forest—185, of which 44 were fatal. Next came the Royals with 118 casualties, then the Camerons with 99 men killed or wounded, the Essex Scottish with 74 wounded and 22 killed, the Rileys with 59 casualties, and Les Fusiliers Mont-Royal with 20 casualties. This gave a total casualty rate of 577.[17] A high bill for an operation whose value was, at best, dubious.

While the war diary of the Camerons claimed they had been "partly successful" in cutting the escape routes across the Seine in front of Rouen, and that "thousands of Germans drowned or were killed from our 4.2 [-inch] mortars and arty fire plus our MMGs," the losses inflicted by the fire from Moulineaux were clearly far fewer.[18] In fact, the Germans in the forest had largely controlled the development of the battle, and the resulting heavy Canadian casualty rate left 2nd Division's combat readiness greatly diminished. Unlike the Canadians, who had been plagued by bad maps, making it impossible for them to get an accurate reading of the forest terrain, the Germans had used their knowledge of the ground skilfully and to best advantage. All too often, they were fighting from heights that overlooked the Canadian lines of attack. Their withdrawals were always orderly, as they simply pulled back to another well-placed fighting position. And counterattacks against the Germans were less effective than usual because ground lost did not seriously weaken their overall defensive positions. Even when the heights at Moulineaux were lost, the Germans were only required to suspend ferrying operations during the day—something they were doing anyway because of the threat posed by Allied fighter-bombers. Night ferrying continued under the noses of the Canadians.

As the Canadian army's official historian later wrote, the three days of fighting in Forêt de la Londe saw 2nd Division unable to make "any important impression upon the strong enemy positions . . . The hard-fighting Germans holding them carried out their task of covering the river crossings at Rouen, and withdrew only when it had been completed."[19]

The question remained: Why did Major General Charles Foulkes—who had at least once considered ceasing offensive operations in the forest—continue to insist on renewed attacks that had little prospect of success? Major Doug McIntyre of the Essex Scottish found the "piece-meal" destruction of 4th and 6th Brigades impossible to understand. Past experience in Normandy had made him believe that Foulkes had a "stubborn haughtiness and apparent disregard for the well-being of an infantry regiment." He was left wondering if Foulkes might have been acting on "some kind of a fierce, rules unwritten, Patton/ Montgomery type competition between divisional commanders to be the first to reach Rouen?"[20]

ULTIMATELY, THE GERMAN withdrawal from Forêt de la Londe was forced by events immediately to the east. Here, in the meander that was the reverse of that of the forest and came to a narrow point at Elbeuf, the 3rd Canadian Infantry and 4th Canadian Armoured Divisions had managed by August 28 to break the main German defensive position. Both divisions had forced crossings of the Seine the previous day and established significant bridgeheads in the face of stiff fighting.

German resistance here was anchored on Point 88 to the northeast of Sotteville-sous-la-Val in the 4th Armoured Division sector. But the Germans also had strong positions in 3rd Infantry Division's operation-al area to the west. Because of the narrow confines of the meander, 3rd Division was able to deploy only its 7th Infantry Brigade. Meanwhile,

4th Armoured Division attacked with just the infantry of 10th Infantry Brigade because the engineers were delayed in making rafts that could accommodate armour operational at Criquebeuf-sur-Seine.

On the morning of August 28, 7th Brigade's advance focused on seizing the railway-road hub of Tourville and Point 80 behind it. Advancing on the left, the Regina Rifles were to clear the small, skinny wood called Bois de Tourville and also clear Tourville. The Canadian Scottish Regiment, meanwhile, would advance past Tourville on the right and take Point 80. Once the Can Scots won this height, the "Little Black Devils"—as the Royal Winnipeg Rifles were called because of the devil image on their cap badges—would pass through and advance to the point where the river bent and then flowed in a direct line to Rouen.

The Lincoln and Welland Regiment of 10th Infantry Brigade, meanwhile, were tasked with seizing Point 88. Upon its capture, the Argyll and Sutherland Highlanders would carry the brigade's advance farther and seize another height of ground northeast of Sotteville—Point 95. It was hoped that by the time this latter attack began, tanks of the South Alberta Regiment would have managed to cross at Criquebeuf to lend support.[21]

The Can Scots advanced at 1215 hours with 'C' and 'D' Companies leading. Opposition was slight, and the troops quickly passed by undefended Sotteville and gained Point 80's summit.[22] On the left, the Reginas also swept forward without meeting any real opposition. Between 1430 and 1530 hours, all its objectives were reported taken and forty-two prisoners rounded up for a loss of only ten casualties.

On 7th Brigade's right flank, however, 10th Brigade's Lincoln and Welland Regiment ran into stiff opposition from the outset. All four companies were committed, with 'B' Company directed on Point 88 from the west, 'A' Company headed for a rail junction at the base of the hill's right flank, 'C' Company making for another transportation junction between Point 88 and Point 95, and 'D' Company tasked with securing a road and rail junction on the outskirts of Igoville.[23] Advancing at 1400 hours behind artillery and smoke concentrations, 'C' Company was closing in on its junction objective and out in the open when it came under heavy mortar and machine-gun fire. Its commander, Captain Laurence Edwin Earl Snelgrove, was killed.[24]

As Snelgrove was the company's only officer, Lieutenant J.G. Martin dashed over from 'A' Company and led the men to their objective. 'B' Company suffered severe casualties as it was lashed by concentrations of 88-millimetre shellfire and also shells coming from an unidentified heavier-calibre artillery piece. Despite its losses, the company gained the summit of Point 88 at 1700 hours. The Germans launched a half-hearted counterattack that was easily fended off. For the next hour, the company endured continuous shellfire.[25] At 1815 hours, the Can Scots arrived to take over the position, and the Lincs happily handed off, retiring to Igoville. Under intensive shellfire, the Can Scots hurriedly started carving out slit trenches, prompting the battalion war diarist to write, "Digging and digging and digging seems to be the troops' occupation these days. They grumble and sweat and dig." The German artillery and mortar crews, he added, "do all they can to annoy us. Slit trenches are definitely still on the high priority list." Despite the fire, the Can Scots suffered only one man killed and one officer and twelve other ranks wounded on August 28.[26]

At 1930 hours, meanwhile, the Argyll and Sutherland Highlanders moved out, following a thirty-minute artillery concentration, toward Point 95. Rolling along in support were the Shermans of the South Alberta Regiment's 'C' Squadron.[27] The tankers had only arrived shortly before the attack began, having been much delayed in getting across the Seine at Criquebeuf. Engineers there had managed to erect a Bailey bridge to an island mid-stream. From there, rafts ferried the tanks the rest of the way. Such was the width of the river that only four or five vehicles per hour were getting across.[28]

Lance Corporal Harry Ruch of 'A' Company's No. 7 Platoon was on the battalion's extreme left flank. The company was badly depleted, and Nos. 8 and 9 Platoons had been amalgamated. A mortar farther to the left was dropping rounds near Ruch's section. As no rounds were ranging beyond his men, Ruch figured the mortar was firing at its maximum range, which still left his men at risk. When a round landed very close to two men without hurting them, the section went to ground and took a few minutes to catch their breath. When they started running forward again, a round landed directly behind thirty-six-year-old Private Gerald Joseph Corcoran and nineteen-year-old Private

Stanley Dickenson, instantly killing both men. Because of the disparity in the two men's ages, the others in the platoon had nicknamed them Pop and Junior. Ruch and the others ran on, gaining the objective.[29]

'A' Company's arrival on Point 95 came several minutes after the Argylls' other three companies had cleared it in a line-abreast assault that had burst out of a covering smokescreen so quickly that the snipers, artillery observers, and mortar crews on the summit were overrun in an instant. The Argylls counted fifty German dead and took another fifty prisoner while losing only ten men killed or wounded. Digging in, the Argylls braced to fend off counterattacks, which never materialized.[30]

Shortly after Point 95 fell, the Algonquin Regiment passed by and advanced a short distance northward. Moving close behind a creeping barrage, they met little resistance, the regiment's war diarist crediting this to "the magnificent work" of the gunners. Some prisoners were taken, and the Algonquins were surprised to find most appeared to be Japanese or Mongolians, apparently conscripted from somewhere into the German army.[31]

The Algonquin line of advance had carried it northeastward and away from 3rd Division's 7th Brigade—the two divisions beginning to put some distance between each other to make room for more troops to enter the bridgehead. This gap was to widen even more as the Royal Winnipeg Rifles struck out to the northwest from a position north of Tourville. 'C' Company led the advance and had just crossed the start line when it came under heavy fire from tanks, mortars, artillery and small arms. Major Norm Wilson-Smith was wounded but refused to be evacuated until his second-in-command, Captain Fred Allen, came up from Left Out of Battle to take over.[32] As the advance continued through what seemed a series of defensive lines, Lieutenant Douglas Alden Kirkpatrick was killed. When 'C' Company reached the battalion's intermediate objective, 'D' Company leapfrogged it, and its Lieutenant Morris Marvin Soronow was fatally wounded. After advancing a total of about a mile, the Little Black Devils dug in for a night spent under intermittent shelling.[33]

The August 28 advances by 3rd Infantry and 4th Armoured Divisions made the German position at Rouen untenable. Accordingly, as 3rd Division's 9th Infantry Brigade entered the bridgehead and led the advance toward the city on August 29, they met only "persistent but light" opposition. To 3rd Division's right, 4th Armoured Division started driving northeastward, with 4th Armoured Brigade's tank regiments leading.[34] Here, the Germans readily gave way. The tankers ended the day having advanced about seven miles and only about the same distance from Buchy, almost on a direct line inland from Dieppe.

On August 30, the 9th Brigade's Highland Light Infantry of Canada loaded 'A' Company onto the Bren carriers of the battalion's carrier platoon, and Major J.D. Sim led the unit into Rouen. They shot up a large group of Germans spotted fleeing up a side street.[35] At 1800 hours, Brigadier John "Rocky" Rockingham and the brigade's intelligence officer, Captain G.E. Franklin, entered the city in an armoured car. A group of civilians told them where the Germans were still operating a ferry downstream of the city. Sim's unit was instructed to shut the operation down. They managed to cut off the escape of about a hundred Germans, killing many and taking the rest prisoner.

Rockingham, meanwhile, was approached by several more civilians, who complained bitterly about the city having been bombed by the Royal Air Force. The group made him wonder if the Canadians were in for a "cool reception here," Franklin wrote later. By the time Rockingham's scout car reached the city's main square, however, "thousands of people crowded so closely that it was impossible to move; people overcome with joy laughed, cried and cheered, pushing forward, eager to touch the car or to shake your hand. Some of the more eager jeunes filles were not content with handshakes and were determined to place kisses on your cheeks. At last the crowd was persuaded to let the car through, and everywhere we went we were stopped by cheering people . . . By this time the car became so bedecked with flowers that it resembled more closely a float in a May Day parade than a weapon of war."[36]

Like Ink on a Blotter

DURING THE NIGHT of August 29–30, a Canadian patrol had intercepted a German motorcycle dispatch rider en route to deliver orders issued by LXXIV Corps for withdrawal of its 331st and 334th Infanterie-Divisions and 17th Luftwaffe Feld Division from the Seine. The latter division comprised anti-aircraft and aircraft maintenance personnel deployed as infantry. First Canadian Army intelligence staff gleaned from the orders that the German command had concluded "that further efforts on this part of the front would yield no dividends, [and so] decided . . . they had had enough and withdrawal was the only 'hope.' Their intention is to reach the comparative safety of the land to the north of the Somme."[1]

By the morning of August 30, a relatively clear picture had developed of the German forces opposing II Canadian Corps at the Seine. During the initial Forêt de la Londe fighting, the Germans had deployed elements of 2nd SS Panzer Division and 116th Panzer Division to contain the situation until 331st Infanterie-Division could relieve them. Repeated delays in this handover resulted in the last SS troops not departing until late on August 28. In the meantime, 17th Luftwaffe had held the easterly meander facing Elbeuf.

On the 29th, LXXIV Corps reported to Fifth Panzer Army that the advances gained by 3rd Canadian Infantry Division and 4th Canadian Armoured Division were decisive. Considering the German "pronounced shortage of artillery ammunition and the lack of reserves of any kind, a breakthrough at Rouen seems inevitable." Accordingly, 331st Infanterie-Division was ordered to withdraw across the river. Colonel Walter Steinmüller had anticipated this timing. By the 29th, all divisional vehicles had been ferried across the river. This enabled him to withdraw the remaining infantry during the early-morning hours of August 30. His was the last German division to cross the Seine. Steinmüller boasted that during the extraction, "no man and no vehicle fell into the hands of the enemy."

That might have been true, but when the division assembled on the north shore, it was much reduced. Having lost its entire 558th Grenadier Regiment well south of Rouen, the remaining 557th and 559th Regiments reported being respectively 25 and 30 per cent under-strength. All other divisional units had suffered similar losses.[2]

Still, the 331st Division was better off than most German formations that had retreated across the Seine. The river's shores were clogged with destroyed vehicles and corpses of horses and men. Much of this destruction had been wrought by the Allied air forces operating daily except when poor weather grounded the planes during the period August 20–23. This enabled Fifth Panzer Army's engineers, working flat out, to evacuate about 25,000 vehicles. The majority of these, however, were only horse-drawn wagons. August 24 dawning clear, and the next three days remaining so, permitted large-scale air operations that inflicted terrific damage on the Germans and reduced their ferrying operations to a trickle.[3]

To avoid being caught on open water, the Germans generally confined ferrying operations to nighttime. But as Canadian and British troops pressed closer to the river the perimeter shrank, and the German forces within became more densely concentrated and more vulnerable. The Rouen-area crossings were particularly targeted. One motor-transport park detected west of the city was attacked by RAF medium bombers dropping 270 tons of bombs. On another day, bombers struck a ferry at Duclair—just west of Rouen—with 105 tons. During several missions carried out in this three-day period, bomb tonnage was recorded at 1,200 tons, and 2,000 rocket projectiles were discharged by 2nd Tactical Air Force Typhoons and Spitfires.

In a weekly summary for the period August 24–31, British analysts reported that 1,450 motorized vehicles, 70 heavy-duty trucks, 54 tanks, 45 armoured-fighting vehicles, 21 staff cars, 50 horse-drawn wagons and 110 horses were destroyed. Forty ferrying barges were also sunk.[4]

Having lost their grip on the Seine, the Germans could no longer coherently resist First Canadian Army's advance. The only favourable defensive feature was the flat-bottomed, marshy valley of the Somme River, which varied from one to two miles in breadth. Its thinly forested banks rose to about 150 feet on either side. All the other rivers between the Seine and the Somme were short enough to be easily outflanked.[5]

By August 29, Oberbefehlshaber West Generalfeldmarschall Walter Model no longer believed an effective stand at the Somme was possible. The situation was deteriorating too quickly. On the German left flank, the Americans were moving so swiftly that he feared his Fifteenth, Seventh, and Fifth Panzer Armies might all end up encircled from the rear. Hitler was meanwhile demanding that a succession of mobile formations attack the American right flank somewhere between the Seine and the Marne Rivers. Model knew this idea was hopeless, and so it proved when xxxxvii Panzer Corps advanced its 3rd and 15th Panzer Grenadier Divisions between the Aisne and Marne on August 31, only to collide head-on with advancing Americans. The Germans hurriedly retreated.

The same day, British Second Army was spreading, as one official report put it, "like ink on a blotter" through northern France.[6] At Vernon, the 43rd (Wessex) Infantry Division had won a bridgehead across the Seine on the night of August 25–26 and had since expanded it to a depth of four and a half miles. This provided sufficient elbow room for xxx Corps to deploy the 11th Armoured Division north of the river. At first light on August 29, Lieutenant General Brian Horrocks ordered this division "to press forward at maximum speed regardless of the progress of troops on their flanks. Local resistance will be by-passed." Understanding that the Germans anchored a defence on the Somme, Horrocks intended to punch 11th Armoured Division and the Guards Armoured Division through to the river at Amiens.

As 11th Armoured led off its tanks, surprised Germans on roads running east from Rouen enjoyed "some good shooting at staff cars and lorries." Forging through heavy rain, by evening the division's armoured regiments had travelled about twenty-five miles without meeting any serious opposition. The following day, the Germans offered a fight at Talmontier but, conforming to orders, the tankers dropped a single tank squadron to contain the enemy and the division rolled onward. This squadron was soon relieved by a regiment of 159th Infantry Brigade. At 2130 hours, 11th Division halted to refuel. Then, moving nose to tail at five miles per hour, the tanks pushed through the night, using only tail lights for illumination. There was no resistance, the only Germans encountered being teamsters aboard horse-drawn wagons, which the tanks shot up without pausing. At 0630 hours on August 31, the leading regiment reached the outskirts of Amiens and soon captured two intact bridges over the Somme. To the right of Amiens, the Guards Armoured Division also reached the Somme by late morning and won three undamaged bridges.[7]

The bridgeheads at Amiens ended any hope the Germans had of mounting a delaying action at the Somme. The situation for the Germans was so chaotic that Fifth Panzer Army's headquarters was overrun by a British reconnaissance troop at Saleux, three miles south-west of Amiens. General der Panzertruppen Hans Eberbach and seven staff members were taken prisoner. Eberbach, who had been promoted to command Seventh Army on August 24, had arrived only hours earlier with orders to merge Fifth Army into his formation. Learning of Eberbach's loss later in the day, Model had to promote General der Panzertruppen Erich Brandenberger to acting commander of the combined Fifth and Seventh Armies.[8]

On the British right, the Americans were blasting through one imaginary defensive line after another, supposedly held by equally imaginary German formations, both existing only as lines on Hitler's maps. Model feared there might be no end to the withdrawal short of the Siegfried Line (or West Wall) defences along Germany's western border. Attempting to delay the Allies was now less important than saving troops and moving them to positions where a true defensive line could be formed, even if this was ultimately on the German border.

Model had little to work with. His panzer divisions had been mauled, each fielding by August 30 no more than five to ten operable tanks and only a single artillery battery. Infantry divisions mostly reported having just a single artillery piece left. Morale was crumbling in the face of "the enemy's superiority in matériel." At midnight on August 29, Model sent Hitler a summation. "The troops coming from Normandy," he wrote, have "few heavy weapons and generally nothing but their rifles . . . The low degree of mobility in the face of a highly mechanized opponent, and the lack of tactical reserves with assault guns and heavy anti-tank guns [has] resulted in a state of complete tactical inferiority requiring quick remedial action." He proposed sending five exhausted and hence useless infantry divisions to Germany for rest and rebuilding. Remnants of the eleven remaining infantry divisions could be cobbled together into four, but equipment to outfit these formations was needed. His remaining six ss and five army panzer divisions were paper tigers, each sufficient in numbers to operate as a regiment. Even then, reinforcements and additional tanks were required.[9]

The British crossing of the Somme on August 31 severely worsened the German situation. Model's retreating armies were in disarray, with many units being overrun each day. Nothing seemed to stand between the British and Antwerp. Realizing the threat, Model issued orders on the night of August 30 that Commander Armed Forces in the Netherlands rush the 719th Infanterie-Division—a formation intended for static coastal defence only—from around Dordrecht to block the British advance near Brussels.[10]

ON AUGUST 31, General Bernard Montgomery met with his two army commanders at Twenty-First Army Group tactical headquarters. Lieutenant General Harry Crerar flew to the meeting in his three-seater Auster light aircraft. He was feeling unwell, dogged by lingering dysentery.[11] As he entered the meeting, First Canadian Army was shaking loose from the Seine, with 4th Armoured Division occupying Buchy to the north. The 17th Duke of York's Royal Canadian Hussars—3rd Infantry Division's recce regiment—reached St. Saëns, about twelve miles almost due north of Rouen. Armoured car squadrons of 2nd Infantry Division's 14th Canadian Hussars gained Tôtes—halfway between Rouen and Dieppe. Crerar's attention was fixed on Dieppe.

On August 30, he had directed 11 Canadian Corps to make its liberation the priority, with a secondary thrust toward the Somme. He also planned to stand 4th Armoured Division down at Buchy for a four-day rest and refit.[12]

With U.S. Second Army having reached the Somme, Montgomery cancelled Crerar's plan to rest 4th Armoured Division. Instead, it was "to be pressed forward with the utmost speed." Second Army's Lieutenant General Miles Dempsey advised that he had directed 11th Armoured Division to push westward along the Somme from Amiens to seize bridge crossings at Pont Remy and Abbeville. Montgomery wanted Crerar to immediately drive forces forward that night to seize these two places on September 1. This would free Dempsey to turn his entire army northward toward Arras and St. Pol.

Crerar said he would get 4th Armoured Division marching immediately and have 1st Polish Armoured Division, which had just crossed the Seine and was considered fit for action, follow it. He also offered Montgomery the tantalizing news that it seemed possible that Dieppe might fall to 2nd Infantry Division without a slow and likely costly "set piece" attack. At 1745 hours, Crerar was back in his plane being flown to 11 Canadian Corps headquarters near the village of Boos.[13] Forty-five minutes later, the plane crashed while attempting to set down in a too-small field adjacent to Lieutenant General Guy Simonds's headquarters. Shaken but otherwise unhurt, Crerar told Simonds that he wanted 4th Armoured Division to reach the Somme by daybreak to take over the bridge crossings at Abbeville and Pont Remy from 11th Armoured Division.[14] Simonds said there might be a delay while 4th Armoured's tanks were refuelled, but he would have the division moving before daybreak.[15]

At 0030 hours on September 1, 4th Division's Major General Harry Foster convened an Orders Group at Brigadier Robert Moncel's headquarters. 11 Corps recce regiment's 12th Manitoba Dragoons would lead the advance, with Moncel's 4th Armoured Brigade following. Lieutenant Colonel Jim Roberts told Foster there was no sense in more than one Dragoon armoured car squadron leading the charge. Having all the armoured cars out front would only mean they would be in the way should a fight develop. Roberts selected 'D' Squadron for the task.

'D' Squadron would be followed by the brigade's Canadian Grenadier Guards, with Roberts planning to hitch his battle headquarters to the rear of this regiment's Shermans. Instead of an armoured car, Roberts travelled in a small truck equipped with a wireless set powerful enough to communicate with 'D' Squadron.

Back at regimental headquarters, Roberts advised Major Gerry Price of 'D' Squadron's task and then asked him to assign Lieutenant George Taylor to lead the point troop, with Lieutenant Bayard Goodday serving as his relief. This meant it fell to Taylor to keep the entire armoured column on course. Roberts had singled out the officer for this task because his older brother, Thomas, had been killed on August 23. He hoped that giving Taylor such a responsible task would focus the young officer's attention away from his grief. Being the lead guide for such a large and long column was always daunting. This time it was even more complicated because of the lack of large-scale maps for the region. All Roberts could hand Taylor and Goodday were 1:250,000 maps, akin to "following a tourist map of the whole of France!"[16]

The advance started at 0400 hours with 'D' Squadron's nine armoured cars leading. By 0950 hours, the column was two-thirds of the way to the Somme, and as the war diarist for the Grenadiers recorded, "it looked like a roll for Abbeville."[17] That was when the Canadians drove into Hornoy and collided with 7th Armoured Division of XII British Corps. Simonds had specifically ordered 4th Armoured Division to follow a route through Hornoy and onward to the Somme at Pont Remy. But the British claimed this route was theirs and produced sufficient paperwork to convince Moncel that their priority was clear.

He tucked his column behind 7th Division's 4th Armoured Brigade and in this manner the two intermingled divisions lurched about ten miles to Airaines. This important junction town proved heavily held by the Germans. A lengthy debate ensued over which brigade should attack the place. Again claiming their priority status, the British launched an attack, which was driven back. They then pounded the town with medium artillery. Moncel, meanwhile, slipped his column away on a northeasterly route.[18]

Because of the opposition at Airaines, Roberts shifted 'D' Squadron to reserve and advanced his other three Dragoon squadrons to the front in order to screen the main column from flank ambushes. Roberts also sensed that Taylor and Goodday were exhausted. They had each been standing in their respective Staghound turrets, trying to simultaneously read maps and keep a watchful eye out for the enemy.[19]

It was 2000 hours, and Dragoons and Grenadiers alike soon groped forward in darkness. The recce troop of the Grenadiers, equipped with light Stuart tanks, led the tank formation, followed by Major Hershell "Snuffy" Smith's No. 3 Squadron and 'B' Company of the Lake Superior Regiment. In the dark, the tankers lost touch with the Dragoons and Smith was also out of contact with the recce troop. "Where are you now?" he called over the wireless to the troop's commander. "At a small bridge east of a village," came the reply. "I think it is Allery." Looking at his map, Smith saw Allery was about two miles almost due west of Airaines—an unlikely spot. "Where are you now?" he inquired again. "Frankly, I don't know," was the response.

Giving up on the recce troop, Smith led the regiment northwest on a road leading from Airaines to Pont Remy, with the village of Wanel midway between. As No. 3 Squadron closed on Wanel, three anti-tank guns fired from it. Smith ordered his two leading troops to fan out in line abreast and open fire. The village soon burned. Dismounting from their vehicles, the Superiors entered Wanel and reported all three guns silenced and the enemy in flight. Moments later, a truck loaded with ammunition roared out of the village. One tank blew it up with a direct hit, while other Shermans mowed down fleeing German infantry with their machine guns.

As Smith re-formed his squadron, two 75-millimetre guns from Sorel-en-Vimeu, about half a mile to the north, opened up.[20] In the dark, Smith figured the gunners were firing half blind—just pointing their guns toward a tank's moving shadow and blasting away. One shell struck the ground ahead of his Sherman and ricocheted over the turret. Smith ordered the leading No. 4 Troop to deploy in a line alongside his tank, "and we just let fly at where the guns were. Next thing the town was on fire."[21]

Both guns were also silenced. When the Superiors once again dismounted and rushed the village, they took fifty prisoners.[22] As No. 3 Squadron started past Sorel, what seemed to Smith like a swarm of Germans—some on foot and others in trucks—poured out right across the path of the tanks. The tankers lashed out with main gun and machine-gun fire. Smith's gunner blasted a round into a nearby ammunition truck, which blew up spectacularly. A piece of shrapnel from the vehicle slammed into Smith's face, pierced his upper lip, and knocked out a tooth, which stuck into the roof of his mouth. Although the wound was painful, Smith was surprised there was no blood. Then he realized that the piece of metal had been so hot it cauterized the wound.

For several minutes chaos reigned, as tankers continued raking the fleeing Germans—concentrating particularly on wrecking the trucks. Seeing this, the Germans piled overboard and ran every which way. As the shooting slowed, the Superiors arrived and started rounding up prisoners. A couple of men brought a German medical officer over to where Smith stood beside his tank with one of the crew ineffectively trying to bandage his wound. The German's "hands were shaking so badly," he could hardly examine the wound properly. "Finally he managed to pull the tooth out of [Smith's] mouth with tweezers," leaving a hole about the size of Smith's little finger.[23] He and another officer, whose foot had been broken when it was caught in his turret's traverse ring, were evacuated by scout car to the Regimental Aid Post. The other officer was twenty-two-year-old Lieutenant William Graham Shaughnessy who, as Lord Shaughnessy, had formally taken his seat in the British House of Lords just six weeks before the Grenadiers deployed to Normandy in early July.[24] Both men would soon return to duty, Smith after only two days.

With the action at Sorel ended, the Grenadiers pressed on about three more miles to high ground overlooking Pont Remy and the Somme—arriving at 0330 hours on September 2. "It was now pouring down in buckets," the regiment's war diarist recorded, "and the boys turned in tired and wet but well pleased with their effort."[25] As 4th Armoured Brigade established its regiments in a line running west from Pont Remy to Abbeville, 10th Infantry Brigade concentrated behind the tankers. The brigade's Lincoln and Welland Regiment, however, was sent to confirm that Airaines was now free of Germans.[26] As the truck convoy carrying the Lincs approached Airaines, it was met by a number of civilians who assured Lieutenant Colonel Bill Cromb that the Germans had fled. Tenth Brigade's Brigadier Jim Jefferson also reported the town clear and that the regiment should just drive rather than waste time dismounting to search it. Dubious, Cromb stopped to consult with some officers of the British 7th Division. Earlier that night, they said, a British officer had taken a jeep into the town and been "blown up." Cromb decided to "dust up" the place. Artillery and 3-inch mortar fire was called down before the Lincs advanced at 0500 hours to find the Germans had this time truly flown.[27]

WHILE 4TH ARMOURED Division had been advancing to the Somme on September 1, 3rd Canadian Infantry Division had left the Seine for the coast at Le Tréport. This village stood at the mouth of Bresle River, about twenty miles northeast of Dieppe. Seizing Le Tréport would isolate both Dieppe and Le Havre, cutting off their German garrisons. Equally, it would outflank many v-1 flying bomb launching sites that had pounded Britain since June 13—killing more than six thousand people and wounding over seventeen thousand. Closing down these sites was a First Canadian Army priority.

The division advanced on a broad front, each brigade following a different series of roads.[28] There was little opposition, most delays caused by the jubilant citizenry of each village or town passed through. "They lined the roads," 7th Brigade's war diarist wrote, "cheering and waving—throwing flowers and all sorts of fruits at us—handing us wines and hard boiled eggs and generally overwhelming us with their kindness. Union Jacks, Stars and Stripes and in one case the Canadian Flag fluttered from nearly every house in the villages—old and young alike came out to welcome us and give us their best wishes and speedy 'bon voyage' to our destination."[29]

On the outskirts of Bure, about twenty miles southeast of Dieppe, 9th Infantry Brigade paused to let the 17th Duke of York's Royal Canadian Hussars armoured cars get a couple of miles out in front. Several civilians approached Brigadier Rocky Rockingham's jeep and reported seeing several wagonloads of Germans fleeing along the main road, heading inland from Dieppe. Rockingham and his intelligence officer, Captain G.E. Franklin, set off to investigate. They quickly closed on "two wagons filled with Germans proceeding at a gallop" around a bend about six hundred yards distant. Realizing they had only a pistol and a Sten gun between them, Rockingham "reluctantly turned back" and sent the Stormont, Dundas and Glengarry Highlanders carrier platoon in pursuit. At 1400 hours, the Glens returned with all the Germans as prisoners. An hour later, the Glens also overran and captured about forty naval personnel who had fled the Le Havre garrison. Then the North Nova Scotia Highlanders reported capturing an officer of 84th Infanterie-Division's headquarters who was carrying orders for that formation to withdraw to the Somme.[30]

Ranging far ahead of the division's infantry brigades, the Duke of York's 'B' Squadron reached Le Tréport at noon, while 'A' Squadron entered Eu a couple of miles inland. The Germans had recently vacated both communities. 'C' Squadron, however, ran into an ambush at Incheville. This village was about seven miles east of the coast and alongside the Bresle River. The Germans sprang their ambush with heavy fire from the opposite bank of the river, as the squadron closed on a partially destroyed bridge. Dismounting, Lieutenant E.W. Smith's assault troop succeeded in driving the Germans away from the bridge in bitter, close-quarters combat. This enabled another troop to also dismount and sufficiently repair the bridge to allow the Staghounds to cross. When the first armoured cars gained the opposite side, the Germans broke off the engagement. By the time the shooting ceased, it was getting dark and the squadron stood down for the night.

Having been relieved by 9th Infantry Brigade, the other two squadrons had raced northeastward, reaching the Somme near Abbeville. Midnight found 'B' Squadron's assault troop on the river's west bank still looking for a bridge. "So," the regiment's Captain Walter G. Pavey later wrote, "another phase came to an end after an exceedingly long march in rough weather and at high speed."[31]

By nightfall, 9th Brigade had crossed the Bresle at Eu and encamped. The division's other two brigades also formed up around Eu but on the river's opposite shore. Major General Dan Spry's intention was for the entire division to cross the Somme the next day. From there, it would enter the Pas de Calais to seize the fortified ports of Boulogne and Calais and eliminate the coastal guns at Cap Gris Nez.[32]

WHEN LIEUTENANT GENERAL Harry Crerar had advised Montgomery on August 31 that Dieppe might fall without a set-piece attack, he was drawing on a message decoded by Ultra—the top-secret organization intercepting and decoding the German Enigma machine transmissions—from Admiral Kanalkuste (Channel Coast) Vizeadmiral Friedrich Rieve, ordering the Dieppe port commander to demolish the harbour facilities. As similar orders were not being given to the fortress commanders at the other coastal port cities, Crerar's intelligence staff believed a withdrawal was under way.[33]

Although optimistic, Crerar was not yet prepared to cancel the major assault plan for Dieppe. Operation Fusilade had been planned months before and envisioned an all-out assault from the east by a Canadian division supported by heavy bomber attacks and offshore naval shelling to shatter the German defences. Like all the French ports, Dieppe had been designated a fortress by Hitler and was to be defended to the last man. Unlike its neighbours of Le Havre or the large ports in the Pas de Calais, Dieppe's fortifications to stave off a landward attack were not well developed. The Dieppe garrison was not large, centred on a single regiment of 245th Infanterie-Division, supported by naval personnel and Luftwaffe anti-aircraft gunners.[34] However, the rest of this division was deployed nearby on either side of the port, which served as the centre point.[35] Consequently, despite the port's inherent smallness and poor defences, it was still feared that the Germans could muster sufficient manpower to offer a stiff fight that would further deplete 2nd Infantry Division's already much reduced regiments. Expecting the operation to begin on September 1, army planners predicted it would take at least until the following day for the port to be secured.[36]

If Fusilade was launched, Dieppe would certainly suffer extensive damage. The naval bombardment was to be fired by two battleships, two monitors, four cruisers, and eight lighter ships. An initial air bombardment was to be directed against batteries of 170-millimetre guns facing seaward to enable the ships to provide fire support seven thousand yards beyond the shoreline. As 2nd Division advanced on Dieppe, more bombers would be on call to attack any artillery batteries or other defensive positions encountered.[37]

Fortunately, 2nd Division and Dieppe were spared a major battle by the intervention of Fifteenth Army's General der Infanterie Gustav von Zangen, who had taken command of this formation on August 27. The army consisted of two corps—LXXXIX and LXVII. Having been deployed to coastal defence duties extending from Le Havre to the Scheldt Estuary, this army was still strong. But the LXXXIX Corps was stretched along the coast from Le Havre to the Somme when the Allies forced the crossings of the Seine. The day after he assumed command, Von Zangen issued orders for the divisions of that corps to immediately vacate their coastal positions and run for the Somme. Accordingly, all of 245th Division in Dieppe and nearby loaded up horse-drawn wagons on August 31 and headed north in good order before 3rd Infantry Division gained Le Tréport and closed the northward roads. Hours before leaving, engineers had attempted to destroy all of Dieppe's quays, bridges, and blockhouses to render the port unusable.[38] All of Von Zangen's LXVII Corps escaped north of the Somme save one of 226th Infanterie-Division's two-battalion-strong regiments, a fusiliers battalion, one artillery battalion and two engineer companies, which Von Zangen ordered to bolster the garrison at Le Havre.[39]

In ordering this withdrawal—while still ensuring that not only Le Havre but also Boulogne, Calais, and Dunkirk were strongly garrisoned—Von Zangen hoped to escape being encircled and destroyed by the rapidly advancing British and Canadian armies. In his mind, "there was no longer any sense in staying at the Channel."[40] The battle for the French northern coast was lost—the fortress ports left to their fates. If he moved fast, there was a chance to save the army for deployment in the defence to come at the Dutch and German borders.

As a result of Von Zangen's actions, when elements of the 14th Canadian Hussars recce regiment entered Dieppe at 0730 hours on September 1, they found the Germans gone. The streets were lined instead with civilians eager to welcome the Canadians back as liberators, rather than as vanquished prisoners following a disastrous failed raid. The commander of the lead squadron was Major D.S.F. Bult-Francis, who had been wounded during the August 19 raid. Among the first Hussars were two soldiers on motorcycles, who were mobbed by the crowd. "At this moment," a Dieppe newspaper reporter wrote, "the enthusiasm of the people reached its height. The crowd ran forward to meet them and was so dense that both men could advance no further. Women threw themselves on them and kissed them. All the citizens then gathered around the Monument to Victory, where both soldiers had gone to deposit the flowers given them. There, ceremonies took place and the crowd sang, 'La Marseillaise,' 'God Save the King,' and 'Tipperary.'"[41]

While this joyous welcome was under way, 2nd Division headquarters staff were making hurried calls to scrap the planned Bomber Command attack on Dieppe. It was cancelled with just twenty minutes to spare.[42] By nightfall, all of 2nd Division had arrived, and the celebrations became frenzied. At the same time, teams of First Canadian Army and British engineers began determining the extent of damage the Germans had inflicted on the port facility. The demolitions were found to have been far less destructive than feared.[43] Although the Germans had sunk three ships to block the harbour mouth, and the harbour itself was littered with eighteen wrecks, the engineers sweeping the water for mines and the docks for explosive charges turned up nothing.[44] Work to render the facilities serviceable started immediately, and minesweepers set to clearing the harbour. On September 6, Dieppe would be declared open for shipping, with the first ten-ship convoy arriving the following afternoon carrying three thousand tons of petrol, ammunition, and other supplies.

Although the Germans had given up Dieppe, the garrisons elsewhere on the French coast were not expected to surrender. On the Biscay coast, Lorient, St. Nazaire, La Rochelle, and a number of other minor ports had been surrounded by small Allied forces, and their garrisons were simply contained—most not surrendering until near war's end. In Brittany, Brest was besieged by a large American force. In First Canadian Army's sector, the garrisons Le Havre, Boulogne, Dunkirk, and Calais were clearly prepared to make a stand. In Belgium, Ostend and Antwerp had not yet been reached by Allied troops.

At Le Havre, the 49th (West Riding) Division leading the 1 British Corps advance reached the outer defences on September 2 and, as expected, found them heavily held.[45] While hoping that preliminary aerial and naval bombardments to soften up the defences, combined with a leaflet campaign, might so deteriorate morale that the Germans would surrender, Crocker reported that the earliest a full-scale assault could be mounted was September 9.[46]

As for 11 Canadian Corps, Crerar had outlined his intentions to Lieutenant General Guy Simonds on September 1. On the following day, Simonds issued instructions that called for 3rd Infantry Division to mop up any Germans between Le Tréport and St. Valéry-sur-Somme at the river's mouth. It would then cross at Abbeville and move into the Pas de Calais. Just coming back into the line after rebuilding from its heavy losses incurred in closing the Falaise Gap, 1st Polish Armoured Division would also cross the river in the Abbeville sector and advance toward Ypres in Belgium. As 4th Armoured Division and 2nd Infantry Division had both seen heavy fighting, Crerar and Simonds planned to allow each a brief rest to reorganize and absorb reinforcements. The 4th Division would rest east of Abbeville and 2nd Division at Dieppe. When ordered, the latter division would pass through 3rd Infantry Division to join operations in the Pas de Calais.[47]

Crerar was well pleased with his army's advance to the Somme. In eleven days—August 21 to September 1—the army had marched 137 miles, from Trun to Dieppe, despite heavy fighting that had cost it 8,036 casualties. To his right, meanwhile, British Second Army had covered even more ground—202 miles. Together, across a wide 50-mile front, the two armies had pushed forward an average of 10 miles per day. Such advances would not have been possible had the Germans not suffered staggering losses that left their formations reeling and unable to recover.[48] So Crerar thought his decision to slow the pace entirely reasonable and necessary.

PART TWO

THE DAYS OF UNCERTAINTY

[10]

Let Us Get on with the War

O N SEPTEMBER 1, Bernard Montgomery was made a field mar-shal and the same day was demoted from commanding all Allied ground forces in northwest Europe. His responsibility was henceforth confined to the command of Twenty-First Army Group. General Dwight D. Eisenhower took overall charge. This change accorded with SHAEF's original post-Normandy invasion plan, but nobody was surprised when Montgomery tried to retain control of the ground war. The rift between Montgomery and Eisenhower on future strategy was only widening. In the last days of August, Eisenhower had made clear his intention to attack Germany on both sides of the Ardennes. While Montgomery's northern thrust toward the Ruhr was to be made with the greatest strength and priority on supply, Lieutenant General Omar Bradley's Twelfth Army Group would carry out a secondary advance through the Saar. This effort would be supported by the American and French divisions approaching from the Mediterranean. Montgomery vehemently opposed this plan, arguing for a single thrust north of the Ardennes. Keeping the Allied armies together, he believed, would enable them to power through the Ruhr and on to Berlin in just two to three weeks. But to succeed, the operation had to be executed by a single commander. Although Montgomery claimed that he cared not whether he retained overall command and would happily see Bradley given the duty, this was clearly untrue. Montgomery wanted the ball and considered nobody else competent to carry it to victory.

Eisenhower no longer believed an autumn victory possible. On August 31, he flew to London from his Granville headquarters on the west side of the Cherbourg peninsula and met Prime Minister Churchill. Then, in the afternoon, Eisenhower held a news conference where he outlined the new command structure. Asked what lay ahead, Eisenhower told the reporters there would "certainly be one major battle before we broke into Germany—this would be through the Siegfried Line to the Rhine." After the conference, his naval aide, U.S. Naval Reserve Captain Harry C. Butcher, asked if Eisenhower thought the Allies "would be able to move supply fast and far enough to keep our armies moving until they broke into Germany." Eisenhower said he "feared we would inevitably be checked." Port capacity was insufficient, the roads were clogged with transport, many bridges were out, and signal communications were bad.[1]

To solve the supply riddle, the Allies needed a major port close to the advancing front. That port was Antwerp—a point Eisenhower had repeatedly emphasized through late August. Montgomery had acknowledged the importance of "securing [Antwerp] as a base" in various orders to Lieutenant General Harry Crerar and British Second Army's Lieutenant General Miles Dempsey. Antwerp, of course, could only be used if both banks of the fifty-mile-long Scheldt Estuary connecting it to the sea were cleared of enemy troops. On its northern flank, the estuary was bordered by the islands of South and North Beveland, and at its mouth by Walcheren Island. All three, but Walcheren in particular, had been heavily fortified to block Antwerp's use even if it fell to the Allies. With the German Fifteenth Army now retreating toward the estuary and hoping to cross it to safety, the Scheldt's strategic importance was even more acute.

Montgomery had emphasized in his August 26 directive that First Canadian Army's "main business" was to open Antwerp. Yet four days later, he started weighing the port's necessity to his future operations. It was really a mathematical question. There and then, Montgomery later wrote, he decided "to rely on the early capture of a Channel port such as Dieppe or Boulogne [and] to cut down our imports from an average of some 16,000 tons per day to 7,000 tons per day."[2] Dieppe's capacity was between 6,000 and 7,000 tons. With just this one channel port in hand, Montgomery believed he could supply the single thrust to the Rhine and on to Berlin. War won, securing Antwerp as a base to supply Allied operations ceased to be relevant. Eisenhower and his American generals, with their broad-front strategy, needed Antwerp's massive capacity. Montgomery did not.

"Although the broad front policy restricted our present aims to reaching the Rhine," he later wrote, "I continued to plan the concentration of such resources as I had into a drive that would hustle the enemy straight through to that river; in order to jump it quickly before the Germans could seriously oppose us. The degree of difficulty which this project involved was directly dependent on the vital factor of speed; for this reason I considered it worthwhile to employ all our resources for its accomplishment, at the expense of any other undertaking." For Montgomery, opening Antwerp was now an expendable undertaking.[3]

Dieppe's falling to the Canadians without a fight on September 1 and the news that its port facilities would be able to receive ships within six days convinced Montgomery he had the minimum capacity required for Second Army to cross the Rhine.[4] It was also possible that Montgomery might have more ports faster than expected. RAF tactical reconnaissance flights were returning photographic intelligence that led 3rd Canadian Infantry Division's Major General Dan Spry to begin his operational instruction for the planned September 3 advance into Pas de Calais with the alluring prospect that Boulogne, Dunkirk, and Calais had all been deserted by an enemy now withdrawing to the east.[5] Were this true, Montgomery would have more capacity than he strictly required.

Reducing supply consumption could only be achieved by cutting Second Army's actual fighting strength. Earlier, Montgomery had grounded VII Corps and its two infantry divisions at the Seine—stripping away most of its transport to move supplies forward to the other two corps. Leaving this corps in reserve enabled him to transfer most of its supplies while providing more than enough transport for his needs.[6]

While Montgomery was independently making his plans, Eisenhower flew to Twelfth Army Group's headquarters at Chartres on September 2. Bradley, Third Army's General George Patton, and First Army's Lieutenant General Courtenay Hodges were all present. Eisenhower told them that the main thrust was to be in the north and involve the xxx British Corps and Hodges's First Army's xix and vii Corps. Third Army would also advance, but on a more limited scale. Even though he grudgingly agreed that the northern advance showed more promise than that to the south, Bradley joined Patton in objecting to Third Army's secondary role. Eisenhower was sympathetic, but insisted the problem was one of insufficient supply.

At this point, Lieutenant General J.C.H. Lee, Eisenhower's deputy commander in charge of SHAEF's Services of Supply department, claimed—without any supportive data—that both the main northern thrust and Patton's southern one could be adequately supplied. This prompted Eisenhower to agree to Patton's striking through the Lorraine region toward the Rhine at Mannheim and Frankfurt.[7]

Meeting concluded, Eisenhower learned that mechanical problems had disabled his personal airplane—a two-engine Douglas c-47. His crew had, however, rustled up a single-engine two-seater Stinson l-5 Sentinel observation plane. Eisenhower and his c-47 co-pilot, Captain Dick Underwood, flew off for Granville. The weather soon deteriorated, with high winds and cloud reducing visibility. Unable to find the airstrip at SHAEF headquarters, Underwood landed on a beach next to Eisenhower's small villa. Although the landing went fine, the rising tide threatened the little aircraft. In pushing the plane across the sand to get above the tide line, Eisenhower wrenched a knee. Treating the injury required encasing the knee in a plaster cast that left his leg immobilized. This necessarily hampered the supreme commander's ability to visit his forward commanders.[8]

Consequently, on September 3 at 1300 hours, it was Bradley and Hodges who appeared at Dempsey's Second Army tactical headquarters six miles southwest of Amiens to brief the British on the decisions made the day before at Chartres. Montgomery was incensed by Eisenhower's absence. His temper flared higher when Bradley advised that the American main effort was now directed by Third Army toward

Frankfurt, while First Army would simply maintain contact between his army group and Montgomery's, rather than being attached to Twenty-First Army Group for a combined drive to the Rhine.

"I have not seen Eisenhower since August 26 and have had no orders from him," Montgomery fumed in a cable to General Alan Brooke that evening, "so I am making my own plans for advancing against the RUHR." No longer expecting help from the Americans, he advised Brooke that both 1st British Airborne Division and 1st Independent Polish Parachute Brigade would be required to seize bridges over the Rhine and hold them until his armoured divisions arrived.[9]

Before cabling Brooke, Montgomery issued a directive to his army commanders. Second Army, he said, was advancing to secure Brussels, Ghent, and Antwerp. Brussels had, in fact, been liberated earlier that day by xxx Corps's Guards Armoured Division, and its recce units were already advancing northward from the Belgian capital. First Canadian Army was beginning its task of clearing the coastal belt. Montgomery's intention was "to advance eastwards and destroy all enemy forces encountered," and then "occupy the Ruhr, and get astride the communications leading from it into Germany and to the seaports." Because he planned to allocate most resources to Second Army's operations, once it had cleared the coastal belt, First Canadian Army would "then remain in the general area Bruges-Calais until the maintenance situation allows . . . its employment further forward."

On September 6, Second Army would advance from a line running between Brussels and Antwerp, with its main weight directed toward the Rhine at Arnhem and Wesel. "One Division, or if necessary a corps, will be turned northwards towards Rotterdam and Amsterdam. Having crossed the Rhine, the Army will deal with the Ruhr and will be directed on the general area Osnabrück—Hamm—Münster—Rheine."

As for Twelfth Army Group, Montgomery said its First U.S. Army would move its left flank forward in conjunction with his advance and "assist in cutting off the Ruhr by operations against its southeastern face, if such action is desired by Second Army." No mention was made of securing Antwerp as a base.[10]

IN THE MIDST of strategic planning for a drive to the Rhine, Montgomery had got into a nasty spat with Crerar. It started with a signal from Montgomery at 1530 hours on September 2 asking Crerar to meet him at Second Army's tactical headquarters at 1300 the following day. This was the meeting attended by Bradley and Hodges. But nothing in Montgomery's cable indicated the high-level nature of the agenda or participants.

On the morning of September 2, 2nd Canadian Infantry Division's Major General Charles Foulkes had visited Crerar's headquarters and requested his attendance at a religious service the next day—a Sunday—at the cemetery outside Dieppe, where about eight hundred Canadians killed during the 1942 raid were buried. Following lunch with town officials, the division planned a formal march past, and Foulkes hoped Crerar would take the salute.[11]

As 2nd Division was stood down and was to remain in Dieppe for several days to rest, refit, and absorb about one thousand reinforcements, Crerar told Foulkes that "this opportunity, suitably to mark a gallant and historic episode in Canadian military history, had my entire approval." Unless "urgent operational matters intervened," he would certainly attend.

When Montgomery's signal arrived, Crerar thought the phrasing indicated "a personal meeting, rather than a formal conference." Crerar had just met Montgomery the previous day and nothing of significance had developed on First Canadian Army's front since. Consequently, he asked Montgomery by signal if the meeting could be pushed back to 1700 hours so that he could attend the Dieppe ceremonies. From "a Canadian point of view," he wrote, it was "desirable I should do so. Will however conform to your wishes. Advice requested."[12]

Although expecting Montgomery's concurrence, Crerar did arrange for any reply to be forwarded immediately. If necessary, Crerar would leave the ceremonies on a moment's notice.

In the morning, Crerar departed his headquarters at 0830 hours for a seventy-mile flight to meet Simonds at 11 Canadian Corps headquarters. Montgomery had not yet responded to his signal. After their meeting, Simonds left by car at 1000 hours for the Dieppe ceremony. As he was flying, Crerar lingered another twenty minutes in case a signal came from Montgomery. When none arrived, he assumed that the 1300 hour meeting "had been altered . . . to meet my request." He would go to Dieppe as planned.

Arriving at 2nd Division headquarters at 1050 hours, Crerar told Foulkes he was expecting an important message from Montgomery that might curtail his participation in events.[13] Having arranged for any message to be rushed to him, Crerar and the other officers then left for the ceremonies.

The small cemetery outside Dieppe had been meticulously maintained ever since the majority of the Canadians killed in the raid had been buried there. Often people slipped in at night to avoid being identified by the Germans and laid flowers on the graves. Late on this Sunday morning, a Protestant service was held, with one of the division's priests presiding. Companies from each regiment that had participated in the raid attended.

At about 1440 hours, every 2nd Division soldier formed up and the march past began. Although no public notice had been issued, thousands of citizens lined the Rue Claude Groulard to watch the troops pass. A bagpipe band formed from five different regiments led the procession. When Crerar mounted the podium to take his place alongside Foulkes, Simonds, and various local dignitaries, the crowd let out a tremendous cheer. On either side of the platform, members of Dieppe's FFI were assembled. Six by six, the Canadian soldiers passed in a long, disciplined column. "It was a magnificent sight, that gave a sensation of power," a local reporter wrote.[14]

Shortly after the parade began, a messenger had passed Crerar a note. It was from Montgomery, insisting he attend the meeting at 1300 hours. "As the time when it would have been possible for me to comply . . . was long past, no corrective action on my part was possible. I therefore completed my agreed part in the Dieppe ceremonial . . . and departed immediately afterwards." Crerar flew to British Second Army's tactical headquarters. He found nobody there other than Dempsey, who said that except for the breach in formality on Crerar's part, no operational disadvantage had resulted. The conversation had focused entirely on operations of Second Army and the Americans.

Crerar then travelled by car to Montgomery's headquarters, just a couple of miles away. Montgomery was having tea and Crerar joined him. They then went together to Montgomery's caravan. The moment they were inside, Montgomery abruptly demanded why Crerar had not attended the meeting. "I kept myself under control," Crerar wrote afterward, "and briefly, with occasional interruptions, gave him the explanation." Montgomery said "he was not interested" in explanations and that the Dieppe ceremony "was of no importance compared to getting on with the war." A signal summoning Crerar to the meeting had been sent to First Canadian Army's tactical headquarters at 0615 that morning, he said. And whether Crerar had got the signal or not, he should have attended the meeting regardless.

Both men were speaking sharply, Crerar saying he could not accept Montgomery's attitude. Crerar declared he had "a definite responsibility to my government and country, which, at times, might run counter to [Montgomery's] wishes. There was a powerful Canadian reason why I should have been present . . . at Dieppe that day. In fact, there were 800 reasons—the Canadian dead buried at Dieppe cemetery. I went on to say that he should realize, by our considerable association, that I was . . . not unreasonable, but that, also, I would never consent to be 'pushed about' by anyone, in a manner, or direction, which I knew to be wrong."

Montgomery reiterated that Crerar had failed an instruction from him and then announced that "our ways must part." Crerar replied that he assumed Montgomery would take up the matter immediately with higher channels and that he would report the situation to his government. Hearing this, and knowing that the Canadian government would not take well to Crerar being fired over an incident likely to seem trivial from a distance, Montgomery changed tactics and announced the matter closed. Crerar balked, wanting the air officially cleared. But Montgomery would not be drawn further.

Instead, he briefed Crerar on the gist of the meeting, which clearly had no relevance to First Canadian Army operations. Crerar decided that the intention was to emphasize that his only responsibility was to Montgomery. "The Canadian ceremony at Dieppe was not of his ordering, nor to his liking." When Montgomery found that "I would not retreat from the stand I had taken—that I had a responsibility to Canada as well as to [him], he decided to 'consider the matter closed.' It was not a willing decision, nor one . . . I . . . assume will be maintained.

However, though our relations have obviously been strained, I trust that the situation is temporary and I shall do what I can to ease them, though without departing from what I consider it my duty to do, or not to do, in my capacity as a Canadian."[15]

In the aftermath, some commentators would maintain that Crerar's presence at the meeting had been necessary. Montgomery's biographer went so far as to argue that Crerar's absence meant he could not "point out the difficulties in seizing quickly the Channel ports," whose rapid capture would provide Montgomery with sufficient supplies to steamroll into Germany. As a result, Eisenhower authorized the "other Army commanders . . . to mount their own offensive thrusts into Germany, each virtually independent of the other—Dempsey north of the Ruhr, Hodges south of the Ruhr on each side of the Ardennes, and Patton via the Saar."[16]

Such a claim was nonsense. On September 3, Crerar had no intelligence to offer as to what difficulty First Canadian Army might have in opening the ports. Instead, he possessed the same aerial reconnaissance data that led 3rd Canadian Infantry Division's Major General Spry to understand that the garrisons at Boulogne, Calais, and Dunkirk were fleeing—joining Fifteenth Army's escape north across the Scheldt Estuary. Nothing Crerar would have said was likely to have altered Montgomery's decision to ignore securing Antwerp in exchange for the calculated gamble of a dash to the Rhine.

On September 7, Montgomery would attempt to mend fences with Crerar. He sent a hastily scribbled note. "I am sorry I was a bit rude the other day, and somewhat outspoken. I was annoyed that no one came to a very important conference.

"But forget about it—and let us get on with the war. It was my fault. Yours ever, Monty."[17]

ON SEPTEMBER 3, Ultra intercepted a message from Hitler to OB West Generalfeldmarschall Walter Model, which was passed to Montgomery the following day. With the British closing on Antwerp and its probable loss, Hitler emphasized the "decisive importance" of holding Boulogne, Dunkirk, and Calais, as well as "Walcheren Island . . . a bridgehead round Antwerp and the Albert Canal as far as Maastricht."[18]

He directed Fifteenth Army "to bring the garrisons of Boulogne and Dunkirk, and the Calais defense area up to strength by means of full units.

"The defensive strength of the fortresses is to be increased by means of additional ammunition supplies from the supplies of the 15th Army, especially anti-tank ammunition, by bringing up provisions of all kinds from the country, and by evacuating the entire population.

"The commanders of the Calais defense area and of Walcheren Island receive the same authority as a fortress commander."[19]

It was too late for Model to defend Antwerp. At noon the following day, 11th British Armoured Division's tanks had rolled into the city centre and were met by the Belgian resistance. The three miles of docks that fronted the Scheldt Estuary were captured intact. Bridges across the Albert Canal that connected to the remaining twenty-seven miles of port facilities north of the city were also intact. But when the British attempted to cross the bridges, they were met by 88-millimetre and 20-millimetre artillery fire and pulled back, despite the Belgians insisting that the Germans were too weak to offer sustained resistance. In the absence of orders from Montgomery to force a crossing, win the port facilities there, and seal off the north side of the Scheldt Estuary by securing the exit route to the mainland from South Beveland, xxx British Corps commander Lieutenant General Brian Horrocks ordered no more than a consolidation of his hold on Antwerp itself. Recognizing that Antwerp alone was an empty prize, Horrocks later regretted not ordering his troops forward on his own initiative. Instead, three days later, he turned the corps eastward and away from Antwerp in order to prepare for Montgomery's drive on the Rhine. Ultimately, it would fall to First Canadian Army to fight a prolonged autumn campaign to win the estuary and open the port to Allied shipping.*

Had Hitler decided earlier on the strategy to hold the channel ports, Dieppe would not have been given up without a fight. And already

---

* The story of that operation is told in the Canadian Battle Series title *Terrible Victory: First Canadian Army and the Scheldt Estuary Campaign, September 13–November 6, 1944.* Hereafter, details of operations by First Canadian Army formations with regard to that campaign are not addressed in this volume.

it was too late for German Fifteenth Army's General der Infanterie Gustav von Zangen to do much to bolster Boulogne's defences. On September 4, his LXVII Corps had mostly withdrawn to a general line stretching from Calais on the coast to St. Omer inland, LXXXVI Corps east from St. Omer to Aire, and LXXXIX Corps from Aire to just north of Douai. There was no thought of this line holding. Von Zangen's focus was directed on getting his battered army across the Scheldt Estuary.[20]

The Boulogne commander Generalleutnant Ferdinand Heim had been briefly led to believe that the headquarters of LXVII Corps with the 64th Infanterie-Division under command was to reinforce him. But by September 5, that formation had streamed past, leaving behind only one of the division's artillery batteries, consisting of nine guns and part of an engineer battalion. This left him with about ten thousand men.[21]

As for Calais, Von Zangen offered its commander no additional support. Fifteenth Army was increasingly disorganized. A huge gap had developed between its left flank and the right flank of what remained of Seventh Army. Through this gap the British had dashed to Brussels and then on to Antwerp. Model had hoped to plug the gap with Fifth Panzer Army and re-form a coherent line. Oberstgruppenführer Joseph "Sepp" Dietrich, now commanding this army, was too far along in withdrawing to Germany to reverse course. The gap kept widening.[22]

With Fifteenth Army pulling away from the ports, the fortress commanders were also no longer able to look to the German navy for either support or resupply. In August 1944, the Germans had five flotillas of E-boats, with one each stationed at Brest, Cherbourg, Le Havre, Boulogne, and Ostend. Each flotilla consisted normally of nine boats, with six generally operational and the other three either undergoing maintenance or being used for training. Somewhat larger than the British motor torpedo boats, E-boats (designated Schnellboot or S-boot by the Germans) had a wood hull wrapped around a steel frame and were capable of 43.8 knots (fifty miles per hour). Armed with two torpedo tubes and two anti-aircraft guns, they were manned by thirty sailors. Largely operating at night and either protecting German coastal convoys or ranging out to attack Allied shipping, the E-boats had proven a formidable force—particularly within the channel.

In the last week of August, British and American naval forces had set about driving them out of their channel port harbours and isolating these from continued supply by the German navy. Two Hunt-class destroyers were added to the Royal Navy patrols previously conducted by a couple of frigates and motor torpedo boats. A number of fierce engagements with German E-boats protecting small, fast coastal convoys ensued. Suffering heavy losses, the Germans decided on August 29 to withdraw their coastal flotillas from Le Havre entirely.[23] On September 4, the E-boats at Boulogne and Ostend also left—all being shifted to bases at Rotterdam and Ijmuiden.[24]

AT 0600 HOURS on September 4, 3rd Canadian Infantry Division crossed the Somme River with the intention of driving straight through to Boulogne. Expectation was still that the German garrisons at both Boulogne and Calais had joined Fifteenth Army's flight toward the Scheldt Estuary. The 17th Duke of York's Royal Canadian Hussars recce regiment led with three of its squadrons. 'B' Squadron was on the left, 'A' Squadron in the centre, and 'C' Squadron to the right.[25] Each squadron was accompanied by a troop of 6th Canadian Anti-Tank Regiment's 56th Battery.[26] These troops had been recently equipped with the 17-pounder self-propelled M10 tank destroyer.[27] The armoured cars and SPs made rapid progress, advancing about twenty-three miles to the Authie River at Nampont St. Martin—thirty-three miles south of Boulogne. Finding the bridge in the village blown, the squadrons spread out and soon found an intact crossing. The dash continued. As 'A' Squadron rolled into Montreuil, next to the Canche River, Germans fled across the village's bridge, which then blew up in front of the leading armoured cars.

While the rest of the regiment formed inside Montreuil, Lieutenant Colonel Thomas Cripps Lewis jumped into a jeep and headed to the east in search of an alternative crossing. About three miles from Montreuil, Lewis spotted a small stone bridge with no roads leading to it, which appeared not to have been used for years and so had been overlooked by the Germans. In short order, the Hussars were trundling over the bridge and pushing onward.[28]

Meanwhile, 9th Infantry Brigade, leading the main body of 3rd Division, had reached Montreuil. Unaware of the bridge the Hussars had found, the men—after a lengthy search—finally turned up a crossing via, as the brigade's intelligence officer Captain G.E. Franklin wrote, "an extremely fragile looking concrete bridge." By the time the brigade reached the other side of the river, it was 1500 hours. Major General Dan Spry's orders called for the brigade to push through to Boulogne before nightfall, but that was clearly impossible. So Brigadier Rocky Rockingham halted the column for the night at Hubersent, on the southern edge of the more rugged and wooded country surrounding Boulogne.[29]

The 17th Hussars had gone six miles farther north to Samer, just twelve miles southeast of Boulogne. As 'C' Squadron with the 56th Battery's 'D' Troop entered an orchard short of the town, it took fire from anti-tank guns hidden amid the trees. The M10s ground into the orchard with their deadly 17-pounders and machine guns blazing. In minutes, two German gun positions, one machine-gun post, and a number of infantry were wiped out. One of the M10s was struck four times by Panzerfaust rounds fired by the infantry, but suffered little damage. When German snipers started firing from a building on the edge of the orchard, the M10s lashed out with high-explosive rounds, and soon it "blazed furiously." A few minutes later, a horse-drawn convoy was spotted passing the other side of the orchard, and the M10s destroyed six wagons.[30]

Retreating Germans were everywhere. Leading the Hussars' 'A' Squadron, Lieutenant A.E. Doig crested a hill overlooking Samer and spotted a long column of horse-drawn wagons.[31] His troop opened fire and were joined by the M10s of 'F' Troop. Eight wagons were smashed to bits.[32] "Then, paying no heed to the burning mess on the road, [Doig] bashed right through them or over them, smack into the middle of the town. The rest of the squadron, commanded by Major [W.C.] Bowen, close on his heels came into the town spraying the buildings with Besa [machine-gun] and 37-millimetre fire to cover the arrival of the self-propelled guns who quickly demolished buildings from which fire was coming and putting out of action . . . two anti-tank weapons," Captain Walter Pavey reported.[33]

Still hoping to gain the objective, 'A' Squadron continued on the main road leading from Samer to Boulogne, until brought up short by a heavily mined concrete roadblock covered by 155-millimetre guns positioned on high ground either side of the road. Shells from the armoured cars' 37-millimetre guns bounced harmlessly off the roadblock, but the M10s ripped into it with armour-piercing shot, followed by heavy explosive rounds that shattered the obstacle. With the 155-millimetre guns zeroing in, however, discretion was called for, and the Canadians beat a hasty retreat.[34]

The Hussars and 56th Battery settled for the night near Samer, while 3rd Division headquarters staff mulled the situation over. By first light on September 5, it was obvious to all that Boulogne and Calais were still strongly fortified and fully manned. Both were going to be tough nuts to crack. Accordingly, the Hussars and 56th Battery did "a quick right wheel," with 'B' Squadron moving to a position where its guns could cut the Boulogne to Calais main road. 'C' Squadron, meanwhile, cut the coast road leading to Dunkirk at the village of Oye-Plage, about eleven miles northeast of Calais, and was reinforced there by 'A' Squadron.

Lieutenant Colonel Lewis considered the entire operation to have been "carried out with dispatch, few orders and mainly, a keen appreciation of the division's intention. The success of the last two days was directly due to the high standard of leadership of the [squadron commanders]. Major C.W. MacLean's rapid concentrating of his squadron, moving to a flank to cross a bridge—then quick deployment, was a piece of traffic management and control of very high standard. Major W.C. Bowen's offensive and enthusiastic leadership on the centre line, kept the main road open at all times despite stiff resistance, and Major E.R. Allen's personal energy and drive in the recce for bridges probably speeded the advance of the division by hours, if not a day."[35]

Now, however, 3rd Infantry Division's chase was over. Before it stood the fortresses, which must be taken by siege.

11

Trouble Galore

A T 1900 HOURS on September 6, Lieutenant General Harry
Crerar received a cable from Field Marshal Bernard Montgomery.
"Would be grateful for your opinion on the likelihood of early capture
of Boulogne," it read. "It looks as if port of Antwerp may be unusable
for some time as Germans are holding islands at mouth of Scheldt.
Immediate opening of some port north of Dieppe essential for rapid
development of my plan and we want Boulogne badly. What do you
think are the chances of getting it soon?"[1]

Earlier in the day, Twenty-First Army Group's chief of staff, Major
General Francis Wilfred de Guingand—Freddie to friends—had
warned Montgomery that it appeared the Germans were determined to
hold the channel ports for as long as possible. He considered Boulogne
most important not only for its large port facility but also because it was
ideally positioned to serve as a delivery hub for a planned cross-channel
fuel pipeline from England to the Pas de Calais.

Crerar agreed with the importance of rapidly securing Boulogne.
The previous day, he had instructed II Canadian Corps Lieutenant
General Guy Simonds to rank this port first in importance, with
Dunkirk to follow and then Calais. Simonds was to identify his requirements to achieve these goals. At the same time, however, Crerar
had expressed his understanding that "additional support and ammunition" would be restricted "pending liquidation [of] Le Havre."[2] There

was simply insufficient heavy artillery, bomber, and naval assets to enable First Canadian Army to break the defences of more than one port at a time.

Simonds turned to this task reluctantly. He would have preferred to simply rope off the ports with minimal forces and send the rest of his corps pursuing the German Fifteenth Army before it could escape across the Scheldt Estuary. Simonds also recognized the importance of clearing the Germans away from the estuary so that Antwerp could be opened. In his mind, these should have been the priorities for First Canadian Army, and he blamed Crerar for "just not minding the shop."[3] Typically, Simonds chose to criticize Crerar, while ignoring the fact that it was Montgomery who had given the channel ports priority over either the destruction of Fifteenth Army or the opening of Antwerp.

Like Montgomery, Crerar considered the channel ports and their potential to provide the necessary supplies of greater importance. "It follows that a speedy and victorious conclusion to the war now depends, fundamentally, upon the capture by First Canadian Army of the channel ports which have now become so essential," he wrote. With the ports as priority, Crerar acknowledged that destroying Fifteenth Army was necessarily "secondary in importance."[4]

Montgomery believed that if Eisenhower agreed to divert to British Second Army three thousand tons of cargo from the American-assigned port of Le Havre, and the Canadians were able to deliver the shipping capacity of Dieppe, Boulogne, Dunkirk, and Calais, then he could punch through to Berlin. Failing all this, and if only "one good Pas de Calais port" was available, the xxx Corps drive to Arnhem would still be viable if he received a daily airlift of one thousand tons from Britain and an additional allotment of motor transport running supplies forward from the base at Bayeux. Reaching Berlin would not be possible, but Montgomery could still punch deep into Germany and win a triangle anchored on the cities of Münster, Rheine, and Osnabrücke.[5]

For the first time in his long service as Montgomery's chief of staff, de Guingand disagreed with his commander. In August 1942, when Montgomery had taken command of British Eighth Army in North Africa, he had recognized the forty-two-year-old staff officer's innate management ability and made him his chief of staff.

Leaving de Guingand to run the army's overall administration freed Montgomery to concentrate on command. As Montgomery's star rose, de Guingand had followed as chief of staff and had also assumed an additional, unofficial role. Besides his administrative responsibilities, de Guingand endeavoured regularly, through his close relationship with SHAEF's chief of staff, Lieutenant General Walter Bedell Smith, to smooth relations between Eisenhower and Montgomery.

This left de Guingand privy to the ongoing dispute over strategy, and he was dismayed by Montgomery's insistence that a single hammer strike to the Rhine could win the war in 1944. Any lodgement Montgomery might win over the Rhine, de Guingand feared, would be unsustainable. With some reluctance, he also believed that Eisenhower's insistence on the broad-front strategy was the correct course to take—both strategically and politically. Nevertheless, he recognized that Montgomery was going to roll the dice, and there was no stopping his making a run for the Rhine.[6]

IN THE EARLY morning of September 5, Simonds issued new instructions to his II Canadian Corps commanders. The 4th Armoured Division and Polish Armoured Division were to continue pursuing the Germans toward the Scheldt Estuary. His two infantry divisions, meanwhile, would focus on the channel coast. While 3rd Division continued concentrating around Boulogne and Calais, 2nd Division was to clear the coast from Dunkirk to the Dutch frontier.[7]

At 1700 hours, Major General Charles Foulkes convened an Orders Group of 2nd Division brigadiers and battalion commanders at his Dieppe headquarters.[8] If required, Foulkes planned to take Dunkirk in a pincer attack, with 6th Brigade hooking up to the northeast of the city and then advancing south along the coast to capture the outlying villages of Furnes (Veurne in Flemish), La Panne, and Nieuport. Simultaneously, 5th Brigade would approach from the southwest. While initially in reserve, 4th Brigade was to be ready to break northeastward up the coast to Ostend on a moment's notice. Whether the division would have to fight for Dunkirk or walk in as it had at Dieppe was unknown. For now, 5th Brigade would lead the division's advance and concentrate in Forêt d'Éperlecques, seven miles south of the village of Bourbourg. This village lay about twelve miles southwest of Dunkirk, and together with nearby Gravelines was believed to constitute the first line of defence on this flank.[9]

During the Forêt de la Londe battle, Les Fusiliers Mont-Royal commander Lieutenant Colonel Guy Gauvreau had become acting brigadier of the 6th when Brigadier Fred Clift had been wounded. Gauvreau's subsequent promotion to brigadier had been confirmed on August 30. If a fight for Dunkirk was required, this would be his first real brigade command test. He was, however, a seasoned veteran, having led the Fusiliers through Normandy.

Forêt de la Londe had cost 2nd Division another brigadier—4th Brigade's Eddy Ganong—but not due to a wound. In the battle's aftermath, Foulkes—who had obstinately insisted on the 6th and 4th Brigades continuing piecemeal attacks, which whittled their battalions down to no good end—had shifted all blame to Ganong and demanded his head.[10] Simonds and Crerar consented, transferring him on August 30 to a staff position at army headquarters. Later that morning, Fred Cabeldu took over the brigade.[11] Cabeldu had led 3rd Division's Canadian Scottish Regiment ashore on June 6 and proven both a competent and popular combat leader. "We were . . . sorry to lose our wonderful leader," the regiment's war diarist wrote that day, "but feel he is deserving of 'better things.'"[12]

As soon as Brigadier Bill Megill returned to 5th Brigade headquarters, he reported that the unit would leave Dieppe in a matter of hours. The move was not unexpected and the battalions rushed to get ready. "Trouble galore arose here," the Calgary Highlanders' war diarist wrote, "because many of the lads had gone downtown into Dieppe for the evening and all means of communication were used to 'herd' all the boys together and back into our own area to await final orders to move." At 0100 hours, September 6, the Calgaries boarded trucks and were away.[13]

Racing ahead were the armoured cars of 11 Canadian Corps's 12th Manitoba Dragoons and 2nd Division's own 14th Canadian Hussars. Both were out to test the defences around Dunkirk. 'C' Squadron of the 14th Hussars soon discovered that both Gravelines near the coast and Bourbourg farther inland appeared strongly defended. They also found that the bridges over both the Aa Canal passing Gravelines and the Bourbourg Canal had been blown.[14] Gravelines appeared to be held by at least 150 Germans and Bourbourg by even more.[15]

Lieutenant Colonel Jim Roberts had thrown his Dragoons out by squadrons to approach Dunkirk from the south, east, and north. 'B' Squadron confirmed the German defences that the 14th Hussars had detected at Gravelines. Reaching Bergues—an old fortress town— in the early afternoon, 'D' Squadron found it encircled by "a rather determined defensive ring."[16] Bergues stood on high ground over- looking the surrounding flat country. Every attempt to bypass the town on nearby roads was detected by German artillery observers within the fortress, who drove the armoured cars back with shellfire. Casting farther afield to roads outside the view of the Germans in Bergues only brought the squadron's troops against heavily defended positions guarding the roads leading to Dunkirk. Major Gerry Price decided the only course open was to withdraw the squadron out of artillery range and take up a position from which his men could ensure that the Germans inside the defensive positions stayed put.[17]

Farther north, 'C' Squadron managed to force its way into Nieuport against slight resistance. Just as the Dragoons confidently prepared to hold the town until infantry could arrive to fully secure it, the Germans opened up with heavy artillery firing from batteries on the coast. The falling shells being of a calibre clearly capable of destroying their armoured cars, a hasty withdrawal was ordered. Two armoured cars, however, were trapped when shells destroyed bridges behind and ahead of them. Lieutenant J.A. Irvine and eight other men were cut off. Irvine set off on foot and managed to find another route out of the village. By the time he returned to the armoured cars, however, both had been immobilized by shellfire and would require a wrecker to come forward and pull them out under cover of darkness. Although Irvine's party suffered no casualties, three crewmen in another armoured car were wounded when it was knocked out by a hidden 75-millimetre gun at a range of thirty yards.[18]

While Roberts's Dragoons had probed Dunkirk's defences, his regimental headquarters had been slowly packing up next to Forêt d'Hesdin for a planned move that would carry it through to Ostend,

Belgium. The small forest lay about nineteen miles southeast of Montreuil. Roberts was in no hurry to get moving; the squadrons would not head for Ostend until the next day. The woods struck him as lovely, so he and several officers followed a trail into their heart. A few minutes later, they "came upon a hidden and empty enemy installation of considerable proportions. There were large underground concrete shelters, all heavily camouflaged with netting and boughs." Roberts soon realized they had stumbled upon an abandoned launching base for v-1 flying bombs. It pleased Roberts to think that the Canadian advance into the Pas de Calais had "contributed to the easing of the load carried by the long-suffering and gallant British civilians," who had been forced to endure the renewed blitz of their cities.[19]

The Germans had in fact withdrawn from all launching sites in the Pas de Calais by September 1. Approximately three hundred sites had existed in France. Although some were on the Cherbourg peninsula, the majority had been concentrated in a broad crescent between Rouen and the Pas de Calais.[20] From these sites the pilotless bombs, each carrying a ton of explosives and powered by a jet-propulsion system that produced a top speed of four hundred miles per hour, had first been launched against London and southeast England on the night of June 12–13. Over the next ten weeks, until the sites were abandoned, hundreds of what the British nicknamed "doodlebugs" or "buzz-bombs" because of the engines' characteristic popping sound, had been fired. Now the skies over England were largely clear of this danger, except for a few fired from German aircraft. The first such air attack was launched on September 5, when fourteen were fired at London. The air-launched bombs proved highly inaccurate, and none reached the city.[21]

On September 7, as Roberts was inspecting the v-1 installation in the forest, BBC Radio formally announced "to the people of England that the menace of the flying-bomb had ceased to exist." The last ground-launched rocket had been released from a site in Belgium the previous day.[22]

ONCE THE RECONNAISSANCE regiments had confirmed that both Gravelines and Bourbourg were strongly defended, 5th Brigade advanced toward them on September 7 with the Black Watch leading. The troops marched through "very heavy rain," battered also by a high, cold wind. It was, wrote the Black Watch war diarist, the "coldest day we have known for a long time."[23] The countryside east of Dunkirk was generally land claimed from the North Sea over centuries of dyke construction and draining by farmers. The result was a nine- to twelve-mile-wide strip of polders that was dead flat and cut by a maze of drainage ditches linked to larger canals. German engineers had breached many dykes, flooding the farmland to depths ranging from a few inches to several feet. Consequently, the Canadian advance was confined to roads that had been constructed on berms or canal banks to prevent their inundation. Having channelled any attacker onto these exposed roads, the Germans blocked their use with heavy defensive positions. Mines had been liberally placed on the road surfaces and verges, while artillery and mortar formations had registered and taped them to enable accurate fire along their length. The ditches on either side were deep with water and generally useless as cover. As movement on the exposed roads in daylight invited immediate and deadly response, the men were forced to slog up the ditches in hip-deep water or await the cover of darkness.[24] For the Canadians, this battlefield was but a precursor to the gruelling conditions they would encounter in the Scheldt Estuary and Rhineland to come.

Advancing against spasmodic German shelling, the Black Watch reached a bridge across the Aa, two miles west of Bourbourg, but found a forty-foot gap blown out of its centre. Engineers from 7th Field Company were to effect repairs.[25] Tasked with providing the necessary bridging equipment was 2nd Canadian Infantry Division's Bridging Platoon, commanded by Lieutenant Geoffrey Charles Barrington Bourne.[26] Bourne had a reputation for tenaciously getting bridges in place quickly despite often working under shell and mortar fire. That day, just finding the required materials challenged his patience. Having been informed that they were stored at the main forward Abbeville dump, he rushed a truck convoy there, only to learn the materials had been moved forward and left at the Calgary Highlanders' headquarters. Finally catching up to the bridging materials, Bourne had to work rapidly but with great precision, because—as his subsequent October

Member of the British Empire (MBE) citation read—"the absence or wrong loading of a single piece of equipment [could] cause the failure of the complete operation."[27]

Bourne's run around the country, heavy rain, and intermittent shelling during construction resulted in the bridge not being ready until well after the assigned noon completion. Brigadier Bill Megill ordered Le Régiment de Maisonneuve to lead the advance into Bourbourg. The Calgary Highlanders would then pass through to capture the village of Loon-Plage, five and a half miles to the northwest and eight miles due west of Dunkirk.[28]

Understrength by 272 front-line infantrymen, the Maisies remained woefully weak, each of its four companies numbering just sixty men.[29] It wasn't until 1600 hours that the regiment started the advance.[30] No sooner had the Maisies crossed the bridge than they were lashed by heavy machine-guns and fire from two 88-millimetre guns covering the entrance into the town. The church tower in Bourbourg's centre provided an excellent observation post from which spotters directed deadly accurate artillery and mortar fire.[31]

Lieutenant Colonel Julien Bibeau ordered his men to take cover until darkness fell. They would then advance behind an artillery barrage provided by 5th Field Regiment. Promoted from major to battalion command on August 28, after its previous commander was lost to illness, the thirty-six-year-old Bibeau had immediately placed his mark on a regiment bedevilled by heavy casualties and constant manpower shortages. Fluently bilingual, he was able to function adeptly within the unilingual world dominant—outside of the French-Canadian battalions—throughout First Canadian Army.[32]

At nightfall, the Maisies attacked. Having discovered several small rowboats, 'B' and 'C' Companies ignored the bridge and rowed across the canal. Unable to find oars, Major Jacques Ostiguy's 'C' Company broke boards into makeshift paddles. Each boat could hold only two or three men at a time, so the crossing was protracted. Major François de Salle Robert, meanwhile, guided 'D' Company without incident across the bridge. Coming under fire from a gun covering the approach to town, Robert led his men in overcoming the weapon. Major Alexander Angers then passed 'A' Company forward, but his men were quickly pinned down by two 20-millimetre anti-aircraft guns covering the entrance to the market square at the town's edge. The rapid fire of these guns made the street a death trap, and 'A' Company dived for cover. No one made any effort to renew the advance, until Sergeant J.P. Leblanc sprinted into the centre of the street with a Bren gun, dropped to a prone position, and threw out such intense and accurate fire that the gun crews abandoned their weapons. The Maisies slowly pushed into the town against fierce resistance, which continued through the night and into the following day. Complicating matters was the fact that each time a block of street was cleared, the civilians who had been hiding in their cellars burst forth and tried to welcome the still embattled, and battling, soldiers as liberators. Townsfolk thrust flowers, bottles of wine, and chunks of meat at the men, while women dashed out to offer hugs even as gunfire raged just around the next corner.

By noon, most of Bourbourg had been cleared, with the Calgary Highlanders having come up alongside the Maisies to advance past the exhausted French-Canadians.[33] The Maisies had three men killed.[34]

WAITING ALONG THE road from St. Folquin to Bourbourg for the Maisies to clear the town, in the late-night hours of September 7, the Calgaries had suffered hellish conditions. The sodden ground made digging slit trenches impossible. Detected by the Germans, the strung-out column was subjected to fire from heavy mortars and even some of Dunkirk's powerful coastal guns, which ripped great holes out of the ground around them. "More than once prayers were said quite openly," Lieutenant Stuart Moore recorded. When a coastal gun's shell tore a building apart near where Lieutenant Colonel Donald MacLauchlan stood with some of his headquarters staff, the blast spun him completely around two or three times.[35]

At about 2245 hours, MacLauchlan was ordered by Brigadier Megill to push through to the railway station. The station could serve as a firm base for the Calgaries to continue on to Loon-Plage. Separated from the town by a canal, the small red-brick station stood on the far side of a plaza, from which the main road running north to south through Bourbourg exited. Just north of the station was a bigger brick warehouse. Control of the station and warehouse would secure the roads running to Loon-Plage and Gravelines.

MacLauchlan advanced 'A' and 'C' Companies, attempting to out-flank the Germans still fighting the Maisies in the town and take the station from the north. The Calgaries immediately attracted heavy machine-gun and 88-millimetre fire from Germans defending the station and from inside the town. As the Maisies gained ground in Bourbourg, the Germans there rushed to join those at the station. 'A' Company struggled through to the station, despite suffering steady casualties, but whether it could hold in place was uncertain.[36]

Word came that the Maisies were advancing two companies to bolster the Calgaries. 'A' and 'B' Companies did try, in the words of the Maisonneuve war diarist, "to give a hand," but they were soon stopped cold on the town's outskirts by smothering artillery fire that also drenched the Calgaries. At 0145 hours, Lieutenant Colonel Bibeau ordered the two companies to fall back. 'A' Company's Major Alex Angers was wounded in the knee. This brought their total casualties for the action to five men dead and nineteen wounded.[37]

Megill kept peppering MacLauchlan with signals to "crack on" to Loon-Plage. This was clearly impossible with the fight for the station hanging in the balance. Instead, the Calgary Highlanders command-er moved 'C' Company forward to a defensive position north of the station and 'B' Company in to reinforce the two leading companies in their fight. 'B' Company's No. 11 Platoon consisted of three-quarters inexperienced replacements, facing their first firefight and wavering badly under the incoming heavy machine-gun fire and shelling. Its commander, Sergeant Kenneth William Deans, scrambled through the rubble of the now shattered station to rally each new man for an attack. Once he had the platoon organized by sections, he led it in a charge that overwhelmed three machine-gun positions. Many a Calgary later believed this action tipped the fight toward the Canadians. Moments later, the Germans seemed to start giving way on their hold over the town and station. Dawn found the Calgaries dug into the rubble of the station and adjacent warehouse.[38]

At 0700 hours on September 8, responding to Megill's hectoring, 'D' Company shook out to the front with 'C' Company, 'B' Company, and then 'A' Company following in train. The plan was to advance by "bites." Once one such point was taken, the company behind would leapfrog to the front and make for the next objective.[39] Supporting the advance were armoured cars of 14th Canadian Hussars' 'C' Squadron.[40] They rolled along the road with the infantry marching alongside. To everyone's surprise, 'D' Company reached the first "bite" at 0840 hours. This was Les Planches, a little clutch of houses halfway to Loon-Plage. 'C' Company passed through and pushed hard for the next point—a road junction six hundred yards ahead. Despite stiff opposition along the way, the company gained its objective. As 'C' Company started digging in because of the heavy shellfire coming down, which was probably being directed by a spotter in the church tower looming above Loon-Plage, 'B' and 'A' Companies continued the advance.

Megill was again demanding a faster pace, insisting to MacLauchlan that Loon-Plage was reported clear of enemy. The Calgary Highlanders commander doubted this. He would stick with the slow and careful approach. 'B' Company cautiously set off with 'A' Company close behind, and immediately shells smothered the road and ground around them. Despite men being cut down in both companies, the advance continued.[41] "Movement forward became very slow and tedious," Lieutenant Moore reported. Had it not been for the supporting artillery fire of 5th Field Regiment, the heavy 4.5-inch mortars of the Toronto Scottish Regiment, and the battalion's own 3-inch mortars, he added, the advance would surely have crumbled.[42] The Toronto Scottish's No. 3 Platoon had set its mortar tubes in the wide-open middle of a roadbed, because the surrounding ground was too sodden to provide a stable firing platform. Between 1200 and 2200 hours, the platoon fired 217 bombs while under "heavy retaliation from the enemy." At 2000 hours, No. 4 Platoon added its mortars to the show with thirty-six bombs. Three Toronto Scottish were wounded by the German counter-fire.[43]

In the early afternoon, most of 5th Field Regiment briefly ceased firing in order to relocate two batteries to a closer range inside Bourbourg. When 73rd Battery resumed shooting, it immediately drew spasmodic fire from what the artillerymen realized were the nine-inch coastal guns at Dunkirk. Seventeen men were wounded, but the gunners kept at their guns. By 1600 hours, each gun had averaged forty-three rounds of high-explosive in support of the Calgaries.[44]

Despite the German shelling, Captain Mark Tennant pushed the battalion support company's 6-pounder anti-tank guns forward to snipe at enemy positions over open sights. As soon as the guns were in range, they accurately shot the church tower in Loon-Plage to pieces.

Hoping to find another way forward, MacLauchlan ordered 'D' Company to hook leftward from where it had been holding at Les Planches and work cross-country to enter Loon-Plage from the west. By this time, the Calgaries were being subjected to a rain of 75-millimetre and 88-millimetre gunfire, as well as Dunkirk's naval guns. Despite suffering a number of casualties, the company got within about five hundred yards of Loon-Plage before the fire became so intense that the company fell back to a cluster of farm buildings about a thousand yards from the village. Here they hunkered down under heavy artillery fire and with machine guns pouring bullets into the buildings, which provided scant protection.

Finally, at about midnight, MacLauchlan ordered the companies to break off the attack and withdraw to Les Planches. The Calgary Highlanders war diarist considered this "drawback necessary from several angles, one of which was the low company strengths." 'A,' 'B,' and 'D' Companies had been reduced to about thirty men each. It had also been forty-two hours since the front-line troops had eaten, and everyone was exhausted.[45] One of 'A' Company's wounded was Private Bill Rawluk. A machine-gun burst that struck a nearby tree had splattered Rawluk and two other men with shrapnel. Then he took a bullet in the right shoulder and a piece of shrapnel "the size of a dime" in the jaw. Rawluk had gone into France with the Calgaries in early July, but now his soldiering days were done.[46]

The men spent an uneasy night sleeping fitfully in shifts. Nobody knew what the morning would bring. Germans had been spotted digging in along the railroad that paralleled the axis of the Calgaries' position about three hundred yards to the east. There was continual machine-gun fire into the Canadian position, and all the companies reported eliminating snipers trying to infiltrate their positions.

September 9 dawned with clear skies, but colder temperatures that bit through the men's sodden uniforms. Sensing a changed atmosphere at Loon-Plage, Major Dalt Heyland sent some men from 'C' Company to probe the German dispositions. The patrol soon reported the Germans gone. Heyland contacted headquarters by wireless at 0815 hours and asked Major Ross Ellis if he could send a platoon and section of carriers in to secure the village. Lieutenant Moore noted that Ellis was "struck dumbfounded" by the thought that the Germans had decided to give up Loon-Plage. As MacLauchlan was at a brigade headquarters meeting with a still impatient Megill, Ellis said, "Go ahead." Soon, Heyland reported that the town was indeed clear. Having returned from brigade, MacLauchlan ordered all four companies at once to secure Loon-Plage.

When Captain Mark Tennant drove into the town seeking a suitable battalion headquarters, he found it in a heavily fortified pillbox "cleverly camouflaged to resemble a large barn and entirely equipped with electrical ventilation system and electric lights, not working as all wires had been cut." Shortly after the headquarters staff moved into the place they decided to give it up. The air stank and nobody could get the electricity working. They moved to a nearby house.[47]

As was now routine whenever the Canadians liberated a town or village, the citizens of Loon-Plage emerged to cheer them by passing around copious amounts of their "famous wine and cheese." MacLauchlan was still wary. He ordered everybody to dig in deep, fearing the town would soon face a hammering from German artillery. He also sent the carrier platoon and infantry platoons out to scout the area for German positions. At 1000 hours, Megill arrived and instructed MacLauchlan to "continue harassing the enemy and to keep on stirring him up." The Calgaries were to maintain an aggressive posture and keep "pin-pricking" German positions wherever they were found, to prevent any attempt to try to regain the town by counterattack.[48]

While the Calgary Highlanders had been advancing northwestward to take Loon-Plage, the Black Watch had been tasked on September 8 with carrying out a short advance from Bourbourg to clear a small hamlet called Coppenaxfort, about five thousand yards east. Because the intervening fields were so deeply flooded, the only viable path was an elevated road that ran straight as an arrow alongside the paralleling Bourbourg Canal right to the hamlet. Only a few trees standing next to the road provided a modicum of cover. Consequently, there was no sense sending the entire battalion forward, so 'C' Company set out with a troop of the 14th Canadian Hussars in support. Moving in a well-spaced formation, the force quickly drew heavy artillery fire that knocked out the lead armoured car and pinned the infantry down just five hundred yards from the start line. Here they stayed until nightfall allowed a withdrawal to a farm on slightly rising ground, where it was possible for 'C' Company to dig in. At first light the next day the advance resumed, and the hamlet was found abandoned.

Veering northeastward, the Black Watch followed the Canal de la Haute Colme to Grand Mille Brugge, which faced another German-fortified town called Spycker. Here, they dug in under heavy artillery fire. "Why this place rates the title 'Grand' is hard to imagine as it is nothing more or less than a row of houses on either side of the canal," wrote the Black Watch war diarist. "The advance was made without much opposition which was fortunate as the fields beside the road are a quagmire, many being completely under water. Here again the retreating Germans have blown the canal bank in many places, and it is impossible for our artillery to set up anywhere near our new positions in view of the ground conditions. Shortly after we had occupied the town the enemy opened up with mortar and 88-millimetre, but casualties were amazingly low since by that time everyone was under cover in the various buildings." Like the Calgaries, the Black Watch's task for now was "to contain the enemy . . . around Dunkirk and to patrol at night."[49]

Megill's 5th Brigade was spent and still facing heavy resistance from Dunkirk's strong garrison.

OPERATING NORTHEAST OF Dunkirk and just inside the Belgian border, 2nd Division's 6th Canadian Infantry Brigade had enjoyed initial success in pushing toward the port town from that flank. In an attempt to maintain control over his far-flung brigades, Major General Charles Foulkes had on September 8 moved his divisional headquarters into

Belgium to a point about five miles inland from the coast and 6th Brigade's immediate operational area. On the same day, 6th Brigade's battalions had also entered Belgium to begin their thrust back toward Dunkirk, creating a very fluid situation with battle lines far from clearly drawn.[50]

Taking advantage of the situation, Lieutenant Colonel Jim Roberts decided to advance the 12th Manitoba Dragoons through to Ostend with hopes of seizing the Belgian port without a major fight. "Rapidly, with roaring engines, we dashed across the Belgian frontier . . . [and then] proceeded more cautiously." Skirting Furnes—6th Brigade's first objective and a village that the Dragoons had determined the previous day was German-held—Major Ron Mason's 'B' Squadron slipped well out to the front, with the rest of the regiment in trail.

As Mason closed on Ostend, he decided to first reconnoiter canal crossings south of the city. Pausing at Pervijze, about ten miles south of Ostend, he sent two troops commanded respectively by Lieutenants Charlie Phelps and Ken Jefferson four miles ahead to Slijpe. Here the road was blocked by a minefield that extended into the adjacent fields and consisted of heavy naval shells wired with pressure-triggered detonators. Each troop consisted of two Staghound armoured cars and one Lynx scout car. Realizing the Staghounds were too heavy to move off the road because of both the minefield and the inundated fields, the two officers decided to get forward with just the 9,370-pound scout cars. One Staghound in each troop carried a pair of steel trackways. After finding some lumber planks nearby and laying these carefully on top of the shells, the steel tracks were added, and each officer then gingerly inched his Lynx over the mines.

Rejoined by the scout cars' drivers, the two officers set off in their Lynxes to find a clear route that the Staghounds could follow. After only a short distance, the lightly armoured scout cars attracted heavy artillery fire from inside Ostend. When the two lieutenants reported this to Mason, he ordered them to get out of range.

By this time, however, 'A' Squadron was probing the major Belgian city of Bruges and had contacted Belgian White Brigade resistance fighters—so known for the white butchers' coats its members wore for identification purposes. They reported that Ostend was only lightly held and arranged for Mason's squadron to rendezvous with the port's resistance leader, who would guide them into it. Consequently, at 1100 hours, 'B' Squadron rumbled into the centre of Ostend and took the port city without firing a shot.

"Pandemonium broke loose," Roberts later wrote. "The city went wild." The squadron's Staghounds and Lynxes were soon stranded within a sea of joyous citizens. Eventually, things calmed down sufficiently for the squadron to search the city. They managed to capture a group of German engineers setting demolitions on port facilities. Even as the engineers were taken, however, "loud explosions and high rising smoke clouds were heard and seen. The explosions were the result of previously set time bombs that the German engineers had placed in the submarine pens in the harbour and in the canal locks."

Roberts arrived just as the explosions began and sent a wireless message to 11 Canadian Corps reporting the city taken. He then had one squadron seal the city from approach out of the south, as this was a logical escape route should the garrison at Dunkirk decide to give that city up. Roberts then visited city hall, where he asked officials to clear the citizens off the streets so the Dragoons could sweep the city to make sure it was truly free of Germans. It was a futile request. No authority could possibly get the citizenry to cease their celebration.[51]

During the sweep, a party of Dragoons came upon a Canadian ambulance jeep parked outside a hospital in the eastern part of Ostend. The officer leading the party discovered Private William McGregor, a medical orderly with 2nd Division's 11th Field Ambulance, and his driver inside the hospital. McGregor explained they had arrived at the hospital the night before with three wounded civilians—a young woman and her two daughters.

Early the previous evening, the field ambulance had parked some distance outside of Ostend and just behind the Essex Scottish Regiment of 4th Brigade, which was closing on the city in the wake of the Dragoons. Streaming past their encampment were large numbers of refugees who had fled Ostend and Bruges for fear that a fight for these cities was imminent. McGregor had just realized the nearby grassy roadside verges had been liberally sown with s-mines when the woman triggered one that blew off one of her feet. Her two daughters were peppered in the legs by shrapnel. McGregor and his driver quickly bandaged the wounds to stop the bleeding, loaded the woman and girls into their jeep, and rushed them to the Essex Regimental Aid Post (RAP) for treatment. The doctor there determined that the woman's wound was too serious to treat at the RAP and the Canadian surgical teams that could save her were too far in the rear to be reached in time. Stabbing his finger at a map, the doctor pointed out a hospital inside Ostend that was just two miles away.

If McGregor were to make a dash behind German lines to the hospital, the woman might just live. It was up to McGregor to decide if he was willing to risk capture or death to save her. McGregor and his driver volunteered, and were soon driving into Ostend's streets. They reached the hospital without incident, and passed the woman and girls into the care of the emergency ward doctors. Nurses then offered the two Canadians a hot meal, a bath, and a bed to sleep in. "We woke up in the morning to find all our clothing washed and ironed. Then we had breakfast with the hospital staff."

When the Dragoons appeared later that day, the officer in command told McGregor to return to his unit forthwith. McGregor didn't agree. He and the driver were comfortable and safe, so why not stay put until Ostend was secured and then find No. 11 Field Ambulance? The two doctors who had treated the woman and her daughters, meanwhile, gave McGregor a handwritten note that read: "The best wishes from Belgian friends to the first Canadian that arrived in Ostend."[52]

WHILE THESE EVENTS played out in Ostend, 6th Brigade had advanced into its assigned battleground. It closely resembled the one 5th Brigade faced—level fields crisscrossed by canals, with blown dykes to inundate the fields and scant cover. Extending as it did from Gravelines in France to Nieuport in Belgium, Foulkes was worried about how widely dispersed his division was becoming. And as his 4th Infantry Brigade was about to move out of reserve and advance on Bruges, the situation was only going to worsen. At that point, the divisional front would be stretched along eighty-five miles. It helped little that, because of the priority that British Second Army had on fuel and ammunition, both commodities were in short supply, with fuel restrictions requiring his quartermasters to impose "stringent measures . . . with regard to the use of all vehicles."[53]

Having concentrated east of Calais around the villages of Louches and Autingues, 6th Brigade started moving on the morning of September 8, with Les Fusiliers Mont-Royal leading at 0715 hours. The entire brigade was loaded into trucks and jeeps, bound for a debussing point at the village of Hondschoot on the Belgian border—a distance of about thirty-eight miles via a route passing through St. Omer.[54] At 0835 hours, the long column attracted the attention of German artillery as it passed Bergues, and several casualties resulted.[55] At noon, the Fusiliers unloaded and started marching for their objective of Furnes, eight miles distant. The advance took six hours, but no Germans were encountered and the Fusiliers quickly set up defensive positions around the town.[56]

Coming up behind, the South Saskatchewan Regiment passed through and marched hard for Nieuport, six miles north. Intelligence reports indicated the town was garrisoned by coastal artillery troops, who had mined the bridge crossing the adjacent canal. Expecting to bump opposition, the leading troops approached by a narrow dirty trail on Nieuport's side of the canal to avoid having to cross the bridge. For the drivers of the supporting carriers and jeeps groping through the "pitch blackness in rain and mud, over broken culverts and all manner of hazards," it was an exhausting and nerve-wracking experience.[57]

Nieuport was found already cleared by White Brigade fighters, who had suffered some casualties. The battalion's stretcher-bearers provided immediate first aid, and the more badly wounded were evacuated through the RAP to a Field Ambulance unit. By 2300 hours, the town was reported secured.[58]

The Queen's Own Cameron Highlanders had, meanwhile, joined Les Fusiliers Mont-Royal at Furnes with the intention of advancing on the coastal village of La Panne in the morning. No sooner had the Camerons arrived, however, than 6th Brigade received an emergency message at 1800 hours from Major General Charles Foulkes. He and a small party of divisional staff had been pinned down by German machine-gun and rifle fire while passing a small wood between Nieuport and Furnes. The party had apparently been attempting to link up with

Brigadier Guy Gauvreau's headquarters, but taken a wrong turn and overshot it. Gauvreau immediately ordered the Fusiliers and Camerons to dispatch their carrier platoons to the rescue. They were soon met on the road by Foulkes, who said the sound of the carriers prompted the Germans to break contact and enabled his party to escape.[59] Despite this narrow brush with the enemy, Foulkes continued the following day to venture out to visit his brigade and battalion commanders.[60]

At 0100 hours on September 9, a White Brigade officer arrived at the South Saskatchewan Regiment headquarters in Nieuport and warned Major George Buchanan—who was commanding the regiment—that roads in the vicinity were heavily mined. "He then produced a detailed plan of the enemy's defences and mined areas." The Germans, he advised, had about four hundred men west of the nearby Yser River and another two or three hundred on its eastern bank. These troops were primarily part of an artillery battery that had been stationed in the area for the past three and a half years, but they had been recently bolstered by a mixed bag of men who had retreated from Dieppe and positions on the Seine.[61]

The brigade plan was to clear the Germans out of the eight-mile coastal stretch of ground between Nieuport to the north and La Panne to the south. The area was known to contain a number of strongly fortified positions. Yet with Belgian resistance members providing vital intelligence on the defences, the operation proceeded like clockwork. The Queen's Own Cameron Highlanders advanced at 0300 hours and occupied La Panne by noon, despite there being spasmodic fire from an 11-inch coastal gun. During the evening, the battalion's intelligence officer, Captain Bruce Valentine Marshall, and his batman, Private L. Torlacius, took a wrong turn in a jeep while heading back to brigade headquarters. The two drove straight into an 88-millimetre gun position guarded by machine guns, and twenty-three-year-old Marshall was killed. Torlacius found cover in a ditch and then worked his way back to the Camerons' lines.[62] Marshall's death due to blundering into a strong German position served as yet another warning that the defenders of Dunkirk were determined and strong enough to offer a real fight. The quick successes enjoyed by 6th Brigade were over, and the days ahead promised to be costly.

12

Fateful Decisions

FOR THE WESTERN Allies, September 10 was one of the most decisive days of the war. This was not due to any battlefield successes.
It was entirely due to the outcome of a meeting between Field Marshal
Bernard Montgomery and General Dwight D. Eisenhower. The evening before, Montgomery had learned that a new type of missile—the
v-2—had fallen on west London during the morning of September
8. Three civilians had been killed and seventeen injured. The new
rocket differed radically from the v-1. Powered by liquid fuel, forty-six
feet long, weighing thirteen tons, and carryng a one-ton warhead, it
reached Mach 1 speed less than thirty seconds after launching and
attained previously unimagined altitudes of fifty to sixty miles in five
minutes. This combination of altitude and speed made the missile
undetectable until it smashed into the ground and exploded with
tremendous force.

The September 8 missile was believed to have originated from a
launching site near La Hague identified earlier by Allied intelligence.
It was this information that Montgomery had acted upon with his
September 3 directive that proposed sending on September 6 one
corps, or at least a division, toward La Hague and Rotterdam, while
his main effort remained concentrated on crossing the Rhine. Up to
now, Montgomery and his staff had not settled on this thrust's precise
route. They were still weighing the pros and cons of making for a

crossing at either Wesel or the more westerly point of Arnhem. Now that the Germans had unleashed the new and more powerful missiles, however, Montgomery decided on Arnhem.[1]

Even as he reached this conclusion, British Second Army's Lieutenant General Miles Dempsey arrived to argue the case for Wesel. Dempsey's intelligence staff had reported the Arnhem and Nijmegen areas were experiencing increased rail traffic and an ongoing deployment of more light and heavy anti-aircraft batteries. More troubling, Dutch resistance reported that a number of battered panzer divisions were being sent to Holland for refitting. Some were thought to be in the Nijmegen and Eindhoven area. This was precisely where Montgomery planned to go.

Dempsey wanted to bounce the Rhine as badly as Montgomery did, but he felt the growing German forces potentially barring the path at Arnhem, combined with other potential problems, made this route too risky. Montgomery's Arnhem plan envisioned dropping 1st British Airborne Division in packets to seize the bridges in the vicinity of Eindhoven, Nijmegen, and Arnhem, while xxx British Corps advanced a column, heavily weighted on armoured divisions, sixty-four miles. The column would relieve each packet as it moved through to Arnhem. Now Dempsey no longer believed xxx Corps could get through quickly enough, because it would be confined to elevated roads surrounded by inundated polders that denied his tanks freedom of movement. To reach Arnhem, xxx Corps must cross five minor water bodies and three major rivers—the Maas (Meuse) at Grave, the Waal (as the Dutch called the Rhine) at Nijmegen, and the Nederrijn (Lower Rhine) at Arnhem. Despite the challenges inherent in winning crossings over three major rivers, this route had the advantage that the airborne forces would likely face fewer losses from anti-aircraft fire. Montgomery had already been warned that the Wesel plan would require the aircraft transporting the airborne troops to fly past the gunsights of thick anti-aircraft defences covering the Ruhr industrial area.

Dempsey, however, argued that the risk to the airborne division's planes was offset by the advantage xxx Corps gained in having its right flank guarded by the First U.S. Army. In fact, striking at Wesel would see his and the American army fighting side by side.[2] This accorded well with the "colossal crack" Montgomery had earlier proposed as a counter to Eisenhower's insistence on a broad-front strategy.

Montgomery was not to be swayed. He proceeded to brief Dempsey on the final vision for Operation Market Garden developed earlier that morning. No longer would there be just one airborne division. Instead, there would be three, and each would seize bridges to enable xxx Corps to quickly cross the minor waterways near Eindhoven, then the Maas, the Waal, and the Nederrijn. Not having to worry about bridges, xxx Corps could advance in a divisional column right through to Arnhem within two days of launch. And from there, Montgomery still hoped to strike out for Berlin. Dempsey was skeptical. He thought Arnhem was just too far away, given that the corps was confined to the road.[3]

His concerns were dismissed. All that remained was for Montgomery to get Eisenhower's approval. He planned to do so that very afternoon. On September 7, Montgomery had requested a meeting with Eisenhower to discuss the logistical problems Twenty-First Army Group faced. Eisenhower had agreed to meet him at Brussels airport. His leg still immobilized in a cast, Eisenhower made the trip strapped into a litter aboard a twin-engine B-25 bomber. Also on board was his chief logistical and administrative officer, British Lieutenant General Sir Humphrey Gale.

As Eisenhower was unable to disembark, the meeting took place inside the tight confines of the plane. Although Eisenhower thought he was in Brussels to discuss logistics, Montgomery immediately insisted that Gale exit the plane, even as he brought his own administrative officer, Major General M.A.P. Graham, on board. Probably hoping to keep the meeting civil, Eisenhower sent Gale away.

Pulling copies of Eisenhower's recent signals, Montgomery bluntly tore into the supreme commander for not reining in General George Patton's Third Army and failing to divert from the American supply stream the supplies required to support Twenty-First Army Group's promised priority. Was Patton in control or Eisenhower? Furthermore, continuing the double-thrust strategy was doomed to fail and the opportunity to end the war in 1944 lost.

As Montgomery's "tirade gathered fury," Eisenhower sat silently and seemingly emotionless. When Montgomery paused for a breath, however, he leaned forward and placed a hand on the field marshal's knee. Quietly and firmly, Eisenhower said, "Steady, Monty! You can't speak to me like that. I'm your boss."

A chastened Montgomery muttered, "I'm sorry, Ike."

Although adopting a more diplomatic tone, Montgomery stuck to his guns. There needed to be a single thrust, and logically that was toward Arnhem. By that route he could reach the Ruhr and possibly Berlin. Eisenhower disagreed. The advance to the Rhine must continue on a broad front. He believed sufficient supplies existed to enable the Allies to break through the Siegfried Line and overrun not only the Ruhr but also the Saar and Frankfurt regions. As he would write in a directive three days later, Eisenhower intended a "drive forward through the enemy's western frontiers to suitable positions on which we can regroup while preparing the maintenance facilities that will sustain the great bulk of our forces on the drive into Germany." The decisive blow into Germany's heart would come only after Antwerp was opened.

Montgomery, however, knew that for Twenty-First Army Group, the choice now was either Arnhem or opening Antwerp. By diverting xxx Corps away from Antwerp at the beginning of September to position it for the drive on Arnhem, he had sacrificed any chance of an early opening of the port. From Ultra decryptions of naval signals traffic, Montgomery knew that the German Fifteenth Army had managed by the night of September 7–8 to ferry 25,000 men, 350 vehicles, and 50 tons of equipment across the Scheldt Estuary. These troops seriously bolstered the defences on the estuary's north bank. At the same time, Fifteenth Army had been instructed by Hitler to form a strong bridgehead around the German coastal batteries on the south bank, in what would soon be known as the Breskens Pocket. These batteries were also to be surrounded by a belt of water and bog created by "ruthless inundation." On the night of September 8–9, the navy also began mining the estuary. If—as seemed increasingly likely—Antwerp could not be regained, the German high command was determined to deny its use by the Allies for as long as possible.[4]

While Montgomery was looking to First Canadian Army to clear the Germans away from the Scheldt, his first priority remained for it to open the channel ports—a task just starting in earnest this very day, with 1 British Corps assaulting Le Havre and 2nd Canadian Infantry Division continuing attempts to invest Dunkirk.

Sitting inside the bomber, Montgomery sketched out the details of the Arnhem operation. He described the carpet of airborne troops through which xxx Corps would race. The confined nature of the roads, the five small streams that must be crossed in addition to the three great rivers, and the hindering of movement presented by the sodden polder and marsh countryside were dismissed. So, too, were the reports that German forces in the area were growing. Eisenhower listened, and decided to believe. "I not only approved it," he reiterated in 1966, "I insisted on it. What we needed was a bridgehead over the Rhine. If that could be accomplished I was quite willing to wait on all other operations."[5]

Seizing his moment, Montgomery renewed his attack on the broad-front strategy. He badly wanted First U.S. Army guarding his thrust's right flank. Again he sought to have that army placed under his command and shifted westward so that it could advance alongside British Second Army. Between the two armies, Montgomery would have sixteen divisions in addition to the carpet provided by the three Airborne Army divisions. Without First Army, he told Eisenhower, breaking through to the Ruhr might not be possible. Montgomery also wanted Patton's Third Army stopped. He needed the supplies that were going to it, and he wanted the eastward drift of the American advance halted so that First Army could support Market Garden. Lieutenant General Courtenay Hodges's eight divisions were currently strung out across a nearly 150-mile front to cover the gap between Dempsey's Second Army and Patton's Third Army. Unless Patton shifted divisions westward to take over some of the line to his left, Hodges would be unable to support Dempsey.

Patton, however, was actively extending his right flank ever farther away from Montgomery, and Eisenhower had no intention of stopping this. Eisenhower was anxious for Patton to create a strong junction with Sixth Army Group, now marching north from Marseilles and scheduled to come under the supreme commander's direct command on September 15. All Eisenhower would give Montgomery was authorization to use the Airborne Army for Market Garden and a promise that the Americans would make good any supply shortages he faced. But Patton's advance would continue.[6]

Save for the divisions of the Airborne Army, the British would have to bounce the Rhine alone. Montgomery and Eisenhower knew that if Market Garden was to have any chance of success, it must happen quickly, or the Germans might regroup and become too strong. A week was agreed. The airborne troops would drop from the skies, and the tanks of Lieutenant General Brian Horrocks's xxx Corps would roll up the narrow roads toward Arnhem on September 17. Both men knew they took a grave risk, but they thought it a calculated one with good odds of yielding decisive results.

When Eisenhower returned to his headquarters at Granville, he had a long discussion about the meeting with his naval aide, U.S. Naval Reserve Captain Harry C. Butcher. In his diary, Butcher reported that Eisenhower "is thinking in terms of advancing on a wide front to take advantage of all existing lines of communication. He expects to go through the Aachen gap in the north and the Metz Gap in the south and to bring the Southern Group of Armies (6th) to the Rhine south of Coblenz. Then he thinks he should use his airborne forces to seize crossings over the Rhine, to be in position to thrust deep into the Ruhr and to threaten Berlin itself . . . Ike has decided that a northern thrust toward the Ruhr under Montgomery is not at the moment to have priority over other operations."[7]

EISENHOWER'S CONFIDENCE THAT he could continue the broad-front approach and gain several lodgements inside Germany before the year's end stemmed largely from a SHAEF intelligence summary issued for the week ending September 9. The German situation was dire. So much so that Hitler had reinstated the formerly disgraced Generalfeldmarschall Gerd von Rundstedt as Oberbefehlshaber West on September 4 and demoted Generalfeldmarschall Walter Model to command of Heeresgruppe B (Army Group B). Von Rundstedt had previously served as Oberbefehlshaber until he had demanded a free hand in early July to oppose the Allied advance in Normandy. When such independence was refused, Von Rundstedt had told Hitler's chief of staff, Generalfeldmarschall Wilhelm Keitel, that the outcome would be a disaster and suggested he come from Berlin and take over. Not about to do that, Keitel had whined, "What shall we do?" To which Von Rundstedt calmly replied, "What shall you do? Make peace, you idiots. What else can you do?" Incensed, Hitler had immediately sacked Von Rundstedt.[8] But now, with the German army again in crisis, the old warhorse was back, and too much the professional soldier to do less than his best to rescue the situation.

The SHAEF summary happily reported that Von Rundstedt had precious little to work with. The number of German divisions facing the western Allies was estimated at just forty-eight. Fourteen were panzer or panzer grenadier divisions, with the remaining thirty-four being infantry. Most of these divisions, however, were "shattered." Bundled together, SHAEF intelligence staff considered their true strength amounted to four panzer and twenty infantry divisions. Four of the infantry divisions were isolated in the French coastal fortresses, so presented no threat to Eisenhower's drive toward Germany. When his staff considered the "enemy capabilities," they exuded optimism. Von Rundstedt, they concluded, "might expect not more than a dozen divisions within the next two months to come from outside to the rescue." For the present, he was left with "the true equivalent of about fifteen divisions, including four panzer, for the defence of the West Wall [Siegfried Line]. A further five or six may struggle up in the course of a month, making a total of about twenty. The West Wall cannot be held with this amount, even when supplemented by many oddments and large amounts of flak."

Although the Germans were scrambling to reorganize, they faced equipment shortages that were worse than the weakness of their fighting troops. On September 7, having taken the measure of his restored command, Von Rundstedt had signalled Keitel. "In the face of the Allied strength, all German forces are committed," he reported. "They are badly depleted, in some cases crushed. Artillery and anti-tank weapons are lacking. Reserves worth much do not exist. Army Group

B has about 100 tanks in working order. Considering Allied armoured strength the implications are clear."[9]

Despite the defeatist tone, this time there were no recriminations from Berlin. Keitel knew Von Rundstedt would try to rescue the situation from disaster and that must suffice. Von Rundstedt had few options. The Allies, he knew, were trying to maintain a situation of fluidity across their entire front. His only chance was to get enough strength into the Siegfried Line to impose a deadlock. The other priority was to keep Antwerp bottled up. To some extent, Eisenhower's broad-front strategy served Von Rundstedt's needs. Nowhere was he facing a powerful thrust by overwhelming mass. Instead, the Germans faced local penetrations that could be sealed off without committing reserves that Von Rundstedt lacked. Should a powerful armoured breakthrough occur, Von Rundstedt had too few tanks to block it with a fire brigade. The one spot in the line from the North Sea to the Swiss border where Von Rundstedt was strong lay in front of Patton's Third Army. Here German First Army had been rebuilt to eight divisions of some quality and strength. They were deployed on a front running from Thionville through Metz and Nancy to Épinal. Patton was facing them with six divisions.[10] If he could contain Patton and deny the Allies Antwerp, and did not face an immediate powerful thrust elsewhere, Von Rundstedt might buy sufficient time to stabilize the situation until bad winter weather brought some relief.

ALTHOUGH MONTGOMERY HAD been pleased that Eisenhower had given full approval to Market Garden, he was displeased by his refusal to stop Patton and give Montgomery absolute priority on supply. Consequently, on the day following the Brussels meeting, Montgomery fired off a signal to Eisenhower. "Your decision that the northern thrust towards the Ruhr is not repeat not to have priority over other operations will have certain repercussions which you should know. The large-scale operations by Second Army and the Airborne Army northwards towards the Meuse and Rhine cannot now take place before 23 September at the earliest and possibly 26 September. This delay will give the enemy time to organize better defensive arrangements and we must expect heavier resistance and slower progress. As the winter draws on the weather may be expected to deteriorate and [we will see] less results from our great weight of air power. It is basically a matter of rail and road and air transport and unless this is concentrated to give impetus to the selected thrust then no one is going to get very far since we are all such a long way from our supply bases. We will do all that is possible to get on with the business but the above facts will show you that if enemy resistance continues to stiffen as at present then no repeat no great results can be expected until we have built up stocks of ammunition and other requirements."

This shot across the bow brought immediate action. Eisenhower's chief of staff Lieutenant General Walter Bedell Smith raced to meet Montgomery on September 12. Eisenhower, Smith advised, would instruct the U.S. Communication Zone to "make every effort to transport 500 tons of supplies per day to the Brussels area by motor truck." The trucks would be made available by grounding several American divisions. This was to be considered an emergency solution and one kept in place only until Market Garden breached the Rhine and Montgomery opened Antwerp to shipping. The arrangement would be sustained until the beginning of October.

Montgomery was satisfied. Market Garden would be launched on September 17.[11] As for Antwerp, in the days immediately following the Brussels airport meeting, both Montgomery and Eisenhower issued various directives declaring the urgency of opening its port. But neither expected this to happen anytime soon. They were fixated on Arnhem and recognized that between continuing the broad-front strategy and executing Market Garden, Antwerp's opening must wait for the over-stretched Canadians—still tasked with reducing, literally one by one, the channel port fortresses.

13

Bold Ruthless Action

BECAUSE THE RESOURCES required to assault a major port were limited, it was impossible for First Canadian Army to launch simultaneous attacks on the channel ports. This fact had been appreciated as early as March 1944, when Twenty-First Army Group planners first undertook a preliminary study of the challenges faced in opening the Seine ports of Le Havre and Rouen. They projected that an assault on Le Havre could probably begin ninety days after the first Allied landings in Normandy. Yet as the breakout from the beaches had gone terribly awry, it was sheer coincidence that on September 3—eighty-nine days after the June 6 landings—1 British Corps commander Lieutenant General John Crocker unveiled plans for seizing Le Havre.[1] After spending the morning setting up shop in the village of Foucart, about thirty miles east of Le Havre, Crocker began the meeting at 1430 hours.[2] Attending were Crocker's senior staff, First Canadian Army senior planners, a Twenty-First Army Group liaison officer, representatives of the Royal Navy and Royal Air Force, and Major General Percy Hobart. The armoured support provided by the so-called Funnies of Hobart's 79th British Armoured Division was deemed essential to any attack on a fortress.

Details about German strength and defences remained unclear. Crocker understood there were between three thousand and five thousand fighting men in Le Havre, and that morale was low. But the intelligence was conflicting.[3] Another estimate held that the garrison numbered twenty to thirty thousand and its commander was determined to fight to the last man and bullet.[4]

Crocker thought this last estimate unduly alarmist. Having seen both Rouen and Dieppe fall virtually unopposed, he was optimistic that the Le Havre garrison would go the same way. He told the meeting that it "should not be necessary actually to deliver a full scale attack, but . . . obviously it was necessary to take the necessary measures to mount a full scale attack." The Germans must see such an attack assembling, and that would entail demonstrations of force by both the navy and Bomber Command.

The day before the meeting, the 49th (West Riding) Infantry Division had brushed Le Havre's outer defences. This division, Crocker said, would now extend its line northward and westward to the accompaniment of heavy artillery support in a show of strength that should convince the garrison commander his situation was hopeless. In fact, as soon as the meeting concluded, Crocker intended to "invite the enemy garrison to surrender, offering . . . the alternative of a full scale heavy bombing attack which, it will be stated, will follow in the course of 48 hours unless the surrender has been received."

Should the Germans foolishly refuse, the bombing would proceed and be followed by a renewed call for surrender with a second round of bombing threatened. "If, after two warnings followed by two attacks by heavy bombers, the enemy has not then surrendered he will be warned that he is now to receive a full scale attack of 1 Brit[ish] Corps supported by the RN and RAF."

Both Bomber Command's representative and that of the navy warned they could not deliver heavy attacks until September 5—just barely meeting the first deadline. The navy was also "reluctant to use battleships" because Le Havre's approaches were heavily mined. HMS *Erebus* and HMS *Roberts*, both monitors mounting 15-inch guns, would have to suffice. *Erebus* was promised for September 5 and would deliver harassing fire against targets designated by 1 British Corps.

In wrapping up, Crocker emphasized his intention to take Le Havre with the "minimum expenditure of Allied resources." He hoped the surrender demands combined with propaganda efforts using pamphlets and amplifiers would cow the garrison into surrendering. Failing that, surely two rounds of heavy bombing interrupted by surrender demands would do the trick. All this was going to take time, however, so in the unlikely event that an actual full-scale attack was required, it could not happen until September 8 at the earliest.[5]

EFFORTS TO ATTAIN localized surrenders and demoralize the garrison were already under way. Aircraft showered the city with thousands of leaflets detailing the hopelessness of the German cause, and, rather than explosives, artillery fired hundreds of shells loaded with such notices onto enemy positions. Amplified broadcasts exhorted soldiers and officers alike to give up or desert.

Avoiding costly fighting was the order of the day. Consequently, when 49th Division's 146th Infantry Brigade bumped into stiff resistance at Gainneville, about five miles east of the city, Brigadier John Walker held the 4th Lincolnshire Battalion back and called on the local German commander to surrender. The officer replied that "only his higher commander in Le Havre could . . . surrender his troops." Walker unleashed his battalion, and the position fell quickly with 23 prisoners taken and several Germans killed in exchange for 14 men wounded. Under questioning, the prisoners—who belonged to the 1041st Grenadier Regiment of 226th Infanterie-Division—reported Le Havre's garrison numbered between 5,000 and 10,000 men. Their regiment was cited as consisting of two battalions made up of four companies apiece. Each company had an average strength of about 120 men.

Not long after Walker forwarded this intelligence to corps, several officers sent by Crocker turned up. It was 1930 hours of September 3, and they carried Crocker's first surrender demand. Loaded into an armoured car streaming a white flag, the officers passed through the lines of the brigade's 1/4th King's Own Yorkshire Light Infantry and delivered the ultimatum to the senior opposing officer. As a gesture of goodwill, all firing across the entire brigade front was halted for a two-hour period. The fortress commander was given until 0900 hours the following day to respond.[6]

Fifty-five-year-old Oberst [Colonel] Eberhard Wildermuth was tall, naturally skeletally thin, and bald. Born in Stuttgart, he had been called up as a reserve lieutenant in the Great War and returned to a career in banking during the inter-war years. By 1939 he was a member of the board of directors of Berlin's influential Deutsche Bau und Bodenbank. Recalled on August 26, 1939, he served in the invasion of France, fought in Russia, and held both the Knight's Cross and the German Cross in Gold. On August 14, 1944, Wildermuth was tasked with defending Fortress Le Havre.

It was a duty for which he was ill suited. First Canadian Army intelligence officers considered his appointment "inexplicable." If the army high command had been "looking for a fanatical, zealous, feverish young Nazi to inspire German troops to fight to the end, they could have chosen no one less likely to fit the role." Wildermuth "was not young, he was not inspired, he was not a soldier and what was most important, he was not a Nazi. Nevertheless, this polite, tired, efficient bank director was . . . ordered to perform a fight-to-the-death task for the glory of the Fatherland."

All their intelligence depicted an officer "who carried efficiency and ability into battle . . . in much the same way as he would have used them to draw up a balance sheet." They believed him "not mentally prepared to sacrifice the lives of his men for a philosophy in which he only half-heartedly believed." This perception of Wildermuth's psychology contributed to the extended effort to convince him to surrender and avoid the inevitable casualties of an assault.

Wildermuth had been given charge of Le Havre only because the previous commander had fallen ill. Offered no alternative, he had duly sworn to hold the city to the last man and surrender only if high command granted permission. He inherited a staff of officers who were all elderly reservists. Yet Wildermuth considered them competent enough. With the enemy sure to turn up any day, he realized there was little time to supplement the existing defences.

Because the garrison had been both depleted and reinforced as Fifteenth Army had retreated past, Wildermuth had only a vague idea of how many men he actually commanded. He thought the garrison totalled about 8,000 men, of which 4,500 were trained infantry. In fact, there were more than 11,000 German army, naval, and Luftwaffe personnel inside the fortress. His best troops came from two divisions that Fifteenth Army had left him. The 1041st Grenadier Regiment of 226th Infanterie-Division numbered about 1,400 men. This division had been cobbled together in July 1944 from Russian-front personnel enjoying leave in Germany. Although mostly combat veterans, they lacked regimental cohesion. They also had no experience in fighting from fixed defences and were unfamiliar with Le Havre's defensive works. Deployed in Le Havre for a longer period, the 936th Grenadier Regiment of 245th Infanterie-Division was better prepared for the forthcoming fight. On August 28, two other units—the 226th Fusiliers Battalion and III Battalion of the 5th Sicherungs [Protective] Regiment —had reinforced the 900-strong 81st Fortress Depot Unit. It was all these units that gave Wildermuth his 4,500-man fighting teeth.[7]

What Wildermuth lacked in manpower, however, was largely compensated for by Le Havre's natural advantages and the years spent on its fortification. As only Marseilles boasted a larger French port, Le Havre had a long history of commercial and military importance dating back to its establishment by King Francis I in 1517. By the end of the eighteenth century, its importance as an international centre for French trade was well established. When the Germans occupied the city in 1940, its population stood at 164,000.[8] From its occupation to the arrival of I British Corps on its outskirts, the city had endured 132 Allied bombing raids. As the raids intensified, many civilians had fled to the country. By September 1944, the civilian population had shrunk to 50,000.[9]

The city was divided into two distinct sectors, separated by a natural escarpment that varied in height from two hundred to three hundred feet. In the sixteenth century, a broad belt of silt-clogged riverbed, marshlands, and mudflats had been drained to create the original city and port. Over time, the city expanded onto the plateau overlooking the lower town from the escarpment. Its commercial, administrative, and industrial centres remained in the lower town, which—along with the port facilities—had suffered the greatest weight of bombing.

In much the same way as the city had been created by draining, the port was constructed by excavating a series of dock basins out of the silt belt on the north side of the Seine estuary. These basins varied greatly in size and ability to accommodate various sizes of shipping. All were bordered by extensive dockyards, and some of the basins were separated by dock gates, locks, or narrow passages. The Canal de Tancarville was also accessed from within the port and provided an important navigable link to Rouen. The port was sheltered from storms by a natural earthen breakwater alongside the river. Entrance to the port was provided by a gap facing the channel. Constant dredging was required to enable the port to handle deep-water ship traffic. Until just before the war, the entrance was only about 10 feet deep, but was deepened then to 35.5 feet to allow the great French liner *Normandie* access during any tidal phase. Artificial breakwaters were extended outward to create a wider 820-foot entrance.[10]

The Seine to the south and the channel to the west provided natural defensive barriers. Due east lay the steep-sided, u-shaped Lézarde River valley, which the Germans had inundated. North of the city, high ground at Octeville-sur-Mer overlooked all nearby lines of approach. And an unbroken line of 300-foot-high cliffs faced the coast.[11]

Although the city was heavily fortified against naval attack, its land-ward defences were incomplete. A continuous defensive line extended west and roughly paralleled the Lézarde River to Montivilliers, about six miles northwest of Le Havre. Here the line turned due west to pass through Doudenéville and Octeville before reaching the coast. These northern approaches were blocked by minefields, barbed wire, and a deep anti-tank ditch that was twenty feet wide, ten feet deep, and had near vertical sides. Cutting across this ground to flow into the Lézarde River was the smaller Fontaine River. It was bordered on two sides by small plateaus respectively identified as the Southern Plateau and Northern Plateau. Also southwest of the Fontaine, Forêt de Montgeon presented a natural obstacle. Because water blocked approaches from the other three directions, it was obvious to both 1 British Corps planners and the German defenders that any attack must come from the north. So it was here that the Germans had concentrated their efforts. The Northern Plateau alone contained eleven of fifteen major infantry strongpoints.[12] All included within their perimeters deep shelters made of reinforced concrete and were protected all around by wire and mines. Each strongpoint was designed to accommodate reinforced platoons or company groups well supplied with machine guns. Close support weapons, especially anti-tank guns, were limited by shortages.

Several strongpoints were large enough to include 88-millimetre guns. Le Havre itself contained two large forts—Fort de Tourneville and Fort Ste. Addresse—as well as many roadblocks, pillboxes, and fortified buildings. Anti-tank guns covered all main routes.[13]

When Wildermuth took command, he was initially impressed by the garrison's artillery strength. To his dismay, however, he discovered that all but one of the large coastal guns could only fire seaward. So although there were thirty-five long-range weapons—most being ten or fifteen centimetres in calibre—they were largely useless. This was particularly true of the Grand Clos Battery north of the city. It housed one 380-millimetre and two 170-millimetre guns, but only one of the latter could fire inland. Deployed about the defences and facing in the right direction were twenty-four 150-millimetre and ten 105-millimetre guns. The coastal and fortress artillery units also had a number of guns intended specifically for close defence against ground forces. But these were mostly 15-centimetre Czech-made howitzers, for which there was little ammunition. Until the end of August, when Fifteenth Army confiscated them, the garrison had been equipped with a variety of French guns. The Czech guns had been handed off as a replacement. In the haste of the retreat, most of the ammunition for the French guns had been left behind. So Wildermuth had "large piles of French ammunition" cluttering up his gun areas and posing a serious "explosive danger to the garrison." Wildermuth was able to bolster his landward artillery by deploying thirty-two anti-aircraft guns. Most of these were 88-millimetre, but four were 128-millimetre. In all, the garrison had about 150 guns.

Wildermuth considered his biggest handicap to be a lack of heavy anti-tank guns. His defensive line stretched over fifteen miles, but he had just thirty 88-millimetre and 75-millimetre guns to defend it. Only seven of these were self-propelled.

As for supplies, the garrison was relatively well stocked. On September 1, Wildermuth's quartermasters reported sufficient food to last fourteen thousand men eighty-eight days. There was also enough food to feed the civilian population for forty days. Ammunition was not plentiful, but the stocks could keep the guns firing for a short time. In Wildermuth's more optimistic moments, he hoped the Allies would simply besiege the city—particularly as they had surely detected that the garrison's naval personnel had begun demolishing the port facilities on September 1. More rationally, however, he realized that the Allies were unlikely to leave Le Havre alone. There was no prospect of repelling a determined attack. He figured that even a single infantry division reinforced with tanks could shatter the garrison in a mere twenty-four hours. If circumstances were more favourable—such as if the Allies proceeded with a slow and methodical assault—Le Havre might stand for three days.

On September 3, when the Allies roped off the city and Crocker sent his surrender demand with the threat of bombing to be followed by an all-out ground attack, Wildermuth knew the end was near. Honour meant he must refuse to surrender, but the coming battle could only end in defeat.[14]

JUST BEFORE 0900 hours on September 4, all firing along 146th Infantry Brigade's front ceased. From the German lines, a small group of officers emerged, passed through the 1/4th King's Own Yorkshire Light Infantry positions at Mont Cabert, just east of the town of Harfleur, and were escorted to a nearby building. They were met by Brigadier John Walker. Wildermuth was not present, but the senior German officer passed Walker his written reply. Wildermuth refused the demand, stating that the garrison "would fight to the end." Despite the definitive response, first the 49th (West Riding) Infantry Division's commander and then Lieutenant General John Crocker himself came to the house.[15] Through an interpreter, discussion turned from the issue of surrender to a request by Wildermuth that a ceasefire enable the remaining civilian population to leave Le Havre. He proposed that the British commander select a point in the front lines through which the evacuation could occur. Agreeing to an evacuation would significantly delay the assault, so Crocker refused.[16] The Germans returned to their lines, and at 1130 hours, 146th Brigade reopened hostilities with artillery fire from its 69th Field Regiment.[17]

On both sides, attention turned to preparing for the coming fight. For the Germans, the emphasis was on destroying port facilities. From three observation positions across the Seine and five miles from the port itself, 1 British Corps's Survey Regiment personnel monitored the destruction. They were able to pinpoint more than one hundred individual demolitions that would together seriously hamper the Allied ability to restore port operations.[18]

Extensive aerial reconnaissance, meanwhile, enabled Crocker's staff to develop a comprehensive overprint of the garrison's defences. This was constantly supplemented by intelligence gathered from continued aerial operations, ground reconnaissance patrols, FFI resistance fighters, and the reports of more than three hundred civilians who had recently fled the city. Interrogations of Germans captured by patrols or deserters also added to the knowledge base. One deserter even brought plans detailing the defensive strongpoints on the Northern Plateau, the layout of minefields across the entire northern sector, the German artillery's pre-plotted defensive fire tasks, and the arcs that various artillery positions could cover.[19] The amount of detail contained on the overprints was invaluable, but it also showed a scale of defences that the 34th Armoured Brigade officer compiling notes for its history found "terrifying in their horrific detail. All true too."[20]

Every night brought more German deserters, most risking getting killed or wounded in the minefields to reach the British lines. On the night of September 3, an entire company of III Battalion of 5th Sicherungs Regiment slipped out of posts in front of 146th Brigade and surrendered.[21] Several prisoners taken by patrols confessed "that were it not for their officers they would offer no resistance."[22]

Such information fostered Crocker's continued hope that the garrison might capitulate once it had been significantly "softened up." This process began on the day after the surrender rejection, when HMS *Erebus* steamed into range and opened fire with its two 15-inch guns mounted in a single turret. The Grand Clos Battery immediately lashed back and scored a direct hit that flooded the ship's after hold. *Erebus* limped back to Portsmouth for repairs.[23]

At 1800 hours, RAF Bomber Command arrived overhead. For almost two hours, the southwest section of the old town was pounded because intelligence reports indicated Wildermuth's headquarters were situated there.[24] The attack was made by 348 aircraft—313 Lancasters, 30 Mosquitos and 5 Stirlings of Nos. 1, 3, and 8 Groups. Altogether, 1,820 tons of high explosive and 30,000 incendiaries were dropped.

A square mile containing the town hall, exchange palace, post office, grand theatre, two municipal museums, and the churches of St. Joseph, St. Michel, and Notre-Dame was decimated when fires spread to engulf most of the lower town. Civilian casualties were horrific—781 killed and another 289 missing. Thousands of homes were lost.

The following evening, 344 aircraft struck the Southern Plateau and Forêt de Montgeon with 1,500 tons of explosives targeting defensive works and ammunition depots. While the Germans remained relatively unscathed in their deep concrete bunkers, another 655 civilians died and 10 went missing. A single bomb that struck the southern end of the Jenner Tunnel accounted for many deaths. Still under construction, the tunnel was to connect the two parts of the city. The explosion blocked the entrance, trapping 326 people within. Just 7 were dug out and rescued; the other 319 perished mostly due to asphyxiation.[25]

While Bomber Command showered Le Havre with explosives, other aircraft continued dropping thousands of leaflets calling on the garrison to surrender. Near the front lines, large speakers continued to broadcast the merits of deserting and the dire consequences for those who stood and fought. Acoustical conditions were so good on the evening of September 6 that a broadcast from a station east of Harfleur was reported by deserters as clearly audible three thousand yards away, where their No. 8 Company of 1041st Grenadiers was positioned. Eighteen men deserted the German lines. Wildermuth responded by withdrawing a number of units considered of doubtful loyalty and replacing them from his garrison reserves.[26]

At 0730 hours on September 8, the bombers returned. The weather was bad and visibility poor. Of the 333 bombers involved, only 109 dropped bomb loads, for a total of 535 tons. The attack focused on the northwestern flank of the German defences. *Erebus* also returned during the day, but was again struck by shellfire from Grand Clos Battery and forced to withdraw. Although there would be another Bomber Command attempt on September 9, thick cloud so obscured the ground that the attack was called off and all 272 bombers returned to Britain without dropping their loads. But Le Havre had suffered dreadfully from the three successful attacks. About 4,000 tons of ordnance had been dropped and 2,053 civilians killed.[27]

Despite the civilian casualties—the extent of which was not realized at the time—consensus within the command chain of First Canadian Army was that the bombings had accurately struck the designated targets, caused significant damage, and greatly shaken German morale. Lieutenant General Harry Crerar sent a personal message to Air Chief Marshal Sir Arthur Harris congratulating Bomber Command for its accuracy, wherein "the targets were hit just as the Army wanted it."[28]

Soon after the bombers turned back on September 9, a second ultimatum passed through the lines to Wildermuth. In the evening, two German officers emerged, were blindfolded, and brought back to 146th Brigade's headquarters. Once again a ceasefire had been imposed. The German officers, however, told Brigadier John Walker that their instructions were to refuse the surrender. Wildermuth again requested a cessation of hostilities to permit civilian evacuation, but was rebuffed. Again blindfolded, the officers were returned to the German lines.[29]

That evening, Crocker green-lighted the assault on Le Havre to begin the following day. The city would be taken by full-scale assault.

Wildermuth, meanwhile, could only watch from the ramparts of his fortress as "large groups of artillery and tanks" gathered. His only intelligence came from a few French fascists recruited as spies. They reported that the Allies consisted of just the British 49th (West Riding) Infantry Division and the Belgian Brigade. The presence of the 51st (Highland) Infantry Division was not discovered. Wildermuth's communications with Oberkommando der Wehrmacht were sporadic and so confused that Berlin issued a September 9 report that the battle for Le Havre had begun earlier in the day. It "described in glowing terms the gallantry of the defenders, and even gave figures as to how many Allied guns had been knocked out." Upon receiving this report, Wildermuth wired Berlin that the attack had not started, and that to date, German artillery fire had been observed to have hit only three tanks and two armoured cars.

As for his gallant defenders, Wildermuth tried frantically to bolster their slumping morale. Surrounded and with no prospect of escape, many questioned sacrificing themselves to defend a worthless port.[30] In an Order of the Day, Wildermuth announced his refusal to surrender. "I expect that every man in the fortress will carry out his duty," he wrote. In another order, Wildermuth cautioned that the "national sense of loyalty of the troops must not dry up now. The military situation does not permit lectures or discussions. The [political officers and unit commanders] must visit individual strongpoints and carry out Nazi education there. The object to be shown is that every soldier grasps the spirit of this battle as a Nazi and sets himself without looking back for the fight with heart and hand. Also our fight in the Fortress is not unmeaning—it is a simple and clear object. It concerns our homes and our state . . . Political leaders will give a short talk daily in the front line for the guidance of troops."[31]

CROCKER'S PLAN FOR Operation Astonia, as the Le Havre assault was code-named, entailed a heavily concentrated thrust by both divisions against the narrow sector bordered by Montivilliers on the left and Fontaine-la-Mallet on the right. The 49th Division with 34th Tank Brigade would strike to the left, while 51st Division punched forward on the right, with 33rd Armoured Brigade in support. Because of the narrow frontage, the 49th Division would lead off with a daylight attack, with 51st Division joining the operation when darkness fell.

Astonia would proceed in four phases. In the first phase, the 49th Division's 56th Brigade would drive forward in a virtual wedge through the German outer defences, seize the Northern Plateau and establish a bridgehead on the Southern Plateau. The second phase would see the division's 147th Brigade exploit out of this bridgehead to win the Southern Plateau. Meanwhile, 51st Division would advance to a base on the northern edge of Forêt de Montgeon. Phase three called for 49th Division's 146th Brigade to open a new front by punching in from the east to take Harfleur. At the same time, 51st Division would wheel to the right out of Forêt de Montgeon toward the channel, destroying all German fortifications and gun positions south of Octeville and thus gain the high ground on Le Havre's northwestern outskirts. Phase four would, as Crocker put it, have both divisions "exploit relentlessly into the town."

Vital to the attack was the support to be provided by 79th Armoured Division's specialized armour. The 49th Division would be supported by the 22nd Dragoons' mine-sweeping Flails—Sherman tanks with forward-projecting rotating drums mounted with chains that literally pounded the ground ahead to detonate mines. A squadron of the 42nd Assault Regiment provided Churchill tanks that mounted a short-barrelled 12-inch gun called a Petard, which fired a 40-pound round to demolish fortifications or breach obstacles such as concrete walls. The regiment also deployed other Churchills equipped with various types of bridging gear, such as the unfolding scissors bridge. Because of the variety of vehicles the 42nd Regiment fielded, they were jointly designated as Armoured Vehicle Royal Engineers (AVRES). A squadron of flame-throwing Crocodiles was also provided by 79th Division.

The leading infantry, meanwhile, would be carried into battle inside the protective armoured hides of forty-four Kangaroos provided by 1st Canadian Armoured Personnel Carrier Squadron.[32] Still considered a novel invention, the Kangaroo had been conceived by Lieutenant General Guy Simonds during the lead-up to First Canadian Army's launch of Operation Totalize—the drive from Verrières Ridge toward Falaise. The Kangaroos were modified American 105-millimetre M-7 self-propelled guns that had been temporarily exchanged for the 25-pounders of 3rd Infantry Division's artillery regiments to provide a high level of mobility during the initial stages of the Normandy invasion. As the M-7s were being phased out, Simonds realized that removing their gun would create room inside to carry infantry. Thickening their armoured hides would also increase the provided protection. The resulting Kangaroos were then able to carry infantry forward at a pace that matched the fastest speed of advancing tanks. The Kangaroos had gone into operation on August 7, but the Canadian squadron was not formally created until August 28 when it was attached to the 79th Armoured Division. Although the M-7-based Kangaroos would soon be replaced by a version utilizing the chassis of the Canadian-made Ram tank, these would not come into service until the end of September.[33]

Assisting the 51st Division would be Flails provided by the 1st Lothians and Border Yeomanry, two squadrons of AVRES, and a squadron of Crocodiles. When phase one was completed, twenty-four Kangaroos would shift from 49th Division to support the 51st Division's night attack.[34]

The main task of Major General Hobart's "Funnies" was to breach the minefields and create crossings over the anti-tank ditch. Two gaps had been detected in the ditch within the narrow front between Montivilliers and Fontaine-la-Mallet. One was four hundred yards wide and the other, two hundred yards. It was through these gaps that the main assault would pass. Eleven gapping teams would each create a lane through the minefields. The 49th Division would have eight lanes and the 51st Division three. Each lane was given a special code name, with those of the 51st being Gin (Lane 1), Rum (Lane 2), and Ale (Lane 3), while the 49th's were Laura (Lanes 4–6), Hazel (Lanes 7–9), and Mary (Lanes 10–11).[35]

A great weight of artillery was deployed. In addition to the two divisions' inherent six field artillery regiments, six medium and two heavy artillery regiments were available. Besides timed concentrations, Crocker could order—and his divisional commanders could request—"Victor" targets—which would see every unengaged gun capable of ranging on the target joining an immediate shoot.[36] A searchlight battery was positioned so that it could provide "artificial moonlight" on the night of September 10 to illuminate the battlefield for the 51st Division.

Attention to detail was extensive, and most units were provided with sand-table and cloth models to plan their role in the minefield-breaching operation. On the evening before the attack, 51st Division's 152nd Brigade rehearsed by breaching a twenty-foot-wide ditch that had been bulldozed to a three-foot depth. AVRES were used to realistically bridge the ditch. The brigade's infantry battalions also practised using twelve lifebuoy flame-throwers and working with three Wasp flame-thrower Bren carriers.[37] The lifebuoy flame-throwers were operated by a single soldier and so nicknamed because of the doughnut-shaped rings that contained the fuel and propellant.

The biggest worry facing 1 British Corps was the weather, which had hampered the bombing raid of September 8 and scotched entirely the one of September 9 while dumping rain that left the surrounding countryside a muddy bog. Crocker had intended to launch his assault on September 9 but pushed it back a day in the hope that the ground would dry slightly. Finally, he decided to delay the attack until 1745 hours on September 10 to allow as much time as possible for the ground to firm up, so that the tanks—particularly the Flails—would face less risk of getting stuck.

On the night of September 9–10, the armour that would support 49th Division crossed the Lézarde River by four tank tracks and assembled on the reverse slopes southwest of Fontenay. To confuse the Germans as to where the attack was to fall, additional tanks and heavy equipment ground back and forth on the fronts east of the Lézarde and also across 51st Division's entire front to the north. Incorporating so much special equipment within the infantry battalions preparing for the attack was complex and at times bewildering. First Gordon Highlanders second-in-command Major Martin Lindsay sat down after dinner on the evening of September 9 to draft marching orders for his battalion and "the mass of queer vehicles" that was to accompany it. "We are to have Crocodiles, AVRES, tanks, and flails. All very complicated, too complicated in fact, and I have been trying to persuade [Lieutenant Colonel Harry Cumming-Bruce] to leave some of this menagerie behind as I fear they will get stuck in the woods we have to go through . . . It is going to be very difficult to control this zoo . . . We shall have fifty-four vehicles and they are all being lined up tonight. I hope to goodness they mark the route well, and especially the minefields, so that we cannot go wrong in the dark. Our column is being led by a sapper sergeant . . . in charge of a scissors bridge to put across the first anti-tank ditch. It seems a great responsibility to give [a non-commissioned officer]."[38]

Dawn broke on September 10 to clear skies, and soon warm sunlight bathed the fields. A dry easterly wind blew across the heavy clay soil and promised to harden it sufficiently for the tanks to roll freely. In England, 1,057 bombers were loaded with explosives.[39] Offshore, *Erebus* and the battleship *Warspite* closed on the coast.[40]

Even with battle about to be joined, Crocker still hoped to win a quick victory without a lot of casualties. Repeatedly, he impressed on every unit commander that "bold ruthless action, carefully planned, might result in the enemy chucking in his hand at an early stage . . . With tanks and other armoured weapons at their disposal, brigade commanders had the means of taking such action."[41]

14

Flails to the Front

"THIS EVENING," THE 49th (West Riding) Infantry Division's intelligence officer wrote on September 10, his division had spearheaded "the biggest set piece assault on a prepared defensive position which any formation has been called upon to carry since the Allied Expeditionary Force landed in France. With a Churchill [tank] Brigade under command, a veritable Noah's Ark of destructive armoured vehicles, and massed artillery of the RA and RN, Bomber Command, with a large force of heavy bombers, played the overture and raised the curtain on the attack at 1715 hours."[1]

In truth, Operation Astonia's opening curtain had lifted at 0800 hours that morning with the arrival of sixty-eight bombers that attacked Grand Clos Battery. Much smoke rising from the battery led to hopes that the air attack had silenced it. Two hours later, however, when *Erebus* returned for its third matchup with the battery, the German guns erupted into life. This time, the monitor was accompanied by HMS *Warspite*. First launched in 1913, *Warspite* mounted eight 15-inch guns in four twin-gun turrets and was more of a match for the battery's 380-millimetre and two 170-millimetre guns than *Erebus*. Aloft in aircraft over the batteries, spotters for the two ships ably and accurately directed their fire.[2]

While *Erebus* concentrated on other "casemated guns on perimeter defences of [Le] Havre," *Warspite* engaged in a short gun duel with the Grand Clos guns that ended with all silenced at no cost to the battleship. The two ships continued to pound German defensive positions for the next six hours. By the time they disengaged at 1400 hours, *Warspite* had fired 304 rounds. *Erebus* had added 130 rounds to the bombardment, and the aerial spotters reported that 30 of these had successfully struck enemy positions.[3] In all, the two ships had engaged nine designated gun batteries.[4]

At 1645 hours, the final bomber raid on Le Havre began with 992 aircraft involved—521 Lancasters, 426 Halifaxes, and 45 Mosquitoes. The two-engine Mosquitoes served as pathfinders, marking the designated targets for the three attacking waves. The first wave struck Le Havre's western defences, the second hit defences around Octeville and on the Northern Plateau, while the third concentrated on the Southern Plateau. A total of eight major strongpoints had been identified and marked by the pathfinders for destruction. In all, 4,719 tons of explosives were dropped.[5]

Only one aircraft was lost, crashing on the return to Britain. To the watching British troops, the raid was heartening. "Our troops were highly impressed with the weight and precision of the bombing and estimated its effect on the defenders as very considerable," one report commented. "Prisoners subsequently stated that the bombing was very frightening, but comparatively few casualties were caused to the German troops . . . due to the excellent shelters, including those designed for the civilian population, of which they made use. A certain amount of damage was done to weapons, but the most important result was a breakdown of enemy communications, which, for example, prevented the German artillery commander, Oberst Erwin von Steinhardt, from controlling his resources and precluded centralised direction of the defences as a whole."[6]

Later examination by RAF Flight Lieutenant R.F. Delderfield—subsequently one of Britain's most famous and successful novelists—revealed that the bombardment had wrought considerable damage on batteries with open emplacements but little to those in concrete positions. In the area around Fontaine-la-Mallet and within Forêt de Montgeon, Delderfield found extensive evidence of heavy bombing wherein German barracks had received direct hits. There was also evidence that ammunition depots within the woods had been destroyed by bombs. The commander of the 51st (Highland) Infantry Division's 154th Brigade, Brigadier James Oliver, told Delderfield that the RAF "bombing of the outskirts . . . was remarkably effective and accurate." While Oliver acknowledged that the latest bombing raid had led to additional civilian deaths, he believed it had prevented "a great number of casualties among the troops."[7]

Although the bombing had damaged German defences, it was less destructive than the British artillery, which first opened fire in full during the night of September 9–10. As the day progressed, Oberst Eberhard Wildermuth was increasingly stunned by the ferocity of the "drum fire" that was striking the "whole extent of the fortress from north and east, from heavy batteries south of the Seine, and from the sea." Oberst Steinhardt, the artillery commander, estimated that the Germans were being shelled by six to eight artillery brigades. He also reported that the surviving coastal artillery was unable to range far enough seaward to counter the fire from *Erebus* and *Warspite*, while the landward-facing guns could barely respond because of the intensity of counter-battery fire coming their way. Further, the landward-capable artillery had been badly diminished. Of seventy-two weapons, fifty-two remained in action. There was little the Germans could do but hunker down and try to survive the firestorm until the assaulters approached.[8]

AS THE LAST bombers dropped their loads and turned homeward precisely at 1745 hours, the 49th Division's ground assault began. Lieutenant Colonel W.A.C. Anderson, whose 22nd Dragoons led the attack on the right, had been "much perturbed as to the effect of the sodden ground on the speed" of his Flails. He feared the Sherman tanks would be incapable of even one mile per hour. Speed powered the Flail chain's rate of revolutions and the depth of ground penetration. Decreased speed meant shallower penetration and the probability that deep-seated mines would be untouched until the tank itself passed over and its weight detonated them. Anderson had wanted the attack further delayed to give the ground more time to firm up. His superior, 30th Armoured Brigade's Brigadier N.W. Duncan, agreed and had taken the matter to 49th Division's Major General Evelyn Barker, who kicked it up to Crocker. With First Canadian Army's Lieutenant General Harry Crerar making it clear that the 79th Armoured Division's "special devices" were needed as soon as possible to enable attacks on Boulogne and Calais, Crocker knew the slow buildup of the Le Havre operation was already trying patience. The "operation must take place at the time arranged," he announced, in order to allow 30th Armoured Brigade to "be released as soon as possible for employment elsewhere."[9]

So, struggling through the mud, the Flails churned forward with chains pounding. As the Sherman's 75-millimetre gun turret had to be reversed when flailing, Churchill tanks from 7th Royal Tank Regiment followed to provide fire support. As the tankers crossed the start line of the lateral road running from Montivilliers to Fontaine-la-Mallet, they saw before them a shallow basin of open fields with the Fontaine River at the bottom. From the river, more fields rose gently to meet the woods of Forêt de Montgeon to the right and the heights of the Southern Plateau on the left. Great gaps had been torn out of the woods by the bombing, and many standing trees were badly shredded.

It was 1815 hours when 'A' Squadron crossed the road and started cutting the three lanes designated as Laura on the division's right flank.[10] The lanes led directly to a fortification identified as Strongpoint 5, which was anchored around a concrete bunker, contained three anti-tank guns and numerous mortars, and held about forty men believed to be amply supplied with shoulder-launched Panzerfausts.[11] At 1818, 'B' Squadron crossed the road. While most of the squadron was focused on the left-hand lanes, one troop was to clear the way in the centre, where a squadron of AVRES would then bridge the anti-tank ditch. Because of gaps in the ditch, no bridging was required on either the right or left flanks. Initially, all went well. By 1835 hours, 'A' Squadron reported its three lanes were halfway cleared, with German opposition limited to "slight shelling." Slower getting off the mark, 'B' Squadron's Flails started work five minutes later. The Flails operating in the three centre lanes designated Hazel reported "plenty of mines . . . going up" as they proceeded, while those clearing the two left-hand lanes code-named Mary encountered no mines or opposition. At 1848 hours, 'A' Squadron was almost done and still under only light shelling.[12]

Suddenly, an anti-tank gun hidden in a wooded depression well right of 'A' Squadron opened fire. The gun lay outside 49th Division's operational area and was part of Strongpoint 8, which had been assigned to be cleared by 51st (Highland) Infantry Division in its forthcoming night attack. On 'A' Squadron's extreme right, the troop commanded by 2nd Lieutenant Charles Neil was flailing Lane 4. The leading tank's turret was blown off and the entire crew became casualties, while a mine disabled the Flail immediately behind. The three surviving Flails in this troop continued clearing the lane right through to Strongpoint 5. Twenty-year-old Neil's tank took a direct hit here, bursting into flame, and all aboard were killed. The surviving two tanks were ordered to widen the lane, but moments later, one was knocked out by a mine.[13]

'A' Squadron had opened two lanes to a width of sixteen feet and the third to twenty-four feet. But the price was steep. It had lost three Flails "burnt out and destroyed." A further nine Flails and a Sherman command tank were disabled by mines or anti-tank fire.

In the centre, progress was slowed by the many mines. At 1843 hours, the right lane was reported as being three vehicles wide. But when an AVRE deployed a scissors bridge across the ditch, the bridge took a direct artillery hit and collapsed. Intelligence reports had determined the ground where Hazel's middle lane was to be created to be free of mines, so no Flails had been assigned to it. But when a Churchill bridge-layer AVRE closed on the ditch, it struck a mine that broke a track. Engineers of 49th Division with hand-held minesweepers rushed into the lane to sweep through to the disabled AVRE, which was then towed clear to make room for another bridge-layer. In Hazel's left lane, meanwhile, all five Flails were disabled by mines. An AVRE bearing bridging equipment was then hit, and its load blocked the lane completely. Efforts to open this lane were abandoned.

To the left in the two Mary lanes, the right lane was declared abandoned at 1947 hours because all but one Flail and following tanks had detonated mines and were disabled. The left lane, however, was successfully widened to twenty-four feet by 1908 hours. Three AVRES, four Crocodiles, and two troops of 7th Royal Tank Regiment's 'B' Squadron hurriedly passed through, but then two following tanks were knocked out by mines and blocked the lane until cleared at 2028 hours.

The 22nd Dragoons had done their job, but the cost was thirty-four Flails put out of action and three destroyed by fire. Two Sherman command tanks were also disabled. Anderson's fears had been borne out. Most of the losses resulted from slow speeds yielding only 900 to 1,100 revolutions per minute instead of the minimum requirement of 1,500 for successful flailing.[14] At 1955 hours, the 22nd Dragoons' war diarist recorded that all flailing efforts had stopped and that those lanes opened had already been used by leading infantry headed for their objectives. Some Flails disabled close to German positions fired their 75-millimetre guns in support of the infantry. Most were soon abandoned in the minefield, with only ten able to withdraw. Of these, just five were deemed capable of assisting 49th Division's 147th Brigade for the forthcoming phase two of Operation Astonia, which was scheduled for the following day.[15]

The state of the lanes changed constantly, "owing to the heavy going and churning up of the ground by tanks" that rendered them "often impassable" except to tracked vehicles. Undiscovered mines continued to damage and disable vehicles. Engineers soon discovered that this was due not only to the inability of the slow-moving Flails to cut deeply enough to trigger deep-seated mines, but also to German cunning. Many mines were found to be buried more than a foot deep with a stick extending upward that when pressed by the weight of a vehicle detonated the charge. As Le Havre's defences had been completed long before the attack, other mines were simply unstable and might not explode until a number of vehicles passed over them.

Consequently, at 0815 hours on September 11, the "state of gaps" was reported as being five blocked or entirely abandoned, one blocked but scheduled to reopen by 0900 hours, one usable by tanks, and one being used for wheeled vehicles. By that time, however, the lanes had largely outlived their usefulness, the battle having moved the evening before beyond the Northern Plateau.[16]

THE NORTHERN PLATEAU fight had begun at 1940 hours, when 56th Infantry Brigade's infantry battalions moved through the lanes toward their various strongpoint objectives. Two of the brigade's three battalions led with strong support from Crocodiles and Churchill tanks of 7th Royal Tanks. The 2nd South Wales Borderers went in on the right and the 2nd Battalion, Gloucestershire Regiment, the left. Once these two battalions had cleared most of the Northern Plateau, the 2nd Battalion, Essex Scottish Regiment, would pass through to secure the last remaining strongpoints and establish a bridgehead on the Southern Plateau.

'D' Company led the Borderers, followed by 'A' and 'B' Companies. In front of the infantry, five Crocodiles and two troops of tanks headed straight for Strongpoint 5. The Crocodiles "soaked" the position "in flame. It was a magnificent and awe-inspiring sight," the infantry reported.[17] 'D' Company, commanded by Major Douglas Talmage, ran through a gauntlet of artillery and small-arms fire from the woods where Strongpoint 8 lay to the right. Talmage fell dead.[18] Most of the company managed to get through the lane, and after an intense eleven-minute fight, Strongpoint 5 fell. In the midst of the action, a platoon of German infantry was caught in the open by a Crocodile and entirely "wiped out by flame." A prisoner stammered that the Crocodiles had devastated the defenders' morale.[19]

Despite being equipped with three anti-tank guns, a profusion of mortars, and many Panzerfausts, most of the Germans offered little resistance. About forty had fled to the safety of the concrete bunker in the strongpoint's centre. Here, they meekly waited until called upon to surrender.

As 'A' Company passed to the front and headed for Strongpoint 6, a heavy concentration of artillery fire from Strongpoint 8 fell directly into the midst of the soldiers, and sixty men—basically half the company's strength—were killed or wounded. Only one platoon section managed to reach the objective in an organized state, but the men were too few to overrun the position. The leading platoon of 'B' Company, which was to take Strongpoint 7 beyond, had been pinned in the open lane by the artillery concentration. Seeing this, Major Donald Collins quickly diverted the rest of the company into another lane to slip past the artillery—which seemed to be firing on a predetermined fire plan rather than under observer direction. With Crocodiles in support, 'B' Company assisted the section from 'A' Company in taking Strongpoint 6 and then seized Strongpoint 7.[20]

On the 56th Brigade's left flank, meanwhile, the 2nd Gloucesters had at 1855 hours advanced 'D' Company, preceded by two troops of tanks, toward Strongpoint 1, while 'B' Company assaulted Strongpoint 2 on the battalion's right flank. Tanks from 'B' Squadron 7th Royal Tanks were in support, as were two troops of Crocodiles and six AVRES of 617th Assault Squadron's No. 3 Troop. Two Crocodiles were immobilized on the start line and another disabled by a mine as it passed down Lane 11—the only one in sector Mary to be opened. The Crocodiles and AVRES preceded the infantry, with the tanks bringing up the rear. As the AVRES exited the lane, one fell prey to a mine. Then two Churchill tanks strayed from the path beaten by the Flails, struck mines, swung back into the lane, and blocked it for the hour required to tow them clear.[21]

This mishap failed to slow the attack's impetus. By 1922 hours, 'D' Company had overrun Strongpoint 1, and eighteen minutes later Strongpoint 2 fell to 'B' Company with three AVRES in support. 'A' Company leapfrogged into the lead with one infantry platoon out front, then a Crocodile troop, a half troop of AVRES, and the rest of the infantry in line behind. Twenty minutes later, Strongpoint 2A was taken. Strongpoint 3, facing the centre of the Gloucester advance, offered more resistance, but the Crocodiles burnt its defenders out. 'C' Company took the lead and headed to the right toward Strongpoint 4, but its Crocodiles wandered astray because of thick, blinding smoke that covered the ground. The infantry got tangled in a sharp action that was brought to an end when two Petard AVRES rumbled up and pounded the concrete bunker with heavy shot. Thirty Germans surrendered at 2115 hours.

While this fight had been under way, a mixed party of infantry from 'A' and 'B' Companies along with a Crocodile and troop of tanks had bulled onward and overrun Strongpoints 9 and 10 at the southern edge of the Northern Plateau. Realizing these positions had actually been assigned for capture by the following 2nd Essex, the force hurriedly withdrew to avoid a friendly-fire incident.

Resistance at most strongpoints had been quite minor, and the Gloucesters claimed four officers and forty-seven other ranks taken prisoner with an unknown number having been killed—primarily by Crocodile flame.[22] Some of the German prisoners seemed to have just waited passively in slit trenches for the opportunity to surrender—emerging with their personal kit in hand and ready to begin a new life.[23]

The 2nd Essex had been carried to their start line by the Canadian Kangaroo Regiment, which were to have taken them right through to their strongpoint objectives. But by 2130 hours, so many lanes were closed or in such bad condition that brigade ordered the infantry diverted to Lane 7 in Hazel's sector and to then advance on foot. They were followed by two carriers bearing wireless sets and an artillery officer in a tank from which the gun had been removed to make room for his equipment.

As Strongpoints 9 and 10 had already been attacked by the Gloucesters, these were secured easily by 0030 hours. 'A' and 'B' Companies, which had respectively carried out these assaults, continued on to clear the Northern Plateau's escarpment overlooking the Fontaine River valley. One platoon of 'A' Company descended to seize two intact bridges. By now it was fully dark, and the 2nd Essex were scattered over a wide area of the Northern Plateau and in the valley. Lieutenant Colonel Geoffrey Elliott decided that continuing on as planned to establish a bridgehead on the Southern Plateau was no longer feasible. The secured bridges would suffice to enable the forthcoming advance by 147th Brigade.[24]

By 0200 hours, 56th Brigade had consolidated its grasp on the Northern Plateau. Brigadier M.S. Ekins reported that more than 250 prisoners had passed through his headquarters, which roughly accorded with the intelligence estimates of German strength in the fortifications defending his sector of the plateau.[25]

THROUGHOUT 56TH BRIGADE's operation, its battalions—particularly the Borderers on the right—had been under fire from Strongpoint 8. As it lay outside 49th Division's operational area and was to be cleared later by the 51st Division, plans had been developed to suppress it with artillery. Consequently, from 1745 to 1915 hours, 600 rounds of high-explosive shells and 200 rounds of smoke shells had been fired by the 3-inch mortars of the Borderers. Another 1,400 rounds of smoke had been added by the brigade's 4.2-inch mortar battalion. Yet this fire appeared to have had no effect on the Germans or their ability to bring artillery fire to bear on the brigade's right flank.[26]

During the advance itself, 'A' Company was to have been accompanied by an artillery forward observation officer (FOO) of the 274th Field Battery, 185th Field Regiment, who could have directed counter-battery fire against Strongpoint 8. Captain W.A. Thompson and his small team had gone into the advance in a Bren carrier, only to have it disabled for a short period when a rolled-up blanket got caught in a bogie wheel. After much "sweating and bad language," the carrier was again on the move, but ended up diverting outside of the assigned lane when it was blocked by a mine-damaged Churchill tank. As Thompson wrote in a later report, the artillery team arrived at the other side of the minefield, separated from 'A' Company and "feeling rather lonely." The artillerymen soon encountered a small group of Borderers who were beginning to engage Strongpoint 7 and told them to stay put until that job was finished. Someone would then return to guide them up to the battalion, as it re-formed to carry on the advance.

After waiting a half hour, Thompson realized something had gone awry and decided to go forward on foot to see "what was cooking." Spotting an infantryman in an orchard, Thompson ran after him and then heard a voice shout, "Come here, boy." Thinking it was the infantryman, Thompson approached and found himself staring down the barrel of a Luger pistol. Hoping to alert his men to the danger, the captain loudly asked if there was anybody about who could speak English. The warning failed, and his men were soon brought in as captives. Thompson realized any attempt to resist or escape was hopeless. The Germans numbered one officer, one warrant officer, and twenty-six men. There was nothing to do but put hands on heads and walk down the hill as directed toward Fontaine-la-Mallet.

En route, the party came under heavy shelling by British guns. Prisoners and captors all hugged the ground, as pieces of shrapnel shrieked overhead. After one near miss, Thompson's driver managed to stay out of sight. When the Germans and other captives moved on, he returned to the carrier and drove back to the British lines. In this way, the cause of Thompson's disappearance was made known to the Borderers.

Thompson and the rest of his crew, meanwhile, had been detained at a combined company headquarters and regimental aid post. They were handed into the care of a Hauptman Kurt Langner. Thompson learned that Langner was thirty-four and had seventeen years of military service. With "all his iron crosses, medals and clasps," Thompson thought him "a very imposing sight. He shook hands and made me very comfortable with a bottle of Champagne, and informed me that he had entertained 2 RAF officers the previous night."

As night settled in, their discussion was frequently interrupted by "various people bringing in reports—the heel-clicking remained well up to standard and was a continual source of interest. Two miserable specimens were also brought in after having made an attempt to desert to the British, they got their faces slapped in the best Hollywood manner and were taken round the back to be shot later; this threat was never carried out and they were later released as stretcher bearers."

Throughout the night, Thompson kept warning Langner that their situation was to be shortly reversed. At first light, as all the news coming in from the front was entirely negative, Langner realized "that he was in fact about to be my prisoner. Finally with great ceremony they stripped off their revolvers and the battle of Fontaine was won. He informed me of the location of his [battalion commander and adjutant] and asked me to go along and collect them which I decided to do, leaving my two signallers to look after the remainder of the party. I also sent out messages to the sector posts for all men to come back to HQ. The Hauptman and I set off to HQ and when about halfway there he implored me with tears in his eyes to allow him to surrender in his greatcoat and peaked hat. These we retrieved from his room and went off to see the commandant. The latter had, however, already flitted with his adjutant and so we went back to our original company HQ. I arrived back to find my two signallers rather dazed and wondering how to look after the forty-seven prisoners who had been foregathered at this HQ. They had helped themselves to Boche arms but had no ammunition and certainly no idea how the weapons worked.

top · A Universal Carrier tows a 3rd Anti-Tank Regiment 6-pounder with 3rd Division infantrymen hitching a ride during the rush to the Seine. Donald I. Grant Photo. PA–132421.

bottom · Private G.R. MacDonald of 2nd Division's Toronto Scottish (MG) gives first aid to an injured French boy in Brionne on August 25, 1944. Ken Bell Photo. PA–135956.

top · Private H. Hackett of 18th Field Ambulance offers a drink to Sapper K.J. Pratt during his evacuation from Bourgtheroulde on August 26, 1944. Ken Bell Photo. PA–137293.

top right · Lance-Corporal W.H. Harris, Canadian Provost Corps, stands guard near bodies of German soldiers in Bourgtheroulde on August 27, 1944. Ken Bell Photo. PA–131360.

bottom right · The Regina Rifle Regiment crosses the Seine at Elbeuf on August 27, 1944. Donald I. Grant Photo. PA–136016.

top · Royal Hamilton Light Infantry soldiers on patrol pass abandoned German wagons in Elbeuf on August 27, 1944. Ken Bell Photo. PA–138276.

top right · As the Germans tried to escape across the Seine, 2nd Tactical Air Force strikes destroyed thousands of vehicles and killed or wounded many of the soldiers aboard them. Donald I. Grant Photo. PA–141883.

bottom right · Sergeant B. Shaw overlooks Rouen from the Forêt de la Londe ridge on August 31, 1944. Ken Bell Photo. PA–131223.

left · Sherman tanks of 4th Canadian Armoured Division cross the Seine via a pontoon bridge at Elbeuf. Donald I. Grant Photo. PA–113660.

top · On September 3, 1944, the 2nd Canadian Infantry Division regimental highland pipe bands led a march through Dieppe to commemorate the members of the division lost during the raid of August 19, 1942. Photographer unknown. Photo in the author's possession.

bottom · A Churchill bridge-layer tank and Flail tank can be seen behind British infantry during the opening of the attack on Le Havre. Photographer unknown. Photo in the author's possession.

top left · Tanks of the Royal Tank Regiment advance toward Le Havre on September 10, 1944. Photographer unknown. Photo in the author's possession.

bottom left · Engineers of 7th Field Company clear a road near Bergues during the attempt to seize Dunkirk. Ken Bell Photo. PA–137307.

top · A group of 79th British Armoured Division soldiers is briefed on September 16, 1944, before the attack on Boulogne. Visible is a Sherman tank and behind it a Churchill Crocodile with fuel trailer attached. Donald I. Grant Photo. PA–176982.

bottom · On September 17, 1944, Mont Lambert outside Boulogne is subjected to heavy bombing. Donald I. Grant Photo. PA–136245.

top · By September 19, Boulogne's citadel had fallen and was quickly transformed into 9th Canadian Infantry Brigade's headquarters. Photo shows the citadel interior as seen through its main archway entrance. Donald I. Grant Photo. PA–136014.

bottom · Personnel of 'C' Company, Stormont, Dundas and Glengarry Highlanders, advance toward Le Portel on Boulogne's southern outskirts on September 22. Donald I. Grant Photo. PA–131231.

top · This and the other heavy guns at Fort de la Crèche were capable of rotating 360 degrees to fire on the attacking Canadians. The fort fell to the Queen's Own Rifles on September 21. Photo from Vol. 235C3.013(D2), Official Photos of Boulogne, LAC.

bottom · German prisoners march through streets near the citadel. Donald I. Grant Photo. PA–136333.

top left · Boulogne Docks after the battle. Photo from Vol. 235C3.013(D2), Official Photos of Boulogne, LAC.

bottom left · As soon as Operation Wellhit ended, Canadian engineers began cleaning up rubble to open roads through to the harbour facilities. Photo from Vol. 235C3.013(D2), Official Photos of Boulogne, LAC.

top · Despite the destruction, citizens of Boulogne soon returned and attempted to resume a normal life. Photo from Vol. 235C3.013(D2), Official Photos of Boulogne, LAC.

top · A Canadian soldier examines the inundated area southeast of Calais that funnelled Operation Undergo's line of advance toward the coastal approaches. Donald I. Grant Photo. PA–131247.

bottom · North Shore (New Brunswick) Regiment soldiers advance on a cross-channel gun position west of Sangatte during Operation Undergo. Donald I. Grant Photo. PA–133139.

top · As the Canadians tightened the noose on Calais, a twenty-four-hour ceasefire was declared on September 29 and most of the twenty thousand civilians still inside the city were evacuated to safety. Donald I. Grant Photo. PA–133946.

bottom · Calais, like the other channel ports, suffered serious damage. On October 1, smoke was still rising from the wreckage of the harbour area. Donald I. Grant Photo. PA–133943.

top · By October 14, despite extensive damage to Dieppe's harbour, Allied freighters were offloading thousands of tons of supplies to the city daily—greatly easing the matériel shortage faced by Twenty-First Army Group. Photographer unknown. Photo in the author's possession.

"By now the 51st Division had arrived and by means of waving a tea towel in the air we stopped them from shooting the lot of us." Leaving the medical officer, an orderly, and seven wounded, Thompson escorted the others toward the British lines. Along the way a stray German shell fell that killed Langner and four other men. Thompson soon turned the rest over to some men of the 51st Division.

During his time in Fontaine, Thompson had been impressed by the effective British shelling of the place. "The arrival of shells . . . was incessant—there was no pause between salvoes and the noise factor was very disquieting even below ground. There is certainly no truth that the Boche has got used to arty fire as they seemed to be even more disturbed then we were. Particularly effective were the LAA Bofors firing low airbursts; they did not know what this was and referred to it in hushed whispers as 'Panzers.' The tracers seemed to have a great moral effect."[27]

AS 56TH BRIGADE wound up its operations in the dying hours of September 10, the 51st (Highland) Infantry Division launched Astonia's phase two with 152nd Infantry Brigade's 5th Seaforth Highlander Battalion leading. The division was to eliminate Strongpoint 8 and establish a firm base on the northern edge of Forêt de Montgeon. Because the Flail and AVRE teams tasked with opening the division's three lanes through the minefield were to begin their work also at midnight, the Seaforths advanced down the rightmost lane in the 49th Division's Laura sector. As Strongpoint 8 could directly threaten the gapping teams, the Seaforths were expected to silence it before the Flails and AVRES reached the anti-tank ditch and came within range of its anti-tank guns.[28]

When the Seaforths reached the entrance to their assigned lane, its condition was reported as impassable to either wheeled or tracked vehicles. Consequently, although its attack was to have begun at 2359 hours, the battalion's commander ordered an immediate advance forty-four minutes early. 'C' Company led the way, with 'D' and 'A' Companies close behind. Persistent artillery fire dogged the men as they manhandled the heavier equipment, such as anti-tank guns, down the lane and across the anti-tank ditch where the earlier bridge had been destroyed. Still tracked by the German artillery, 'C' Company reached its forming-up position—the captured Strongpoint 5—at 0040 hours. The company then crept undetected along a communication trench that led directly from this strongpoint to the southern edge of Strongpoint 8. 'D' Company, meanwhile, closed in on the German position to 'C' Company's right at 0230 hours. Here the barbed wire fronting the position had been flattened by artillery fire. 'A' Company leapfrogged the two leading companies and within an hour reported Strongpoint 8 taken without serious fighting. Eighty per cent of the German weapons were found incapable of firing in the direction of the Seaforth's approach. The battalion rounded up 160 prisoners and many weapons, including two 88-millimetre guns. Its own casualties were 20 killed and 28 wounded, most due to artillery fire.

While the Seaforths had been carrying out their attack, three Flail troops of 'D' Squadron, 1st Lothians, and three AVRE troops from 16th Assault Squadron had started creating the division's three lanes through the minefield. The lanes were to be fifty yards apart, with Gin to the right, Rum in the centre, and Ale on the left. As the lane cutting was to occur in absolute darkness, artificial moonlight was employed for visibility. Engineers had also gone ahead of the teams to deploy green lights along the routes, and Bofors anti-aircraft guns fired tracer rounds to mark the boundaries of each lane for the thousand yards from the start line to the anti-tank ditch.

It was a very dark night with little cloud, so there was nothing for the searchlights creating artificial moonlight to reflect their beams off. This greatly diminished their effectiveness. Complications deploying the lights and some inaccurate firing by the Bofors caused the gapping teams to stray off course. The centre team ended up working in the area of the right-hand lane, while the team that should have been there was pushed west to a point where the anti-tank ditch bent away. Only the third team went to work in the right area.[29]

This third team was commanded by 16th Squadron's Major Ronald Watson. The Flails were 'B' Squadron's No. 1 Troop under Lieutenant Peter Carter. At 0010 hours on September 11, Carter realized the centre team was actually bearing on the lights marking the right lane. The lights that should have denoted the left lane were not seen at all. But Carter recognized from the configuration of the ground that they needed to be farther left and not drawn into the area where the centre lane was to be opened. Going ahead of the team on foot, Carter kept looking for the lights marking the left lane and finally concluded they must have been destroyed by artillery fire. Blundering through the dark, the lieutenant finally stumbled on the anti-tank ditch—having missed a track that was to have served as an early-warning marker.

An AVRE deployed its bridge across the ditch. Back in his Flail, Carter led No. 1 Troop over the bridge, and the tanks started flailing. They advanced and cleared a two-hundred-yard-long stretch of lane without detonating any mines. Carter ordered the operation ceased and directed the tanks toward 'B' Squadron's rally point. As the troop approached this point, it came under intense mortar and machine-gun fire. At the same time, the tank immediately behind Carter's blew up on a mine. Carter pulled back about fifty yards and reported the situation to Watson.

The centre team was commanded by 16th Assault Squadron's Major John Willott, with the Flails of 'B' Squadron's No. 2 Troop under Lieutenant William Loreham. Initially finding it easy to follow the green lights and the Bofors marking the same route, it was only as Loreham's tank came to the last light that he decided they were too far to the left and the Bofors were now firing in a different direction. Loreham decided the tracer fire was marking the correct route and advised Willott of this. The team changed direction, only to have Loreham realize as they approached the anti-tank ditch that they were now too far right. That they were well off course was confirmed by the presence of a large house that should not have been there. Skirting to the left of the building, the leading AVRE crew soon informed the team that they had fallen into a hole. This was actually the anti-tank ditch. Willott ordered a type of Churchill called a Snake forward. This tank bore a long hosepipe filled with explosive that could be pushed into a minefield and set off. The Snake deployed its hosepipe beyond the anti-tank ditch, and the charge was detonated. As the ground immediately beyond the ditch was now deemed cleared by this explosion, another AVRE deployed its bridge.

Up until then, Loreham later wrote, "the operation had gone without a hitch." But now his Flail was unable to get onto the bridge because there was a gap between the structure and the ground. Fascines were quickly deployed to fill the gap, and Loreham rolled across the bridge and started flailing. A few minutes later, Loreham realized his tank had bellied out on a stump and stopped. The tank behind moved past to take the lead, but was disabled when a two-inch pipe locked around its rotor. The three remaining Flails continued about twenty yards before two blew up on mines. With only one Flail remaining, Loreham directed it to join the Gin team to the right. The tank set off, creating a tank-width lane between the Rum and Gin lanes.

The Gin team was commanded by Major John Bromfield of 284th Assault Squadron, with the Flails of No. 4 Troop led by Lieutenant David Melville. This team, Melville later reported, had "arrived at the ditch exactly where we were meant to, but found the centre lane there, so we moved round the corner." Here they used a Snake and deployed their bridge. Again fascines had to be used to enable the Flails to gain the bridge deck. Melville crossed and flailed a lane through to the Montivilliers–Fontaine-la-Mallet road, where his tank blew up on a mine. Two Flails passed to the front, while another reported that its rotor was not working. Melville took over command of the last functioning Flail and began widening the path cleared by the two out front. Reaching their final assigned clearing point, Melville swung his tank about to widen the lane farther and was disabled by a mine. One of the other two Flails started to pass by and also blew up on a mine. Then both the tank that had experienced problems with its flail and the one following Melville were knocked out by mines. Melville and his crews abandoned their tanks and headed back to the ditch. En route, two men were wounded by shrapnel from shellfire.[30]

In the end, Gin and Rum lanes merged a short distance past the anti-tank ditch to form one lane, with Ale being about a hundred yards left of it. All of 'D' Squadron's Flails were out of action, and a field company of engineers came forward at 0225 hours to ensure the lanes were clear. Working under sporadic artillery and mortar fire, the engineers declared Rum in the centre clear to where it merged with Gin and continued to the south side of the minefield. At 0400 hours, the lane was declared fit for "marching personnel and by 0435 hours for vehicles."

First out of the lane were the 5th Battalion, Queen's Own Cameron Highlanders with 'D' Company leading, but its movement was slowed by heavy shelling. By 0600 hours, however, both 'D' Company and 'C' Company were relatively in the clear and closing on Strongpoint 11—the last significant German position on the Northern Plateau. A short firefight broke out, during which the Camerons found the No. 77 phosphorous grenade "very useful in mopping up this area which was honeycombed with emplacements and concrete shelters." About a hundred prisoners were taken.[31]

'D' Company's Major Alfred Parker, meanwhile, had established his headquarters in a concrete observation post on the edge of the strongpoint. Soon after, a telephone rang. Somewhat fluent in German, Parker answered and determined that the call was a routine check to ensure the line still functioned. Spontaneously, Parker asked the German if he could put the Le Havre garrison commander on the line. Although somewhat surprised, the German said he would ring back shortly. A few minutes later, the phone rang and Parker was speaking to Oberst Eberhard Wildermuth. Parker asked if "he wished to surrender."[32] A bemused Wildermuth replied "that his job was to lead the defence, that at the moment he was fairly busy, and that he had no time for interviews. He then hung up."[33] A report on the incident noted that there was "good reason to believe that other subscribers listened to this conversation and were thereby encouraged to expedite their arrangements for surrender." The report also noted that throughout the following day, there was no attempt by German artillery or mortar crews to fire on Parker's captured outpost. First light, meanwhile, found both the Camerons and Seaforths firmly ensconced in the outskirts of the heavily bomb-damaged ruins of Fontaine-la-Mallet.[34]

In the early-morning hours of September 11, Oberst Wildermuth was left frantically trying to develop a clear picture of what was developing in the centre of his defensive line. He soon realized the Northern Plateau was lost and the Southern Plateau jeopardized. Throughout the night, a vast dome of light cast by huge searchlights had eerily illuminated the German defences, "and under this artificial moonlight infantry and flame-throwing tanks" were "continuing their break-in . . . Command during the hours of darkness was almost impossible with means of communication, wireless and roads, hopelessly damaged. Companies thrown in for relief reached their assembly points late, and with considerable casualties." Hoping to retrieve a situation he considered probably doomed, Wildermuth placed the fortress reserve—3rd Battalion, 936th Grenadiers—under command of the teetering 1041st Grenadiers. The 936th were instructed to take up position on heights northeast of the road from Harfleur to Octville in preparation for launching a counterattack to regain control of Fontaine-la-Mallet.

Wildermuth had little artillery with which to support any counter-attack. At dawn, he was advised that only seventeen field and medium guns, along with six anti-aircraft guns able to fire landward, remained operational. Although his coastal artillery was intact and the gun crews there had suffered few casualties, the weapons were useless to him.[35]

15

Trifling Opposition

O PERATION ASTONIA'S NEXT stage called for a methodical advance by 152nd Infantry Brigade of 51st (Highland) Infantry Division west from Fontaine-la-Mallet to Les Monts-Trottins and then northwest to the village of Doudenéville. This would establish a large lodgement through which 153rd Brigade would then neutralize the gun positions west of Forêt de Montgeon.[1] But as both his division's attack and that of the 49th (West Riding) Infantry Division had gone so well, Major General Tom Rennie decided to cut straight to the 153rd Brigade's phase. At 0425 hours, Rennie ordered this brigade's 1st Gordon Highlanders to initiate the advance. 'B' Company was to push through Fontaine-la-Mallet and secure a bridgehead across the Fontaine River to the northeast of the forest. The rest of the battalion would pass through the forest and sweep up the gun positions to the northwest.

The Gordons were to be supported in this task by a tank squadron, two Crocodile troops, an AVRE troop, and a Flail troop, but the gaps through the minefield and anti-tank ditch were by this time so blocked with congestion, damaged equipment, or collapsed bridges that only the marching infantry could pass through. At 0615 hours, 'B' Company emerged from the last surviving gap in 49th Division's Laura area, while the rest of the battalion used Ale lane. Following behind the Gordons was 153rd Brigade's 2nd Battalion, the Seaforth

Highlanders—also lacking any supporting vehicles. Work, however, was under way to get the lanes cleared and pass the equipment through as quickly as possible.

As the Gordons entered Fontaine-la-Mallet, they met a strong German force, which 'B' Company tackled with a bayonet charge. The threat of cold steel prompted two hundred Germans to surrender at the cost of four or five British casualties. By 0750 hours, the Gordons had secured a bridge crossing the river east of the village's church. Forward movement through the village was complicated by the main road being completely obstructed by the rubble of buildings destroyed by bomber raids. 'B' Company was also tracked by fire from heavy machine-gun positions to the south and southeast of the village.

At 0730 hours, the skies overhead became cluttered with 171 bombers, arriving to carry out Bomber Command's last attack on Le Havre. They dropped 864 tons of bombs on the western part of the city.[2] With the skies clear, 2nd Tactical Air Force's rocket-firing Typhoon fighter-bombers were in constant action engaging targets "with their spectacular hissing projectiles," as one report described them.[3] In the 49th Division's operational sector alone, between 1015 hours and 1545 hours, Typhoons carried out directed rocket attacks on one pillbox, two strongpoints, two identified lightly defended positions, and a suspect large building.[4]

Much impressed by the bomber operations, Crocker thanked Air Chief Marshal Sir Arthur Harris. "Attack on Le Havre is going well," he signalled, "but is bound to be a slow and intricate business . . . Nobody could have given a better start than we were by Bomber Command. All ranks unanimous in their praise of absolute accuracy of bombing and timing on every occasion. Prisoners testify to its efficacy. On behalf of all ranks I [British] Corps wish to thank you for your whole-hearted co-operation. Would much appreciate if all crews taking part could be informed of admiration, appreciation, and gratitude of us all."[5]

In the Fontaine River valley, meanwhile, the Gordons' 'A' Company had passed through 'B' Company at the bridge and ran into a sharp fight on the eastern edge of the forest, when the 936th Grenadiers attempted to carry out Oberst Eberhard Wildermuth's ordered counterattack. The German counterattack was quickly broken, and the regiment's commander was among the "large numbers" of those who surrendered." As the Gordons proceeded through the forest, the 2nd Seaforths advanced out of Fontaine-la-Mallet on both sides of the road leading to Les Monts-Trottins. By 1100 hours, they had two companies on either side of the road lying in position to assault the small German blockhouse containing a gun position on Les Monts-Trottins.[6] That assault was put in at noon following a short artillery barrage, and soon the German positions at Les Mont-Trottins were declared clear—the defenders eager to surrender. The Seaforths carried on to Doudenéville, where hundreds of Germans, completely demoralized by the aerial bombardments and persistent artillery shelling, gave up.[7] A total of 634 Germans surrendered, while the Seaforths reported four men killed and ten wounded during their advance.[8] The Seaforths were now a thousand yards south of the German coastal defences near Octeville-sur-Mer.[9]

At 1230 hours, the nearby Gordons were reinforced by 'B' Squadron of the 144th Assault Squadron. This squadron consisted of a troop each of AVRES, Crocodiles, and Flails. Infantry patrols started moving westward into Forêt de Montgeon, as the Gordons' commander went forward on a reconnaissance to determine the best way of attacking the gun areas to the west.

Advancing along two tracks through the woods, the Gordons assaulted three suspected gun positions. Prior to the advance, the battalion commander asked for artillery support. This was denied, as it was believed some friendly forces might be in the area. The battalion, one report noted, replied that the "'friends' were shooting very accurately with 88-millimetre guns." In the end, it hardly mattered. The attack went in at 1430 hours, and by 1600 hours, all positions had been taken and another four hundred prisoners bagged.[10]

The two other battalions of 153rd Brigade, the 5th Black Watch and 5/7th Gordons, quickly passed through the forest and by early evening had penetrated, without serious opposition, into Le Havre's northwestern outskirts on the upper bench.[11] At the same time, the 154th Brigade's 7th Black Watch reached the edge of Le Havre's neighbourhood known as la Hève in reference to the adjacent Cap de la Hève, where a German coastal gun battery was situated. The infantry rode to the edge of town in Canadian Kangaroos but to continue the advance dismounted, as the streets were so badly blocked by bomb-destroyed buildings. Although they entered the heart of the built-up area at 2130 hours, it was decided to leave mopping up and capturing the gun positions until morning.[12]

JUST AS 51ST Division had pushed out from Fontaine-la-Mallet, 49th Division had simultaneously launched a two-pronged advance. On its left, 147th Brigade was to seize the Southern Plateau. To the right, the 146th Brigade would punch through Harfleur and close in on Le Havre from the east. The Lézarde River ran between the two brigades.

Harfleur was defended by four strongpoints, of which two dominated the road running from the town to Le Havre and were considered the most important objectives. The main strongpoint to the right was code-named Oscar and the one on the left, Oswald. The first was believed to be held by fifty Germans and the other by seventy. The ground from the British lines to the strongpoints sloped gently downward. An orchard that would have provided some cover had been completely cleared away by the Germans, so any daylight movement could be seen from the strongpoints and also from the Southern Plateau. Intelligence had believed that a minefield protected the front of the strongpoints. When patrols failed to find any trace of it, however, the brigade's intelligence staff decided the field, "on somewhat inadequate evidence," could be written off as containing only dummy charges.

Because of the open ground, Brigadier John Walker decided to attack at 0530 hours—just before first light. The attack was supported by a thirty-three-minute artillery concentration on the strongpoints.[13] Leading the attack was the 1/4th King's Own Yorkshire Light Infantry, followed by Churchill tanks of 'A' Squadron, 9th Royal Tanks; two Flail troops of the 22nd Dragoons' 'C' Squadron; a Crocodile troop of 'A' Squadron, 141st Royal Armoured Corps; and the AVRES of No. 2 Troop, 222nd Assault Squadron.[14] One tank squadron was to provide covering fire from overlooking high ground, and the Flails were kept in reserve for deployment in daylight should a minefield be discovered.

The continued insistence that there was no fear of a minefield was baffling. During the night, 'B' Company—which was to attack

Oswald—had attempted to probe the strongpoint with a patrol that stumbled into a minefield and sustained thirteen casualties. The company commander, Major A.B. Little, had immediately asked for the attack to be delayed and the Flails deployed as soon as it grew light. Walker refused, because that would mean losing the artillery support, the timing of which could not be altered.[15]

At 0530 hours, 'B' Company crossed its start line and advanced into the cleared orchard area. Within moments, it was mired in a minefield, and nine men became casualties to s-mines.[16] As the men picked their way through the minefield, the Germans in the strongpoint offered no resistance. But when the company reached the wire fronting Oswald, its garrison came to life with automatic weapons firing at short range, which pinned the British troops in place.[17] Two of 'B' Company's three officers—including Little—were wounded. Reorganizing into two platoons, the company scrambled back to its start line. In all, the company suffered fourteen casualties.[18]

On the left, 'C' Company had come to within six hundred yards of Oscar before getting hung up in a minefield at 0627 hours and then pinned down by machine-gun and mortar fire.[19] Lieutenant Colonel Thomas Harrison-Thompson ordered the company to also fall back to the start line, so he could organize a new effort supported by tanks and led by Flails.[20]

The renewed effort was quickly assembled, with 'A' Squadron's 9th Royal Tank Regiment's Churchills leading and bringing heavy fire to bear on both strongpoints. Their fire was so intense and accurate that it seemed to silence the German garrisons.[21] As the tanks took up position to provide covering fire, three Flails of No. 4 Troop started opening a lane through the minefield. Despite two Flails bogging down, the lane was cleared at about 0830 hours. 'C' Company, following hot on the heels of the Flails, burst through, and Oscar was taken by 0930 hours.[22] Oscar yielded fifty-seven prisoners.[23]

With Oscar silenced, the new attack on Oswald was to begin, with 'D' Company replacing 'B' Company. More Flails were to create a lane through which the infantry and supporting tanks and Crocodiles could pass. Just before the attack started, a message from Oswald's commander was received. He sought a one-hour armistice to allow evacuation of wounded and burial of German dead. The commander was identified as being in charge of No. 6 Company of the 1041st Grenadiers.[24] Walker rebuffed the request but offered a respite until noon to surrender.

At 1230 hours, with tanks again providing covering fire, a troop of Flails entered the minefield and cleared two lanes while detonating fifty mines.[25] Although two Flails were disabled by mines, the moment the lanes were opened, at 1305 hours, the Crocodiles rumbled through with 'D' Company in trail. When the Crocodiles flamed the forward edge of the strongpoint and two outposts on either side, the garrison immediately surrendered.[26] At 1335 hours, sixty-three prisoners emerged with hands raised.

Both Oscar and Oswald were found to be "of considerable strength, having deep concrete dugouts and including two 81-millimetre mortars and one 75-millimetre anti-tank gun in their armament. The battalion considered that 'if the defenders had been determined to fight to the end, great difficulty would have been experienced in capturing them.'" Instead, both positions had fallen relatively easily. With their capture, the other two strongpoints soon surrendered. The British infantry battalion had suffered a total of fifty-six casualties, about 70 per cent men who were wounded or killed by mines.[27]

With the strongpoints eliminated, 146th Brigade's advance into Harfleur proceeded rapidly, as the 4th Lincolnshire Battalion advanced into the town by two routes. Although four roadblocks barred the main road, 'A' Company took this route. To help breech the roadblocks, the infantry was supported by two AVRES, an armoured bulldozer, and sappers of the 294th Field Company. The sappers deployed bee-hive-shaped explosive charges powerful enough to penetrate concrete fortifications. These and the fire of the AVRE Petards made short work of the roadblocks. The bulldozer then cleared away the debris and filled numerous craters to open the road to vehicles.

The main body of the Lincolns skirted to the south of Harfleur via a narrow lane and cross-country movement. Although harassed persistently by machine-gun fire from concrete bunkers inside Harfleur, only fourteen infantry casualties were suffered. Each bunker was systematically eliminated by AVRES.[28] From Harfleur, the Lincolns found four intact bridges that enabled easy crossing of the Lézarde River. They then advanced south along a line that paralleled the Canal Vauban and by nightfall had penetrated into the outskirts of Le Havre due east of the port.[29]

WHILE 146TH BRIGADE had been fighting through Harfleur, 49th Division's 147th Brigade had tackled clearing the Southern Plateau to the immediate north. This brigade was to advance alongside the left flank of the division's 56th Brigade from Montivilliers, cross the Fontaine River, and then secure the plateau. The advance was to be led by the 11 Royal Scottish Fusiliers (RSF). As the road running from Montivilliers to a Y-junction close to the river was found to be heavily mined, the operation got off to a slow start. Although the RSF started advancing at 0800 hours, their pace was a virtual crawl as they waited for sappers ahead to clear mines. It took two hours to reach the junction.

Thereafter matters proceeded briskly, as they found the 2nd Essex holding the bridge won the night before and were able to establish a secure bridgehead on the Southern Plateau by 1300 hours. Expecting only slight opposition, the RSF commander volunteered to carry on the clearing operation, rather than lose time having the 7th Duke of Wellington Regiment pass through according to plan. The RSF went forward on a broad front with six AVRES in support. By 1440 hours, having met "practically no opposition," the RSF had advanced about a mile and a quarter. They carried on to where they were looking down on Harfleur to the south. It was 2030 hours and the battalion was meeting nothing "but trifling opposition." That changed at dusk, when the leading company came under fire from a heavy machine gun and was forced to take cover. With night closing in, the battalion commander decided it was too late for a coordinated attack on the position, so the RSF withdrew out of range and awaited the dawn to finish clearing the Southern Plateau.

The RSF taking over operations on the plateau had presented Brigadier Henry Wood with an opportunity to advance the 49th Division's operational schedule with a direct thrust by the 7th Duke of Wellington Regiment (7 DWR) through to Le Havre's outskirts. At 1115 hours, this battalion advanced from Montivilliers with two companies riding in the Canadian Kangaroos and the other two marching. When two Kangaroos were damaged by mines, the entire battalion continued on by foot. As mines disabled several more vehicles, it became clear the track they were following would have to be re-swept to allow safe usage. The regiment was directed to return to Montivilliers and pass through to the Fontaine River via the still-operational Mary gap on the brigade's extreme left.[30]

Fortunately, standing by next to the bridge held by 2nd Essex were the 2nd Gloucesters of 56th Brigade. Learning of the 7 DWR's setback, the Gloucesters' Lieutenant Colonel Francis Butterworth volunteered to carry out the planned advance and was quickly placed under 147th Brigade's command. 'C' Company mounted onto tanks of 7th Royal Tank Regiment's 'B' Squadron to lead off.

Unbeknownst to the Gloucesters, out at their front was a small party led by 34th Army Tank Brigade's Brigadier W.S. Clarke and artillery officer Lieutenant Colonel M.W. Pope. The two men and a few aides walked up the road leading to Le Havre and "decided there was no obstacle to proceeding into the town." Hurrying back to where two of the brigade's tank regiments had assembled, Clarke drafted a reconnaissance troop equipped with turretless Stuart tanks, known as Honeys. With Clarke in a jeep and Pope in a scout car bearing a wireless set registered on his artillery regimental net, the small force rushed toward Le Havre. Zipping around the southern edge of Forêt de Montgeon for a distance of almost two miles and into the city out-skirts without incident, Clarke's group was flagged down by civilians who warned there were two anti-tank guns about four hundred to a thousand yards ahead that were hidden from sight behind the crest of a small hill. Clarke suggested that he and Pope go forward on foot to situate the guns. As the two men started out, a group of Germans were spotted crossing a side street to the left. The crews of the Honeys engaged the fleeing Germans with small-arms fire. Immediately, a high-explosive shell burst nearby, confirming the presence of the anti-tank guns. Pope ran to his scout car and called for a "Mike" target shoot—entailing all the regiment's 25-pounders—on where he thought the gun was hidden. He then had the artillery walk two more full "Mike" concentrations of fire along the road at two-hundred-yard intervals.

Dashing into a house and upstairs to an upper room, Pope "located an anti-tank gun about four hundred yards away in the area of the first Mike target and saw Germans attempting to bring up a truck to get the gun away. Another burst . . . on the original target location put the Germans to flight," Pope wrote later.

Clarke's party had by now been joined by 'C' Company and 'B' Squadron. One of the Churchill tanks rumbled up the street, with Clarke and Pope walking alongside. Pope pointed out the anti-tank gun's location, but before the Churchill could engage it the German gun crew snapped off two rounds that fell short. The Churchill crew lashed back with Besa machine-gun fire and two 75-millimetre armour-piercing rounds. The anti-tank gun ceased firing, and a white flag popped out of the entrance to a civilian air-raid shelter next to it. Twenty-four Germans, including two officers, emerged and Clarke took their surrender. A second 75-millimetre gun was discovered on the opposite side of the road from the knocked-out weapon. This gun was "hidden beneath a pile of timbers and boards from a wooden house brought down on top of it by the shell fire." A small 20-millimetre anti-aircraft gun was also discovered nearby.[31]

Except for this "incident," as one 49th Division report referred to it, no further opposition was encountered, and by 1815 hours the Gloucesters and tankers had reached their assigned objective.[32] This was the Place de la Liberté, a square in the northeast sector of Le Havre, where the British troops were met by a small group of civilians and a larger force of FFI fighters. The latter proved useful in helping escort the growing number of German prisoners back to the British rear.

Lieutenant Colonel Butterworth soon arrived and gained permission from division to continue the advance through to Fort de Tourneville—one of the two main German defensive positions within the town. 'D' Company, mounted on another troop of tanks, pushed through to the large Sainte-Marie Cemetery immediately east of the fort without incident, but was then fired on by a gun positioned in the fort's southeast corner. The infantry piled off the tanks, which then engaged the gun. Advancing through the cemetery, using crypts and tombs for cover, a platoon closed on the fortress wall. The platoon's sergeant then engaged and damaged the gun with three shots from a PIAT gun.[33]

Meanwhile, a hastily formed "battle group" of infantry and tanks had worked round to the north side of the cemetery. But when the infantry jumped down from the tanks, they found the ground littered with s-mines, and heavy fire started coming from the northeast corner of the fort. With darkness closing in, Butterworth ordered a withdrawal into the cemetery, with plans to launch a coordinated assault come morning.

The 2nd Gloucesters now reverted to command of 56th Brigade, whose other battalions had followed close on their heels. Between the cemetery and the original objective within Le Havre, the 2nd South Wales Borderers established a defensive line, while the 2nd Essex were concentrated next to the southeast corner of Forêt de Montgeon.[34]

BY LATE AFTERNOON of September 11, Oberst Eberhard Wildermuth was receiving nothing but a "toll of bad news." Forêt de Montgeon was lost, the main defensive line to Doudenéville was rolled up, and tanks were breaking into the upper part of Le Havre and overrunning numerous battery positions. Hoping to establish a resistance base in the suburb of Graville, immediately south of the Canal Vauban and east of the port facilities, Wildermuth went to the 1041st Grenadiers (1041 GR) headquarters there. He was still en route when British troops broke into the area from the forest and from Harfleur. After initially hiding out in a church, Wildermuth spent several hours returning to his original headquarters. Twice he narrowly averted capture only because civilians warned him where the nearby British troops were situated. Any thought of continued organized resistance was abandoned. At nightfall, Wildermuth shifted his battle headquarters to Fort Tourneville.

The early-morning hours of September 12 brought only more gloom. Local defences in the Graville area had been smashed. Tanks were growling outside Fort Tourneville and seemed to prowl freely wherever the British liked. Wildermuth's artillery commander, Oberst Erwin von Steinhardt, was isolated in Fort Ste. Addresse. He understood that the batteries of Cap de la Hève were lost. A grenade there had reportedly ignited the ammunition of one of the large coastal guns and blown the "battery commander and his men to Kingdom come. Nothing was heard from Octeville or the eastern sector. The writing was clearly and boldly on the wall. Organized defence of the fortress had come to an end.

"Together with the commander of 1041 GR, the local flak commander, and a few men, Wildermuth set up his last stand in the gardens between Fort Tourneville and the Naval Intelligence Station. When daylight came artillery fire had almost ceased and only intermittent rifle fire could be heard." Wildermuth waited on the British.[35]

Realizing the Germans were nearly finished, both the 51st and 49th Divisions set out at first light to mop up "with vigour" the remaining resistance.[36] A 49th Division report caught the tenor of September 12 operations. "Whereas the first 24 hours of the battle produced much hard fighting and our troops often met determined resistance," the report stated, "the last 24 hours was a period of small isolated local engagements in built-up areas and of wholesale surrenders."[37]

On every front, when the British approached an objective still strongly defended and capable of a determined fight, the Germans simply surrendered or did so after only token resistance. On the 51st Division front, an ad hoc force that had assembled during the night headed toward the German military airport at Octeville with orders to then cut west to the coast. Led by Major Gray Skelton of the Northamptonshire Yeomanry's 'A' Squadron, with an infantry section from the Derbyshire Yeomanry, this unit was dubbed Grayforce. Approaching the airport at 0900 hours, Grayforce swept past the airport and closed in on the nearby large coastal guns and bunkers, where they were greeted by a flurry of white flags. Three officers and 357 Kreigsmarine artillerymen were taken prisoner without a shot fired, and this strong portion of Hitler's Atlantic Wall was eliminated.

At Octeville, more than a thousand Germans were dug in around the town and the nearby coastal battery. This was the 2nd Seaforth's objective. Supporting the infantry was 'B' Squadron of the East Riding Yeomanry under command of Captain Henri Salman, a Belgian who spoke fluent German. Approaching the major German strongpoints, Salman dismounted and with revolver drawn led the force forward while shouting at the Germans to come out. They emerged in droves with hands raised.

Inside Le Havre itself, the 154th Brigade's 7th Black Watch cleared up resistance in the la Hève area. This meant little more than rounding up prisoners who surrendered as soon as the supporting tanks shot at any concrete pillboxes encountered. By 1100 hours, Cap de la Hève and the surrounding neighbourhood were declared secure, with more than eleven hundred Germans captured.[38]

In the 153rd Brigade's sector, the only opposition was at Fort Ste. Addresse. As the 5/7th Gordons closed on the fort, the Germans detonated a series of electronically ignited mines. This gave the Gordons sufficient pause, and they decided to bring up supporting armour that included Flails and Crocodiles. During the wait, the battalion's anti-tank guns and mortars banged away at the fort. In the late morning, an explosion—believed to be the result of a lucky mortar hit on an ammunition dump—tore a breach in the stout outer wall. At 1500 hours, the Gordons with supporting tanks and Crocodiles were ready to punch through the breach. The moment the advance began, however, a white flag shot up. Seven officers and 242 other ranks surrendered. Among them was Wildermuth's artillery commander. A well-stocked wine cellar was discovered, which the brigade's second-in-command quickly secured.[39]

For 49th Division's 146th Brigade, the greatest complication consisted of trying to find a usable route from the eastern flank of the city through to the port. The combination of Allied bombing and German demolitions had rendered all bridges over the canals and railroad impassable. A cross-country route between the main road leading in from Harfleur and the Canal de Tancarville was finally found. At 0800, the 4th Lincolns, with 'B' Squadron of the 9th Royal Tanks on the right and the Hallamshire Battalion supported by 'C' Squadron and two AVRES on the left, advanced. They soon entered the lower part of Le Havre—a maze of high-rise worker flats, warehouses, repair shops, and adjacent docks. This area was overlooked by the escarpment where the higher, newer part of the town was situated, and some fire came from positions there that had yet to be cleared. The Lincolns also encountered a number of German strongpoints containing anti-tank guns and machine guns, but most fell after only a short fight. Cratering of roads caused by the bombing and debris from ruined houses had to be circumnavigated, and progress was consequently slow. But finally, the Hallams were well into the dockyards, where the last German ges-ture of defiance was to set off several enormous explosions to destroy some sluice gates.[40]

The final act in Le Havre's capture had begun at 0800 hours. Simultaneously, the Gloucesters with 7th Royal Tanks 'B' Squadron supporting, and the South Wales Borderers backed by the 7th Royal's 'A' Squadron, started advancing—in the words of a 34th Tank Brigade report—in "a race through the town to the sea."[41] The race began slowly for the Gloucesters facing Fort de Tourneville. Mines blocked the road leading to the fort, and an anti-tank gun started shooting the moment infantry and tanks moved out from the cemetery. The tankers lashed back with a ten-minute 75-millimetre gun bombardment. That was enough to persuade the garrison to surrender. Most of the four hundred Germans bagged had been waiting passively out of the line of fire, with bags packed and ready to go into captivity.[42]

At 1200 hours, Wildermuth—who had been wounded in the left thigh by a splinter from a tank shell fired during the bombardment—learned of the garrison's surrender at his nearby headquarters in a concrete bunker. The strongpoint at his bunker no longer had a functioning anti-tank gun. Wildermuth knew it was over and ordered the surrender. He had no intention of asking infantry to fight "tanks with bare hands." In this way, his British interrogators concluded, he "had transformed the High Command's precept of a fight to the last man to his own concept of fight to the last" anti-tank gun. "The difference was fundamental. It marked the civilian from the soldier."[43] Found in bed, wearing pajamas adorned with his medals, Wildermuth surrendered to a troop commander of the 7th Royal Tanks 'B' Squadron.[44] Although he formally offered the Le Havre garrison's surrender, Wildermuth was not able to broadcast such an order to the isolated pockets of Germans still holding out. So each had to be dealt with in turn.

Scattered resistance continued throughout the day, particularly in the vicinity of the port. But at 2220 hours, when Lieutenant Colonel

Hart Dyke commanding the Hallams led a platoon of men onto the port's mole to tackle the bunkers there, they found eighty Germans only waiting to surrender. The battle for Le Havre was over.[45]

ALTHOUGH THE STRONGPOINT on the mole was not secured until the evening, 1 British Corps conveniently declared Le Havre's fall to have happened within forty-eight hours of the opening of ground operations in the late afternoon of September 10. Field Marshal Bernard Montgomery set this declaration in stone, writing, "Le Havre constituted one of the strongest fortresses of the Atlantic Wall and had been provided with most elaborate concrete defences, extensive minefields, but it had been reduced after forty-eight hours of fighting."[46]

An official British report declared there was "no doubt that the speed and comparative ease with which the operation was accomplished were largely due to the absence of a determined will to resist on the part of the garrison, and that this condition was created by a sense of complete isolation by land, sea, and air, culminating in the concentrated and undisturbed bombardment of the defences by the Royal Artillery, the Royal Navy, and above all, the Royal Air Force. The Corps plan, both in its conception and execution, made full use of this condition; all available arms were employed to their best advantage; the momentum of the assault was never permitted to relax; before it had time to recover the garrison was overwhelmed."

One analyst observed that the operation entailing two infantry divisions heavily supported by the Funnies of 79th Armoured Division "afforded a first large-scale opportunity to practice the armoured assault-team technique which formed part of the inspired conceptions which had led to the setting up of that novel formation, Flails . . . to thresh a path through the minefields, AVRES with their bombardment Petards and miscellaneous equipment to bridge and overcome . . . anti-tank obstacles and Crocodiles to bring terror to the heart of the defenders, constituted a redoubtable trio which carried all before them. Despite very bad going and by virtue of great gallantry [of 79th Armoured Division crews] the formidable fortifications were overrun and the lives of many infantrymen were saved. The enemy condemned the Crocodiles as unfair and un-British and one officer reported that a whole platoon caught in the open had been burned to death. A Crocodile commander who witnessed this episode, one of few occasions throughout the campaign when the enemy stood up to flame in the open without instantaneous surrender, has described the horror of the blazing, shrieking, demented Germans. Some of his crew were physically sick at the sight."[47]

Although it was clear the Crocodiles seriously reduced the German will to fight, their presence might have inadvertently reduced the actual numbers of enemy that would have been killed had each strongpoint been taken by infantry assault alone. Out of a garrison finally set at about 12,000, only about 600 were believed to have been killed. This included those who died during the Allied bombing raids. The final surrender tally was 11,302, of which the 49th Division accounted for 6,900 and the 51st Division 4,400.

In comparison, 1 Corps losses were amazingly light. The 49th Division reported only 62 men killed, 3 missing, and 208 wounded, while 51st Division had 35 fatalities and 103 wounded. The supporting armoured units had just 16 men killed and 32 wounded.[48]

FIRST CANADIAN ARMY staff were quick to embark on studying what had worked well and what less so during the operation. The bombing was clearly disappointing, serving more to shake morale than cause significant German losses or damage to fortifications and weapons. On September 15, Squadron Leader Abel of 2nd Tactical Air Force's Operational Research Section toured various German positions pinpointed for bombing. Damage to one battery containing four 155-millimetre guns in open emplacements was typical. Two of the gun emplacements had a bomb strike next to them, with a resulting large crater from which a mass of soil and debris had then been thrown upon the gun. While each gun remained serviceable, its crew had been unable to either fire or traverse it owing to the debris that they were unable to clear away before the position was captured. The third emplacement was untouched. A direct hit in the centre of the fourth emplacement resulted in the large gun being "blown clean out of" it. The gun "appeared to have landed close by and right side up without having sustained severe damage, although the wheels were badly smashed." Of two twin 20-millimetre flak guns attached to the battery, one was unscathed, and the other "wrecked by a near miss."

Abel also examined several heavily protected coastal batteries and found that little damage had been caused to these concrete and steel emplacements. One battery had been the subject of a fifty-bomber attack on September 10, but none of the guns had suffered damage. A direct hit on the steel roof of a 360-millimetre gun still under construction did hole the roof and tear up some steel flooring, but the gun was untouched. One battery's concrete emplacements had a crack running about fifteen feet across it that was a few inches deep, but the "inside of the emplacement was entirely undamaged despite a near miss twenty feet from the opening."[49]

Ultimately the analysts, while admitting the bombing caused little damage to targeted guns or casualties, took heart in its demoralizing effect, emphasizing the confession of one prisoner that being bombed had been the "most depressing experience of his life." They also learned from field examination and interrogation of artillery officers that damage to lines of communication had been so extreme that artillery commander Oberst Erwin von Steinhardt had early in the battle "lost practically all communication with his subordinates and found it impossible to control his resources." Communication loss appeared to add to the "demoralizing feeling of isolation among his men."

Without considering the great destruction the bombing wrought on Le Havre itself and civilian casualties, the analysts were concerned with the negative impact the bombing had on battle operations. Fontaine-la-Mallet had deliberately been subjected only to bombing by fragmenting explosives to prevent deep cratering that would obstruct the advance. Yet the town was "reduced to a shambles and was a serious obstacle for some hours. This type of bombing removes landmarks, such as small clumps of trees, and covers tracks with thick dust. This tends to cause lack of direction in the dark. Cratering again put a number of tanks and AVRES temporarily out of action."[50]

Whatever the military advantage gained by the bombing, the cost to the people of Le Havre was terrible. Eighty per cent of the city lay in ruins, nothing but vast swaths of rubble from which a lone structure—often just a gutted shell—rose. About ten thousand homes had been destroyed along with most public buildings, five churches, two hospitals, and thirty-four primary schools. The final count yielded 5,126 citizens killed and another 31,000 rendered homeless. "We are liberated," one civilian said, "but we no longer have houses." A rumour circulated that the city and its port had been deliberately destroyed so that after the war it would not compete for shipping business with Southampton.[51]

Artillery had contributed little additional damage to the city and its effect against the German strongpoints again largely only added to the demoralization factor. The Germans had expected the 77,000 estimated mines encircling Le Havre to seriously delay the Allied attack. So the appearance and effectiveness of the Flails in opening lanes through the minefields was a nasty shock.

So too was the attack's speed, scale, and unrelenting intensity. The analysts attributed much credit to time taken "for planning on all levels, and for the complete integration of all sub-units who have to work together ... Three full days were available on this occasion. This was ample for the gun tanks and infantry, but only just sufficient for the Flails, AVRES, and Crocodiles."

Although lanes through minefields had been successfully created, it was realized that this had been a close-run thing and that in future such undertakings should be more fully planned. "For a variety of reason, Flails may be severely handicapped. AVRE bridges may be laid but are easily dislodged by traffic; snakes are unwieldy and may be prematurely exploded. A reserve of all these weapons is essential, and reduces the number of lanes which can be attempted. To ensure against complete failure, both in the initial stage and as the operation progresses, it seems essential that some crossings and lanes should be made by [engineers operating] behind a local infantry bridgehead."

They also were less pleased with the night attack. While Astonia proved that night operations were "practicable," they considered it "open to question whether this is preferable to a daylight assault. It has the advantage of affording concealment during the forming up and approach phases, but once started, the inevitable noisiness of a mechanized assault makes further concealment of the point of attack unlikely. Darkness will not then prevent the enemy's defensive fire and fixed-line weapons being effectively applied. Conversely, the accurate application of the fire of our supporting troops is prejudiced.

"A mechanical assault is inherently a complicated business, and the difficulties of control, of maintaining direction, of adjusting errors and overcoming unforeseen hazards are immensely greater at night. It is believed, in principle, that the conditions in which it is staged should be those which make for ease of control and co-operation, i.e. the ground and timing must be selected primarily to suit the specialist mechanized units concerned. The simpler and more limited the task or objective, the more practicable it is to assault in darkness. It is certain, however, that at least one rehearsal over an exact model of the enemy defences, will be essential if, for some reason, night is chosen for the mechanized 'break-in.'

"The main lesson in the use of Flails was that they cannot be expected to provide anything like complete clearance. In spite of their heavy casualties, however, they made possible the 'break-in' on both divisional fronts."

One sobering fact was that in the initial phase of the break-in, infantry "must be prepared to operate . . . without any vehicles at all and therefore without their close support weapons, tanks, and Crocodiles."

Another point the analysts emphasized was that "although actual defences were formidable and well-sited, the degree of resistance put up by the defenders was not impressive. In particular, the scarcity of effective anti-tank guns was noticeable, and the failure of the counter-artillery measures (due largely to the dislocation of communications as a result of air and counter-battery bombardment) was almost complete. Without these factors, i.e. a half-hearted garrison and a thorough subjugation of hostile artillery, success would have been less rapid and much more costly."[52]

All this analysis was intended to provide information and guidance for First Canadian Army's forthcoming operations to reduce the other channel ports of Dunkirk, Boulogne, and Calais.

16

A Lot to Crack

OVER THE COURSE of September 13, the 49th (West Riding) Infantry Division and 51st (Highland) Infantry Division both pulled out of the ruins of Le Havre to rest areas. The city was turned over to the British 4th Special Service Brigade. By 0940 hours, No. 41 Commando had taken control of the city's upper half and No. 48 Commando the lower half. The commandos quickly put German prisoners to work excavating civilian dead from the ruins and burying them. Receiving a report that there were civilians buried alive in one area of ruins, two hundred Germans tried in vain to find them.[1]

Teams of American engineers assigned to get the port up and running also arrived. Le Havre's capture had not provided Field Marshal Bernard Montgomery the port he so badly needed, because SHAEF had long ago designated it for American use. Montgomery, who could normally be counted on to dispute any decision that compromised Twenty-First Army Group operations, lodged no objection, because Le Havre was almost as far to the rear as the main British Rear Maintenance Area at Bayeux. With the Germans still firmly in control of the Scheldt Estuary, and thus denying use of Antwerp, Montgomery's immediate need for a channel port remained acute. Boulogne was more important to him than either Calais or Dunkirk. Only Boulogne could serve as a terminal in France for a Pluto cross-channel fuel pipeline.

First Canadian Army had not been able to move against Boulogne until Le Havre was taken, however, because all the specialized and mighty armour and artillery formations required for breaking into a fortress were tied up there.[2] The day Le Havre fell, 79th Armoured Division units started reorganizing for an almost immediate move toward Boulogne. The 1st Lothians and Border Yeomanry, for example, spent two days recovering their salvageable Flails from the battlefield and then left for Boulogne on September 15. 'B' Squadron was the exception. It had been so badly shot up during Operation Astonia that re-equipping was necessary, so the decision was made to have 'B' Squadron sit out the attack on Boulogne and then lead the following assault on Calais.[3]

In Le Havre, meanwhile, the extent of damage to the port was such that the American engineering teams were hard put to render it operational. Harbour basins and quaysides all had to be swept for mines and demolition charges. In three days the entrance to the port was cleared, and this enabled ships of up to 2,500 tons to offload troops and supplies onto adjacent beaches. Three days later the port, according to one Royal Navy report, was "declared clear of mines with the exception of a few one ton demolition charges, fortunately unexploded, which could be hoisted on to the quays and rendered harmless without difficulty. One hundred and sixty-five wrecks, wrecked bridges and other obstructions, however, still blocked the waterways, and for some time the port was of limited value for the landing of supplies."[4] It would be October 9 before the first large American Liberty freighters began to make deliveries. Even then, as the cranes had all been demolished, the heavy crates in which the supplies were packed had to first be landed in Britain, then unpacked, put into smaller packets, and ferried across to Le Havre. Daily deliveries would seldom exceed five thousand tons, but Le Havre was still considered vital to the American supply stream.[5]

EVEN AS THE battle for Le Havre had been under way, 2nd Canadian Infantry Division had continued its effort, begun on September 7, to wrest Dunkirk from German hands. The lack of 79th Armoured Division's specialized tanks and heavy artillery support, however, turned this into a dispiriting and costly undertaking. Worsening matters, the ten-thousand-strong German garrison was clearly made of sterner stuff than that of Le Havre. Extensive flooding of the low ground complicated movement and channelled it onto raised roads, and the fortified outposts guarding the city were well positioned and strongly held. Two of the division's brigades had been tasked with taking Dunkirk. From the southwest and south, 5th Brigade had managed to force the Germans out of the fortified villages of Loon-Plage and Coppenaxfort by the evening of September 9. This success little reduced the size of the German perimeter or its defensive strength. Virtually the entire ten miles of the perimeter, which extended an average of three miles from the town's centre, was protected by an extensive network of outer defences. In the 5th Brigade sector, the German defences were anchored on Mardick—three miles northeast of Loon-Plage and near the coast—and Spycker, which lay a mile to the northwest of Coppenaxfort. The Calgary Highlanders were concentrated before Mardick, and the Black Watch faced Spycker—each patrolling aggressively to gather intelligence on their defences in preparation for all-out assaults. Throughout this interlude, which lasted until September 12, all three regiments endured during the day near constant shell and mortar fire that was accurately directed by observers stationed in the strongpoints overlooking the Canadian-held ground. Some of this fire came from coastal batteries capable of rotating landward. German infantry was also constantly infiltrating into ground cleared earlier, requiring renewed mopping-up exercises.

Operating in the coastal area north of Dunkirk, 6th Brigade had also made little progress. Having by September 9 cleared an eight-mile stretch of coast from Nieuport to La Panne, the brigade's main effort on September 10 had focused on continuing an advance toward a two-mile-wide line from the coast next to Bray Dunes Plage inland to the village of Ghyvelde. The Queen's Own Cameron Highlanders were to advance along the coast. Operating on their left would be Les Fusiliers Mont-Royal. The day before this advance, the Camerons had discovered a series of deserted casemates just inside the Belgian border. That night, they provided a welcome shelter when the Germans started blasting their position with a heavy coastal gun and several anti-aircraft guns likely of 88-millimetre calibre from positions near Bray Dunes Plage.

At the same time as these two regiments advanced toward Dunkirk, the South Saskatchewan Regiment was to clear the coastal area to the north and northwest of Nieuport, where the Germans held a series of fortifications. Movement here was difficult because the sand dunes and beaches were thickly sown with mines and covering machine-gun posts. A mile up the coast from Nieuport stood a fort known to be held in strength and designated as the battalion's objective for September 10.[6]

This main fort was a large cement bastion well camouflaged amid the sand dunes, with gun ports facing in all directions. It was pro-tected by several smaller strongpoints and concrete pillboxes. 'A' and 'B' Companies advanced at 0400 hours, but were driven back by intense fire well short of the fort and withdrew after suffering light casualties.[7] The company commanders reported to battalion commander Major George Buchanan that the pillboxes and main fort appeared to be linked by tunnels.

A new attack was planned for 'A' Company to tackle the fort alone at 1930 hours, with two artillery batteries of 6th Field Regiment, the 6-pounders of the anti-tank platoon, and six 40-millimetre Bofors anti-aircraft guns providing fire support.[8] To plan the artillery shoot, the regiment's intelligence officer, Lieutenant B.A. Urquhart, and the 6th Field's FOO, Captain George McLean, set up in the steeple of a church that provided good observation of the German position. When Urquhart momentarily let the end of the telescope he was using slip out to where it reflected sunlight, a German crew manning a 6-inch gun responded immediately with an armour-piercing shell that ripped into the steeple just inches below where the two men were perched. "Never did men scramble down ladders so fast and hardly had they reached the ground floor when the steeple was torn off completely by a second shell," Buchanan wrote.

In the afternoon, Brigadier Guy Gauvreau arrived to discuss the operation with Buchanan and "decided to send in an ultimatum to the fort rather than use up more lives attacking the cement walls." Having discovered a Belgian woman who admitted being the fort commander's girlfriend, Gauvreau drafted a note to the commander and sent her to deliver it. The note demanded he surrender or face being subjected to aerial bombardment.[9] The bombardment was an empty threat, as a request for 2nd Tactical Air Force to attack the position with Typhoons had been rejected. The German major's response stated in German, "There is no question of it," and added in English, "It is indisgustable."

As the time for the attack neared, FOO McLean delivered the unwelcome news that each field regiment was restricted to firing just twenty-five rounds per gun per day.[10] This was because First Canadian Army, particularly II Corps, had been put on serious ammunition rationing in order to free supply for the forthcoming Operation Market Garden and the attack on Le Havre. The two batteries supporting the Sasks had already fired their allotment, so there would be no gun support prior to 'A' Company's advance. Buchanan decided that the advance would occur in two stages. First, it would gain the bank of sand dunes that formed a kind of ridge looking toward the fort. Here gun positions would be identified for the 6-pounders and Bofors, which would then be in range to provide direct fire support.

At 1930 hours, Sergeant M. Faille ordered his two 6-pounders to start firing while 'A' Company's 2-inch mortars threw out smoke rounds. Captain Ken Williams led his men forward. Although they were met by machine-gun and 20-millimetre anti-aircraft guns, the rounds all went high or wide and caused no casualties. The sand-dune ridge was secured by 2145 hours, and Williams started selecting spots for his supporting guns, while a detachment of the battalion's pioneer platoon swept the area for mines.

When the Bofors had not arrived by 0300 hours on September 11, Buchanan decided to attack without them. Instead, 'B' Company would join the attack from the right of 'A' Company's position. At 0400 hours, the 2-inch mortars fired flares, "turning night into day." This enabled the two 6-pounder crews to spot their targets and commence firing. Several direct hits were scored. Williams led 'A' Company to a row of houses, and thirty minutes later 'B' Company joined the advance. Both companies were met with heavy machine-gun and rifle fire. An artillery piece also started shelling the advancing infantry, but 6th Field's

Captain McLean—it being a new day and a new ammunition ration having been dispensed—was able to silence it almost immediately with counter-battery fire. The small-arms fire continued to build, however, and both companies were pinned down short of the pillboxes screening the main fort. At 0615 hours, an artillery smoke and high-explosive screen was laid down directly between the two trapped companies and the Germans, despite it squandering most of the day's shell allotment. Under its cover, the Sasks escaped at 0700 hours, taking their wounded with them. Williams had been hit in the forehead by a shrapnel splinter, but was not seriously injured.

At 0800 hours, Buchanan huddled with his company commanders and the platoon section leaders of 'A' and 'B' Companies. The consensus was that with just infantry and limited field artillery, "the strong point was going to be plenty tough to take out." They even figured that medium artillery might make no impression on the concrete structures. What they needed was rocket-firing Typhoons. After some negotiating, several Typhoons put in an attack at 1800 hours, but failed to hit the fort.

The situation had clearly stalemated. Even the arrival of the Bofors supplied by the division's 3rd Light Anti-Aircraft Regiment failed to give the Sasks a stronger hand. So they spent most of September 12 harassing the German positions with fire and patrolling for some way to enter without being cut apart.[11]

Fortunately, the tides of war playing out that day just a few miles to the northeast and about midway between Dunkirk and Ostend inadvertently turned things in the Sasks' favour. At Middelkerke and Westende-Bad, the Germans held two other large fortified positions, which were besieged by 4th Brigade's Essex Scottish Regiment, with each two-company battle group supported by a gun troop of the 3rd Light Anti-Aircraft Regiment and the 17-pounders of a troop of 2nd Canadian Anti-Tank Regiment. These positions closely resembled the one besieged by the Sasks in construction, weaponry, and garrison size. Having been subjected to two days of "accurate, observed shooting with mortars, anti-tank, bofors and field guns," the garrison of about three hundred men at Westende-Bad surrendered at 1215 hours on September 12.[12]

The fortification at Middelkerke soon followed suit after fire from the AA troop's 40-millimetre guns killed eight Germans manning a gun position and raked the command post with accurate fire that penetrated through its gun slits. About 280 Germans surrendered.[13] Except for the fortress besieged by the Sasks, this eliminated the last German resistance pockets between Ostend and the Dunkirk garrison. Avoiding a direct assault saved Canadian lives. "I personally thanked God for this bloodless victory," Essex Scottish's Major Donald Mackenzie wrote. Total casualties "for the whole show were two killed and three slightly wounded."[14]

At 1600 hours, Brigadier Gauvreau appeared at the South Saskatchewan Regiment's headquarters bearing the pay book of the officer who had commanded one of these fortifications. Urquhart and a Belgian civilian dressed in a Canadian uniform carried it to a position in the dunes overlooking the besieged German fortification and called out to speak to its commander. When Major Gunther von Gündell appeared, Urquhart passed him a surrender demand and the German pay book.

The ultimatum warned that if he failed to surrender the position, Bomber Command's heavy bombers would "plaster the place." This was, Buchanan observed, "pure bluff."[15] He was also told that Le Havre and Calais had both surrendered "and it was no use" continuing to resist. Gündell asked for fifteen minutes to talk with his officers. Punctual to the minute, his interpreter returned and offered a surrender on the morning of September 13, if the wounded could be evacuated now, the prisoners guaranteed protection from the Belgians, and officer baggage allowed to accompany them. These conditions were accepted.

At 0830 hours on September 13, 8 officers and 270 men emerged from the fort and surrendered. The Sasks "were pleased . . . as it would have been a lot to crack that fort."[16] Von Gündell was transferred to 2nd Division headquarters, where Major General Charles Foulkes with Lieutenant J.W. Henley interpreting attempted "to induce him to call on another strongpoint . . . to surrender. This, Gündell refused to do." The Germans manning this strongpoint, however, soon gave up after it was pounded by artillery. Another 150 Germans marched into captivity.[17]

WHILE THE SIEGE north of Nieuport had been under way, the other two 6th Brigade battalions had been inching their way toward Bray Dunes Plage and Ghyvelde across a two-mile-wide front. To the left of Ghyvelde the ground was fully flooded, preventing any possibility of flanking the German positions. The Germans met the Queen's Own Cameron Highlanders and Les Fusiliers Mont-Royal with fierce resistance. On September 11, the Fusiliers attempted to break into Ghyvelde. The village turned out to be strongly held, the regiment's war diarist wrote, and the Fusiliers were "repulsed by heavy enemy fire and suffered heavy casualties."[18]

To the right, the Camerons were, in the words of their official historian, directly assaulting "through the sand and minefields . . . the huge concrete forts that formed part of the German west wall, the guns of which were now, in most cases, turned landwards. Artillery preparation and repeated heavy bombing had little or no effect on these immense fortifications. They were nearly all connected by deep underground tunnels. They were well stocked with stores and sumptuously appointed so that the German defenders had most of the advantage on their side. Nothing short of a direct hit from a shell made an impression on these fortresses—bombs, in fact, were less effective than shells. This was the area where Hitler and his Generals had been sure the original Allied invasion attempt would be made, and they had poured into these all of the ingenuity and defensive knowledge they had. In addition, the range tables of the Nazi artillery could pinpoint virtually every square foot of the surrounding terrain with deadly accuracy."

The Bray Dunes Plage bastions consisted of a number of early 1900-era French casemates that the Germans had improved upon and integrated into those of their own construction to create a formidable position. Hoping to isolate them and thus render them indefensible, the Camerons swung slightly inland toward the adjacent village of Bray Dunes. Ill fortune dogged them at every turn. On September 11, 'C' Company's Major Ronald Rainey Counsell—who had earned a Military Cross when just a lieutenant for his role in the fighting at Green Beach during the Dieppe raid—was killed when his entire company headquarters was wiped out by an artillery shell. The company's advance fell into disarray. On the battalion's right flank, 'B' Company had advanced through the dunes only to lose wireless contact with battalion headquarters and then have all its Bren guns jammed by fine sand. 'A' Company, with remnants of 'C' Company, attempted to support 'B' Company, but the attack collapsed.[19]

Ground was gained neither that day nor the next. Even night patrols were "pinned down by mortaring and machine-gun fire, brought to bear with the aid of illuminating flares."

II CANADIAN CORPS COMMANDER Lieutenant General Guy Simonds issued a new order on September 12. "Complete the investment of Dunkirk," he insisted.[20] To increase pressure on the German garrison, Simonds had ordered 2nd Division's 4th Infantry Brigade moved from the area of Bruges and Ostend in Belgium to take up position between the other two brigades at Dunkirk and besiege Bergues, five miles southeast of the port. Simonds was directing the full might of 2nd Division against Dunkirk in an attempt to force its submission.[21]

Accordingly, Major General Charles Foulkes ordered both 5th and 6th Infantry Brigades to renew attacks. On the 5th Brigade front, the Black Watch was to seize Spycker, while Le Régiment de Maisonneuve worked to the east of the village to clear the ground between it and Bergues. From Loon Plage, the Calgary Highlanders would push toward Mardick near the coast. Meanwhile, on Dunkirk's northeastern flank, 6th Brigade's Queen's Own Cameron Highlanders would attack through the sand dunes with two companies, while a third infiltrated Bray Dunes by road to "pave the way for the remaining company to fight its way through the town."[22]

The Black Watch was first off the mark, attacking Spycker on September 12 at 1800 hours. Spycker was a small village surrounded by farm buildings frequented by German snipers. As the village church was centrally located, the Black Watch plan called for 'B' Company to seize the buildings to its right, and 'C' Company those to the left. The attack started with artillery firing smoke rounds to provide concealment, while mortars dropped high-explosive bombs on suspected German positions. Crossing the start line just outside Grand Mille Brugge at 1805 hours, the two companies stuck close to the creeping smoke. When the barrage ceased at 1815 hours, the infantry were closing on the village. One platoon of 'C' Company advanced so briskly through Spycker that it overshot its objective by four hundred yards. In trying to fall back from what quickly proved an untenable position, its commander was killed and several other men wounded. These losses persuaded 'C' Company's Major Alex Pinkham to concentrate in several houses somewhat short of the church. 'B' Company also advanced farther than its objective, which left it vulnerable to a counterattack that fell "in such force that most of it returned to Grand Mille Brugge." Only a small number of men remained in a building east of the church, providing slight coverage of 'C' Company's right flank.

About thirty minutes after 'C' Company's arrival in Spycker, around thirty Germans counterattacked from a barn northwest of the village. The counterattack was easily repelled. Meanwhile, the battalion commander, Lieutenant Colonel Frank Mitchell, had reorganized 'B' Company and sent one of its platoons back into Spycker to bolster the force there. Shortly after midnight the Germans attacked again but were driven off. Then, at 0400 hours, a German party came in from the right and started a systematic house-clearing attempt, with an officer directing the operation from the centre of the street. The Germans arrived so suddenly that a small group of Black Watch in one building, who were all new recruits, were taken prisoner. But three grenades lobbed out the window of the next house in line sent the Germans packing. By 1000 hours, Germans had infiltrated throughout the village, and one non-commissioned officer was killed on a garden path just five yards from Pinkham's company headquarters. An attempt to reinforce the position with two armoured cars failed when one was knocked out by a Panzerfaust and the other mired in a ditch. The roads leading into the town were all mined, and no vehicles could get through to evacuate the wounded or bring up supplies. Pinkham advised Mitchell that his position "was not tenable unless assistance could be brought to clear the right [side] of the town." Maintaining only a tenuous hold on Grand Mille Brugge itself with the meagre strength of the Black Watch, Mitchell had nothing to offer. So at nightfall, 'A' Company came forward to assist in evacuating the wounded and to cover the withdrawal from Spycker. By 0200 hours on September 14, the Black Watch were gone from the village.[23]

The situation in Grand Mille Brugge had also deteriorated, as it was subjected to almost constant shelling and mortaring that included rounds from coastal guns firing landward. By noon of September 13, Mitchell's headquarters had suffered five direct hits, and the Regimental Aid Post was struck by one round. Eight of the battalion's vehicles and six motorcycles were burning wrecks. Amazingly, only one man was wounded, and that was nothing more than a small cut to his forehead due to flying debris. Brigadier Bill Megill decided there was no chance of holding the place, so he authorized the Black Watch to fall back five miles westward to Bourbourg. Consequently, as soon as Pinkham's force arrived from Spycker, Grand Mille Brugge was abandoned at 0330 hours.[24]

This marked the end of any real attempt by 5th Brigade to push in the Dunkirk defences. The best its battalions could do was to continue patrolling and harassing the Germans before them.[25]

17

They Could Have Blasted Us

O N THE 6TH Brigade front, meanwhile, the Queen's Own Cameron Highlanders' attack on Bray Dunes had gone in during the early-morning hours of September 13. Both 'B' and 'C' Companies were stopped virtually on their start lines. Major J.J. Gagnon's 'D' Company, however, reached its first objective of a crossroads outside the town at 0530 hours and seized a roadblock there "after a short very one sided battle with a few enemy sentries." The crossroads was surrounded by several buildings. Gagnon included some of these within the company's perimeter, but others stood just beyond. During this initial action, No. 18 Platoon led by Lieutenant A.S.C. Williams knocked out an 88-millimetre gun with a PIAT round and then overran several machine-gun positions in and around the buildings. Twenty minutes after the fighting ended, the company's officers were getting the platoons organized to meet an expected counterattack when Gagnon heard horses approaching from the north, outside the Dunkirk perimeter. Gagnon quickly passed word that the men were to hold fire until he gave the word. Out of the murk of pre-dawn, a number of horse-drawn wagons filled with ammunition appeared, and Gagnon shouted for the men to start shooting. Machine guns and rifles slashed into the fifteen wagons, killing horses and teamsters alike in a fierce slaughter. Soon afterward, two Germans on bicycles approached the roadblock and were killed by the company sniper. Then, at 0730 hours, two German officers riding horses turned up. One was shot dead, but the other was called upon to surrender. Instead he pulled out a stick grenade, and several men gunned him down. An hour later, the expected counterattack came, but it was easily thrown back, with heavy casualties inflicted. Gagnon estimated his men had by this time killed about 150 Germans.

But 'D' Company was also completely surrounded, with Germans infiltrating behind their positon around the roadblock. Fortunately, the company's jeep had been brought forward, and aboard was a good supply of emergency rations. Gagnon was also in contact with battalion headquarters via his No. 18 wireless set, although as the afternoon wore on, he worried that the single battery available would die.

With the Germans subjecting the position to heavy mortar and shellfire, 'D' Company's situation was perilous. At 1230 hours, the Germans counterattacked again. This attack was beaten back at the cost of one Cameron killed and three wounded. Shortly thereafter, a German ambulance blundered into the position, and two first-aid men were captured. As night fell, 'D' Company staved off another counterattack. The Germans than set fire to the buildings outside the company position. But, Gagnon said later, "there was no wind and we weren't burnt out." One of the buildings was some form of seniors' residence, and the company safely evacuated five nuns and four elderly citizens. While rescuing the civilians, one infantryman discovered a sizeable cache of food inside. He made several return trips to the burning building to carry out the haul.

Throughout the day, the battalion's other three companies tried repeatedly to fight through to the isolated unit. Every attempt was repelled. Gagnon's only communication link remained the wireless set, so he kept signals to a minimum. He was desperately worried that the battery would go flat and leave him completely cut off. Miraculously, the day's fighting had yielded just the three men wounded in the second counterattack. But Gagnon had no idea how long 'D' Company could hold on its own.[1]

ABOUT THE TIME the Camerons launched their assault, during the early-morning hours of September 13, 4th Infantry Brigade had started moving from around Ostend and Bruges toward Dunkirk and the fortress of Bergues. Transport for the infantry was in short supply, so many Royal Regiment of Canada men were conveyed by 4th Field Regiment. This, Bombardier Ken Hossack confided to his diary, was a first. "We load infantry on the vehicles, guns and trailers, and they hail this as much better than walking . . . we take turns buying drinks at a café which opens early as our convoy halts. A long and tiresome trip takes us back over the French border and down to Rexboede, near Dunkirk . . . Regardless of the fact that we are moving away from the main front, Belgians and Frenchmen still line the street to cheer us and offer food and drink." Dropping the infantry a few miles from the assigned artillery position, the gunners carried on while the Royal Regiment trudged on foot to face Bergues. The 4th Field's gun position was about four thousand yards back. Hossack and the other gunners got to work with their shovels, hacking out gun positions and slit trenches as "heavy enemy shells began to whine" overhead.[2]

Soon Hossack's 'A' Troop commander, Captain George Blackburn, was dispatched as a FOO. He stared grimly at "Bergues' medieval-walled heights, looking awfully formidable on that solitary hill humped up on the pancake-flat landscape." From his first view of this new battleground, with its "watery landscape," Blackburn "despaired of troops managing a successful assault on Dunkirk." The "one road to Dunkirk—a skinny seven-kilometre-long causeway stretching through the water to infinity from this spit of land forming the far bank of the canal, under observation every foot of the way—must surely become a road to suicide." Blackburn understood from a Maquis report that Bergues was held by a garrison of three hundred ss troops, which only made it less likely that it could be taken by assault.[3]

Brigadier Fred Cabeldu also studied Bergues with a wary eye, noting how well fortified it was, "with a high sloping brick wall and partly surrounded by a moat." With the ground to the southeast completely flooded, the only "approach was very limited. Minefields were also known to exist." He ordered the Royal Hamilton Light Infantry (Rileys) to check out a church tower in the village of Quaëdypre, about three miles east of Bergues, which might enable observation over the fortress walls. The Royal Regiment (Royals) was to patrol the Canal de la Basse Colme to see if it could be crossed and Bergues thus outflanked.[4]

Having only reached their assigned position near the village of Warhem at 1630 hours, the Royals had little time for reconnaissance before nightfall. Their headquarters staff was also perplexed by the general plan. This seemed to entail containing the huge German garrison whose outer defences apparently centred on Bergues, which they now faced, and by doing so somehow "force their surrender. Should they prove too strong it would be necessary to keep pressure bearing on them until our heavier arty could be released from the siege of the other channel ports: Le Havre, Boulogne and Calais."[5] On the one hand, great urgency was being expressed as to how quickly Dunkirk was to be taken in order to free 2nd Division for operations back in Belgium. On the other, it appeared the division might be hunkering down for an extended siege.

At 1600 hours, Quaëdypre was found to be undefended. The Rileys established their battalion headquarters there, and 4th Field's Major John Drewry set up an observation post in the church steeple. From here, he "commenced to register targets in Bergues." The Rileys were temporarily under command of Lieutenant Colonel Bill Ritchie, as their commander, Lieutenant Colonel Denis Whitaker, had been wounded back in Normandy and was not expected to return to duties until September 17. Ritchie was baffled as to how to take Bergues. The sloping walls were twenty feet high. The flooding left only the narrowest and most obvious axis for attack. And the ground between water and wall was choked with barbed wire and undoubtedly mines. Aggressive night patrolling and all through September 14 turned up no other route of approach. Ritchie decided the only option was, as the regiment's historian later wrote, "a night attack. Patrols would cut gaps in the wire and lift mines under cover of darkness, if possible, without alerting the enemy. A platoon of engineers would blow the wall and [Major H.A. "Huck"] Welch's 'B' Company [would carry] ladders for scaling, but it was obviously going to be a costly operation, if the Germans decided to fight it out."[6]

BY THE EVENING of September 13, it seemed certain the Rileys and the rest of 2nd Division's battalions were destined to continue slugging it out with the Dunkirk garrison. Early that morning, Field Marshal

Montgomery had advised Lieutenant General Harry Crerar by note of his decision to launch Operation Market Garden in four days' time. After congratulating Crerar on Le Havre's capture, Montgomery got down to Market Garden's implications for First Canadian Army operations. "The things that are now very important," he wrote, "are: (a) Capture of Boulogne and Dunkirk and Calais. (b) The setting in motion of operations designed to enable us to use the port of Antwerp. Of these two things, (b) is probably the most important." But, Montgomery added, he was "very anxious that (a) and (b) should both go on simultaneously if you can possibly arrange it, as time is of the utmost importance. I wonder whether you could possibly use one Corps HQ to control the operations from Boulogne to Dunkirk, and the other Corps HQ to control the opening of Antwerp. Perhaps you would let me know what you think of this." Montgomery promised lavish air support for operations to open Antwerp.

Crerar had replied the same day that it was going to take II Canadian Corps ten days to two weeks "to finish its allotted tasks and clear the coast up to the west bank of the Scheldt." It would also, he wrote, require "at least ten days to move [I British Corps] to . . . Antwerp and this would only be possible if extra transport was allotted from Army Group resources and I was given a minimum of one clear route through Brussels. Apart from the question of transport and routes, this delay in getting down to the business would be serious." As an alternative, Crerar proposed that XII British Corps come under his command or that the 53rd British Infantry Division currently holding Antwerp remain there to join the estuary-clearing operation.

None of this was to Montgomery's liking. He responded at 1810 hours that XII Corps and 53rd Division were both to be involved in Market Garden. He wanted I British Corps with its 49th (West Riding) Infantry Division "brought to Antwerp as early as possible." The 51st (Highland) Infantry Division would be grounded so that all its transport could help move 49th Division. This move was necessary to enable First Canadian Army to relieve 53rd Division from guarding Antwerp.[7]

Ninety minutes after this signal, Montgomery sent another, offering a new solution. "Early use of Antwerp so urgent that I am prepared to give up operations against Calais and Dunkirk and be content with

Boulogne," he announced. Montgomery wanted to discuss this idea in person with Crerar early the next morning.[8]

On the morning of September 14, Crerar, still plagued by dysentery and weakening more each day, gathered his staff and advisers from Bomber Command, 2nd Tactical Air Force, and the navy to discuss the feasibility of this idea. The question for the naval liaison officer was whether Boulogne could be used if Calais remained in German hands. The officer replied that any shipping trying to use Boulogne would be dangerously exposed to the guns of Calais and Cap Gris Nez. Dunkirk was a different matter. The garrison there could be bottled up and left to rot—its coastal guns easily avoided. So Calais and Boulogne must either both be taken or not be taken at all.[9]

Soon after this meeting, Crerar flew to Montgomery's headquarters. Later that afternoon, Montgomery issued a new general directive. While covering all Twenty-First Army Group operations, there were three key elements for First Canadian Army. First, Boulogne and then Calais were to be captured. Second, Dunkirk would "be left to be dealt with later, for the present it will be merely masked." Third, the "whole energies of the Army will be directed towards operations designed to enable full use to be made of the port of Antwerp."[10]

EVEN AS THIS decision to give up besieging Dunkirk was being made, Canadians were still fighting and dying before its fortifications. On the 6th Brigade front near Bray Dunes, Queen's Own Cameron Highlanders' 'D' Company remained cut off at the roadblock. The morning of September 14 found Major J.J. Gagnon still marvelling that his wireless set kept working. He considered it "miraculous" that the battery lived and also that the fires from the still-burning buildings had not spread into the company perimeter. Via the wireless, he knew the battalion's other three companies were trying to carve a path through to him.[11]

By 0120 hours, 'C' Company was mired in a fight just three hundred yards south of 'D' Company. At the same time as they exchanged gunfire with some Germans, others came forward to surrender. The company commander sent a plea back to battalion headquarters at 0750 hours for help getting thirty-five prisoners out of his hair. At 1000 hours, the company had crept another hundred yards closer to

Gagnon's men. 'A' Company, meanwhile, had run into opposition from about fifty Germans and was taking fire from light machine guns and mortars. With casualties mounting, an urgent call was sent out for stretcher-bearers and stretchers. It was 1130 hours, and 'B' Company was also meeting stiff resistance.[12] The company's commander fell wounded, and Company Sergeant Major Frank Breakey took over. He immediately went forward under fire to determine the location of the enemy positions pinning the company down. Seeing the Germans ensconced in a group of buildings to the company's right, Breakey led an attack against the enemy's left flank. Armed with a PIAT launcher and three bombs, Breakey charged across open ground to attack the buildings at close range. As his Distinguished Conduct Medal citation recounted, "The enemy . . . opened fire on him wounding him in the head. With great determination and despite his suffering, he continued to move forward to within fifty yards of the enemy position. From this point he fired the three bombs through windows in the building causing terrific casualties to the defenders."[13]

Despite this success, 'B' Company was still unable to reach 'D' Company. But during the night, 'C' Company slipped a patrol through to Gagnon's lines. At dawn, a jeep was able to use the path opened by 'C' Company to evacuate the company's three casualties. 'D' Company had been cut off for forty-eight hours, and Gagnon's wireless set still worked.[14] September 14 cost the Camerons four fatal casualties.

Also during the night of September 14–15, the South Saskatchewan Regiment had attempted to relieve pressure on the Camerons' 'D' Company with an attack through the coastal dunes to seize Bray Dunes Plage. 'C' Company led the effort, followed by 'D,' 'B,' and 'A' Companies. It was so dark, with the men winding their way "in and out of the sand dunes," that 'B' and 'A' Companies became separated from the two ahead. After much blind stumbling about, Major George Buchanan reorganized the battalion, and a general attack was put in on the village at 0600 hours. 'D' Company overran a pillbox housing a 75-millimetre gun, and from this firm base provided fire support for the other three companies. Bray Dunes Plage fell quickly, as it proved only lightly held, but several men stepped on German wooden s-mines and were wounded. By 1500 hours, Bray Dunes Plage was declared clear.

The Sasks then extended their lines to take over the area held by the Camerons' 'D' Company to enable them to withdraw. In the fighting of the previous days, the Sasks' war diarist recorded, the Camerons "had been badly shot up, but had accounted for quite a few Jerries." While the Camerons were withdrawn, the Sasks were to continue active patrolling to maintain pressure on the Germans in this sector until 2nd Division was relieved from the masking duties it had now assumed.[15]

ON THE MORNING of September 14, Brigadier Fred Cabeldu convened an Orders Group in which he set out 4th Infantry Brigade's plan to overcome the stout fortress of Bergues. It entailed a night attack by both the Royal Hamilton Light Infantry and the Royal Regiment. The Rileys were to assault Bergues directly, while the Royals would cross the Canal de la Basse Colme to the right and outflank the fortress.[16] Both battalions were to be supported by engineers of 2nd Field Company. Accompanying the Rileys, No. 1 Platoon would sweep for mines and then breach the fortress walls with demolition charges. No. 2 Platoon was to clear mines to enable the Royals to reach the river and then handle the boats for the crossing. Once the Royals had established a bridgehead across the canal, No. 3 Platoon would sling a Bailey bridge across. During the day, the engineers attempted to reconnoiter the selected bridging site, but were driven away by heavy fire from two machine guns and several light automatic weapons. The Germans doing the firing were all within fifty yards of the proposed crossing site. Royals and engineers alike feared they were in for a hot reception come nightfall.[17]

In the afternoon, the Royals advanced 'B' and 'D' Companies to the canal, where they dug in. At nightfall, 'D' Company was to make its crossing, while 'A' Company came up to cross the canal through 'B' Company's lines. Just after dark, as 'A' Company was readying its raft, five Germans from the 588th Grenadier Regiment swam the canal and surrendered. At about 2200 hours, Major Hank Caldwell led 'A' Company down to the water. A stealthy crossing followed as the men pulled the rubber raft back and forth with ropes attached to either canal bank. About two thousand yards to the left, Major Bob Suckling's 'D' Company also crossed undetected just after midnight. Both companies crept out from the canal, 'A' Company stopping two or three hundred yards beyond. 'D' Company continued to a crossroads about half a mile to the northwest. Quietly, the Royals dug in and awaited the dawn.[18]

Just before midnight, meanwhile, the Rileys had formed to directly assault Bergues. 'B' and 'D' Companies, with the platoon of engineers carrying explosive charges, were getting ready to advance, when suddenly the Germans ignited a large petrol dump about three hundred yards northeast of the selected breaching point. At 0200 hours, the fires were blazing brightly and illuminating the line of advance. Two hours later the fires still burned and, with dawn approaching, the two companies withdrew.[19]

Dawn of September 15 found the Royals' 'A' and 'D' Companies still dug in across the canal and undiscovered by the Germans. When two Germans peddled into the midst of one section at the crossroad, they were taken prisoner. As the light improved, the Royals discovered German positions within a hundred yards of their respective company lines, the regimental war diarist wryly noting that "had they been keeping a proper watch or possessed the will to fight, they could have blasted us in a few moments. Also the positions they were occupying were well-camouflaged in haystacks . . . so as to prove a problem if resolutely defended."

Shortly after dawn, the Germans responded with heavy fire across the canal toward the companies holding the crossing points. The Royals summoned a troop of 3rd Light Anti-Aircraft Regiment's Bofors, and a duel erupted at ranges of three hundred to four hundred yards.[20] Then a large German force was spotted massing to counterattack 'A' Company. Major Caldwell hurriedly linked in with the 4th Field Regiment and a mortar platoon from the Toronto Scottish, and both caught the Germans in the open with heavy fire.[21]

After this attack was broken, the Germans lashed back at 4th Field Regiment's positions with extremely accurate fire from coastal guns near Dunkirk. As the regiment's batteries had been forced to deploy in the open to be within range to support 4th Brigade, the gunners were badly exposed to German observation from Bergues. In his diary, Sergeant Bruce Hunt recorded, "Command posts, troops and kitchen—each in turn receives a well-directed vicious effort." Tires and gas tanks on vehicles were punctured, and "all sorts of kit blown to oblivion." Yet the

2nd and 26th Batteries escaped any casualties. Not so lucky, 14th Battery suffered five men wounded, and Gunner John S. Sherwood was killed.[22]

Twice more, the Germans tried mounting counterattacks, only to be sent running by the artillery and mortars. At 1115 hours, after the third attempt broke, one officer with twenty-five men surrendered. Then, at 1300 hours, another officer and nine men gave up. Ninety minutes later, the Royals' watch on the Bergues side of the canal was ended by immediate orders for the two companies to withdraw. Brigadier Cabeldu, having just received word from division, announced that 4th Brigade was ceasing offensive action in order to move immediately to Antwerp. The Royals brought out two dead—nineteen-year-old Private Edward Barry and Private Lars Ingvar Larman—and two men wounded. But five were also missing and presumed captured or killed.[23] By 1500 hours, both 4th Brigade battalions had moved beyond range of the Germans. An hour later, Cabeldu and his battalion commanders turned their attention to organizing the move from Dunkirk, slated to begin at 0800 hours on September 16.

As 4th Brigade departed in the morning, 'C' and 'A' Squadrons of the 14th Canadian Hussars deployed their armoured cars into the vacated front lines to provide a confining screen. Across the entire front, the Hussars enabled 2nd Division's orderly departure. From inside Bergues, large explosions could be heard, and 2nd Division sent an urgent request for 'A' Squadron to determine what was going on. Carefully, 'A' and 'C' Squadrons approached the town and found all bridges leading into it blown. Men sent forward on foot managed to cross a bridge on its intact foundation. They entered Bergues in time to see a large building to the left of a church explode with such force that it brought down a tall spire at the church's back. They found the town heavily mined and the town hall riddled with booby traps, but clearly the Germans had vacated Bergues. Four men from 'A' Squadron were wounded by mines. Before Bergues would be safe for soldiers or the milling civilians, it would require thorough mine sweeping.[24]

On September 16, the British 4th Special Service Brigade arrived. The brigade was to contain Dunkirk's garrison. A week later, this commando unit was itself relieved by the 154th Brigade and engineers of 274th Field Company, both from 51st (Highland) Infantry

Division.[25] First Canadian Army retained responsibility for Dunkirk, but on October 7, the 1st Czechoslovak Independent Armoured Brigade assumed the actual task of containing the German garrison within its hundred-square-mile confines. Two days later, the Czechs had relieved the 51st Division troops. Major-General Alois Liska had under command not only the Czech troops but also several British units. This included one tank and one artillery regiment, plus an anti-aircraft brigade. Serving in the latter was 2nd Canadian Heavy Anti-Aircraft Regiment. This formation was formally designated Dunkirk Force.[26]

Prior to the Czechs taking over, negotiations by the International Red Cross had resulted in two ceasefires—September 20 and October 5—which enabled the civilian population to be evacuated. About 6,000 left in September and 19,000 in October. Just 820 French civilians stayed. There were also 60 British and Canadian prisoners being held along with a handful of Maquis in the town jail.[27]

Given the number of Germans caught inside the Dunkirk pocket and their being armed with about 170 artillery pieces of varying calibre, the Czechs were ordered to avoid direct assaults. Their task was instead to keep the garrison contained and to entice its surrender. This entailed "active patrolling, artillery bombardment and psychological warfare and . . . preventing reinforcements or supplies from being sent in by sea or air." The Czechs soon put their distinctive spin on how "active patrolling" was defined. On Czechoslovakia's October 28 Independence Day, they attacked with vigour, killing about two hundred Germans and taking another four hundred prisoner. On November 5, they followed this attack with another raid in force that yielded two hundred more captives.

On November 27, Dunkirk Force switched from First Army Command to that of Twenty-First Army Group. The Canadian anti-aircraft unit remained on station at Dunkirk until February 8, 1945, when it returned to duty with First Canadian Army. Not until May 9, 1945, did the Germans in Dunkirk finally surrender.[28] A few days earlier, there had been a popular uprising in Prague that liberated the city, but on the same day that the Czechs accepted the German surrender in Dunkirk, Soviet troops entered the Czech capital and brought the nation under their control.[29]

PART THREE

THE PAS DE CALAIS BATTLES

[18]

A Lost Outpost

O N SEPTEMBER 17, Twenty-First Army Group launched two dra-matically different operations. At 0955 hours, First Canadian Army's 3rd Infantry Division attacked the German fortress at Boulogne. Then, at 1300 hours, American and British paratroops drifted down onto landing sites at Eindhoven, Veghel, Grave, and Oosterbeek in history's largest airborne drop. Two of the three airborne divisions were American, with the 101st Airborne descending on Eindhoven and Veghel, while the 82nd Airborne came down at Grave. At Oosterbeek, near Arnhem, 1st British Airborne Division landed. As the paratroops went into action, the Guards Armoured Division led the xxx British Corps advance at 1435 hours out of a small bridgehead over the Meuse–Escaut Canal just short of the Belgian–Dutch border. In front of the British tanks stretched sixty-four miles of narrow road that crossed several major waterways before coming to the Nederrijn at Arnhem. Operation Market Garden was a bold gamble that called for xxx Corps to punch through to Arnhem in no more than four days, or fewer if possible. Operation Wellhit at Boulogne was another beast entirely, a methodical reduction of well-prepared defences held by a garrison under orders to fight to the last man. Running parallel to each other, the two operations required a vast commitment of Allied resources, and it was the Canadians facing Boulogne who were left wanting.

Under its command, xxx Corps had the Guards Armoured Division, 43rd (Wessex) Infantry Division, 50th (Northumbrian) Infantry Division, 8th Armoured Brigade, and the Royal Netherlands Brigade. Its left flank was to be screened by xii Corps with 7th Armoured Division, 15th (Scottish) Infantry Division, and 53rd (Welsh) Division under command. On the right was the 11th Armoured Division, 3rd Infantry Division, 4th Armoured Brigade, and 1st Belgian Brigade of viii Corps.[1]

For the attack on Le Havre, which had been neither as heavily fortified nor as naturally suited for defence as Boulogne, First Canadian Army had deployed i British Corps with two infantry divisions, two armoured brigades, and the specialized armour of 79th Armoured Division under command. To invest Boulogne, Lieutenant General Harry Crerar could muster only two infantry brigades of 3rd Canadian Infantry Division; the tanks of the Fort Garry Horse regiment; avres of 87th Assault Squadron, Royal Engineers; and three armoured assault teams of 31st British Tank Brigade. Artillery support, however, was lavish, and each formation had begun shelling the fortress as it arrived.

Although Field Marshal Montgomery repeatedly stressed his urgent need for Boulogne, Lieutenant General Harry Crerar was not to be rushed. On September 13, he had written Montgomery that he did not want the effects of Le Havre's capture "neutralized by an unsuccessful attack on Boulogne." He therefore "had ordered [Lieutenant General Guy] Simonds to take extra time if necessary in planning and mounting the operation in order to ensure a decisive assault."[2]

A key component that Crerar wanted confirmed was air support from Bomber Command. Yet on September 13, when 3rd Division's Major General Dan Spry issued his operational order for the assault, he could only say that "heavy bombers would support the attackers." Details of timings, target areas, and safety bomb lines were still being determined, and there was no confirmation that Bomber Command would assign aircraft to the task.[3] The following day, the raf Bomber Command liaison officer failed to attend a scheduled meeting at First Canadian Army headquarters. Anxious to get the bomber-support issue settled, Simonds and his chief of staff, Brigadier Church Mann, flew to Allied Expeditionary Air Force (aeaf) headquarters at Versailles.

Here they consulted with Air Vice Marshal Victor Groom of No. 84 Tactical Group and an air vice marshal from Bomber Command. Simonds was determined to nail down bomber support for both the Boulogne and later Calais assaults.

Things got off to a rough start. As the 11 Canadian Corps diarist later wrote, "There was considerable reluctance to use more than 300 [to] 400 RAF bombers for each port supplementing them with such medium bombers as might be available from the various other priority tasks which AEAF had at the moment on their list." Unexpectedly, Air Chief Marshals Sir Arthur Harris and Arthur Tedder, along with Air Marshal Trafford Leigh-Mallory, joined the conference. With RAF's three most powerful commanders all in the room, Simonds seized the moment and frankly set out his army plan and air-support requirements. "The Air Marshals agreed with little hesitation that if Boulogne and Calais were to be captured forthwith and air support was necessary, then it should be given in full measure." Simonds had his bomber support.[4]

ON SEPTEMBER 5, 3rd Infantry Division had cordoned off Boulogne and cut the coastal road connecting it to Calais. Since then, the 8th and 9th Brigades had been steadily gathering intelligence on Boulogne's fortifications and garrison, while 7th Brigade had positioned itself on high ground dominating the coastal road and set for an attack northward on Cap Gris Nez. Until Le Havre fell and the specialized assault armour, artillery, and bomber support required could be released, there was little the Canadians could do beyond reconnaissance.

About five miles from the city, 9th Brigade's front extended southeast and east from Hardelot on the channel to the southern edge of Forêt de Boulogne. The 8th Brigade was concentrated across the eastern flank of the port.

The Canadians quickly discovered, as one intelligence analysis reported, that Boulogne was "a formidable fortress with strong outer defences built on a ring of high features that encircled the port and protected it against landward attack. The strongpoints in this system, which had originally been constructed by the French and further strengthened by the Germans during the occupation, were mutually supporting to a marked degree and commanded all the approaches to the city. All contained substantial reinforced concrete gun emplacements, dugouts and underground passages, while on the surface they were hedged with wire and linked by extensive minefields. In addition to these infantry defended localities, a number of coast defence batteries and fortified radar stations strategically placed about the area combined to make Boulogne one of the most strongly defended ports on the channel coast.

"By far the strongest links in the chain of defences were the Mont Lambert and Herquelingue features which together covered the landward approaches to Boulogne from the east and southeast. The steep slopes of these two hills, each over 150 metres high, were studded with small fortresses made up of casemated guns and guns on open emplacements, trenches, weapon pits and pillboxes." On Mont Lambert's summit, an observation point provided excellent visual coverage outward to about two thousand yards in all directions. "The main belt of defences, each strongpoint in which was to become a Canadian objective in the assault, ran through Fort [de la] Crèche, Bon Secours, and St. Martin Boulogne in the north; Mont Lambert and Herquelingue in the centre; then across the flooded Liane River to Mont St. Etienne and Nocquet in the south. Well to the north, centred on La Trésorerie and Wimereux, were more defences, while west of the Liane, at the tip of the Outreau 'peninsula' was the fortress of Le Portel."[5]

The German headquarters was inside the Boulogne citadel, a medieval French fort located in the eastern corner of Haute Ville, the town's older section. Haute Ville was atop a hill adjacent to the east bank of the Liane River. In the thirteenth century, this part of Boulogne had been surrounded by high ramparts with four gates allowing access and seventeen towers adding to its defences. Three centuries later, the rampart and towers were lowered to allow the use of artillery, and embankments were constructed against the inside of the walls to strengthen them against the battering impact of cannon fire. The citadel itself was surrounded by a moat. As Boulogne had grown over the centuries, its population spilled beyond Haute Ville's walls and down the hill's steep slopes to the low ground alongside the river. West of the river, the small industrial zone of Capécure had developed. The port had two parts, an outer deep-water harbour and a more sheltered inner harbour for smaller vessels.

Montgomery hoped the port would considerably improve his supply situation. In 1937, more than a million tons of cargo had moved through it. But once it became clear that the port was of no further value to them, the Germans began its destruction. Several small coastal and fishing vessels were sunk across the channel mouth, barring access to, as one 3rd Division engineering report noted, "all but shallow draft boats at high tide." Only one dockside crane avoided complete destruction. The locks that provided access to one of the larger sections of the port were badly damaged by explosive charges. Not all this destruction was caused by the Germans. The port had also been subjected to years of Allied bombing that contributed to the demolition of 60 to 70 per cent of its submarine pens and severely damaged several major quays. By mid-September, only a small part of the port had escaped serious damage, and even there the quays had several sunken fishing boats alongside that would have to be raised and removed to enable their use.[6]

Boulogne's garrison was commanded by fifty-year-old Generalleutnant Ferdinand Heim, who had joined the army in 1914, fought through the Great War, managed to continue military service during the inter-war years, and was serving as Generaloberst Heinz Guderian's chief of staff when Germany invaded Poland. When Hitler decided to invade Russia, Heim became one of the operation's chief planners. On November 1, 1942, he was promoted to Generalleutnant and took command of the XLVIII Panzer Corps headquartered on the outskirts of Stalingrad. When the corps's Rumanian Panzer Division was torn asunder by the Russians, and the German Sixth Army was consequently encircled and forced to surrender, Heim was made a scapegoat. Arrested in January 1943, he was imprisoned for five months without charge in a German Investigation Prison. Upon release, Heim was put on a military pension. It appeared his career was over until August 1944, when Heim received orders to take command of Fortress Boulogne.

Heim arrived at Boulogne just as the Fifteenth Army flowed past, and the fortress was completely isolated by September 2. There was no time to coordinate Boulogne's defences with those of Cap Gris Nez or Calais before the coastal road north of the town was cut. As the Germans had feared an Allied invasion on the Pas de Calais, all the town's main weapons faced seaward. Heim set about converting his defences from an anti-sea role to an anti-land one. An anti-tank ditch was dug on the heights east of Mont Lambert, which dominated Boulogne. As he told Allied interrogators later, he considered "this high ground to be of critical importance, and if held by investing forces would make defence of the port impossible." Hundreds of local civilians were forced to dig the trench, "but despite frantic efforts" it was not complete when the Canadians arrived.

Although it was extremely difficult, Heim reoriented most of his artillery to fire landward. All the mobile guns were repositioned in sites facing inland from behind the town. Many guns had been sited inside concrete bunkers with ports facing only seaward. Removing these guns so they could assist in the coming battle was a nightmare that could only be undertaken with the smaller weapons. The large naval and coastal artillery "could not be budged, and remained blinking uselessly at the Channel."

Getting the garrison's infantry "out of their comfortable bunkers facing the coast and . . . digging perimeter strongpoints about the fortress" was easier. Cement emplacements directed westward, however, had to be adapted so there were gun ports facing east. In the citadel, Heim established a reserve that could be sent as needed to any perimeter point under threat. By mid-September, the garrison was as ready for battle as it ever would be. Heim was under no illusion that Boulogne could be held and had no intention to fight to the last man, but only to "the last bullet." Should the situation become "hopeless from a military standpoint," he would "lay down his charge with a clear conscience."

Before Heim lost contact with Fifteenth Army, he had been ordered on September 1 to establish a ten-kilometre-deep defensive ring around Boulogne. Within this area, all bridges were to be blown, buildings levelled, and vast minefields laid. With no more than a handful of engineers, such a task was impossible, and only a little of the work was completed. In a cynical moment, Heim "merely put a big red circle on [his] map to show that the demolition had theoretically been carried out."[7]

By mid-September, Heim had managed to turn enough guns landward to provide a strong artillery presence. There were at least twenty-two 88-millimetre guns and nine 150-millimetre howitzers manned by the garrison's artillery regiment of 64th Infanterie-Division.[8] Heim also had four 75-millimetre Belgian guns. Then there were the guns facing seaward, which ranged in size from 15 centimetres up to 30.5 centimetres. Very few of these could be turned to fire inland. The four heavy guns at Fort de la Crèche were important exceptions.

While Boulogne's coastal batteries were well stocked with ammunition, there was little for the guns arrayed landward. As at Le Havre, there were thousands of rounds for 15.5-centimetre French guns that had been removed from the garrison when its original 47th Infanterie-Division was withdrawn. For the 150-millimetre howitzers, Heim had just a hundred rounds apiece and a thousand rounds per 88-millimetre gun.

When Heim arrived in Boulogne, the 47th Infanterie-Division was still in place and had been there for a long time. In late August, this division was withdrawn and Heim was promised three Fortress Machine-Gun Battalions as an infantry replacement. Soon the 27th, 1407th, and 1408th Machine-Gun Battalions duly arrived, but they had lost about a quarter of their personnel and many weapons in aerial attacks suffered during their journey from Germany to Boulogne. These troops constituted Heim's only infantry force and numbered just two thousand. Heim considered them a sorry lot, consisting "of former office clerks and old men whose training was rudimentary and who could do nothing with the many strange weapons they found in their bunkers," which included French, Belgian, and Czech arms. Although his garrison numbered about ten thousand men in total, most were naval marines, manning the coastal guns, and administrative and supply personnel.

Heim had understood he was to receive reinforcement in the form of 64th Infanterie-Division. But by September 6, only part of the division's artillery regiment and part of one engineer battalion had arrived, and he learned that would be it.

As for morale within the garrison, Heim considered it rather good "under the circumstances." While everyone knew they were part of a "lost outpost," they mostly accepted Heim's explanation that their duty was to "gain time. An early evacuation of the fortress would give the Allies just that much more time to start repairing the damage." Although Heim was personally disillusioned with Nazism, many of his men were not. He "thought that the greatest phenomenon of National Socialism was its ability to convert the German pessimism of the last war into the illusionism of this one. Men between thirty and forty years of age, who had seen the world, nevertheless believed all of Goebbels' propaganda with a naivety and faith difficult to understand." Upon arriving in Boulogne, Heim was asked by some in his command if he had heard "that a new German plane had made losses of Allied planes so high that newspapers did not dare publish the figures anymore.

"This universal faith in a miracle that would be wrought by . . . Hitler, was something Heim found impossible to comprehend. It was the style to be cheerful and hopeful, whereas in the last war it was the thing to be gloomy and disillusioned. This strange reaction existed even though men knew they had not been told the truth about Russia, and that the overall picture was extremely dark. Yet they wanted to believe in a German victory, and nothing could shake them from this conviction."[9]

PERHAPS IT WAS this continued belief in a miracle that had prompted the defenders on the Pas de Gay hill to carry out an almost suicidal charge from their dugouts against 'D' Company of the North Shore (New Brunswick) Regiment when it assaulted their position on the night of September 15–16. The sane thing would have been to remain in the dugouts and force the Canadians to engage in a costly fight to eliminate each one. Instead, the Germans had been cut to pieces and the hill had fallen fairly easily. When the firefight was over, however, the strength of the German defences on the hill and in the hamlet of Wacquinghen, also taken that night, provided convincing evidence that the forthcoming battle for Boulogne would be no walkover. As it was, in that initial opening attack on the Boulogne fortifications the North Shores had eliminated only two minor defensive works.

These lay outside the German wire perimeter screening the network of positions that protected the two major strongpoints on the northern edge of the Boulogne fortress—La Trésorerie and Wimereux. But the effort had rid the 8th Brigade's frontage of two well-situated German observation posts and given the North Shores a "good, firm base" in preparation for the launch of Operation Wellhit on September 17.[10]

The decision to eliminate these two outposts prior to the main assault resulted from the thorough planning that 3rd Division had put into Operation Wellhit. Blessed with time while they waited for Le Havre to fall and the arrival of the siege weapons, Major General Dan Spry and his staff had been able to develop a quite thorough understanding of the defences and how to overcome them. There remained, however, gaps in their knowledge and also some errors. They estimated the size of the garrison, for example, as between 5,500 and 7,000 men, rather than the actual 10,000.[11]

As Spry had only two understrength infantry brigades, which at best numbered 3,500 men apiece, 3rd Division was actually outnumbered by the Germans inside Boulogne. In fact, each battalion of 9th Brigade would attack with individual company strengths of only about 85 men instead of the normal 130, with each platoon section consisting of 6 men commanded by a non-commissioned officer.[12] The situation was better for 8th Brigade, whose three battalions reported being close to normal strength. According to generally accepted military theory, the likelihood of an offensive's success could largely be guaranteed when the number of attackers was three times that of the defenders. The Canadians, however, counted on their infantry being more skilled and resolute than the Germans. Even more, they counted on the colossal power of both the aerial bombardment and the artillery to shatter the German fortifications and the garrison's will to resist.

"Normally an operation should not be thought of as dependent on air support for its success," Spry commented. "Inclement weather should merely deprive an infantry assault of a useful but not essential adjunct." But Operation Wellhit was another matter entirely because the "air component is a requisite." If the weather turned bad, he would have to delay the operation. Wellhit, he cautioned, "could not [be] launched without the air effort."[13]

The attack plan foresaw four primary phases. After a heavy preliminary aerial and artillery bombardment, both 8th and 9th Brigades
would attack from the east between Mont Lambert and Fort de la
Crèche—although 8th Brigade's North Shores would be operating
farther north with an independent attack on La Trésorerie and then
through to Wimereux. In the second phase, the two brigades would
seize the heart of the town and, if possible, a bridge crossing over
the Liane. The third phase entailed capturing the outlying strongpoints of Fort de la Crèche, Outreau, and Herquelingue. Wellhit would
finish with the capture of Nocquet on the coast and the heights of St.
Etienne.[14] During phases three and four, most of the outlying strongpoints, such as Fort de la Crèche and Outreau, were to be attacked
effectively from the rear, as the Canadians would be advancing toward
them from Boulogne.

Each brigadier issued his own operational plan on September 15,
and 8th Brigade's John "Rocky" Rockingham stressed that the "success
of the op will depend upon the speed with which [infantry battalions]
advance after the last aerial bomb has dropped. Timings must be
adhered to in order to take advantage of the heavy bombing and the
initial arty fire plan."[15]

Each brigade was to be supported by a squadron of Fort Garry Horse
tanks, and the specialized equipment of the 79th British Armoured
Division's 31st Tank Brigade moving up from Le Havre.[16] The Flails
of the 1st Lothians and Border Yeomanry 'C' Squadron's Nos. 1 and 3
Troops were assigned to 8th Brigade.[17] So, too, was a troop of AVRES
of 6th Assault Regiment's 81st Assault Squadron.[18] As 9th Brigade
faced the toughest job—winning Mont Lambert and then breaking
through Boulogne to seize a crossing over the Liane River—it was
given additional specialized equipment.[19] The brigade's attack was to
advance in three columns with heavy armoured support. Each column
was to be organized on the same lines, consisting of one Flail troop,
one AVRE troop, one Crocodile troop, a number of Petard-equipped
Churchill tanks, an armoured bulldozer, a Fort Garry Horse troop,
and a platoon of Kangaroos to carry the infantry.[20] As many of the
Crocodiles manned by the 141st Regiment, Royal Armoured Corps,
had only just left Le Havre after completing necessary repairs and

maintenance, the numbers of these per column varied from two to four and were far fewer than desired. From north to south, the columns were numbered A, B, and C.[21] Thirty-six Kangaroos and twenty 17th Duke of York's Royal Canadian Hussars recce regiment's half-track armoured personnel carriers were provided to protect 9th Brigade's infantry and allow it to keep pace with the armour. Each 9th Brigade battalion was also to be closely supported by Wasp flame-thrower Bren Carriers from the 17th Hussars.[22] Each brigade was assigned a field company less one platoon of engineers to clear routes through areas cratered by the aerial bombardment. The engineers would also, where needed, improvise a bridge over the Liane River to enable a proper Bailey to be emplaced, so that armour could join the infantry in the planned bridgehead on the opposite bank. The engineers brought with them four armoured and seven unarmoured bulldozers.[23]

Because the main weight of 3rd Division was concentrated across a quite narrow front facing and to the left of Mont Lambert, a deception plan was developed to convince the Germans that their entire frontage was threatened. Dubbed Klaehn Force because it was commanded by Cameron Highlanders of Ottawa (MG) battalion's Lieutenant Colonel P.C. Klaehn, it consisted of a "hodge podge" of units. At its core were the Camerons' machine-gun companies. But it also included two light anti-aircraft batteries, a battery from 3rd Anti-Tank Regiment, one troop of M-10 self-propelled anti-tank guns, and elements of the 18th Field Company, Royal Canadian Engineers, with the potential for a Fort Garry Horse squadron to be attached as necessary. The guns of the 14th Field Regiment were also on call. And there was a handful of FFI members. Klaehn Force duly set about trying to make as much "noise as an army," the Cameron Highlanders of Ottawa's second-in-command, Major Richard M. Ross, later wrote. "This was accomplished by patrolling, moving vehicles, vigorous harassing and a sound effects sapper section who simulated the sound of mortars being fired by detonating a series of small charges. Quite frankly this noise didn't sound particularly like mortar fire but did add to the cheerful racket."[24]

Operation Wellhit's large and complex artillery-fire plan was worked up by 3rd Division's chief gunner, Brigadier Stanley Todd. With all the heavily constructed concrete fortifications that had to be targeted, Todd knew the 25-pounder shells "would bounce . . . like peas off a tin pan." It was going to require heavier artillery to do the main job. Getting ready for the opening bombardment was a complex process, because the targets could not be registered by a gun firing from its planned position. "We never fired from our regular positions before the attack," Todd said later. "We'd take one gun away 300 yards and fire from there and prove our figures by observation. Then we'd calculate our figures from the position in which we hadn't fired at all because we knew the Germans would have sound detectors all over the place and if we stayed in a position from which we'd done our ranging, they'd knock us out on the day of the attack."[25]

Another problem Todd faced was getting all the ammunition in place. He had 328 guns made up of five field regiments, seven medium regiments, three heavy regiments, and two heavy anti-aircraft regiments.[26] Most of the ammunition was being brought from a depot at Dieppe, with the heavier-calibre shells coming from Bayeux. By September 17, he had managed to get delivered 400 rounds for each of the 120 25-pounders, 150 rounds for each of 112 medium guns, and 100 for every one of 48 heavy guns, plus more ammunition for the 48 heavy anti-aircraft guns. This amounted to 69,600 shells—all having to be squirrelled away safely near the gun lines.[27]

Through 11 Canadian Corps headquarters, Todd also acquired artillery support from across the English Channel, in the form of four large coastal guns stationed east of Dover that routinely duelled with the German cross-channel batteries at Calais and Cap Gris Nez. These consisted of two 14-inch guns, nicknamed Winnie and Pooh, manned by the Royal Marine Siege Regiment, as well as the two 15-inch guns of 540th Coast Regiment, Royal Artillery. The fire of these guns was to be directed by aerial observers flying near the selected targets, which were not part of the Boulogne defences but rather guns near Calais that could be turned to range on the Canadian troops putting in the attack.[28]

Todd and many gunners were grateful that neither the aerial nor artillery bombardment was likely to cause the extensive casualties that had been inflicted on the citizens of Le Havre. Generalleutnant Heim had managed to arrange their evacuation in two groups between September 11 and 13. Persuading some nine thousand civilians to abandon their homes had not been easy. Heim finally had to exert pressure on Boulogne's mayor to actually get the civilians organized to leave.[29]

As soon as Heim notified the Canadians of his intention, First Army Civil Affairs officers arrived to assist. They issued warnings that the civilians must be clear of Boulogne within thirty-six hours. Directions were given to move to a rendezvous point ten miles from the city. About five thousand civilians duly emerged within the required time period, and by September 16, a further three thousand had exited Boulogne. All were carried from the rendezvous point by military transport to camps that Civil Affairs had established about twenty miles from the soon-to-be battle area. "Thus," as one report put it, "a potential source of danger and confusion that might have impeded our operations and jeopardized the successful outcome was removed before the assault started. There seems little doubt that the civilians for the most part were extremely grateful to the Canadian Army for the arrangements made for their welfare and personal safety."[30] Heim, however, regretted being left with "about one thousand stubborn civilians who refused to be budged."[31] Within the fortress, food and water were not plentiful, and now he had additional people to provision. He also worried that many staying behind were connected to the resistance and were "a dangerous element."[32]

One evacuee column had passed through the North Shore (New Brunswick) Regiment's lines, creating a "steady stream of civilians with wheelbarrows and carts and baby carriages, streaming from the city. They seemed quite happy about the whole affair . . . A German soldier in civilian clothes was captured and the French said he had been hiding for a week in their homes."[33]

AS PLANS FOR the forthcoming aerial bombardment were being finalized, medium bombers appeared over Boulogne and showered down 420,000 leaflets entitled "The Lesson of Le Havre for the Defenders of Boulogne." The gist was that resistance was futile, and the Germans were being asked to die for nothing. As the leaflets were fluttering down, forty thousand safe-conduct passes were fired into the city by 25-pounders. Four scout cars equipped with loudspeakers stood in readiness to close in on isolated strongpoints, so that propaganda officers could try talking the defenders into surrendering.[34]

It was through the leaflets that Generalleutnant Heim learned of Le Havre's loss. "It came as a shock that this great fortress had collapsed so quickly and the news offered no bright prospects for [Boulogne's] future." Heim was left in the dark as to how the attack had been conducted. He learned nothing of the use of "flails, flamethrowers and armoured personnel carriers," his interrogators noted. "This failure to pass on information of enemy tactics and to forewarn of new attack methods was apparently quite normal, for Calais in turn did not benefit from any of the lessons learnt at either Boulogne or Le Havre. The only strange equipment of which Heim had been informed, and this from Fifteenth Army, was of a tank that cleared minefields. But so vague was the description that it was necessary for his interrogator at a later date to enlighten him on the appearance and principle" of the Flails.[35]

Meanwhile, the air aspect of Operation Wellhit was pulled together in all its destructive glory. There would be a ninety-minute heavy bomber attack of "a great quadrilateral of country, which included Mont Lambert and St. Martin-Boulogne, and reached almost to Marlborough and Bon Secours. The area to be bombed was over three kilometres in frontage, and a little over a kilometre in depth." This portion of the aerial attack would coincide with the main artillery bombardment. When the last bomb fell, the ground attack would begin. The other bombing was to provide close support and engage enemy guns in four areas west of Boulogne. These were two positions near Outreau—one on a knoll to the west and the other to the south—the strong defences of Nocquet, and a larger area at St. Etienne. This close-support phase was to happen between 1100 and 1250 hours, in what was described as "a form of counterbattery fire from the air," intended to free many artillery pieces to support the main attack.

In addition to the heavy bombing effort, No. 84 Tactical Group was to have fighter-bombers or rocket-firing Typhoons available for immediate call.[36] These aircraft, along with some medium bomber squadrons, had been active in the days immediately before Operation Wellhit, carrying out forty-nine attacks on known battery positions.[37] For September 17, nineteen targets were selected for Typhoon attacks.

Included in these strikes were Fort de la Crèche, La Trésorerie, an assortment of German gun positions, and a couple of strongpoints, along with a suspected signal centre.[38] Thereafter, the method of readiness known as "cab rank" would be at play, with aircraft waiting on the ground at nearby landing strips and able to arrive within thirty minutes of being summoned by ground or air observers to attack assigned targets.

A key component of Brigadier Todd's artillery plan was to "prolong the neutralizing effect of the air bombardment to enable the infantry to reach their first main objective before the [German] gunners could return to their guns. Secondly, to neutralize any strongpoint that might cover the ground over which the infantry was to advance beyond the first objective. Thirdly, to engage targets of opportunity in close support of the infantry."

To achieve this required "a comprehensive fire plan including over 400 predicted targets which covered every known and every possible strongpoint, gun position, and infantry position. These targets were sub-allotted to sixteen field, medium, heavy, and heavy anti-aircraft regiments so as to bring the required amount and most effective type of fire on each specific target. There was a timed program to cover the infantry to their first objectives, from then on pre-arranged tasks were made available on call as the advance progressed and the need arose."

Helping to prolong the air bombardment phase, these timed concentrations would be fired even as bombs were still dropping. The guns would then seamlessly continue as the infantry advanced, "in the hope that the enemy in his shelters would not be able to distinguish it from the bombing." Three medium regiments were also to shell identified German anti-aircraft gun installations to try to prevent their firing on the bombers. Great responsibility rested on the RCAF observation plane crews in their "minute Auster aircraft," as they were to quickly direct heavy bombers on to gun batteries that revealed themselves by opening fire. Three of these light, unarmoured, single-engine aircraft were to be over the battleground throughout the day.

With so much complex staff planning having gone into Operation Wellhit, its actual launch had attracted a great deal of attention throughout the Allied command chain. As September 17 approached, it became clear that this was "a show" attracting a large audience. Orders were consequently issued on September 15 for the accommodation of spectators, who included "naval, military and air force personnel, as well as press correspondents." The order emphasized that "such spectators do not position themselves at an operations headquarters where the staff is engaged in fighting the battle." Instead, they were provided with a "spectators' stand . . . located on very high ground two kilometers east of Neufchatel [that] afforded excellent observation of the Boulogne area, and was within the safety limits of the heavy bomber support." The 3rd Division order ended with a suitably legalistic disclaimer that this "formation accepts no responsibility for spectators within the divisional area."

Because the show was set for September 17, ensuring that it began on time and all the actors performed their respective parts on cue required careful attention to timepieces. For this was to be the day that Double British Summer Time, which had been in effect throughout the Normandy Campaign and which was two hours ahead of Greenwich Mean Time, would revert to regular war time—one hour faster than GMT. Consequently, all watches and other timepieces were to be set back an hour at 0300 hours, "so that there could be no possibility of a fatal hour's error throwing the whole attack into confusion."[39]

19

A Hard Day's Fighting

CLEAR SKIES AT dawn provided ideal weather for the heavy bombers and guns at Dover to do their work. Yet in his forward command post, 9th Brigade's Brigadier Rocky Rockingham was anything but sanguine about the bombers' pending approach. When Lieutenant General Guy Simonds advised him that Operation Wellhit would start with an aerial bombardment, Rockingham responded, "Send the heavy bombers to Berlin. I don't want anything to do with them." The brigadier was hardly the nervous type. He had led the Royal Hamilton Light Infantry into Normandy and immediately distinguished himself as a tough, pragmatic, clear-thinking soldier and first-class leader with a ruthless streak when necessary. Big and muscular with a face bearing scars of war, Rockingham possessed a self-confidence that allowed him to speak bluntly to superiors. In Normandy, a heavy-bomb attack had gone awry, striking part of the 3rd Division and inflicting a great many casualties. Among these was its commander, Major General Rod Keller. It was Rockingham who ripped open shell dressings to bind the leg wounds that ended Keller's military career. Unless Simonds could guarantee that the bombers would not stray over his lines, Rockingham opposed their use. "Well, you've got to do it," Simonds snapped.

A compromise was reached. The 9th Brigade's battalions would stay two thousand yards from the forward bomb line. Rockingham estimated that it would take ten minutes after the last bomb fell for the Kangaroos to carry the men to their first objective. That was plenty of time for the Germans to emerge from their dugouts and come into action. This was especially certain if they cottoned on to the planned ruse wherein the artillery would masquerade as bombers for several critical minutes after the planes departed. But Rockingham had an idea to counter this danger. What if at least some of the bombers circled back for another pass, leaving their bomb bay doors open? He suspected the Germans would think a new wave was arriving and stay hidden. Simonds agreed to arrange this ruse on ruse. He also offered to assign an RAF group captain to Rockingham's headquarters who would maintain constant contact with the bombers and intervene if bombs started falling short. When the officer arrived, Rockingham considered handcuffing the man's wrist to his own. "Don't go anywhere or I'll shoot you," he warned instead.[1]

At 0825 hours, wrote 3rd Division's historical officer, Captain Jack Martin, the "bombers approached us head on. Suddenly huge bursts of dust and smoke plumed out on the slopes of Mount Lambert . . . over the peak of Mount Lambert appeared a tight concentration of low [artillery] air bursts, designed to keep the flak crews there below ground . . . A later wave of bombers, directed on the peak of the mountain was preceded by a Pathfinder which dropped a white smoke marker. The arty seemed also to lay smoke here. A swarm of planes then materialized out of the sky as before, and once again huge clouds of smoke blotted out the shape of the hilltop."

In this attack, 540 Lancasters, 212 Halifaxes, and 40 Mosquitoes unleashed 3,232 tons of bombs on Boulogne. From Rockingham's post, the group captain confirmed that Mosquitoes dropped their pathfinding markers "precisely on the right points . . . close cooperation at its best."[2]

On Mont Lambert, a cluster of casemates were buried by earth thrown skyward. One casemate took a direct hit that cracked the concrete. Later, two dead Germans were discovered inside. One was slumped before the steel door, as if trying to escape. The other sat at a table staring straight ahead. Blood had spilled from his eyes, ears, and nose, indicating that concussion had killed him and his comrade.[3] A German officer scribbled a letter to his wife later in the afternoon, "I was just ready to go to breakfast when we had to run for shelter and we have been there ever since. The bombardment by bombers and artillery was terrific . . . I am looking at your pictures, my loved ones. I am quiet now and resigned to my fate whatever it may be."[4]

Generalleutnant Ferdinand Heim had inherited a battle headquarters in a bunker on Mont Lambert's summit because it afforded excellent views seaward while being a safe distance inland. This headquarters housed Boulogne's central communication hub and most headquarters' wireless equipment. With the attack now coming from land, Heim had realized Mont Lambert was going to be in the eye of the storm so had relocated on September 16 to Outreau. But little of the large communications equipment had been moved before the attack began. When the first bombs struck Mont Lambert, the communication hub ceased working. Heim was suddenly unable to communicate, except sporadically, with the garrison's many strongpoints. He was virtually isolated in Outreau.[5]

Again, as at Le Havre, the actual results of the bombing proved more visually dramatic than effective. Where bombs struck open gun emplacements, the result was decent, with about half of the weapons disabled or destroyed. But the British operational research team that visited after the battle concluded that "against concrete gun positions it is extremely unlikely that any damage [was] caused by the bombing." As before, they sought solace in believing that the "moral effect of heavy bombing may be considerable if followed up immediately on the ground. The only time limit so far available for negligible resistance is within ten minutes of the attack." After that, the Germans generally recovered and assumed their fighting positions. Reassuringly, they added that "bomb craters near strongpoints afford useful cover for attacking troops and reduce our casualties."[6] That these craters also impeded armoured vehicles supporting the attack went unremarked. The moral effect was generally considered important. One German caught in an underground bunker described the experience as "like being in the bottom of a cocktail shaker."[7]

WITH BOMBS STILL falling, 8th Brigade's North Shore (New Brunswick) Regiment launched the ground assault's first phase attack on the coastal battery at La Trésorerie, on the extreme northern flank of the German defences. Although its 12-inch coastal guns could not fire landward, the battery was heavily protected and enjoyed such a commanding view over the main Canadian attack area that it was considered a potent threat. So the North Shores had been ordered to distract the Germans there with a direct attack thirty minutes before the bombardment ended and the rest of the ground assault started at 0955 hours.[8]

'A' and 'B' Companies advanced with a couple of platoons of 'D' Company providing flanking support fire from the summit of Pas de Gay. Each company was deployed in arrowhead formation, with one platoon forward, the other two back, and company headquarters in the middle. Lieutenant Charles Richardson, wounded at Carpiquet Airfield on July 4, 1944, had just returned a few days earlier from convalescing. He led 'B' Company's forward platoon.[9] Richardson had been shocked to find that so many comrades from the early days in Normandy had died, been wounded, or evacuated sick. It "was like walking in on a group of strangers," he recalled. There was no time for Richardson to get acquainted with the ground over which he was to attack or to meet the men he led. His touchstone was veteran Sergeant Ed Gilks.

The decision to attack before the bombers broke away and while the artillery still battered La Trésorerie gave the two companies an initial edge. Going in hard and fast, the North Shores reached the forward slit trenches without pause and rooted out the dazed defenders. A newly constructed pillbox covering the crossroads below the coastal battery was taken without pause. "I thought it was like old times," Richardson said later. In mere minutes of dashing forward through warm sun-shine, and facing no serious resistance, his platoon had reached its intermediate objective on the edge of the hill east of the battery and paused to wait for the others to catch up.

But looking back, Richardson realized his mistake. The rest of 'B' Company was taking heavy fire from the Germans by the battery and were also caught in a minefield his platoon had dashed through unawares. Major Bill Sullivan had a leg torn off by a mine. Taking over, Captain Mickey McCallum managed to lead the rest of the company through to Richardson's position. 'A' Company's Major F.F. "Toot" Moar and most of his men safely negotiated the minefield, but his company headquarters, including the company signaller, froze in its middle and would go no farther.[10] Despite being wounded in four places by shrapnel from an exploding s-mine, Company Sergeant Major Fenton Daley returned to these men and led them out.[11] He then made several further trips into "the mine-infested territory to attend wounded." Daley received a Military Cross, a decoration usually reserved for officers.

From well back, Support Company's Captain Hal MacDonald had at first thought it "awe-inspiring to watch the attacking companies, like ants, moving up the slope under heavy fire and over mines. With every puff of smoke and dirt you wondered what fellow had got it . . . The whole area was a network of mines and booby-traps." He realized that the concrete bunkers and forts were all sited so their fire overlapped to prevent any gaps through which the North Shores could wriggle. Seeing that the attacking companies were in dire straits, MacDonald got his pioneer platoon busy clearing a gap through the minefield to re-establish contact.

Through the morning and into the afternoon, both companies repeatedly tried advancing, but were driven back by heavy fire. Several German machine guns were firing from positions just twenty-five yards distant. "The Jerries had all the advantages and though we tried everything . . . we could not get beyond the trenches we had taken, and in one of our desperate attempts Lieutenant [William Ernest] Tranton was killed," Richardson said. McCallum proposed they retreat. "I pointed out it would be hell to go back through the minefield." Moar agreed, saying, "We should hang on as long as possible."[12]

With 'A' and 'B' Companies stuck under "a storm of airburst" fire from 20-millimetre anti-aircraft guns and the machine guns, the situation only worsened when 75-millimetre guns started ranging in from a position near the village of Wimille to the south. From his forward headquarters in Wacquinghen, Lieutenant Colonel Ernie Anderson felt helpless to assist his embattled companies. By the afternoon the village itself was being heavily shelled, and he could see that the 20-millimetre gunfire was terrifically "effective against infantry, invariably pinning them down. The advance was stopped, all movement being impossible. Enemy defensive fire tasks were brought down over the main road, with such accuracy as it was hard not to admire."

Anderson tried sending Flails followed by Crocodiles through the minefield to the companies, but "such profuse armour-piercing shot met them that they were unable to move up the hill and had to remain behind its cover. Thus no lanes could be beaten through the mine-fields." When several Wasps attempted to pick through the minefields, two blew up and the others retired. The only thing helping was a troop of M-10 self-propelled anti-tank guns firing from a position eighteen hundred yards from the companies. That somewhat countered the 20-millimetre "flak pillboxes which ringed the objective."

At dusk, Moar's 'A' Company closed on the northeasternmost gun battery's casemate and, after a frantic exchange of grenades, wrested half of the large complex from the Germans. Further progress was impossible, so Moar's men settled in for the night and were happily surprised when the Germans failed to cut the power to their area—leaving them with the luxury of electric light and a radio playing. 'B' Company, meanwhile, dug in nearby and started aggressively pa-trolling by sections. One of these sections captured the gun battery's hospital without a fight. The North Shores discovered they were largely able to range freely in the night without encountering any moving Germans. Anderson assumed the "enemy . . . had no stomach for night patrols and was easily panicked by them."

During the night, MacDonald's pioneers cleared a narrow passage through the minefield. Carrying parties passed through with food and ammunition and evacuated the wounded on their return trip. They also took in batteries for the wireless sets, which had all failed. "All in all," Anderson later wrote, "it was a very unpleasant night."[13]

JUST AS THE main attack had started at 0955 hours, the four coastal guns near Dover fired on selected targets near Calais. The 14-inch guns "Winnie" and "Pooh," manned by the Royal Marine Siege Regiment, were each soon throwing a round every thirty seconds across the channel toward targets twenty-three miles distant. Shortly into the shoot, Winnie suffered a misfire that disabled it for thirty minutes.[14] Also joining the firing program were the 540th Coast Regiment, Royal Artillery's two 15-inch guns. Despite nearing the end of their shelf life, the guns still managed to score a hit on a German emplacement in the

Noires Mottes Battery near Sangatte that detonated its ammunition. The resulting explosions wrecked one 16-inch gun's mountings. At 1400 hours, however, shot from the worn barrels of the 15-inch guns was reported falling into the sea well short of its targets. Both guns stood down. They had fired their last shots of the war, having during fifty-six actions expended 1,243 rounds in cross-channel shoots.[15] Winnie and Pooh remained operational.

The fire from the Dover guns hugely impressed the tankers of the 1st Hussars Regiment from 2nd Canadian Armoured Brigade, enjoying a front-row seat from positions outside Calais. Earlier, their commander had been given a map "with a great blue line [that] told us where the danger zone was. Every few minutes one would hear a terrific din . . . Here is about the only time when our shells were a bit unwelcome—mainly because at 21 miles we were uncertain as to the beaten zone and we could just visualize what a Sherman would look like after an encounter with an allied 'freight train.'"[16] Winnie and Pooh would continue supporting the Canadians at Boulogne through to the end of September 20.

AS PART OF the main attack, 8th Brigade's other two battalions advanced on foot. Le Régiment de la Chaudière headed for Marlborough, about two miles west of the start line. Left of the French-Canadians, the Queen's Own Rifles of Canada were bound for St. Martin Boulogne, which stood alongside a main road leading into Boulogne's upper town. The Chauds had an intermediate objective—a hamlet called Rupembert, where a small garrison protected a radar station.[17]

Major G. Beaudry's 'C' Company led the Chauds' advance. Before them, Rupembert burned, and fires also raged in St. Martin Boulogne.[18] There was little opposition, mainly artillery fire covering the roads and crossroads. Minefields were profuse and deep, slowing the marching troops and wrecking or disabling several supporting vehicles.[19] By 1030 hours, 'C' Company closed on Rupembert, and it seemed its garrison was ready to make a stand.[20] Supporting the Chauds were tanks of the Fort Garry Horse's 'C' Squadron. The tankers started shooting from an open field about five hundred yards out and then rolled in with the infantry, using the Shermans for cover. Minutes later, the sixty-strong garrison spilled out of its blockhouse and surrendered.[21] The radar station was taken intact, providing a fine haul for Allied intelligence staff.

As the Chauds passed out of Rupembert, they drew fire from an anti-aircraft gun position, which 'C' Squadron's No. 4 Troop immediately shot up. After this, the infantry shooed the tankers away because their presence was drawing increasingly heavy artillery fire.[22] Moving back, the tankers continued to be dogged by shelling, and No. 4 Troop's commander, Lieutenant J.R. Johnston, and his crew were wounded when their tank was knocked out. Following a different route, the tank squadron tried again to close up with the Chauds, only to be blocked by mines and obstructions on the road. Major C.W. Fletcher sent Lieutenant Wilfred James Stevenson's No. 3 Troop to the southwest, where a ravine might provide a route around the obstructions and then allow them to regain the road. Finding every approach blocked by more mines, Stevenson dismounted to find a way through on foot. The twenty-eight-year-old stepped on an s-mine and was killed.[23] There was nothing the tankers could do but wait for a Flail to come forward and clear a route.

At 1326 hours, the Flails opened a lane, and 'C' Squadron accompanied by 6th Assault Regiment AVRES headed forward to support the Chauds.[24] While passing through the minefield, two more Shermans were knocked out, and two crewmen died.[25] A small creek ran through the middle of the minefield with a thick carpet of mines dug in on the opposite bank. A half troop of AVRES, commanded by Captain T.W. Davis, carried bundles of fascines to make an ad hoc bridge over the creek. Although Davis was wounded while scouting on foot, he managed to find a suitable crossing point. The AVRE crews dumped their bundles of sticks into the creek. Flails then moved over the creek and cleared a path through the mines to open a route for the Shermans.[26]

The Chauds, meanwhile, had encountered a position near Bon Secours consisting of ten reinforced concrete dugouts on a forward slope overlooking their line of advance. About a hundred Germans were inside the dugouts and interlinking trenches. They opened up with a storm of small-arms fire. Separating the Chauds from this strongpoint was a deep, dense minefield. 'D' Company quickly tackled the strongpoint. Commanding one platoon was Corporal Robert Richards, who was wounded in the hip by shrapnel from an exploding mine as soon as the attack began. Refusing to stop and have the wound dressed, Richards led his men through thick fire to close on the dugouts.[27] Nearby, Private Joseph Etienne Ouellet carried a Bren gun in the leading section of one assaulting platoon. Many men with him were either killed or wounded getting through the minefield. Then the section's second-in-command was killed right in front of Ouellet, who pressed on virtually alone. Twenty yards from a German machine-gun post, he was wounded by grenade shrapnel. Ignoring the injury and the volleys of fire coming his way, Ouellet charged the machine-gun post while firing his Bren gun from the hip. Wounding the three-man crew silenced the position. The actions by Richards and Ouellet turned the battle, and about fifty Germans surrendered. Richards received a Distinguished Conduct Medal and Ouellet a Military Medal for their bravery.[28] After this, German resistance diminished, and the Chauds progressed rapidly to Marlborough.

Left of the Chauds, the Queen's Own Rifles had also been slowed by minefields and harassed by shelling. The Queen's Own had under command a platoon of the Cameron Highlanders of Ottawa's 'D' Company, the 52nd Canadian Anti-Tank Battery, a platoon of 16th Field Company engineers, a squadron of Fort Garry Horse tanks, and a squadron of AVRES from the British 6th Assault Regiment. Leading the attack were Captain Robert William Sawyer's 'B' Company and Major R.A. Cottrill's 'D' Company. Facing little resistance beyond artillery and mortar fire, 'B' Company soon reached the outskirts of the hamlet of Wicardenne. Sawyer was slightly wounded. Most of the Germans holding the hamlet surrendered as soon as the company reached it. As a column of prisoners tromped past where Sawyer stood discussing next moves with the Fort Garry Horse troop commander, a German sergeant strayed beyond the marked safe route that had been flailed through the minefield in front of the hamlet and triggered a mine. Sawyer and the German were instantly killed.

'D' Company, meanwhile, had passed out of Wicardenne toward a strongpoint whose defenders were fighting "tenaciously." The ground between the hamlet and the strongpoint had been so badly cratered by bombs that the Shermans could find no way forward. A Petard AVRE managed to negotiate past most of the craters, only to slide into one just short of the strongpoint, where it remained stuck for two days. Despite the lack of armoured support, 'D' Company soon overran the strongpoint and took more prisoners.[29]

Beyond stood St. Martin Boulogne atop a slight hill. This small suburb contained one of Boulogne's main rail stations. A small church stood close to its eastern boundary, where a crossroads cut across the main St. Omer–Boulogne road that 'A' Company was going to follow in its attack. Behind the crossroads were several machine-gun positions in concrete pillboxes. On the west side of the village, a smaller strongpoint protected a couple of artillery pieces, which started shelling Captain Dick Medland's 'A' Company the moment it headed toward St. Martin. Company Sergeant Major Charlie Martin led No. 9 Platoon up the left side of the road, with No. 8 Platoon opposite. Tucked in behind was Medland's headquarters and No. 7 Platoon. That day, however, the last platoon was not made up of Queen's Own Rifles. Instead, the 3rd Defence and Employment Platoon of the Lorne Scots (Peel, Dufferin, and Halton) Regiment, which provided guard protection for 11 Canadian Corps divisional and brigade headquarters, was attached to give it combat experience.

The moment 'A' Company moved into the open, it came "under heavy shelling and machine-gun fire, but we were moving fast, zigzagging, changing speeds and being careful to be well spread out—from the point man at our front to the last section man, our coverage would be about a hundred yards," Martin wrote. "We were lucky to take only a few light casualties."

As the lead platoons came up to the crossroads, the machine-gun and mortar fire from the facing strongpoint pinned them down. They needed tanks, but Martin saw that these were still back about a half mile down the hill, mired amid mines and bomb craters. Flails were working on a lane, but it was clearly going to take awhile. Martin's men were in a loose cluster left of the road, and on its right side was Corporal Joey Carmichael's No. 8 Platoon section. A pillbox housing a machine gun was very close. If it was knocked out, they might be able to move. No. 9 Platoon's Sergeant James "Jimmy" Young and

Rifleman Stephen De Blois decided to attack it together. Both were D-Day veterans. De Blois's two brothers, Lomar and Alex, each served in separate 'A' Company platoons. They came from Cochrane, Alberta. Young led off with De Blois close behind. Halfway across the road, a machine-gun burst killed both men. Young was twenty-five, De Blois twenty-one. No sooner did these men fall than Rifleman Ernie Hackett charged the pillbox with the rest of their section in tow. Although Hackett and several others were wounded, the men managed to throw several smoke grenades through firing slits that brought the Germans out, choking and gasping, to surrender.

With the German opposition lessened, Carmichael's section dashed over the road and eliminated the last machine-gun position. Carmichael suffered a severe leg wound. The rest of No. 8 Platoon pushed into St. Martin and established a defensive position north of the church.[30] A short, vicious firefight erupted, with some of the platoon using tombstones in the small church cemetery for cover. "Move over, Pierre, I think I'm going to join you," one man said as he squeezed hard against a headstone.[31]

'A' Company soon won St. Martin, the Germans either driven off or captured. The wounded were gathered inside the church, while Medland established his headquarters in the adjacent manse. Several nuns appeared and began treating the wounded. Some had tears in their eyes as they tended the soldiers, after first giving each a glass or two of the communion wine.

Martin was seeing to the company's disposition. To his surprise, the Lorne Scots had come through the action without a single casualty. "If they were inexperienced in action, it sure didn't show," he said. He gave them the company's frontal position on St. Martin's western edge, while the other platoons formed an all-round defence centred about the church and manse. The prisoners were confined under guard to several nearby outbuildings.

At dusk, Martin and Rifleman Charlie Bloomfield prepared to go back about two miles to the start line and bring up the company jeep and Bren carrier. They badly needed ammunition and food. Martin wanted to make a quick turnaround, so he contacted the company's acting quartermaster, Rifleman Dick Klintworth, to say they were coming. In the fading light, Martin could see the route to take safely through the minefields and craters. But the return would be in darkness, so he wanted to mark it somehow. Normally, white tape served this purpose, but nobody had any. So he asked an English-speaking nun if she could think of anything that would work. She returned with all the church's pristine linen tablecloths and napkins. "Our priest is giving a special prayer for you and your men," she said.

Tearing the linen into strips the two men duly marked out the trail behind them. Arriving at the start line, they found the jeep and carrier ready to go. The company cook, whom Martin only knew as "Pops," stood by with kettles of hot grub. He insisted on coming along. "I cooked it, I serve it," he grunted. Klintworth drove the carrier, Corporal W. Pennell the jeep. The latter disliked the idea, arguing that the mines, the continuing shelling, and the fact that the lines were still porous with many German outposts having been bypassed, made it all too risky. Klintworth suggested that Martin lead the vehicles on foot to keep them on the safe path. "Where he leads, I follow," Klintworth told Pennell. At 2100 hours, the little group reached the church. Martin knew that without the church linens, he would never have found the way back. Soon thereafter, the Germans launched a small counterattack from Boulogne, which the Lorne Scots easily drove off while gathering in more prisoners.

Captain Medland told Martin he was really worried about the following day. Their assignment was to punch into Boulogne and fight through to the Saint-Pierre district, which looked down upon the Liane River mouth and the port. That meant advancing a couple of miles through a densely built town where many buildings had been destroyed by Allied bombing and the streets were likely choked with rubble. 'A' Company's two normal platoons were down to half strength due to the day's casualties. The Lorne Scots were whole, so would lead the attack. Yet they had little combat experience, and street fighting was among the worst of assignments.[32]

WHILE THE QUEEN'S Own Rifles and Le Régiment de la Chaudière of 8th Brigade had been advancing on the right, 9th Brigade's attack had been put in by the Stormont, Dundas and Glengarry Highlanders

and North Nova Scotia Highlanders. The plan for the Glens was ambitious. They were to be carried forward in Kangaroos through a gap
between two heights of German-held ground. At six hundred feet,
Mont Lambert stood to the right—a low, hulking, heavily fortified
mound that dominated the mostly flat ground surrounding it. Mont
Lambert was the North Novas' main target. Their task was straight-
forward—just carve a way up to the summit. But as the slopes were
heavily defended, and large concrete bunkers on top dominated any
approach, a sharp action was expected. The Glens, meanwhile, were
to slip through the gap and gain control of the road that passed to the
south of St. Martin Boulogne. This would open the way for the three
armoured columns formed by 31st British Tank Brigade troops in their
specialized equipment, with Fort Garry Horse tanks and a platoon
of infantry, to batter their way into Boulogne and drive through to
bridges across the Liane River. The Glens would provide a platoon for
both columns A and B, while the North Novas assigned a platoon to
column C. The rest of the Glens were to breach the wall surrounding
the old part of Boulogne and secure the citadel. For the first phase
of the attack, the Glens had twenty Kangaroos and seven armoured
troop carriers to lift them to the road. Fire support was provided by a
troop of self-propelled anti-tank guns, two troops of Fort Garry Horse
tanks, three AVRES of 87th Assault Squadron, and a section of 18th
Field Company engineers. There was also a section of Wasps of the
17th Duke of York's recce regiment on hand. The Glens carried several
lifebuoy flame-throwers.

The artillery was still firing as the Kangaroos carrying the two lead
assault companies of the Glens charged toward the gap. 'D' Company
was on the right, 'B' Company on the left, and 'C' Company following
on foot, its task being to clear the small La Cocherie wood.[33] As the
Kangaroos swept forward, small-arms fire and shrapnel from exploding German artillery shells and mortar bombs ricocheted off the armoured hulls. Thirty minutes out, the Kangaroos were stopped before
a minefield. The infantry piled out and ran forward.[34] As 'D' Company
entered a draw running south of La Cocherie wood, it got hung up
in a minefield. The objective lay a thousand yards ahead, and men
were being lost to mines and enemy fire. The Fort Garry Horse tanks

were also held up by the minefield, so the company had no armoured support. 'D' Company slogged forward alone under "very heavy and extremely accurate shelling." 'B' Company was also taking fire, but its men managed to get through the minefield and gain their objective "without event."

As per his normal practice, Lieutenant Colonel Roger Rowley was out front with his men. Having taken over the Glens in the last stages of the Normandy breakout, the thirty-year-old had won the respect of the men through his audacious leadership, which often put his own life on the line but also made clear he would do everything possible to keep them from harm, while never failing to achieve assigned tasks. Rowley saw that the "disadvantage of the terrain was now painfully evident." To their right, 8th Brigade's Queen's Own Rifles had not yet seized St. Martin Boulogne. On the left, Mont Lambert was just being attacked by the North Novas. From the southwest, they were clearly visible to German positions across the river at Le Portel and Outreau. "From all three points came heavy artillery fire which made movement almost impossible . . . Under this fire an engineer officer of 18 [Canadian Field Company] did excellent work directing the clearing of the minefield up to the crossroads." As a bulldozer supporting the advance had proven capable of doing only three miles per hour, it had been bypassed by the Kangaroos and other vehicles and now seemed to have gone astray entirely. So all the mine-clearing "work had to be done by hand," using mine detectors and knife-probing techniques to find each buried charge and then lift or detonate it.[35]

Over by Mont Lambert, meanwhile, the North Novas were tangled in hard fighting. The Kangaroos carrying 'D' and 'C' Companies in the vanguard surprised everyone by getting partway up the slope before a minefield blocked them.[36] 'D' Company bailed out thirty yards from the crest, which was actually a saddle linking the main summit on the right and a lower spur to the left. Charging upward, the men got into the saddle, but were then slashed by fire from each of the higher flanks and a pillbox straight ahead. Major Maurice Clennett led his men in two attempts to overcome the pillbox but was driven back each time. To the right, 'C' Company' ran into trouble when it disembarked directly into a minefield. Some men froze, but Sergeant

George Stewart carefully guided them through the mines by ones and twos. Meeting stiff resistance from a series of pillboxes, the company had three men killed and fourteen wounded in winkling out the Germans. 'A' Company soon came up to the left of 'D' Company and went for the lower spur. Lieutenant Caleb Evert Sutherland was at the head of one leading platoon, Lieutenant E.F. Fraser the other, when a shell landed in the middle of the track between them. Sutherland fell dead. The company suffered heavily, but dug in close to the spur's summit.[37] Above them was a network of pillboxes, and continuing on was impossible. 'A' Company, meanwhile, had been pinned down by a strongpoint a short distance up the slope and radioed for support. Two British Crocodiles responded. Closing to within fifty yards, one unleashed its entire fuel load of flame against the pillbox. This caused the Germans inside to lock themselves into a gas-proof chamber, from which they finally emerged after one of the North Novas who spoke German negotiated with them for about five hours.[38]

Throughout the long day's fighting on Mont Lambert, the North Novas encountered "innumerable pillboxes" that had to be eliminated one by one. Twenty of them were overcome by either the North Novas burning them out with the lifebuoy flame-throwers, or the supporting Petards blasting them with their heavy shells.[39] Also in support were several Wasps of the 17th Duke of York's Regiment that had managed to keep up with the infantry. Captain Walter Pavey watched the first two reaching the saddle get knocked out the moment they "poked their noses over the crest."[40] Farther to the right, however, two others managed to get within two hundred yards of a large fortification. With the North Novas providing covering small-arms fire, the Wasps advanced across open ground right into the position and flamed four bunkers. Immediately, the Germans within threw out a white flag, but refused to come out for ten minutes for fear of the lingering Wasps. Twenty-seven Germans surrendered.[41] As night fell, 'B' Company came up behind the three strung-out companies to protect their rear. There were still isolated pockets of Germans scattered about the slopes. When a cluster of about twenty-five Germans was spotted running into the cover of a house, a Petard lumbered over and "brought the place down on top of them." The North Nova's war diarist estimated they had suffered about fifty-eight casualties. Among those killed was Lieutenant James Arthur Affleck. It was his first day in combat.[42]

In the mid-afternoon, two of the three armoured columns attempted "to smash through to the river crossings." Column A was to have advanced via the La Capelle–Boulogne road, but Rowley had gone forward and found it obstructed by roadblocks.[43] The southern route involved poorer roads damaged by bomb craters, but it was decided that a bulldozer could render it passable. At 1630 hours, this route was declared open, and the two columns proceeded one behind the other along it. Travelling with each was a platoon of Glens from 'A' Company. Leading the advance were Flails with some FFI men aboard—while others rode in the column commanders' scout cars—to serve as guides.

"This vital thrust to the river," as one report stated later, "encountered great difficulties from our own bomb craters as well as from enemy road blocks. Craters were from 30 to 50 feet wide and 20 deep. Blinded by the dust that arose from the shelling and from the caterpillar tracks of the columns themselves, many armoured vehicles floundered into these huge holes. Filling them in with the earth blown out was not satisfactory, for it was too pulverized to give the tanks traction. Flails were lost in the dust of their own threshing, and three bogged down in this way. With these obstacles confronting them, and much heavy enemy shellfire coming down upon them, it is not surprising that neither of the two armoured columns succeeded in reaching the bridges to which they were directed. Instead, they spent the night fighting in the streets of Boulogne." One column broke off and joined the main body of the Glens advancing toward the ramparts of the old town.[44] At nightfall, operations ceased and everyone paused to await the morning.

As the army's official historian wrote, "at the end of the first day, a considerable wedge had been driven into the enemy's fortifications in the Highland Brigade's sector, while in the 8th [Brigade's] good progress had been made." But everywhere, the "operation had gone more slowly than . . . forecast." On September 15, a First Army staff report had "assumed that Boulogne would fall in one day . . . and suggested the same troops that attacked Boulogne on the 17th might be able to attack Calais on the 19th. This, it now appeared, was wildly sanguine."[45]

20

Process of Winkling Out

DURING THE NIGHT of September 17–18, Stormont, Dundas and Glengarry Highlanders commander Lieutenant Colonel Roger Rowley realized that the leading armoured column inside Boulogne had only a single platoon of his men providing protection. He decided to send Major J.F. Peterson's 'B' Company to reinforce it. As Captain Jack Watt, who commanded the support company, had been killed earlier in the day, Rowley lacked an experienced officer for that role. He therefore dragooned his 14th Field Regiment FOO, Captain Arthur Dowker, into taking the support-company vehicles, loaded with ammunition and other supplies, through to the armoured column. By the time the support company was ready to go, Peterson's 'B' Company—which was to have accompanied Dowker's vehicles—was long gone.

Buildings burned everywhere, "so the troops were uncomfortably silhouetted as they passed through the streets and there were many German patrols in the area." Finding it impossible to read his map and often unable to illuminate it for fear of attracting enemy attention, Peterson kept getting lost. Finally, after several skirmishes with the enemy, 'B' Company blundered into the armoured column and threw a protective screen around its machines. They arrived in the nick of time, as Germans soon "came in on the Glens in hair-raising fashion, their boots covered with cloth so as to be noiseless and their faces and hands blackened. They were familiar with the paths and alleys . . . and were able to close in to the attack quickly." The Glens drove them off without losing a single tank, but several men were wounded.

Contacting Dowker by wireless, Peterson learned the FOO was lost. Taking three men, he set out to find the artilleryman and the support company. Slipping past houses where Germans were heard talking, Peterson marked each door with chalk so they could be easily located in the morning. Failing to find Dowker, the patrol was just turning about when a German soldier appeared. Peterson shot him, and suddenly small-arms fire struck from all sides. One man fell dead, another wounded, while Peterson and the other man fled back to the column. A patrol quickly went out and rescued the two casualties.

Dowker was soon in touch by wireless to report he had taken another wrong turn but was now headed in the right direction. He led the vehicles along a perilous route that was badly cratered, often mined, and under German shellfire. Getting through to the column just before dawn, Dowker delivered the supplies. The Glens were just about out of ammunition. Dowker received a Military Cross for his work.[1]

During the night, the Canadians and Germans across the front conducted an often confused, sometimes desultory, and at other times fierce exchange. German snipers were active, and their mortar and artillery fire was incessant. The Canadians responded by closing on pillboxes to attack with grenades and machine guns. Most of the time, these positions were too strong to overcome with small fighting patrols. But on Mont Lambert, the North Nova Scotia Highlanders' 'A' Company sent a platoon out to determine the "best way to take their pillboxes" on the summit of the lower spur west of the main summit. Catching the Germans by surprise, the platoon seized two small pillboxes that provided a good base for the morning's renewed attack.[2]

South of Mont Lambert, Brigadier Rocky Rockingham had ordered the Cameron Highlanders of Ottawa's Lieutenant Colonel P.C. Klaehn to send a patrol up five-hundred-foot-high Mont Herquelingue, which dominated the north bank of the Liane River across from St. Etienne, and determine how strongly held were the fortifications surrounding a 155-millimetre battery there. 'C' Company's Lieutenant V. Leatherdale, with three men, climbed up the summit, wormed through wire surrounding the fortifications, and then snuck around quietly, assessing their strength. The patrol returned at 0340 hours, and Leatherdale reported that although the fortifications were occupied, he did not think it was in strength. Based on this information, Klaehn instructed 'C' Company's Major Bill Baird to tee up an attack. At the same time, 'B' Company would start moving northwest alongside the Liane River toward Boulogne—two and a half miles distant.[3]

Before daybreak on September 18, a Cameron Highlanders of Ottawa patrol near the base of Herquelingue picked up four German prisoners—who reported that the battery was held by 150 to 300 men and consisted of two 155-millimetre guns, while the garrison was equipped with twenty light machine guns. Considering this, Baird decided to postpone the attack for a day to plan it correctly. The attack would go in the night of September 18–19.[4]

AT DAWN ON Monday, September 18, the Canadians struck the Boulogne garrison hard. On the 8th Brigade front, particularly at La Trésorerie, the "process of winkling out the immense pillboxes . . . proved a slow task."[5] In the early morning, the North Shore (New Brunswick) Regiment's 'A' Company succeeded in securing the other half of the large casemate on the position's northern corner, half of which they had taken the day before, and then eliminated a smaller gun position with a PIAT round. This led to a weakening of resistance throughout the German position. When a German surrendered to 'B' Company, Captain Mickey McCallum sent the man back with a demand that they give up or face being annihilated by tanks and aerial bombardment. Instead of putting in an attack, Lieutenant Charles Richardson and the other officers "waited on our boy and hoped he was telling a good story. Sure enough, we saw a white flag emerge from the gun emplacement. Then Jerries without arms started hurrying out. When those surrendering troops reached us I asked them if there were any others remaining in the emplacement, and was quickly cautioned not to go near it as the big gun was soon to be 'kaput.' The Jerry who spoke English said, 'The kapitan kaput also to himself.' The import of this did not hit us until there was a sudden deafening roar from the emplacement and we proceeded to explore. We found the commandant had strapped himself into the firing seat of the cross-channel gun together with his second-in-command on the opposite seat, and had used demolition charges to put the guns and themselves out of commission."[6]

With the main position and its 30.5-centimetre guns silenced forever, the German defenders lost heart, and the third strongpoint soon surrendered. By mid-afternoon, all that remained to be cleared were the fortified observation posts on the northwest slope overlooking Wimereux. 'B' Company's platoon commanders managed to talk the men in several of these into surrendering, while others were driven out with phosphorous grenades. Once it was clear that La Trésorerie had been subdued, the Germans opened up a three-sided shelling of the position from batteries at Wimille, Wimereux, and Cap Gris Nez. The North Shores, however, found good protection inside the casemates.

'A' and 'B' Companies had both suffered fairly heavy casualties, and Lieutenant Colonel Ernie Anderson decided their job would be to continue occupying La Trésorerie, while 'C' and 'D' Companies carried out the next task of seizing the two villages of Wimille and Wimereux.

The North Shores had taken 450 prisoners and never bothered counting those Germans killed. "Stronger fortifications could hardly have existed," Anderson said. "The casemates had been unshaken by heavy bombing. Each one contained a complete electric plant and diesel engine, which were kept in running order by a few prisoners who were retained for this purpose. The quarters, well heated and lit, were most comfortable. The garrison was nearly all German; most of them were marines. Perhaps because of the superior facilities of their quarters they looked cleaner and more soldierly than the usual prisoners. Their ammunition supply was in no way depleted. There was an ample stock of food, which might have lasted three months. The battery also possessed a dug-in, well-equipped hospital."[7]

While the North Shores had been quelling La Trésorerie, 8th Brigade's main two-battalion body had continued its operations on the northern outskirts of Boulogne. Le Régiment de la Chaudière's 'A' and 'B' Companies advanced on Bon Secours despite intense 88-millimetre fire coming from the village. Major Hugues Lapointe's 'A' Company soon encountered such heavy resistance that it was pinned down midway to the village. Both companies were eventually stopped by the fire and fell back to their start line. Abandoning further frontal attacks on Bon Secours, the Chauds planned to take it in a flank attack that evening.[8]

At St. Martin Boulogne, meanwhile, the Queen's Own Rifles advanced toward the Saint-Pierre district of Boulogne at 0530 hours. 'A' Company took point with 'B' Company right behind. Because of Captain Robert William Sawyer's death the previous day, Captain H.C.F. Elliott now commanded 'B' Company.[9] As 'A' Company's other two platoons could field only half their normal strength, the unscathed Lorne Scots platoon, commanded by twenty-one-year-old Lt. John Donald Leslie Stewart, was out front. The platoon's normal duty was to guard First Canadian Army higher formation headquarters, so Stewart's first experience of combat command had taken place only the day before. Company Sergeant Major Charlie Martin had been impressed by the officer's courage and situational awareness. So he was not surprised to see Stewart advance his platoon in textbook configuration for the forthcoming street-cleaning operation.

"There was a point man on the right side. Every time he moved forward, two men following twenty yards behind on the left gave him covering rifle fire. And twenty yards back again [were] two Bren-gunners, one on each side of the road. As the point man moved up, so did one of the Brens—only one at a time—and when that small advance appeared secure the second Bren would come up." Just as Martin thought, "we seem to be doing okay," things went to hell. A small German armoured car appeared ahead, and the light machine gun on its cab opened fire. As Stewart shouted at his men to take cover, a hidden sniper armed with a machine gun fired a burst from the flank, and the officer fell dead. Martin and Sergeant Jack Bennett of No. 9 Platoon grabbed a PIAT gun and raced forward. Their first round missed the armoured car, but the second one struck true and knocked it out. Before the two men could get back under cover, Bennett was shot in the chest and badly wounded. As Martin dragged him to shelter, he saw the Lorne Scots advancing without pause despite Stewart's death.[10]

The Queen's Own Rifles were soon inside Saint-Pierre, meeting only light resistance but making slow progress because of extensive bomb damage to buildings and roads. To ensure that no Germans were left to threaten their rear, ruins and intact structures alike all had to be cleared one at a time. Not wanting to leave Stewart's body unattended, meanwhile, Captain Thomas Edgar Parkinson, Company Sergeant Major R. Hess, and a signalman—all from battalion head-quarters—took a jeep out and retrieved it. On the return trip, they took a wrong turn and, as the Queen's Own war diarist recorded, "ended up on a bridge crossing the Liane River where an enemy MG opened up on them, almost cutting their jeep in two." Parkinson and Hess were both badly wounded, while the signalman broke a kneecap rolling out of the jeep to cover.[11] Thirty-five-year-old Parkinson died later that day. A school principal, he had joined the Queen's Own in 1939 and had been a stalwart in its headquarters ever since. The "most willing officer who ever served; he would tackle anything—from keeping an eye on the bugle band to trying to find out why so many cooks went on periodical sprees. His never-flagging enthusiasm was infectious and his good humour a legend."[12]

SEPTEMBER 18 FOUND 9th Canadian Infantry Brigade's regiments divided into two sections, with the Stormont, Dundas and Glengarry Highlanders and Highland Light Infantry both deployed inside Boulogne, and the North Nova Scotia Highlanders still clinging to positions on the slopes of Mont Lambert. Determined that the de-fences on Mont Lambert—which the German garrison commander had deemed the linchpin of Boulogne's defence—must fall quickly, Brigadier Rocky Rockingham had assembled a bold attack by two ar-moured columns consisting of tanks and AVRES, with the North Novas being picked up from their positions along the way. The rightmost column was to charge up to the summit and descend into the valley below for a charge through to the hamlet of Le Chemin Vert, a mile to the southwest. On the left, the second column would seize Mont Lambert's southeast face. As 'A' and 'B' Squadrons of the Fort Garry Horse had been combined owing to earlier losses, a troop from this formation would lead each column's advance. Behind would follow the AVRES and the infantry on foot.

The attack began at dawn, both columns surging through a cover-ing ground haze to reach Mont Lambert. Charging up the slope, the tanks and following AVRES on the right side caught the Germans by surprise and were soon in among their fortifications. The Petards pounded the dugouts and pillboxes with heavy rounds, and all the North Novas had to do was follow along and round up the Germans waving white flags from each position so bombarded. At 1100 hours, Mont Lambert's garrison commander surrendered. To the left, the same scenario had played out, as the tanks covered the Petards in approaching the strongpoints and then blasted them into submission. Although small pockets of resistance continued to be eliminated for the rest of the day, the battle for Mont Lambert was mostly over by noon.[13]

With the summit in hand, 'D' Company was prepared to descend the hill's southern flank to take out several 88-millimetre guns protected by pillboxes. The terrain was such that no armour could support the attack, so Major Maurice Clennett called for a twelve-minute intensive creeping barrage. With one platoon still busy rounding up prisoners, 'D' Company attacked with just two platoons going forward in a straight line "as if on parade" and Clennett in the middle. Seventy-five yards short of the position, the artillery suddenly ceased firing. The North Novas started running, only to have the artillery start up again so that some rounds fell among the men. Clennett and several others were wounded, while the rest dived into bomb craters and shell holes. Seeing the attack broken, Lieutenant Ritchie McVean Grainger rallied the men and then led half of No. 17 Platoon in a head-on charge, while Sergeant Jack MacKenzie brought the rest in from the right. With the shelling done, the Germans had returned to their machine guns and were firing out of the pillbox apertures. Bren gunner Private Clyde Moares stood in the open thirty yards from one pillbox, firing bursts through the gun slit. Standing at his shoulder, Private N.E. Smith steadily passed him a fresh magazine as each was emptied. Under this protective cover, Grainger and MacKenzie closed on the position. Grainger jumped into one dugout with his gun blazing, while MacKenzie's section quickly silenced one pillbox. This enabled Sergeant Herb Murray to bring the other platoon up and overrun the pillboxes to the rear of the position.[14] Although shot in both legs by automatic weapon fire, Grainger staggered into another dugout and killed the Germans there with grenades. Suddenly, the fight went out of the Germans, weapons were thrown down or stepped away from, and hands raised skyward. The paltry ranks of 'D' Company lined up 311 Germans. Despite his wounds, Grainger organized the company to defend the position won. It was found to contain six pillboxes and four 88-millimetre gun emplacements. For his bravery and leadership, Grainger was awarded a Military Cross.[15]

At the southern base of Mont Lambert, 'B' Company and some of 'D' Company's survivors linked up with one of the British-commanded columns of Fort Garry Horse tanks, Flails, AVRES, Crocodiles, and Petards. The "cratering was appalling" on the route leading to Le Chemin Vert, so it was close to nightfall by the time the hamlet was taken. Thereafter, the pace picked up, with a lieutenant from the 1st Lothians and Border Yeomanry out ahead as a guide. As one 1st Lothians officer later wrote, "It was an inspiring sight this madly charging column—off the road, between craters, on the road, off again. The whole time blazing away with 75-millimetre and Besas . . . Germans coming out of the houses [to surrender]. Short pauses when you threw grenades into the houses alongside but no real pause until [the column] hit the Route Nationale."[16]

After meeting some stiff resistance, the column punched through the southern sector of Boulogne to gain the Liane River, only to find the wooden bridge there had been burned.[17]

INSIDE BOULOGNE, THE Stormont, Dundas and Glengarry Highlanders had set about expanding and solidifying its grip on the city. 'B' and 'C' Companies each worked with one of the armoured columns in pushing through to the river.[18] At 0915 hours, one column reached the river at the bridge closest to the harbour mouth. They found it had an 80-foot gap blown in it, but infantry could still cross. The next bridge upstream had a 160-foot gap, but the damage was deemed "bridgeable."[19]

Also during the morning, Lieutenant Colonel Roger Rowley with his battalion headquarters and 'D' Company headed for the citadel. With the Glens were two Petards. The Glens totally misunderstood the citadel, thinking it included everything encompassed by the ramparts enclosing the old town. But 'D' Company soon managed to locate the main gate that gave entrance to the actual citadel. Sergeant

Gerry Bousfield of No. 17 Platoon was looking at the gate and observing that it was heavily manned by Germans. He was thinking what a tough nut this was going to be to crack, when a small Frenchman appeared and asked, "You look for entrance? I show." Bousfield called 'D' Company's Major Jim Stothart over. He and Bousfield's No. 17 Platoon followed the civilian to a tunnel entrance that looked like a big culvert. The Glens warily crept in and were soon inside a large tunnel. Suddenly, a German officer with a pistol popped out directly in front of Bousfield. When the German fired at him, the gun merely clicked. Lunging forward, Bousfield snatched the pistol away and discovered there was no bullet in the chamber. "'I should shoot you, but I can't do it in cold blood,'" Bousfield told the German. "It was my lucky day."[20]

Meanwhile, outside the citadel the rest of the Glens attacked the fortress walls directly with the Petards, raking the ramparts with their Besa machine guns and then blasting the portcullis that blocked the entrance. "The gate was effectively blown in," Rowley later wrote. "At once a host of white flags waved from the walls. To add to the confusion, Major Stothart had now appeared in the midst of the besieged fort, utterly astonishing its defenders."

About two hundred prisoners, including sixteen officers, were rounded up. "Most of them were drunk, and happy to be out of the war. The garrison was commanded by a major, who was as pleased as the rest." As the Glens moved out and combed the rest of the old town within the ramparts, more prisoners were collected, but there was no effective opposition.[21]

With the Glens having taken the citadel and come up alongside the north bank of the Liane River, Brigadier Rocky Rockingham decided to force a crossing of the river with his Highland Light Infantry (HLI). Originally, this battalion had been intended to attack Mont Herquelingue, but as this position was reported lightly held, that task was left to the Cameron Highlanders of Ottawa. Riding in Kangaroos, the HLI began moving at 1500 hours from a position on Boulogne's outskirts. The situation in Boulogne was so fluid that their movement was detected and obviously reported to gun positions outside the city, as the route taken was "laced with fire and air bursts were vicious." It wasn't until 1945 hours that the battalion reached the bridge nearest the harbour mouth.[22]

Rockingham had teed up a wealth of fire support to cover the infantry as it scrambled across the badly damaged bridge. Every available tank, AVRE, anti-tank gun, PIAT team, and machine gun had moved as close to the river as possible. "Their task was to plaster the enemy in the buildings on the opposite bank whilst the infantry crossed, and as soon as they were across, the barrage ceased, and support continued by observation. The commanders of the various weapons were with the [HLI commander] and he controlled the fire through them."[23] Once across the river, the HLI established a narrow bridgehead and dug in for the night in order to protect engineers from 18th Field Company, who started making the bridge passable to vehicles and tanks. With the morning, 9th Brigade would turn its attention southward to eliminate the strongholds on the so-called Outreau peninsula. At the same time, 8th Brigade would begin clearing the remaining strongpoints north of Boulogne.

DURING THE NIGHT of September 18–19, the Cameron Highlanders of Ottawa launched their attack on Mont Herquelingue. It was believed to be defended by 150 to 300 Germans with at least two 88-millimetre guns. Against this formidable force, Major Bill Baird's 'C' Company had about a hundred Camerons and a light anti-aircraft troop serving as infantry. He assigned Lieutenant V. Leatherdale's No. 9 Platoon to seize the fortification itself, while No. 10 Platoon would approach from the southeast flank. No. 11 Platoon and the anti-aircraft troop would provide covering fire and also cut the German escape route west to Boulogne.

No. 9 Platoon numbered just twenty-five men, counting Leatherdale. Creeping up the slope, they were just fifty yards past a building when a German hissed a challenge. Leatherdale and Private Charles Alexander Spratt, who carried a Bren gun, shot the man dead. A few moments later, five more Germans emerged through the gloom. Leatherdale and Spratt again opened fire. This elicited loud yelling, followed by silence. Pressing on, the platoon came to a thick hedge laced with barbed wire and brush that proved impenetrable. Moving along the hedge to find an opening, Leatherdale met up with No. 11 Platoon, which had come forward to find a better fire-support position. Discovering a gap in the hedge, Leatherdale led his men on. Several times they drew fire, and the Germans popped a number of flares to try to illuminate their position. Dividing his platoon into two sections with himself in the centre, Leatherdale waved for the men to charge just as the first hint of dawn tinged the eastern skyline.

Ahead they could see that the fortification consisted of five large casemates from which anti-tank gun barrels protruded, along with a covey of machine guns. "Spratt and I closed to the nearest emplacement," Leatherdale said later, "into which I threw grenades while covered by Spratt with the Bren gun. One man only appeared at the door, he fired at point-blank range and missed. It was obvious that almost complete surprise had been achieved. When loud cries were heard I went to the front door and threw in another grenade. Spratt was firing away with the Bren and excellent results were soon apparent. PW came out and were very docile. On pillbox 2, the same treatment was in order but results not so good. Private Gauvin and the PIAT were brought up and a direct hit through a small aperture at thirty yards brought immediate reaction. Casemate 3 now proceeded to become a definite nuisance when they started to open up with a small mortar. It caused some casualties . . . In the meantime Spratt and Sergeant [Murray Stanley] Dickson pressed home the attack."[24]

Yelling to platoon second-in-command Sergeant Lucas that he was wounded, Leatherdale staggered clear of the fight. Lucas ran over and told Corporal Ivor William Merry-Ship to dress the wound while he found a stretcher. When Lucas returned, he found Merry-Ship lying dead next to Leatherdale with a bullet through his head.[25]

Spratt and Dickson, meanwhile, had been wreaking havoc through the German fortification. With Spratt blasting the front door of each casemate with his Bren, Dickson dashed in and chucked Type 36 grenades through the apertures. Steadily, the two men took out three casemates this way while being fired upon by the mortars, snipers, and artillery shells from a gun position on the hill at St. Etienne. After the grenades exploded, Spratt and Dickson lunged into each casemate, but found only dead and wounded Germans. The wounded had no fight left in them. As they moved away from the third casemate, two bullets pierced Spratt's uniform blouse but failed to penetrate his chest.[26] The two men assaulted the fourth casemate in their tried and true fashion. This was a bigger position, and several men accompanied Dickson in clearing it. When Dickson and three others entered one room, a large petrol tank exploded. Dickson received serious facial burns, and the other men—Privates Warnes, McLellan, and Oscar Couvrette—also suffered burn injuries, along with twelve Germans.[27] Couvrette's burns covered 90 per cent of his body. As Couvrette was carrying a backpack stuffed with dynamite, he was astonished that it failed to explode.[28]

The fifth casemate was unoccupied. A total of 164 Germans were taken prisoner, about twenty of whom were wounded. Seven dead were found. The fortification contained one 75-millimetre gun, one 105-millimetre gun, five 88-millimetre anti-tank guns, one 40-millimetre anti-aircraft gun, and several 20-millimetre guns.[29] Dickson and Spratt both received Military Medals. "For sheer guts in a hand to hand struggle," Cameron Highlanders of Ottawa Major Richard Ross wrote, "this action is paramount in the history of the . . . battalion."[30] Having won the summit, 'C' Company settled in amid the bunkers for a hoped-for rest. Instead, Lieutenant H.B. Jackson wrote, they "spent a weird night" under German fire from St. Etienne—particularly 20-millimetre anti-aircraft guns. One soldier was wounded. When another man rushed to his side, the anti-aircraft gun zeroed in on them. The unhurt soldier managed to prop up a steel plate for cover. They hunkered behind this barrier for several hours as the 20-millimetre spattered rounds off the plate. In the process, the original casualty suffered another wound, and his assistant was also wounded. Finally, the fire eased, and Jackson was able to recover the two men from where they had been caught in the open. Except for those on guard, the other Cameron Highlanders of Ottawa hunkered inside the casemates to avoid the fire. During the fight for Herquelingue, the Camerons suffered one officer—Lieutenant Leatherdale—wounded, one corporal killed, and twelve other ranks wounded.[31]

NEAR THE HARBOUR mouth of the Liane River, an assault section of 18th Field Company's engineers arrived at about 2000 hours on September 18 and worked alongside the Highland Light Infantry's pioneer section on the damaged bridge. The web of both main girders had been blown away near the centre, leaving a ragged, forty-five-foot gap in the decking. Lieutenant R.C. Eddy realized they needed lots of timber to fill the gap. By 2130 hours, a collection of boards of every length and thickness had been gathered. "Then," as the official Royal Canadian Engineer historian recorded, "occurred one of those incidents which frustrate the best of plans. It was discovered that only one hand axe was available! The engineers . . . had been equipped to sweep and lift mines, not to build a timber bridge; the records contain no explanation as to why the infantry pioneers had left behind their glittering parade axes. There were no saws, nails, timber dogs, or even rope to hand. Still, by fitting and piecing, sorting and arranging and carefully stacking and bracing, before 0415 hours a plank deck, over 12 by 12 inch stringers padded up from the sagging steel girders, had been contrived. At 0430 hours, with some trepidation, a jeep was driven over the bridge, then other jeeps, then an empty three-ton truck, then another, then a loaded three-tonner; the relief experienced by the harassed sappers was almost tangible."

By first light, all HLI transport had driven across the bridge. This included its heavy half-tracks. At best, Eddy rated the bridge a Class 5, but it had managed to handle traffic normally requiring a Class 9–rated crossing. Still, Eddy had no interest in trying a tank. So the HLI was on its own for the planned advance out of the bridgehead. Not until much later in the day did 31st Field Company arrive to throw over a proper sixty-foot, Class 40 Bailey bridge.[32]

"We think our 'bridge,' if it can be called one, was a pretty good effort and [we] certainly never expected to build a bridge at any time with timber alone," Eddy said. At 0455 hours, the HLI reported to 9th Brigade headquarters that the bridge was complete and the battalion was "pushing forward now."[33]

The HLI attack was the first of this third day of the battle, and their assignment was to clear the third of the city on the Liane's southern bank and then seize the Le Portel fortification on its outskirts. Getting all the companies organized and the operation under way was not completed until 0630 hours. Wireless communication between companies, battalion headquarters, and brigade headquarters was patchy and confused. Throughout the preparations, German snipers harassed the forward troops. Then, as 'B' and 'A' Companies led off, they came under "murderous fire from all directions which was heavier than the battalion has yet experienced," the HLI war diarist wrote. It was the worst kind of street fighting—buildings and bombed-out ruins providing perfect hides for the Germans, with each position having to be cleared one by one. Sometimes the Germans surrendered as soon as the Highlanders closed in; others fought to the bitter end. Never knowing what to expect added to the stress and slowed the advance. Lieutenant Colonel Nicol Kingsmill had only a scanty idea of what was happening because of continuing problems with the wireless communication. All he knew was that the troops were heavily engaged. Adding to the confusion, many officers were being wounded or killed. At about 1000 hours, 'A' Company's Major Douglas Philips Kennedy stepped out of a building's doorway "and walked into a MG42 firing incendiary" rounds. "He lived only a short time." The twenty-six-year-old Kennedy's brother Major Peter Kingston Kennedy, older by three years, had been killed on September 17 when a shell had struck his company headquarters.[34] Their father would receive the news of both sons' deaths in the same telegram.[35] All three lieutenants leading the platoons of 'B' Company were wounded, and one was taken prisoner.[36]

About midday, Rockingham went to Kingsmill's headquarters to see what was holding up operations. No sooner had he arrived than the building came under heavy shellfire with air-burst rounds exploding everywhere. Rapid-fire anti-aircraft rounds snapped overhead. Rockingham ordered some artillery fire to neutralize the German artillery batteries. He also arranged for Typhoons to attack the German guns with rockets.[37]

At 1400 hours, the Bailey bridge constructed by 31st Field Company opened to traffic. This enabled one armoured column to join the HLI. Once the armour tied in with the infantry, 'B' Company led off at 1520 hours in a hook toward the coast and German fortifications at

Honriville just outside Boulogne's port area.[38] Supporting the infantry were two Crocodiles, several Flails, two Petards, and two Sherman tanks. The force advanced toward a hillcrest behind which a road separated an artillery battery on the right side and several blockhouses on the left.

As soon as the leading Crocodile crossed over the crest, it got stuck in a crater. The following Crocodile tried using a chain to pull the tank free. On the right side of the road, infantry under heavy air-burst fire were repeatedly forced to take cover. Suddenly, the column came under heavy artillery fire from Le Portel, the harbour area, and positions that had not yet been silenced on the north side of the river. Despite this combined incoming fire, one Petard managed to take out the closest two blockhouses, but the other Petard bogged down and was unable to get free. The Crocodile trying to tow its mate out of the crater had its flame-thrower fuel trailer set alight and had to jettison it.[39] When the Flails started clearing a minefield, four were knocked out by mines or incoming artillery. As the Petard moved away from the two silenced blockhouses, a round from a coastal gun at Le Portel punched through the side of its turret, and two mines exploded underneath it. The crew managed to bail out and escape on foot to the river. At this point, the armoured column commander decided to withdraw.[40]

The Highlanders were on their own, but also spent. They had suffered sixty-four casualties.[41] At 2130 hours, the HLI advance halted, and was to resume in the morning.[42] Brigadier Rockingham, meanwhile, had decided early in the afternoon to have the Stormont, Dundas and Glengarry Highlanders cross the river and move through the narrow bridgehead the HLI had managed to carve out on the southern bank. If they could take Outreau and several objectives to its south and east, that would take pressure off the HLI. At 1500 hours, Lieutenant Colonel Roger Rowley received his marching orders at the citadel. In addition to capturing Outreau, they were to eliminate a gun battery on Mont Soleil just south of the village—one that had been subjecting the HLI to heavy shelling and anti-aircraft gunfire. Once this was completed, they were to turn and secure two sugar factories southeast of Outreau that had been turned into a German marine base, and then continue southward to gain control of a water reservoir.[43]

DURING THE EVENING of September 18, 3rd Division Medical Officer Captain Joseph Greenblatt had written to his sweetheart, Frances Trachtenberg. Greenblatt was depressed by the war and had forgotten that the day was Rosh Hashanah (Jewish New Year). Whether he could have attended the ceremonies held at 11 Canadian Corps headquarters more than forty miles away was uncertain. Jewish personnel, he had only belatedly discovered, were entitled to be excused from duty in order to attend. But the unit was very busy treating wounded, so Greenblatt wrote that he likely would not have gone. He then confided to being in low spirits because of all the friends the war had so far claimed. "War narrows a person's horizon and the most important person in a soldier's scope of vision is himself. One does not think too much about another person's sacrifices, although one realizes that the next person is sacrificing as much [as] or more than yourself."[44]

Closer to the front, in the Queen's Own Regimental Aid Post (RAP), situated in a basement under battalion headquarters, Medical Officer Douglas Oatway was treating more German casualties than Canadian. On September 17, he had reported in his diary treating about sixteen Queen's Own and three times that many Germans. Most of these men were marines wounded by their own mines. A couple spoke English. One "was a typical Prussian, another a fifty year old chap from Dortmund who was fed up with war. Two opposite types." Oatway liberated a German watch. He was very tired.

The morning of September 18, he moved the RAP to the outskirts of Wicardenne, only to find German artillery shelling the hamlet. One shell exploded on the RAP's roof. There was no food for either the medical staff or the wounded. Oatway watched about five hundred prisoners, mostly marines, march past in good order. Reports were coming in that the street fighting in Saint-Pierre was going well, "tho' a bit tough."

On September 19, Oatway moved his RAP again, this time into Boulogne, where he set up on the main floor of a large building surrounded by good German dugouts. "Boulogne is a wreck like Caen. Scarcely any civilians to be seen. In afternoon were shelled heavily by own artillery who were shooting short. Brigadier [Ken Blackader] gave them hell in no uncertain terms, but they gave us a bad scare for almost an hour. Quite a few fleas or lice in the building, and the Padre has been the hardest hit so far. (It must be the odour of sanctity!) Called out to see Lieutenant Earl Stoll and two or three other casualties at German hospital nearby. German doctor—colonel—there. Left there after bringing up plasma from RAP. Doctor gave us cognac and coffee, and was quite friendly. D.L. Cregan killed. Payne wounded. Both Company stretcher bearers." Oatway soon learned that Stoll had died.[45]

The number of Canadians dying for Boulogne was sending shock-waves through 3rd Infantry Division. Despite having passed 88 officers and 3,600 men through its prisoner-of-war cages, and knowing that a good number of others had been killed, German resistance seemed to be stiffening even as their grip on the city was lost. September 19, one divisional report stated, had seen 9th Brigade suffer "casualties . . . heavier than expected. There is no doubt that the troops were beginning to get tired, especially in 9th Brigade. They had been fighting for three days and three nights almost continuously with very little food and practically no rest."

With the Germans now consolidated in fortifications to the north and south of the city, divisional intelligence staff were recognizing that "the enemy had concentrated his better troops, which were nearly all pure Germans, in these positions, which were still holding out. They were certainly putting up a hard fight. It was interesting to see PW coming into the Divisional cage on this day. They are much fitter and of a much higher standard altogether compared with the two previous days."[46]

The intelligence staff also noted that these more determined troops were almost uniformly fighting from "thick concrete defences," which "minimize the effect of our fire power." They feared that there were still at least two thousand Germans, "none of whom . . . had indicated any intention of surrendering."[47]

21

Another Fortress Finished

I N THE LATE afternoon of September 19, with a fine rain falling, the Stormont, Dundas and Glengarry Highlanders crossed the Bailey bridge over the Liane and headed toward Mont Soleil. The Highland Light Infantry, the Glens' war diarist reported, were "experiencing much difficulty in proceeding with the work of mopping up and this accounts for our having to seize this added feature."[1] Lieutenant Colonel Roger Rowley's plan was three-phased. First, 'A' Company would secure Outreau, while 'C' Company advanced to the southeast and won the water reservoir. Next, 'D' Company would pass through Outreau or around it to capture the Mont Soleil artillery battery. Finally, 'B' Company would advance eastward to occupy the two sugar factories near the Liane River. Rowley had explained this at the citadel before leading the battalion to the river.[2] As the Glens were exiting Boulogne, the North Nova Scotia Highlanders descended from Mont Lambert to occupy the city's centre.[3]

As the North Novas were arriving, the Queen's Own Rifles also left the Saint-Pierre district for an advance north along the coast road to Fort de la Crèche. They found the way on the outskirts blocked by a strongpoint anchored on a 75-millimetre gun. Captain Dick Medland's 'A' Company attempted to take the position, but was repulsed by heavy fire.[4] After several more fruitless attempts, Lieutenant Colonel Steve Lett informed 8th Brigade headquarters that he "could neither take nor by-pass the enemy infantry and artillery and that the position would require 'special treatment.'"

The Queen's Own were supposed to be closing up alongside Le Régiment de la Chaudière so the two could together overwhelm Fort de la Crèche. But the French-Canadians had also run into problems early in the afternoon when they moved against some enemy positions south of Bon Secours. Despite support from a Fort Garry Horse squadron and several AVRES, at 1750 hours they remained stymied by the German strongpoint, which included a series of blockhouses with steel turrets containing machine guns. Three 88-millimetre guns added to the strong defence.[5] Late in the evening, the attack was abandoned, and the Chauds withdrew beyond German gun range. The Chauds' war diarist was less impressed by the strongpoint than the fact that it stood close to the 174-foot-tall Column of the Grande Armée.[6] Begun in 1804, it commemorated Napoleon's forthcoming and expected-to-be-successful invasion of England. When the invasion fell through, the column underwent a series of redesigns through the 1800s, until it was completed as a sculpture of the emperor standing upon a lofty pedestal with his back to the sea. Some said it had been intended that he should be looking seaward, but the workers installing the statue faced it the wrong way. Whatever the case, many a Chaudière considered himself privileged to see the column and was determined that no harm should come to it as a result of the surrounding fighting.

Back on the southern bank of the Liane River, meanwhile, the Glens had attacked shortly before 1700 hours. As Major F.W. Landers's 'A' Company started out, it discovered the road from Boulogne to Outreau was heavily mined at staggered intervals. Within minutes, Landers was wounded when an approaching runner triggered an s-mine.[7] Shortly thereafter, Sergeant Alexander Sweet, who commanded a mortar section, was killed.[8] With 'A' Company entangled in the mines, Rowley feared the attack was losing momentum. So he directed 'D' Company to make for Outreau immediately, and if opposition there proved light, to then carry on to Mont Soleil. 'A' Company, however, quickly extricated itself from the minefield, reorganized and, staying clear of the road, got to Outreau on schedule. The few Germans there quickly surrendered. 'C' Company, meanwhile, had run into a snag while heading for the reservoir. Its route involved passing the mouth of a railway tunnel, and as the men started past, more than two hundred enemy poured out to surrender. Rowley described the number of prisoners as "embarrassing." They could have done 'C' Company great damage, but instead the Glens were delayed by the need to organize them. Among their number were some thirty fez-wearing black Senegalese conscripts. The Glens had to dragoon clerks, signalmen, and other non-essential headquarters staff to guard them all. Shed of its prisoners, 'C' Company proceeded to the reservoir without encountering any real resistance.

With Outreau in hand, 'D' Company teed up to attack the German gun position on Mont Soleil. This position was believed to contain fifteen different guns, including six 88-millimetres. As his men formed in woods about a thousand yards to the east of the hill, Major Jack Stothart realized the gunners "were engrossed in heavy shelling of HLI . . . and failed to notice" his men. During the artillery-planning phase for Operation Wellhit, Mont Soleil had been marked and code-designated Norway. Consequently, it was pre-registered by one medium artillery and four field regiments. Stothart checked his bearings and the range. He then passed instructions to the gunners that would provide a very close creeping barrage.

The result, Rowley noted, was a "magnificent surprise. The infantry, following the fire closely, swarmed over the hill with bayonets and grenades before the last rounds had fallen. At no time were they more than 250 yards from the bursts."[9] Just before the summit, a German emerged from the shelter of a bunker and fired a Schmeisser burst that wounded Corporal James W. McDonald in the knee. But his comrades cut the German down and the charge never faltered.[10] "The nearest position was overrun and its three 88s taken intact; the troops rushed for the other three, but these were blown up. The action resulted in the taking of 185 PW, but during it Major Stothart's only two remaining officers were wounded. It was now nearly dark and the company consolidated its position and remained on the hill all night."[11]

Because of the initial problems in advancing on Outreau and the reservoir, Rowley had kept 'B' Company in reserve, rather than dispatching it to the sugar factories. That task would wait until morning.

The Glens had no familiarity with the terrain south of the Liane, so a night attack was rejected.

With nightfall, the battleground quieted. As the Germans in Le Portel had seen Mont Soleil fall to 'D' Company, their gunners subjected the summit to intermittent shelling that convinced the Glens to spend the night buttoned up inside the concrete bunkers.[12] Across the 9th Brigade front, there was little active patrolling. The men in all three battalions were exhausted, dirty, and hungry.

North of Boulogne, the situation was about the same for 8th Brigade's battalions. During the day, the North Shore (New Brunswick) Regiment had attempted to take Wimille with Major Jim Currie's 'C' Company. Currie had suspected Wimille was going to pose "a tough job to clear." The village was fairly large and was protected to the north by the Wimereux River. Standing as it did astride a key road running north out of Boulogne toward Calais, Wimille barred any approach from the east toward the coastal town of Wimereux. Inside the village, a bridge over the Wimereux River served as the North Shores' prime objective. During the fighting at La Trésorerie, the North Shores had been slashed much of the time by anti-aircraft fire from Wimille's garrison. Currie's line of approach to the village necessitated advancing along a narrow winding road running through a valley clearly visible to the Germans there.

Lieutenant O.A. Robertson's No. 9 Platoon led, with Currie's company headquarters right behind. Then came Lieutenant Don McPherson's platoon and finally the third platoon, under Sergeant Joe Hennigar. Robertson's orders were simple: advance to contact—which happened at noon, when a number of Germans came forward to surrender. Just when the North Shores figured they were going to easily bag the village, a German officer shouted that he would shoot the next man who tried to give up. Suddenly finding their backbone, the Germans ahead of 'C' Company lashed out with heavy fire. McPherson broke left to gain Wimille's most built-up area. Heavy mortar fire drove the platoon back. Currie knew that without some heavy support, 'C' Company was too weak to win, so broke off the engagement. He was amazed to find that 'C' Company had suffered not a single casualty. Yet he figured they had killed about twenty Germans, wounded twice that many, and taken two hundred prisoners before the officer intervened. That evening, Lieutenant Colonel Ernie Anderson arrived and promised Currie some M-10 anti-tank guns for the morning.[13]

Elsewhere in 8th Brigade's lines, patrols worked to keep the Germans off balance, but they were "met everywhere by fairly strong opposition."[14]

SEPTEMBER 20 DAWNED with cloudy skies and dull rain. In the 8th Infantry Brigade sector, the Queen's Own Rifles were still stuck on the edge of Saint-Pierre in front of the strong German pillbox position. To their right, Le Régiment de la Chaudière were equally blocked by the strongpoint around the Grande Armée column. Both were being urged to push on to assault Fort de la Crèche. The North Shore (New Brunswick) Regiment was teeing up for a major attack on Wimille and a drive toward Wimereux on the coast. South of the Liane River, two of the 9th Infantry Brigade battalions were given minimal tasks because they were so worn out. The Highland Light Infantry turned its attention away from the southward advance on Le Portel and instead concentrated on clearing strongpoints around the harbour docks, while the Stormont, Dundas and Glengarry Highlanders were tasked just with securing the two sugar factories east of Outreau and alongside the river.

It fell to the North Nova Scotia Highlanders to carry out the brigade's main effort. Their objective was a small fortification at Ningles, which lay near the coast in a re-entrant about halfway between Nocquet and Le Portel. Lieutenant Colonel Don Forbes had gone to Mont Soleil to conduct a visual reconnaissance before marching his men directly west of this hill toward Nocquet. He arrived on the summit just as the Germans chucked a hail of fire toward Mont Soleil that swept the open ground the North Novas would be crossing. Forbes reported to Brigadier Rocky Rockingham that his men would be slaughtered if they took that route. Rockingham stared at his map and then told Forbes to take a long circular route, passing through the enemy positions at St. Etienne, Ecault, and then to Nocquet. They were to cross the river by way of a bridge found intact the day before on Boulogne's southern outskirts.[15]

At 0800 hours, several AVRES and Fort Garry Horse tanks "took a crack" at the German pillbox blocking the Queen's Own. Their rounds bounced harmlessly off the position, which was determined to consist of not only the pillbox's concrete walls but also three outer walls of heavily reinforced concrete. After the armour gave up, Captain Ben Dunkelman's mortar platoon moved into range and started dropping 3-inch rounds on the pillbox's roof.[16] The first bomb fired by Sergeant W.T. Corrigan's mortar dropped neatly into a narrow ventilation shaft, and large detonations of ammunition within the pillbox were heard. Even then, the Germans inside refused to surrender.[17]

Brigadier Ken Blackader decided to have one Queen's Own company contain the position while the rest of the battalion moved against Fort de la Crèche on the heels of a medium-bomber attack he had teed up for the afternoon. When the bombers unexpectedly failed to materialize, the Queen's Own stayed put. Le Régiment de la Chaudière was also to have cut around its opposing strongpoints to join this attack. Blackader reorganized, and a new request for the bombers was sent up First Canadian Army's channels to the headquarters of Allied Expeditionary Air Force responsible for approving such attacks. Blackader was soon assured that the bombers would come, and that their failure to arrive so far had been due to a mistaken cancellation of this mission instead of the correct one at Calais.[18]

Rather than sitting quiet and waiting for the bombers, the Chauds' 'C' Company advanced to the left of the Grande Armée column in an attempt to overcome the strongpoints there. Platoon commander Lieutenant C.P. Rutledge sent two platoons out wide to the southeast. Although they met no enemy, the men attracted a shower of various-calibre artillery fire. The precision of this fire astonished the men driven to ground by it. Only later would the Chauds learn that the Germans had an observation post near the base of the column, from which they could monitor the battalion's every move. Company 'B' had also been driven to ground, but it managed to slip a couple of small patrols up to the fortification, and a soft spot was identified. Lieutenant Colonel Paul Mathieu worked out a careful plan that saw 'B' and 'D' Companies put in an attack at noon on September 21. Although a hard fight ensued, within a few hours the German position was won and seventy-five prisoners were taken.[19] The road was then open for the regiment to advance toward Fort de la Crèche.

Outside Wimille, the North Shores Major Jim Currie's 'C' Company had linked up with a troop of M-10 self-propelled anti-tank guns from 3rd Canadian Anti-Tank Regiment's 52nd Battery shortly after dawn on the 20th. Currie's focus was on breaking into the built-up area where Lieutenant Don McPherson's platoon had been stopped cold the previous day. Just before first light, Currie, Captain Ev Gorman, and McPherson had gone forward with two FFI fighters wearing North Shore uniforms to scout the village entrances. The FFI men "showed us the lay of the land and we planned that . . . McPherson would get one M-10 gun, take it and a section of his platoon and shoot holes through the building the Jerries were holding, while Sergeant Joe Henningar would attack down an alley the FFI lads had shown us."

The well-planned effort went off without a hitch. As soon as the M-10 punched a couple of rounds into the building and Hennigar's men let loose with close-range Bren gun fire, the Germans fled. Currie heard Sergeant Art Payne and McPherson both yell, "There they go!" Several made it to a house on the road leading to Wimereux, and a few others were shot down, but most just halted when the gunfire started and raised their arms.

With the third platoon of 'C' Company, Lieutenant O.A. Robertson had advanced more directly along the road approaching from the east. Several civilians warned him that the Germans had a roadblock astride the crossroads on the village's eastern flank. The roadblock proved to be an overturned bus. Motioning the men to take cover, Robertson and two men crept up to the bus. When Robertson rounded the bus he saw several Germans crouched behind it. As they took no offensive action, Robertson settled down out of view next to the bus, and after a few minutes the Germans indicated they wanted to surrender. Soon after, Robertson saw a white flag appear from the window of a ruined building near the roadblock. That gave him sixty prisoners in less than an hour.

Robertson was still wary. Ahead lay a second crossroads with a small wood alongside. He and the two men showed themselves first and drew immediate fire, which also revealed the location of a small pillbox amid the trees. The platoon sergeant came up with a PIAT and Robertson managed to score four direct hits in a row that tore holes in the fortification. Out scrambled the small garrison with hands raised.

As 'C' Company tightened its grip on Wimille, Germans on a nearby hill started mortaring the place. An FFI fighter told Robertson that the hill position consisted of about four machine-gun posts manned by fourteen men. Then a female Red Cross nurse appeared and offered to accompany Robertson to talk the garrison into surrendering. The platoon went up under a white flag, and the woman spoke in fluent German with the sergeant in command. He expressed willingness to surrender, but suddenly a sniper shot rang out, and the FFI fighter fell wounded. Robertson and the others dived into an empty gun pit. The Germans all returned to their weapons. But the nurse continued to call to them and explain the futility of their situation. Finally, the garrison surrendered. "My relief," Robertson said, "was tremendous, for that lady had saved us some very hard fighting and, probably, some North Shore lives."

By noon it was over, and Wimille was secure. The North Shores had captured the village's commander, 37 non-commissioned officers, and 101 soldiers. There had also been quite a number of Germans killed, and some of the prisoners were wounded. 'C' Company suffered not a single casualty. At La Trésorerie, Lieutenant Colonel Ernie Anderson started immediately planning for an advance on the morning of the 21st to Wimereux—the battalion's final objective.[20]

IN THE EARLY morning of September 20, the Stormont, Dundas and Glengarry Highlanders on Mont Soleil spotted movement in a hut at Le Portel, and smoke soon trailed out of its chimney. It was a cool day, and Corporal Don Milne could imagine the Germans inside warming themselves by a fire or cooking up grub on a stove. "Let's put out the fire," he said. On Mont Soleil, they had three captured 88-millimetre guns in perfect working order and lots of ammunition. But being infantrymen, none of them had been trained to fire Canadian artillery, let alone German guns. But what the hell, the breech was open on the nearest gun. So Milne peered down the barrel and then moved the gun about until it seemed to be pointed at the hut. Then they stuffed a shell in, closed the breech, and the rest of the men in Milne's section dived for cover as he pulled the lanyard. The gun fired, the hut disappeared, and the men gave a loud cheer. The stunt garnered Milne a Military Medal.

While Milne had been learning the artillery trade, Major J.F. Peterson's 'B' Company had advanced eastward along the river and easily secured the sugar factories. Heading toward Mont Soleil to re-join the rest of the battalion, the men came to a château that Peterson speculated had likely been Generalleutnant Ferdinand Heim's main headquarters. He chewed on that thought and the probability of good looting all the way to the summit of Mont Soleil. Keeping mum about the château, Peterson suggested to Lieutenant Colonel Roger Rowley that 'B' Company should go back toward the river to protect the battalion's left flank. "Since when were you ever interested in my left flank," a suspicious Rowley asked. Peterson wove "a horrible picture of German infiltration on the left flank" and finally got his way.

As Peterson was leaving, the artillery FOO persuaded Rowley that he should go along, too, in case gun support was needed. Outside, he told Peterson, "Hell, you're not fooling me, you've got hold of something and I'm going to get in on it." Seeing some Germans about the château, 'B' Company teed up a proper two-platoon pincer attack with the third platoon providing suppressing fire. White flags sprouted from several windows, and a chef wearing a tall white hat ran out. The place was quickly secured. Peterson was soon inspecting pots and pans in the kitchen, where he found French fried potatoes and a dozen chickens cooked and ready for eating. Stuffing the pot of chickens in a closet, Peterson went to check on the rest of the château. When he returned, a group of Glens was gathered around the stove finishing off the fries. Seeing they still looked hungry, the major pulled the chicken pot from the closet, plunked it on the stove, and walked out without a word. Once outside, he chuckled at the delighted expressions he'd seen on the men's faces.

The best was yet to come. In a safe obligingly opened by the garrison's paymaster, Peterson found 2.5 million French francs and a half million Belgian francs. Rumours circulated later that the Provost Corps was unable to effectively investigate a Canadian company commander who handed out 25,000 francs to each of his men on a pay parade. The investigators did trace the trail of this rumour back to the Glens, but Rowley dismissed it as "a ridiculous story, for where would a company commander get all that money?" September 20 marked the end of the Glens' role in Operation Wellhit. Taking up position on Mont Soleil, they continued to harry the Germans at Le Portel with 88-millimetre fire and also a captured 80-millimetre mortar, but this was more for sport than an attempt to reduce the fortification. One shot from the 88-millimetre, however, did succeed in knocking out a matching weapon.[21]

In the harbour area, the Highland Light Infantry set about the task "of clearing up numerous pillboxes and strong points along the waterfront." The battalion was organized into two companies and several smaller assault teams assigned specific targets. 'D' Company, meanwhile, established a holding position to the south at Honriville and ended up cut off from the rest of the battalion. Attempts to link up with it were driven back by heavy shellfire. One of the scout cars with a loud hailer system was brought in to encourage the Germans within the harbour to give up. This proved somewhat effective, until shrapnel from a shell fired at the car knocked the hailing system out of action on September 21.

Throughout September 20 and 21, the HLI continued this task. It was slow work, but often as one pillbox was taken, it provided good cover for the men to mount their attack on the one beyond.[22] Finally, late in the day on the 21st, some Highlanders with a Wasp carrier advanced toward the last position in the harbour—a pill-box on the tip of a jetty thrusting out seaward. The Germans there seemed determined to make a suicidal stand, so the Wasp led, with the Highlanders clustered behind its protective hide. After about a hundred yards, the Wasp shot a jet of flame toward the pillbox, but it fell short on the jetty. Advancing another hundred yards, the tank sent out a second burst of flame, which brushed the pillbox exterior. The Wasp quickly put out a third shot, but this just produced a long squirt of fuel that failed to ignite. As its gunner realized that the gas pressure was too low to produce flame and the Wasp was effectively neutralized, a white flag appeared. The supporting infantry, the Wasp commander said later, "advanced through the flames of the burning jetty and literally sat on the fortification until the enemy conjured up sufficient courage to emerge."[23]

With the harbour secure, Brigadier Rocky Rockingham planned to turn the HLI southward on September 22 to renew its advance on Le Portel. The Glens on Mont Soleil would provide supporting fire and possibly a company to attack on the left flank. His attention on September 20 was largely focused on monitoring and supporting the North Novas' drive toward St. Etienne.[24]

THE NORTH NOVA Scotia Highlanders had pushed out from the south-east corner of Boulogne toward St. Etienne, about two miles distant, with Major E. Wright's 'C' Company leading. Shortly, the infantry came under heavy fire from pillboxes on the flank of Herquelingue. Although the Cameron Highlanders of Ottawa had taken the summit of this hill on September 19, they had failed to find these positions. Exposed as the infantry were in open ground, the situation could have been disastrous had they not been supported by No. 3 Troop of the Fort Garry Horse's combined 'A' and 'B' Squadron. The tankers could clearly see the German gun positions, and a rapid volley of fire silenced a heavy field gun and one 88-millimetre gun.[25]

'C' Company pressed on and was soon closing on St. Etienne, where a white flag fluttered from a church tower in the eastern sector. Yet from elsewhere, artillery, mortar, and machine-gun fire greeted the North Novas. They concluded that the village priest was trying to save his church from being shot up. As they closed on the village, the German fire ceased, save for a few rifle shots. Lieutenant D.H. Gurton's platoon was out front. Before him a road stretched up a long slope about twelve hundred yards to the village. Gurton suspected a trap and told his men to be ready to hit the dirt at the first shot. About three hundred yards out, two houses stood alongside the road. The first house was Gurton's waypoint. The platoon reached it without incident and set up inside. Wright arrived and figured Gurton's men were exhausted by the tension of their advance. So he told Lieutenant Ronnie McNeill to take point and secure the second house, which proved empty. McNeill's platoon carried on, crawling up the ditches toward the hill crest. Wright was crawling alongside McNeill and growing increasingly uneasy, suspecting that they were heading into an ambush.

Just short of the crest, McNeill signalled his men to cover, and the two officers went ahead alone. The moment they crossed the brow, machine guns in concrete emplacements opened up. When McNeill's men popped a couple of mortar smoke rounds, the German fire thickened. Realizing the enemy had no observation on the road, Wright ordered the rest of 'C' Company to concentrate by the second house down the slope. He then contacted Lieutenant Colonel Don Forbes by wireless and asked for the tanks.[26]

The Fort Garry Horse No. 3 Troop rushed its four Shermans up the slope and powered over the crest, as Lieutenant Cyril Burgoyne wrote, "with all guns blazing! Jerry was running helter-skelter, jumping in and out of slit trenches, dugouts and pillboxes. The tanks fired steadily for five minutes, and when they stopped, out popped white flags and surrendering Germans." 'C' Company charged in behind the tanks and rounded up two hundred Germans.[27] "Another fortress finished," the North Novas' war diarist wrote. The men took over pillboxes for their night's quarters, "and we all settled down to a good cigar and a restful night. Casualties nil."[28] During the night, the North Novas were not entirely still. Patrols probed the coastal positions at Nocquet and Le Portel to check their strength.[29]

As a result of the North Novas coming under fire from Herquelingue, it had become evident that there remained a strong German force of some sort on its slopes. Their whereabouts, however, remained a mystery until early on September 21, when a dugout door opened and out walked a German major. He reported having about five hundred men underground that he would surrender in the approved fashion of an officer and gentleman. After some back-and-forth negotiations between the German and Brigadier Rockingham, it was agreed that he would take the major's formal surrender at 1300 hours. The Cameron Highlanders of Ottawa, who had been sitting on the summit for almost two days, totally unaware of the presence of this large force, were "more than surprised" when it emerged. Hearing of this development, 3rd Division's Major General Dan Spry dubbed it the "Bargain Basement

Incident," because apparently nobody had bothered to go down into these underground bunkers and search them.[30]

As these Germans were surrendering, 'A' and 'B' Companies of the North Novas advanced toward Nocquet. 'A' Company moved along a ridge with a troop of supporting tanks, while 'B' Company was below and following the road to Ecault. 'A' Company soon drew 20-millimetre anti-aircraft gunfire from a radar station to its north. The company took cover in an abandoned German fort overlooking the station. An attack was teed up for 'A' Company to head straight for the radar station, while 'B' Company flanked it from the left. The tanks provided fire support. As things kicked off at about 1345 hours, the familiar white flags started waving over the station. The lone officer emerged from a doorway, calmly lifted two mines, and then led two hundred men past them to surrender.

'B' Company had not even had to pause at the radar station. It carried on to the coast, marched through Nocquet without seeing a German, and easily secured the small fortification at Ningles. Here the company spent the night hunkered down in the fort's bunkers. Every movement in the open drew anti-aircraft fire from a battery about six hundred yards to the north.[31]

DURING THE NIGHT of September 20–21, a patrol from the North Shore (New Brunswick) Regiment's 'C' Company had found a ford across the Wimereux River, and that settled Lieutenant Colonel Ernie Anderson's plan for the attack on Wimereux itself. The attack would go in at noon with 'C' and 'D' Companies advancing, while the other two companies provided covering fire from La Trésorerie. Just east of the town, 'D' Company would wade the stream and go in south of the river, while 'C' Company approached from the north. 'D' Company was to be supported by two M-10s.[32]

Divisional intelligence staff had told Anderson that all civilians had left Wimereux. Observing the town from La Trésorerie, Anderson had seen signs of life there that led him to believe otherwise. Consequently, he was loath to accept the supporting fire of medium and heavy artillery regiments on offer. Instead, even as he recognized that it was likely too little, Anderson requested fire from just one field regiment and came up with a unique compensatory scheme. Facing Wimereux from La Trésorerie were several 20-millimetre anti-aircraft gun batteries that had been captured intact. Anderson had some men from 'A' and 'B' Companies familiarize themselves with the operation of these guns until they could fire them quickly and efficiently. As the two attacking battalions headed for the town, these guns opened fire. "They made a terrific noise," Anderson later said, "and served to bolster the slight artillery support, without, however, smashing the town so extensively."[33]

Hopes that the flak gunfire would keep German heads down were disappointed. Major Otty Corbett's 'D' Company came under heavy mortar fire as they crossed the start line, and when the lead section reached the river ford, it found the water ten feet deep. Nobody had factored in the effects of tidal flow this close to the river mouth, and at noon it was in full spate. Corbett ordered his men to take cover next to the embankment of a raised railway that ran alongside the river to Wimereux. He then directed the troop commander of the two M-10s to open fire on the machine-gun and mortar positions that were dug into the railway embankment and in front of the town station and were firing at 'C' Company. The targets were eighteen hundred yards distant, and Corbett was impressed to see almost every shot the anti-tank gun crews fired hit home. He spotted two Germans running over the railway embankment, one carrying an MG-42 and the other, two cans of ammunition. They jumped into a slit trench and started threading a belt of ammunition into the gun. Corbett was in wireless contact with the troop commander and advised him of the machine-gun crew's location. The gun had fired only a single burst when an M-10 dropped a high-explosive round a few feet away. Corbett saw one German dragging the other up the embankment to safety, abandoning the MG-42. As the machine gun was silenced, an artillery piece started firing out the door of a railroad boxcar next to the station. A high-explosive shell ripped a chunk out of the boxcar's side, revealing that the gun was surrounded by sandbags. An armour-piercing shot punched through the sandbags, and pieces of the gun—a French 75-millimetre from the Great War, with wooden wheels—went flying.

The supporting fire of the M-10s helped Major Jim Currie's 'C' Company get forward, but it was still tough slogging. Not far from the start line, they ran into a minefield. Several men were wounded, along with a stretcher-bearer who tried carrying one of them to safety. Free of the minefield, the company advanced into the teeth of the fire from the railway station. At 1310 hours, Currie asked Anderson to send the Cameron Highlanders of Ottawa platoon armed with Vickers heavy machine guns to support him. Adding to the din of firing machine guns, 20-millimetre flak guns firing overhead, and the steady thump of the M-10s was the near-constant sounds of exploding ammunition dumps on the south side of Wimereux. Clearly, the Germans knew they could not win, but they continued to fight hard.

"Finally we reached the station and laid siege to a blockhouse close by," Currie said. "The Jerries fired every weapon they had made ready for our invasion and one missile was a large drum of tar which landed on the street beside us and spread out. Our boots were sticky with tar for days. We blasted in the door of that blockhouse before dark and the Jerries filed out with their hands up, badly scared lads. Then 'D' Company moved through us and went on and soon I saw . . . prisoners being brought back . . . It was too dark then to do more and we made our plans for the morning."

At dawn on September 22, the two companies were reinforced by several Crocodiles and Petards. Currie was glad to see them. The mere sight of these machines ready to spout fire and bunker-smashing shot had the desired effect. "White flags went up everywhere and that was it."[34] As the men moved through the town, they were "thronged with civilians, which confirmed [Anderson's] belief and made him glad that they had been able to capture it without the devastating effect of so much artillery." Anderson was glad that the principal German defences at Wimereux had faced seaward and the coastal guns there had been unable to swivel to fire landward. Inspecting the coastal fortifications, he considered them "impregnable."[35]

BY NIGHTFALL ON September 21, the only main resistance points within Boulogne fortress were Le Portel and Fort de la Crèche. Both were expected to fall the following day.

With the improved weather on the 21st, Fort de la Crèche had been subjected to four medium-bomber raids, which started at 1730 hours with eighteen Mitchells striking. Every five minutes, more bombers arrived. The second and third waves consisted of eighteen more Mitchells apiece, and the final raid at 1745 hours was made by twenty-four Bostons. As the bombs were falling on the fort, the Queen's Own Rifles were able to get very close to it.[36] During the night, a troop of M-10s joined them. Originally, Fort de la Crèche had been an objective of Le Régiment de la Chaudière, but that battalion had only just managed to eliminate the last resistance around the Grande Armée column. If required, it would join the Queen's Own. But it was hoped that one battalion with the M-10s providing covering fire could do the job.[37]

At dawn, the M-10s started firing 105-millimetre shells directly at the old fort's walls. Manning a German 50-millimetre anti-aircraft gun, Queen's Own Major Neil Gordon joined in.[38] Nobody in the battalion looked forward to trying to take the place by storm, so a steady rate of shells was thrown at it. There was little return fire, and it was concluded that the Germans inside had been entirely surprised by the appearance of the Canadians literally at their gates. At 1045 hours, just as 'C' and 'D' Companies were ready to put in an assault, white flags rose above the ramparts. More than five hundred Germans surrendered. Soon a Queen's Own corporal marched out of the fortress "wearing a silk hat and playing a violin he had 'liberated.' To the tune of the *Skater's Waltz* the prisoners solemnly jigged along behind him."[39]

During the night, an armoured column had been formed in Boulogne to put in the main attack on Le Portel. As Generalleutnant Ferdinand Heim was known to be inside the fortification and had refused several calls during the day to surrender, a major fight was expected. Shortly after dawn on September 22, the column—made up of all the Fort Garry Horse Shermans of its combined 'A' and 'B' Squadron, a troop each of AVRES, Crocodiles, and Flails, and the Highland Light Infantry on foot—headed toward Le Portel's northern flank. The column soon halted behind the crest of a hill screening it from the fort.[40]

A scout car mounting a loud-hailer system rolled up to the summit, and Brigadier Rocky Rockingham called out a personal message to Heim at 1145 hours: "You have lost the battle for Boulogne. Over 7,000 prisoners have been taken and all form of resistance has ceased except this position. You are completely surrounded by a large force of arms.

"If you surrender now no further casualties will occur on either side and you and your garrison will be treated as prisoners of war and eventually return to your families. If, however, you do not surrender with all your garrison we will attack you with every means at our disposal, during which time we will incur some casualties but there is no way of assessing how many you will incur.

"You have one hour to make up your mind. Come out with a white flag flying, your hands above your heads, and unarmed within one hour. If this does not occur we will commence at once to destroy you and your garrison. You have had your warning, surrender or die from flames."[41] The fortification at Le Portel was made up of two strongpoints, with one at the northern edge of town and the other on the southern side. It was to the northern fort that Rockingham had directed his message, but the same demand was also delivered to the southern strongpoint. While the main force faced the northern strongpoint, the one to the south was to be taken by the Stormont, Dundas and Glengarry Highlanders. From 0715 to 1000 hours, 'A' and 'D' Companies on Mont Soleil had kept this fort under a steady rain of fire with the captured mortars and three 88-millimetre guns. At 1000 hours, this fire ceased to give the Germans the chance to surrender.[42]

Between 1300 and 1500 hours, several false alarms had briefly suggested that a surrender was imminent, so Rockingham ordered no attacks. Finally, at 1500 hours, his patience ended. With Flails leading, four Shermans under command of Lieutenant A.P. Thompson proceeded up to the summit overlooking the northern fort. As the tanks appeared, a great explosion erupted inside the fort that left the tankers blinded by dust for fifteen minutes. Thompson had his tanks fire blind toward the fort. When the dust cleared, he reported white flags were going up.[43]

Heim was determined to be still holding out in the southern fort, so Rockingham sent a German officer to talk him into surrendering. With the Glens closing in and drawing intermittent fire, it looked increasingly likely that Heim would fight. But as the Shermans and Crocodiles moved to join the Glens, the Germans in the fort began to destroy their guns with demolitions. At 1617 hours, white flags sprouted from the strongpoint, and Rockingham signalled a cease-fire. Fifteen minutes later, he signalled over the brigade wireless net, "General Heim has been taken." Ten minutes after that, Rockingham reported, "All folding up. Boulogne has been taken."[44]

"He came out in polished jack boots, sword and cap," Rockingham said of Heim. "I was as usual in an old battle dress. He didn't bring any staff. He came out by himself. I took his sword and [also his] car, which I used throughout the rest of the war."[45]

The six-day battle for Boulogne was over "at a juncture when time was very important," the army's official historian wrote. In all, 9,517 prisoners were captured, 250 of them wounded. How many had been killed was never determined. Allied losses were calculated as 634 killed, wounded, and missing. The six infantry battalions suffered the heaviest losses—462. These were roughly even across the two brigades, with 9th Brigade having 247 casualties and 8th Brigade 215. The Highland Light Infantry suffered most, with 97 casualties, of which 18 were fatal. But more North Nova Scotia Highlanders died—27 of its 96 casualties.

The fall of Boulogne had taken four days longer to achieve than scheduled, and there would be critical comparisons made to the fact that Le Havre had succumbed in two days as planned. But at Le Havre, an only slightly larger garrison had been reduced by the full weight of 1 British Corps with its two infantry divisions, two armoured brigades, and the support of the Funnies of 79th Armoured Division. For Boulogne, only two Canadian infantry brigades of 3rd Division had taken the fortress virtually alone.

Field Marshal Bernard Montgomery had hoped Boulogne would give him the port he so desperately desired. But Heim had been thorough in seeing its facilities demolished. And the aerial bombardments that had done so little damage to the German fortifications had caused much further destruction to the port and city. Extensive repairs were required. Although the Pluto fuel line would be strung across the channel from Dungeness to Boulogne on October 10, the port did not open to major shipping until October 14—doing nothing to relieve the immediate Allied supply problems.[46]

During his interrogation, Heim said it would have been a better use of German manpower to have destroyed the ports of Le Havre, Boulogne, and Calais and then withdrawn along with Fifteenth Army to the Scheldt. He considered the decision to maintain the fortress and thus consign thousands of men to die or be taken prisoner a grave mistake. Looking back at it, Heim said, "the game hadn't been worth the candle." He then considered why so many of his troops surrendered rather than die in their bunkers, as men of a fortress garrison were supposed to do. "The further east you go," he said, "the less important death becomes. The Japanese have no fear of death at all, and the Russians have almost none. In England and America life is very precious, and everything is done to preserve it and prevent its needless waste. We Germans stand in the middle."[47]

During the evening of the 22nd, Rockingham hosted a dinner for his battalion commanders and those unit commanders that had supported 9th Brigade, to celebrate "a task well done." Rockingham knew there would be precious little time for his men to rest and clean up from Boulogne, for every day of extra fighting here had delayed the start of the effort to take Calais.[48] Indeed, while his brigade was to be given a short breather and was also tasked with relieving 7th Infantry Brigade south of Cap Gris Nez, 8th Brigade would have no rest. Even as Brigadier Ken Blackader complimented his troops "on their efficiency and courage" in Operation Wellhit, he issued orders for the units to move the next morning toward Calais.[49]

[22]

With Great Boldness and Efficiency

WHILE OPERATION WELLHIT had been under way at Boulogne, First Canadian Army's Lieutenant General Harry Crerar and his staff had planned two other major operations—the capture of Calais, which included elimination of the Cap Gris Nez coastal batteries, and an invasion of Walcheren Island at the mouth of the Scheldt Estuary. As Field Marshal Bernard Montgomery was increasingly eager to have the port of Antwerp opened to Allied shipping, the Walcheren operation—Infatuate—was given priority. Consequently, during a conference on September 21 regarding details of Infatuate, Crerar asked the Royal Navy officers present the same question he had posed to his naval liaison officer on September 13: Could Boulogne be used if Calais was merely masked by sufficient forces to contain the Germans there and leave them to moulder? Admiral Sir Bertram Ramsay, Eisenhower's Naval Commander in Chief, thought it could, as long as the Gris Nez batteries were taken. Crerar then produced a memo that Captain A.F. Pugsley, a Royal Navy officer assigned to II Canadian Corps, had written advising that Calais must be taken for Boulogne's port to be usable.[1] With everyone wanting to get back to Infatuate, it was finally agreed that "naval considerations made it necessary . . . that Calais and the batteries at Cap Gris Nez and Sangatte be captured, as their larger guns would . . . prevent the free movement of shipping into Boulogne."[2] Consequently, "subsequent to the capture of Boulogne," Lieutenant General Guy Simonds was to quickly "exploit that success and capture Calais." Crerar had still hoped prior to September 19—the date originally scheduled for the attack on Calais—that this port could be taken with a short, sharp operation. He had, however, written to Montgomery on September 15 that should the Calais garrison show "indications of resisting anything but a heavy and prepared assault," 1 British Corps, less its 51st (Highland) Infantry Division, would be moved there to relieve Simonds, so that all of his corps could focus on opening Antwerp.

On the 19th, circumstances changed when it became necessary for 1 British Corps to take over the Antwerp sector. This would free British Second Army's XII Corps to shift eastward to support Operation Market Garden, which had run into serious trouble when the armoured column's attempted breakthrough to the Nederrijn (Lower Rhine) at Arnhem was threatened by German flanking attacks. With 1 British Corps now tied down, Simonds must take Calais. Although Crerar continued for a few more days to think it might still be possible to mask Calais, he formally abandoned that notion on September 23—the day after Boulogne fell.[3]

This was also the day Operation Market Garden began to unravel. Although a thin link to the Nederrijn had been established the day before, efforts to ferry Polish paratroopers in rubber dinghies over to reinforce the embattled 1st British Airborne Division only added five hundred men to a position that was increasingly a trap being closed by German forces. The corridor from Eindhoven was regularly severed by German flanking attacks. There seemed little hope that approximately seven hundred men of 2nd Para, 1st Parachute Brigade, who had managed to reach the Arnhem road bridge on September 17, could either be reinforced or hold out much longer. As for the rest of the airborne division surrounded in a shrinking bridgehead at Heveadorp—a village near Oosterbeek and west of Arnhem—there was no chance of getting men through to their comrades at the bridge.

With this tragic drama playing out to the east and absorbing Montgomery's and Twenty-First Army Group's main attention, First Canadian Army's planning and preparations for Operation Undergo— the assault on Calais—fell into full swing. In the last two days of

Wellhit, various formations of Flails, AVRES, Crocodiles, and other specialized equipment of 31st British Tank Brigade had left Boulogne for Calais. As soon as Wellhit ended on September 22, the rest of the brigade followed, as did all the artillery units, including the field regiments of the British 51st (Highland) Infantry Division seconded from I British Corps to support 3rd Canadian Infantry Division. Major General Dan Spry already had his 7th Canadian Infantry Brigade on the ground in the Cap Gris Nez area about seven miles southwest of Calais. The rest of the division began moving toward the city.

Even though 7th Brigade's Canadian Scottish Regiment had been held as divisional reserve through Wellhit, its other two regiments had managed to steadily push the Germans back toward their three Gris Nez batteries. But on the night of September 16–17, an attempt to capture these batteries with limited support by the 1st Hussars' tanks and two artillery regiments failed to make any impression on the German defenders. On September 18, 7th Brigade handed off the Gris Nez sector to the 17th Duke of York's Royal Canadian Hussars and moved to forming-up positions for the attack on Calais.[4]

The plan for Undergo broadly followed that of Wellhit. There would be very strong air, artillery, and assault-armour support to assist two 3rd Infantry Division brigades—the 7th and 8th. The battleground, however, was not at all comparable to Boulogne. Nor were the German defensive works and garrison equivalent.

Major Bill Matthews of the Canadian Scottish Regiment quickly realized that "the capture of Calais presented a very different problem from that of Boulogne. Whereas the latter fortress had based its defence on the prominent features which enclosed it, Calais was mainly surrounded by low-lying, marshy country." Typically, the Germans had expanded the water barriers by inundation. Only the country to the west offered to Matthews's eye a viable line of approach. Here the Belle Vue Ridge from its highest point at Noires Mottes ran eastward toward the flooded ground around the city. All this ground was heavily defended, but Matthews could see that the country to the east and south of it was too low and marshy "to permit . . . a successful initial attack. The enemy moreover possessed complete command of these approaches.

"Nor could the problem be solved with the reduction of the outer defences alone, as was substantially the case at Boulogne. Within the city . . . were many canals, well-defended, which divided it into islands and imposed further obstacles."[5] Somewhat as in Boulogne, Calais was centred on a medieval citadel, which itself did not provide a major defensive advantage against modern weapons. But the Germans had established a network—bristling with pillboxes, guns in casemates, anti-tank guns, and infantry posts—that took advantage of the many canals and dykes "to make the heart of the position as formidable as its tough outer shell."[6]

Realizing that the ridge provided the logical approach to the city, the Germans had constructed extensive defences to block its use. A network of minefields, concrete pillboxes, and wire obstacles had been emplaced from the coast back to the ridge top to meet an attack from the sea. Key points in these defences were Noires Mottes with its battery of three 406-millimetre naval guns, a smaller battery at Sangatte, and a small battle group at Vieux Coquelles.[7] Strung out along the ridge between Noires Mottes and Sangatte were numerous machine-gun positions and concrete shelters. Just north of Vieux Coquelles, slightly higher ground than the surrounding marshy terrain had been heavily fortified with a variety of weapons protected by wire barriers and minefields. This ground stood astride the main Boulogne–Calais road. The eastern and southeastern approaches were also defended by minefields "and infantry positions supported by field, anti-aircraft and anti-tank artillery. Finally, in the Les Baraques area on the northwestern outskirts of the port, coastal installations were shielded by still more minefields and an anti-tank ditch connecting the inundated areas to the sea." There was no possibility of any movement on the flooded ground, which was deep and looked like "a vast lake."[8]

For hundreds of years, Calais had been subject to conflict between the French and British, with control of the city changing hands several times over the centuries. This had led to construction of a series of fortifications on its outskirts, particularly to the west, where the ridge had provided as good access for medieval soldiers as modern ones. The Germans had used these fortifications to advantage and created a defensive line that ran from Fort Lapin through Les Baraques to Fort Nieulay by the inundated area guarding the western and south-western approaches to the city. Fort Lapin contained a heavy artillery battery protected by anti-tank ditches and minefields. The battery here and one nearby identified as Bastion 11 were reported to be equipped with flame-throwers.[9]

As with Le Havre and Boulogne, Canadian intelligence estimates of German strength were woefully inaccurate and more the product of guesswork than hard intelligence. Estimates ranged from an initial 4,450 to 5,550 to a later revision of 6,000 to 8,000. It was actually about 7,500.[10]

The garrison commander was Oberstleutnant Ludwig Schroeder. Canadian intelligence staff were puzzled as to why and how the equivalent of a lieutenant colonel came to be in charge of "a large-scale, ideological stand." In fact, Schroeder's appointment on August 30, 1944, was purely the result of circumstances that put him in the city at that time. There was nothing in his military background suggesting any special abilities relevant to defending a fortress. At forty-three, Schroeder was large-bodied, long-jawed, and aged beyond his years by wounds and illness. Whereas Ferdinand Heim at Boulogne had a somewhat intellectual bent, Schroeder exuded a "surprised simplicity, and his views on military and political matters were marked by a narrow dullness that bespoke the unimaginative man who preferred to have his thinking done for him."

His war career had eventually led, via a series of plodding advances, to command of the 1035th Grenadier Regiment of 59th Infanterie-Division. This division had been cobbled together after the Normandy invasion with men who were home on leave from the Russian, Italian, and Norwegian fronts. On August 19, its ten thousand troops formed up in the area of Calais and relieved the 64th Infanterie-Division. With the German situation collapsing in France, two of its regiments rushed off to defend the Somme on August 27, and that left Schroeder's regiment to defend a twenty-mile coastline anchored on Calais. On August 30, however, Schroeder's regiment was also sent away. Schroeder, with his regimental staff, was told to remain and take command of Fortress Calais.

Over the next few days, he received various assurances that re-inforcements were on the way. But they never arrived, and he retained nothing from 59th Infanterie-Division but a company of engineers tasked with carrying out demolitions and building defences. In prepar-ing for the inevitable battle, Schroeder did little to become fully familiar with his command. He had only a vague understanding of available artillery—guessing that it amounted to about twenty-two guns varying in calibre from 75-millimetre field guns to 150-millimetre howitzers. His grasp of anti-tank guns was better—about fifty guns total. These consisted of three 88-millimetre guns and then a mix of 77-millimetre, 75-millimetre, and 37-millimetre guns. The naval coastal guns num-bered about twenty and ranged in calibre from 21-centimetre to the huge 30-centimetre Batterie Lindeman guns at Sangatte. Only six of the naval guns could traverse 360 degrees to fire landward, and efforts to physically turn some guns were still under way as the Canadians geared up for Operation Undergo. Schroeder was also able to deploy twenty 88-millimetre anti-aircraft guns and fifty to sixty lighter flak guns for ground combat.

As for troops, his best consisted of the engineer company and a reinforcement battalion of infantry left behind by 47th Infanterie-Division. Initially, the garrison numbered about 6,000, but as the Canadians rolled up more of the coastline, others trickled in to bring it, by Schroeder's calculation, to about 8,000. Schroeder thought the mor-ale of "this conglomeration of troops was wretched . . . They contained a high percentage of Volkdeutsche (Germans living in foreign countries) and Hiwis (foreign volunteers)—who were easily influenced by Allied propaganda." Not only were the troops poor, but his officers were "negligible," and—aside from the artillery staff officer—Schroeder "had very little good to say on their behalf."

Of the core 6,000 men, only 2,500 were available to fight as infantry. The balance was split up, so that 1,000 men manned the coastal guns, 1,000 the port installations, 600 the anti-aircraft weapons, and 1,000 the artillery facing to the south and east. Schroeder doggedly distrib-uted his infantry with anti-tank gun crews in the various strongpoints, with most positions manned by only 30 to 50 soldiers. Schroeder recognized that Calais's topography, with its flooded areas and then the ridge, was well suited to defence because the intervening ground would be difficult to cross in the face of his fire. But he doubted his troops were capable of defending the city for long.

In Schroeder's opinion, defending Calais was not worth the loss of men it would necessarily entail when the inevitable defeat occurred. "If they had been taken back to Germany and given . . . four or six weeks training they would have formed a good division. At Calais, in their raw state, they were mere rubbish," he said.

Capping the whole futility of the effort, the port was not a great asset for the Allies. It was small. Constant dredging was required to render it usable by deep-draught shipping. The Germans had not dredged the harbour for more than a year and used it only for small surface boats. Once Calais was besieged, naval personnel started destroying the harbour facilities. Schroeder figured that between this damage and the dredging need, it would be a long time before the Allies brought the port into service.

Schroeder was also bedevilled by the presence of twenty thousand civilians within the city who refused to budge, despite attempts by the mayor to organize an evacuation before hostilities were likely to begin. The mayor succeeded in persuading only some five to six thousand people to leave. While Schroeder understood there were sufficient rations to feed the garrison troops for fifty-seven days once the assault began, there was insufficient food to also maintain such a large civilian population.[11]

ON SEPTEMBER 17, Allied efforts had begun to soften the German garrison and reduce its already poor morale with air strikes by No. 84 Tactical Group fighter-bombers and rocket-bearing fighters. As at Boulogne and Le Havre, these attacks did little direct damage. Some strongpoints bombed proved to be freshly made with no weapons installed yet. A rocket attack succeeded in detonating the ammunition dump at one emplacement. Several attacks directed at emplacements next to the inundated areas caused no damage, and later investigation by RAF personnel led to the conclusion that the bombs had fallen harmlessly into the water. Oberstleutnant Schroeder's headquarters had been identified as being situated in a building within the wooded Parc Saint Pierre in the heart of the city and just east of the harbour. On September 22, it was targeted by the 341st and 329th Squadrons, RAF. Both claimed bomb hits on the building and some near misses. The building was in fact undamaged by the closest three bombs, which struck within twenty feet, or the four others that landed about seventy yards distant.[12]

While these efforts were under way, 3rd Division's Major General Dan Spry and his staff were still simultaneously fighting Wellhit and planning Undergo. As 7th Infantry Brigade was not involved in Wellhit and so was relatively fresh, Spry assigned it the main job—to "attack and capture or destroy the garrison." This meant seizing Belle Vue Ridge, Vieux Coquelles, and then Calais. At the same time, 8th Infantry Brigade would be responsible for the Escalles area west of 7th Infantry Brigade's operational area. This included the village of Escalles, the battery at Noires Mottes, and Sangatte. Both brigades would attack on a two-battalion front, with 7th Brigade advancing the Regina Rifles and Royal Winnipeg Rifles, while the North Shore (New Brunswick) Regiment and Le Régiment de la Chaudière would lead 8th Brigade's attack. In 8th Brigade's sector, the Chauds would be on the left to capture the high ground east of Escalles and all defences on Cap Blanc Nez. To the right, the North Shores must eliminate "the defences of the whole Noires Mottes area" and then capture the large battery at Sangatte. The 7th Brigade's operation was more ambitious and therefore would unfold in three phases. First, the Little Black Devils would take Coquelles, while the Reginas seized the Noires Mottes strongpoints and batteries. The second phase called for an advance along the coast to eliminate the defensive line running from Fort Lapin through Les Baraques to Fort Nieulay. In the third phase, the brigade would fight its way into and secure Calais.

The "same smashing, battering bombing" as at Boulogne and Le Havre was considered "an integral part" of the whole. Five large target areas encompassed most of the area through which 7th and 8th Brigades would advance. Calais itself was not targeted for the operation's launch, but it was to be bombed in the days leading up to it and as needed once the assault began.[13]

Each assault-date target was assigned a priority number, with targets one and two to be bombed before Zero Hour and the fall of the last bombs marking the beginning of the ground troops' advance.[14] Zero Hour was set for 1000 hours, so the first attack was scheduled to start at 0815 hours with a forty-minute program on target two, then a switch to target one at 0855 hours that would cease at 0955 hours. The third target would be struck at 1025 hours and bombing there ended at 1105 hours. Target four would then be hit until 1125 hours. The last segment would run from 1125 to 1145 hours.[15]

At Le Havre and Boulogne, heavy bombing had produced cratering that seriously impeded the advance of the armoured columns. "Cratering and destruction is essential," stated one Undergo planning document, but there was also interest in seeing if the same "smashing and battering" effect could be achieved with different ordnance.[16] Bomber Command, therefore, proposed on September 18 using target four as a testing ground. Instead of high-explosive bombs, this area would be subjected to fused explosives "for less cratering and more blast."[17] It was hoped that fragmentation bombs "among concrete and earthwork defences" might severely damage them without creating craters that could swallow an AVRE or tank.

The actual start date of Undergo had not yet been finalized, as Wellhit was still under way and the weather appeared to be worsening over both Calais and the bomber bases in Britain. Yet Bomber Command was adamant that Zero Hour, on whichever day it came, must be no later than noon for the program to play out as planned.[18]

WHEN WELLHIT CONCLUDED, the great artillery force gathered outside Boulogne started moving toward Calais on September 23. The regiments took two different routes, both of which exposed them to heavy shelling, especially from batteries at Cap Gris Nez.[19] Brigadier Stanley Todd, 3rd Division's chief gunner, oversaw their deployment into assigned gun positions. "Within three miles of [Calais] every road, every field and every cowshed was covered with mines," he said. "We had a terrible time trying to get the field clear enough of mines to be able to deploy the guns to support the infantry."[20]

A major threat was that the gun lines planned for west of the main Calais–Boulogne road could be observed by the Germans at Cap Gris Nez and brought under fire by four large 100-millimetre guns there.

It was therefore necessary to create a massive daytime smokescreen to blind the German observers. The mines making life miserable for Todd also necessitated concentrating many guns into this site. Between the inundated areas and the minefields, there was little suitable ground elsewhere for deploying artillery.

Captain J.C. Bond, the chemical warfare technical officer of II Canadian Corps, oversaw the smoke operation. He quickly determined that the generators producing the smoke needed to be placed along the road running from Wissant, on the coast, inland to Marquise. This was about four miles southwest of Escalles and roughly midway between that village and Cap Gris Nez. Bond's instructions were to maintain the screen for twelve hours each day. Originally, Bond expected to maintain the screen for only a day and a half, but in the end it continued until September 28.[21] The stretch of road where Bond deployed his smoke generators was three thousand yards long. Initially, there were sixty smoke-points, all manned by twenty-three gunners of the 3rd Canadian Light Anti-Aircraft Regiment.[22] Bond estimated that he needed 2,800 generators a day—exhausting four every hour at each site—to produce sixty-eight tons of smoke. His calculations were based on the worst weather conditions of low humidity, strong west winds, and high turbulence. The gentle sea breezes and pleasant sunshine of a Calais summer were over. Each day, the weather worsened. Bond's crews started producing smoke at 0700 hours on September 23 as the guns began to roll into their assigned positions.

It quickly became apparent that the task was not as monumental as originally conceived, and the number of smoke-points could be reduced. At 0900, Bond cut the number of points to just eighteen, making it much easier for his crews to keep them running. This was possible because the prevailing winds were coming from the west and at a right angle to the smoke-generator line. Putting two or three generators in the same spot at two-hundred-yard intervals produced sufficient smoke to create a continuous barrier in both width and height. On the best day, only twelve smoke-points were required.

A major challenge Bond faced was finding enough generators for the task. As the operation continued, he deployed many captured German

No. KL 42 generators. These, Bond reported, "give approximately two thirds the screening length of a No. 24 [Canadian generator] and vary in burning time from 18 to 28 minutes. 520 German generators were used. They were more difficult to handle, harder to ignite, have a greater percentage of failures, and give a more irritating smoke. The generators were not used as an experiment, but as a necessity."

Over the course of the operation, 8,118 generators would be utilized to produce an average hourly rate of 2.4 tons and 147 tons over the course of the operation.[23]

While the gunners welcomed the protective smokescreen, it only moderated the rate of German shellfire from Cap Gris Nez and rendered it inaccurate. But chance hits still happened. The screen also did nothing to prevent the guns from being observed and fired on by batteries at Calais. At 1445 hours, 13th Canadian Field Regiment deployed near a crossroads at Hauteville, a village about six miles southwest of the city and under constant fire. "The shells were coming from the direction of Calais," Lieutenant William Barrett wrote, "skimming the crest of the hill in front and landing with the mighty 'crump' of a large calibre gun. The work of digging in the guns and building command posts was carried on during the lulls in the shelling. Sergeant [John] Muir of the 78th Battery was killed that afternoon while digging a pit for his gun." Throughout the day, the nearby crossroads was under near constant fire, and many stray shells fell within the adjacent 22nd and 78th Battery positions.[24]

On September 22, 3rd Division's counter-battery officer, Lieutenant Colonel James Hargrave Drummond Ross, distributed fire plans and traces to the various regimental artillery commanders. At forty-seven, Ross was a Great War veteran artilleryman who had been awarded a Military Cross during that conflict. Recognizing that at Boulogne the German batteries had not been effectively smothered by the opening bombardment, Ross was determined this time to avoid that problem. He and Todd planned a heavy bombardment that would last for forty-eight minutes and cease just thirty-five minutes before Zero Hour. Ross meticulously identified twenty-one fixed batteries and arranged for each to be heavily shelled for three minutes at a concentration of fifteen Canadian guns per German weapon.

To protect the RAF bombers, the divisional artillery commanders also created a large counter-flak program to be fired by the medium, heavy, and heavy anti-aircraft regiments against the German heavy anti-aircraft batteries. Air observation posts would be flying overhead to direct observed fire onto enemy guns that became active or had missed being identified. Rocket-firing Typhoons were also to be on call to attack enemy gun positions. As the battle progressed, the guns would fire as directed by FOOs moving with the infantry.[25]

BECAUSE THE BATTLE for Boulogne took far longer than envisioned, Operation Undergo experienced several postponements, which became an almost daily occurrence between September 17 and 22. On September 21, Bomber Command contacted 11 Canadian Corps headquarters to say that owing to other commitments, a firm date for Undergo was needed and suggested either the 24th or 25th. Lieutenant General Guy Simonds replied that the 24th was preferred, and this was accepted assuming favourable weather. At 1642 hours on the 23rd, however, Bomber Command signalled, "Undergo Lemons 24 Sep because of weather. Will plan now for 25 Sep."[26]

With 11 Canadian Corps during these days communicating directly with Air Chief Marshal Sir Arthur Harris and his headquarters, Simonds and his staff decided to cut corners and mount a bombing raid without passing it for approval via the normal channels of First Canadian Army through to the headquarters of Allied Expeditionary Air Force and 2nd Tactical Air Force. On September 20, Simonds's Chief of Staff Brigadier Elliot Rodger had asked Harris directly to arrange for a hard strike on the Escalles area late that afternoon. Harris promptly agreed. A few hours later, learning of the plan, First Canadian Army staff were alarmed that the carefully developed working relationship it had built with Allied Expeditionary Air Force (AEAF) and 2nd Tac Air was being jeopardized. They hurriedly put through a request for the same attack Harris had already approved based on the 11 Corps proposal. Possibly affronted at 11 Corps's cheek, AEAF ordered the attack cancelled. But they applied the order to the wrong attack, cancelling the September 20 2nd Tac Air medium-bomber raid planned for Fort de la Crèche instead—which had left the Queen's Own Rifles waiting for a pre-bombardment that never came and had to be hurriedly re-organized for the following day. Meanwhile, the attack that AEAF had wanted cancelled went ahead in the late afternoon of September 20, with 633 aircraft dropping 3,372 tons of bombs into the Escalles area.[27] "It was too easy!" Rodger scribbled in his diary.

Rather than being chastened by AEAF's botched attempt to exert its authority, Simonds and Rodger decided, in collusion with First Canadian Army's Chief of Staff Brigadier Church Mann, to develop a way "to get bomber support on our direct link without crossing up all the higher HQS." Rodger wrote that "Mann seemed to get a system agreed which should work. Tested it by a message of 23 Sep which got an affirmative reply morning 24 Sep for bombs on Calais about 1800 hours 24 Sep weather permitting."[28]

When the next day Bomber Command scrubbed the immediate start of Undergo, II Corps sought to ensure that the agreed-to Calais bombing at least would proceed. "If factor causing your postpone-ment of 'Undergo' should change to permit bombing later in day, we would welcome any spare effort you can offer . . . for softening Calais defences."[29] At 1020 hours, Bomber Command signalled that weather permitting it would strike five targets in and around Calais between 1730 and 1850 hours. The signal included a stated assumption that "all French" civilians had been "removed from vicinity of these aiming points." As II Corps had no idea and likely suspected the opposite, it did not reply.[30]

Not long before the bombers were to arrive, 7th Canadian Infantry Brigade headquarters was advised that the attack had been cancelled. Consequently, no arrangements were made for artillery to suppress, or "pancake," the German anti-aircraft defences ringing the city. "As a result," the brigade's war diarist recorded, "we lost eight Lancasters. They did a grand job and plastered Calais north from stem to stern but they had to fly through a thick curtain of flak. We felt very help-less watching this attack—the casualties to aircraft could have been lowered if someone along the lines somewhere hadn't messed things up. However one has to expect this sort of thing in war. Patrols were sent out from battalions to try to pick up some of the bomber crew—those we did find were dead."[31]

Captain Vassar Hall of the Regina Rifles had watched the bombers getting shot down from a height of ground. "It was cloudy and the bombers were coming in fairly low and the anti-aircraft gunners . . . had their range just about right . . . One of our company commanders Captain Len Glass . . . was in the forward area . . . and one of these aircraft had been shot just overhead and one of its engines came down in front of his position and bounced right over it . . . It was disheartening to see these bombers being hit like that, although of course many of them got through. We could see the fires starting up in Calais where they were bombing."[32]

As the bombers pulled away at 1850 hours, 7th Brigade reported to 3rd Division headquarters that the northeastern sector of Calais had been struck by many phosphorous bombs. "There appears to be large balls of fire shooting skywards . . . Heavy smoke over northern part of Calais. One fire burning at harbour entrance."[33]

ON SEPTEMBER 23, Lieutenant General Crerar sent a letter to Lieutenant General Guy Simonds advising that he was to receive a Distinguished Service Order. As DSOs were normally granted to officers as a result of some combat action, the award was tied to the period when he commanded 1st Canadian Infantry Division in Sicily. Particular mention was made of "his frequent visits to the forward areas—where under bomb, shell, and mortar fire" he had led the division "with great boldness and efficiency."[34]

Having been away from his headquarters in the afternoon, Simonds found Crerar's letter that evening. "I really don't know what to say about the award of which you tell me," he said in an immediate handwritten reply. "It is gratifying that in doing my duty I have been able to give useful service but I always feel that it is worse than criminal to spare any forethought and trouble to give our troops the best possible break in battle. Given a proper start they *always* succeed. The successes we have had are all theirs and I hope they realize that this award to me is recognition of that fact.

"May I reassure you of my complete and continuing loyalty—and that of every other commander in the corps. You can be certain of the execution of the tasks which you give to us, to the best of our abilities.

If the circumstances of a very extended and varied battle make it impossible to give personal attention to every detail, I hope you will not think that any of us are giving less than that. I have served you for a very great part of my service and may I say that I have never had the feeling that the submission of a suggestion would be interpreted as showing any disloyalty. Your decision is final and will not be argued here and I will feel perfectly free to make suggestions on that basis, if from such limited information as may be available to me, they would appear to further operations."[35]

Even as Simonds sent his note off to Crerar, the First Canadian Army commander's increasing ill health was reaching a critical juncture, and he was scheduled for a September 25 checkup at No. 6 Canadian General Hospital in Saint-Omer. As Undergo was getting started that day, the doctors diagnosed Crerar as suffering from dysentery and a possible blood disorder. He was scheduled for evacuation on the 26th to England for treatment. Simonds would assume temporary command of First Canadian Army, with Lieutenant General Charles Foulkes of 2nd Infantry Division assigned to run II Canadian Corps.

Late on the afternoon of September 24, Regina Rifles commander Lieutenant Colonel Foster Matheson gathered his officers for a final Orders Group. "Spirits were high when he announced the fall of Boulogne with nine thousand POWs," Major Eric Luxton wrote. "In a few seconds spirits and bodies were low as a Jerry 'stonk' came down" on battalion headquarters.[36] For most of the day, Matheson had ensured that his men were "getting as much rest as possible." The arrival of bombers over Calais had surprised him because the weather throughout the day had been so "rough."[37]

While the Reginas' Orders Group had been a modest familial affair, the North Shore (New Brunswick) Regiment's was of gala proportions. Joining the North Shore officers were representatives from an array of supporting arms. Seventy-three men crowded together in the village of Audembert's schoolhouse to study a sand model of their objective—Noires Mottes.[38] The North Shore officers little needed the model. They had spent time examining their objective through binoculars and had not liked the look of it. Noires Mottes had proven to be not a single hill but two closely grouped together and connected by a slight saddle, with both "dominating the approaches to the sea and the blockhouses on the beach itself. The position had about it all the features that make for hard fighting—every advantage to the defenders," the regiment's historian wrote. "The slope leading up to the dugouts was open and devoid of cover as well as being heavily mined. On the other side of the hill leading down to the sea, were large concrete emplacements, mutually supporting. The ground was churned up in an almost unbelievable manner for the position had been subjected . . . to bombing from RAF heavies . . . Enormous craters overlapped each other and not a single road, track or blade of grass remained. So it was plain that after the heights had been gained, armoured support was an impossibility."

To get the North Shores to that summit, the specialists in the room described how their Flails, Crocodiles, and AVREs would operate. Each specialist gathered the North Shore platoon officers and non-commissioned officers around the model and carefully briefed them on how to work in tandem with his machines. Lessons had been learned at Le Havre and Boulogne, where too many elements had been left to be overcome through dash and daring. The 1st Lothians and Border Yeomanry, the 6th Assault Regiment, and the 81st Assault Squadron had lost much equipment and the lives of more comrades in those operations than they felt necessary. This time they were carefully preparing, and the North Shores thought it could yield "handsome dividends" in casualties avoided.[39]

We Will Fight

"WE HAD A quiet night," the Regina Rifles war diarist wrote on September 25, "and most of us woke in morning expecting operation 'Undergo' to be cancelled due to first signs of weather. However, [Zero Hour] is confirmed by brigade and activity speeds up. We have been anticipating this show for some time and are anxious to get our teeth into enemy. Bombers start passing overhead and spasmodic artillery fire starts." Although at dawn the weather had been nasty with low clouds, a high wind off the sea, and cool temperatures, by 0830 hours the sun was breaking through.[1]

It still made for poor bombing weather, and when the first heavies arrived over Calais, many bombardiers were unable to accurately pinpoint their targets. Almost 900 bombers were committed to the air attack, but only 303 actually released their loads, for a total of 1,321 tons of explosives. II Canadian Corps headquarters signalled Bomber Command, "Bombs which were delivered were well timed and on target."[2] This was only partly true. The Reginas' 'A' Company moved at 0850 toward its start line, and 'D' Company followed at 0900. When these forward elements moved into place, they radioed back to battalion headquarters that the "bombing task that was to have covered our objective has missed to the west." Lieutenant Colonel Foster Matheson immediately contacted 8th Infantry Brigade's headquarters to confirm that the attack should proceed anyway, and

Brigadier Ken Blackader immediately responded that the "operation will go on."[3]

At 1100 hours, Air Chief Marshal Sir Arthur Harris signalled 11 Corps, "Regret weather spoilt our op this morning 25 Sep. Please inform us urgently present position and state future intentions and requirements. Will stand by but weather forecast for Tuesday 26 Sep very unfavorable." Despite this forecast, Bomber Command did accept a bombing program of nine targets inside Calais for the 26th to begin at 0955 hours and end at 1255. Because of the weather, Harris cautioned that a two-hour postponement might be required and asked that, to increase the prospects of accuracy, no changes be made to the targeted map references unless submitted no later than 0200 hours on September 26.[4]

Those bombs that were dropped yielded the same generally poor result seen at Le Havre and Boulogne. Few pillboxes and other defences were eliminated or even damaged. The usual claims of battered German morale were made, but the enemy stuck to its defences.[5] Nor did the massive artillery barrage that started at 0845 hours with a forty-minute counter-battery program worked up by Lieutenant Colonel James Hargrave Drummond Ross yield the desired results. A total of 224 guns of eight medium and three heavy regiments, along with two heavy anti-aircraft regiments, weighed in at first. Then, at 1000 hours, the six field regiments joined the bombardment with pre-planned "concentrations and stonks . . . followed by targets fired on call as the battalions began moving forward with their supporting armour," the army's chief artillery historian wrote.[6]

During planning for Undergo, it had been recognized that the Noires Mottes feature dominated the ground over which 7th Infantry Brigade's Regina Rifles and Royal Winnipeg Rifles must advance. So its early seizure was deemed essential. Although the North Shore (New Brunswick) Regiment and their supporting armoured units had undertaken extensive planning the day before, the officers of the 1st Lothians and Border Yeomanry still thought the scheme was based on sketchy and hurriedly gathered intelligence mixed with a great deal of "pious hope."

Still, at 1015 hours, 'C' Squadron's Nos. 3 and 4 Troops rattled across the start line and began flailing toward Noires Mottes. Overlooked by high ground to the left and from the objective ahead, the tankers were surprised when not a shot was fired at them. Both troops quickly flailed out three-track-wide lanes up to where the bomb cratering began. Here No. 3 Troop was confined to flailing "a tortuous course" in single file through to the objective. No. 4 Troop, meanwhile, created another lane back to the start line and then made for the hill that formed the left feature of Noires Mottes, as there appeared to be fewer craters in front of it. This line of approach proved most manageable, with the Flails detonating thirty-seven mines and then chewing their way through two aprons of wire without losing a single tank.[7]

Marching up the lanes behind the Flails, the North Shores' 'A' and 'B' Companies had led the advance, closely followed by 'D' Company. Major Otty Corbett had two of 'D' Company's platoons and his head-quarters section tight behind 'B' Company, while the third platoon, under Lieutenant Hobart Staples, tailed 'A' Company. Once the two hilltops were secure, 'D' Company was to descend the western slope to take out the large coastal guns and then proceed to clear the smaller battery next to Sangatte. The Fort Garry Horse regiment would provide fire support from the right flank. Both of the forward company commanders also rode into the advance, inside a Fort Garry Horse tank to keep pace with the Flails. Each company's second-in-command moved with the troops.

'B' Company followed No. 3 Troop, and despite the difficulty with the craters, reached the German positions first. The lead platoon, under Lieutenant Harry Hamley, dashed through the breach in the wire and paused to wait for the rest of the company. From what he could see looking out the turret hatch of the tank, Major Bill Parker thought the hilltop positions seemed abandoned. Raising Hamley on the wireless, Parker ordered his platoon to head straight through to the objective "without the assistance of tanks or Crocodiles." By the time the rest of the company and the supporting Crocodiles arrived, Hamley's men had taken eleven prisoners. Within an hour, both 'B' and 'A' Companies had consolidated their hold on the two hilltops, having encountered almost no opposition. Most of the dugouts had been unoccupied.[8]

As Corbett's main body of 'D' Company passed over the crest, it was met by a hail of small-arms fire and driven back. "The enemy had given up the crest positions ... but once the initial shock wore off his reactions were quick and effective. An exposure on the seaward slope brought instant and accurate machine-gun fire. Lift a steel helmet on a stick and it would be punctured in ten seconds," Corbett said.

Hoping to break the impasse, Corbett arranged for Crocodiles to advance down the slope. They immediately drew intense anti-tank gunfire and were unable to manoeuvre around the bomb craters. The advance ground to a halt, with one 'D' Company platoon and three Crocodiles pinned in place about three hundred yards downslope. Here the North Shores remained blocked until dusk, when Corbett was ordered to recall the Crocodiles as they would be too exposed out on the slope. Two managed to escape, although the fuel trailer of one was holed by two anti-tank rounds. The third fell into a large bomb crater. Corbett told the platoon to stay with it.[9]

At the same time that the main body of 'D' Company had run into trouble, the platoon under Staples tried to advance from 'A' Company's hilltop and was met by "a violent reaction from the enemy," as machine guns, 20-millimetre flak guns, and several anti-tank guns opened fire. Then a 170-millimetre coastal gun started methodically dropping rounds on the slope Staples and his men were slowly descending. Before starting down, Staples had tried to get tank support, but the Fort Garry Horse officer on the hill said it would be suicide for his Shermans to expose themselves on the skyline. Crawling and dodging from one point of cover to another, Staples and his men managed by nightfall to reach a concrete blockhouse about five hundred feet above the nearest large coastal gun position. Eight prisoners were taken, but the platoon could go no farther.[10]

To the left of the North Shores, Le Régiment de la Chaudière advanced with three companies forward to clear the Cap Blanc Nez area and Escalles. 'A' Company was left, 'B' in the centre, and 'C' right. There was no cover, so the battalion's mortar platoon fired smoke bombs to blind the Germans. Advancing quickly, the Chauds seized Escalles without incident, but as they started up the slope toward Cap Blanc Nez and the gun battery there, the Germans started firing machine guns through the smoke. 'B' Company's Lieutenant A. Maltais fell badly wounded.

On the right, Major G. Beaudry had discovered a narrow coulee and advanced 'C' Company unseen along it to a position where he could outflank three of the series of blockhouses that were pinning down the other two companies. 'C' Company quickly silenced these three positions. Stunned by the rapidity of 'C' Company's attack and obviously thinking Beaudry's force was much stronger than it truly was, the remaining men manning the blockhouses in front of the Chauds hoisted white flags. Three German soldiers then approached and asked to speak to an officer. Accompanied by Corporal R. Chartrand, Beaudry went with the soldiers to the headquarters of the Cap Blanc Nez headquarters. The garrison commander requested two hours' grace from further attack so that he could organize the surrender of his entire force. Beaudry contacted Lieutenant Colonel Paul Mathieu, who accepted the terms.

At 1900 hours, the Chauds advanced into the strongpoint on the cape and found that the Germans had destroyed the gun battery. Most of the approximately two hundred soldiers who meekly surrendered appeared to have spent the two-hour truce getting drunk on wine and other alcohol.[11]

As the Chauds were taking the surrender of a garrison they had expected to offer stiff resistance, it began to storm. On the summit of Noires Mottes, Major Parker and Major Corbett stared down the slope grimly as the ground grew slicker by the minute. The plan had been to renew the attack in the morning, but this was clearly not going to work, as the tanks would surely bog down in the ever-deepening mud.[12]

Among the prisoners was a man named Paul who spoke English with a Brooklyn accent. He had suffered the misfortune of having returned to Germany just in time to get conscripted into the army. Paul was a delighted prisoner. So delighted, he offered to persuade the Germans in a nearby bunker to surrender. There were twenty men there under command of a sergeant. They wanted to give up, but were afraid of being mistreated. Paul assured them they would be treated much better if they surrendered now than after the Canadians had to root them out. The Germans promptly gave up.

The prisoners reported the location of a complete hospital carved into one side of Noires Mottes with a large underground ammunition bunker just beyond. Parker's second-in-command, Lieutenant Charles Richardson, thought "we were riding a wave and that a bold move might pay off, so [I] asked the line of prisoners for a volunteer to act as a guide to the hospital. After no more than a thirty-second pause one chap stepped forward." Paul and North Shore Sergeant Claude Jennings accompanied the volunteer to the hospital. The senior medical officer there told Jennings he was unable to contact the garrison commander by phone because the bombings had severed the wires. So a runner was sent with a demand that the garrison be surrendered at first light. When the runner failed to return, the North Shores could do nothing but wait.[13]

At 0130 hours, the runner returned with a terse response: "We will not surrender, we will fight." The North Shores braced for battle. The rain increased, and any thought of armour support was dismissed. Then, at 0530 hours, two German privates approached and asked to speak to the commander. Taken to Lieutenant Colonel Ernie Anderson, the men said "the Germans wished a conference." Looking down the slope toward Sangatte, the North Nova Scotia Highlanders saw two white flags fluttering over the coastal batteries. After some confusion over how this conference would take place and where, some German enlisted men reported that they had locked their officers in their rooms as soon as the flags had been raised. They had now released one officer to confer with Anderson. A conference ensued, wherein Anderson convinced the garrison commander that "it was useless to fight on." It was agreed that both the positions at Noirs Mottes and the battery west of Sangatte would surrender at noon on September 26. At the designated time, seven officers and 278 men marched out unarmed.[14] The past twenty-four hours, Major Corbett said later, had been "possibly the most fantastic of the whole war."[15]

WHEN 7TH INFANTRY Brigade launched its attack on the morning of September 25, the Regina Rifles led on the left, with the Royal Winnipeg Rifles on the right. The Canadian Scottish Regiment was in reserve with the plan that once the Reginas captured Belle Vue Ridge, they would pass through and push to the coast. Each infantry battalion was supported by a squadron of the 1st Hussars, as well as the specialized tanks of the 1st Lothians and Border Yeomanry.

The Little Black Devils crossed the start line at 1016 hours, with the Reginas getting under way nine minutes later.[16] Major Ronald Shawcross's 'A' Company was on point for the Reginas—its objective the village of Peuplingues, about a mile distant and at the base of Belle Vue Ridge. With Shawcross were sixty-five men and FOO Captain Fred Brown. Between the start line and Peuplingues stretched a wide-open, upward-sloping field. Shawcross considered the field a "deadly" threat and was glad to have a troop of tanks from the Hussars' 'C' Squadron along. "We had to use our flame throwers [Crocodiles] and ... Flails ... and as many tanks as we could get our hands on," he later wrote. The combined force quickly broke into the village, rooting out a thin line of Germans holding dugouts in front of it.[17]

As 'A' Company dug in to turn Peuplingues into a firm base, 'C' and 'D' Companies came up to move through to the ridge. "To appreciate the difficulty of the task," Major Eric Luxton wrote, "it must be realized that the ground and approaches to Belle Vue Ridge were absolutely bare of cover. The rolling nature of the ground gave perfect fields of fire from the German emplacements on the crest." 'D' Company was to advance on the left and 'C' Company the right. The moment they began moving out of Peuplingues, "a terrific shelling began that kept up for the rest of the morning. When supporting tanks moved through, it intensified."

Despite the constant fire, the Reginas gained the summit at 1330 hours. Both companies were "fighting hard for their objectives and calling on the supporting tanks, flails, and ... Crocodiles for cooperation. It was a straight slugging match until the first few pillboxes were taken and then the Jerries began to give up as they usually did once they saw they had inflicted all the casualties possible without greatly endangering their own skins." Their job complete, the Reginas dug in. It had been a costly attack. Ten men were dead, another 61 wounded, and 2 missing. They sent 140 German prisoners to the rear.

Soon investigating the ridge's emplacements, Luxton was astonished to find that many were three hundred feet deep, "and that the bombing and artillery had made no impression on them. Why they did not continue to fight, no one could understand. It was the general opinion that a brigade attack at least would have been necessary if the Huns had fought with determination."[18]

Not all the Germans were ready to give in. The Royal Winnipeg Rifles had gone forward at 1015 hours with 'D' Company on the left and headed for a farm called Les Alleux, while 'A' Company made for Vieux Coquelles.[19] Major Dave Campbell's 'D' Company caught the German defenders at the farm napping and dragged the "terrified, disheveled Germans" out of trench after trench. It was a different story at Vieux Coquelles. From a network of bombproof concrete shelters, the Germans tied up 'A' Company in a bitter close-quarters fight.[20] When 'C' Company arrived to help, its Major Fred Allen was fatally wounded while trying to eliminate two well-sighted machine-gun positions. Lieutenant Leonard Keith Furry was also killed and several non-commissioned officers were wounded silencing these guns. This left 'C' Company badly depleted.

'C' Company's second-in-command, Captain Cliff Chadderton, rushed to Vieux Coquelles to take over. He found that Lieutenants Jimmy Kerr and Norm Douglas had reorganized the platoons in readiness for their advance toward Coquelles. When Chadderton reported to Lieutenant Colonel John Meldram that the company was fit to continue, the Royal Winnipeg Rifles commander ordered an immediate attack.

The scene in the village, Chadderton wrote, was "one of expectancy. A troop of Flails were warming up in a concealed yard beside a burning church. A troop of Shermans from the 1st Hussars ['B' Squadron] were there also, waiting to shoot the attacking infantry onto their objective. Lieutenant Bill Speechly assembled a detachment from the pioneers in some nearby trenches. Each carried a big roll of white tape to mark the path that the Flails would beat through the minebelt. Captain Mac Wright of the 14th Field Regiment . . . had set up his observation post and was ordering his gunners to blanket the German position with a smoke screen. The two forward platoons of ['C'] Company were parked in a ditch, waiting the order to attack. The reserve platoon and company headquarters occupied a farmhouse. German [88-milimetre] shells plunked systematically into the area and everyone was sure that there was quite a battle in the offing."

'C' Company was not heading directly for Coquelles. Its immediate objective was a height of ground dominating the surrounding countryside. The hill was largely wooded, and in its centre stood a large stone mansion called Château Pegache.[21] Canadian intelligence staff had designated the hill as La Basse Normandie. 'B' Company, which would be advancing to 'C' Company's right, was bound for another hill—La Grande Rouge Cambre.[22]

'C' Company advanced with Sergeant Art Kelly's platoon left and Lieutenant Kerr's platoon right. Right behind followed the Flails, "their revolving chains lashing the ground in a furious maelstrom."[23] No. 3 Troop of the 1st Hussars led the charge, with Lieutenant Bruce Edward Caw commanding. That day, Caw was at the centre of every hot spot the Royal Winnipeg Rifles encountered. His troop had smashed into Les Alleux to assist 'A' Company. Now it ground forward at the head of 'C' Company's attack.[24]

The artillery smokescreen began to break up soon after the attack started, the smoke drifting so that the entire slope was covered "with a murky haze." German artillery was heavy and "exploding shells cascaded black earth skyward in a well-laid pattern over the entire hillside. Occasionally an armour-piercing round would whistle through the air as the German anti-tank gunners positioned on the high ground . . . tried for the Flails and Shermans."

With the tankers drawing heavy fire, 'C' Company raced "struggling and sweating to [get] ahead of the armour," Chadderton wrote. At Carpiquet and again at Caen, the company veterans had learned to keep their distance from tanks, as they always drew "unwelcome volumes of fire." Nearing the crest, Kelly and Kerr's men saw the pillboxes—"ominous-looking structures, with black slits just above ground level. No movement was discernible in the German camp and the infantry quickened their pace. The distance to their goal narrowed to 400 yards. On the troops swept, followed by the Flails, churning their path through the waving wheat. At 300 yards, the little pillboxes, still silent, loomed as large as forts out in front of the panting, weary but excited infantrymen.

"Two-hundred-and-fifty yards remained when the heart-chilling chatter of machineguns froze the infantry in their tracks. The awful realization that the enemy had come to life held them momentarily— then they went down, crawling for any kind of cover."

Sustained machine-gun bursts streamed out of the woods and pillbox apertures. To go forward was suicide. Now Chadderton saw Lieutenant Caw's No. 3 Troop rumble past. Bullets and shrapnel ricocheted off their tank hulls. Caw and his men lashed back with 50-millimetre machine guns and 75-millimetre main gunfire. As the Shermans shifted up a gear for "the last mad dash that would take them into the German defences," 'C' Company let out a cheer.

"Several more bursts came from the German guns as the tanks closed in—then the Boche automatics were silenced forever. The big tanks churned and thrashed through the brush that camouflaged the enemy positions, spitting lead and shells in all directions . . . The battle-wagons crunched through the undergrowth, smashing the German earthworks to bits. A few well-aimed armour-piercing rounds put the remaining pillboxes out of commission. Frightened Jerries hiding in the scrub broke for new cover as the tanks neared them, only to be brought down with bursts from the bow guns mounted in the co-driver's seats."

The Little Black Devils charged in on the heels of the tanks, but there was little to do but round up the terrified-looking clusters of prisoners. After clearing some isolated dugouts, Chadderton had 'C' Company dig in.[25]

On the right, 'B' Company's advance had been "hampered mainly by heavy shelling, mines and snipers, which increased as they neared their objective," the Royal Winnipeg Rifles war diarist wrote.[26] Although the approaches to La Grande Rouge Cambre were exposed to fire from 8-inch coastal guns at Calais, Lieutenant Caw's plucky No. 3 Troop raced from 'C' Company's position to join the fray. One tank was knocked out by an enemy shell, but the rest got through, and La Grande Rouge Cambre fell quickly and with few infantry casualties as a result of Caw's timely arrival. For his actions that day, Caw received a Military Cross.[27]

From La Grande Rouge Cambre, 'A' Company moved on Coquelles—the battalion's final objective. As at Vieux Coquelles, the company "met fierce resistance and had to fight their way in and through the village while being subjected to shelling from both their left and front flank. The determined enemy had to be driven back house by house and

'D' Company was sent to assist the much depleted 'A' Company during the final stages. By 2200 hours all the day's objectives were firmly consolidated and the troops prepared to spend the night resting." The war diarist noted that the 1st Hussars and Flails had been unable to assist in taking Coquelles because of extensive minefields and roadblocks and the many 88-millimetre guns covering all approaches. While not recording how many casualties the Royal Winnipeg Rifles suffered, he tallied their prisoner count at about one hundred.[28]

September 25 was a costly day for the 1st Hussars, who "lost several capable crew commanders." Lieutenants Gordon John Christie and Edgar Archibald George Rodgman were killed—the latter by an airburst shell. Lance-Corporal Philip George Maguire and most of his crew died when his Firefly tank ran over a thousand-pound naval shell rigged as a mine, which blew off the turret.[29] Lieutenant R.M. Sample was wounded when he got into a grenade-throwing duel with a dug-in sniper. The second-in-command of 'B' Squadron, Captain Chas M. McLeod, was also seriously wounded when his tank struck the same type of improvised mine that destroyed Maguire's tank.[30] McLeod was blown out of the turret, rescued by some passing infantrymen, and sent to the Casualty Clearing Post suffering severe head wounds.[31]

AT 1815 HOURS, the Canadian Scottish Regiment's four infantry companies had "piled into the Kangaroos" of 1st Canadian Armoured Personnel Carrier Squadron "and roared off in a cloud of dust" from their start line toward Belle Vue Ridge. The road they travelled was under continuous shelling.[32] Captain F.S. Corbeau, who commanded the Kangaroo squadron, had them strung out in a line with a gap of twenty-five yards between each vehicle. It took an hour and fifteen minutes to travel the six-mile route and deliver the Can Scots to the top of the ridge.[33] Here the infantry unloaded.

The Can Scots looked down on Sangatte. Their plan called for an advance through to that village, then "a smart right turn to Calais . . . But the only trouble was," the battalion's war diarist added, "the enemy were soundly entrenched in fortifications all along the road and seemed to resent our presence. They resented us so much that they sent us very insulting 'explosive' remarks." The companies strung out along the ridge to await the morning. Everyone "treaded carefully as there were many minefields and a man makes only one wrong step with them."[34]

Lieutenant Colonel Desmond Crofton thought the night would "long be remembered as one of the dirtiest of the war, ploughed fields and chalk pits, a howling wind off the Channel and a driving rain made the blackness particularly a problem." 'A' and 'C' Companies tried to tee up an attack down the slope into Sangatte village. Each time, they "walked into the enemy lines alone, and finally, completely lost," returned to their start line.[35]

Frustrated, 'A' Company's Major Bill Matthews and 'C' Company's Major Roger Schjelderup left their men at a crossroads and rashly set off to find Sangatte alone. "After stumbling and sliding for about three quarters of an hour (it was then about three in the morning) we became aware that all the noise about us was not the storm," Matthews recalled. "Further investigation proved we were on sandy soil and we could hear the surf beating in. A further recce revealed we had somehow slipped in between the enemy and were very close to our objective. We ascertained the extent of the gap in the 'impregnable' West Wall. Roger then returned to send down 'A' Company to me and bring down his own men. I stayed to recce further the positions for them. My leading elements arrived under [Captain] Doug Gillan and in short order we were tidy on our objective." By first light on September 26, Sangatte was firmly in hand, and the Canadian Scottish were ready to begin the advance along the coast toward Calais. Slightly to the west, meanwhile, the North Shore (New Brunswick) Regiment was preparing to take the surrender of the coastal battery and that of Noires Mottes. When white flags appeared as scheduled on the slopes of Noires Mottes to signal this surrender, Matthews sent Gillan to investigate. He arrived a few minutes before the North Shores and consequently claimed the German garrison surrendered to the Can Scots, which was duly reported in their war diary entry for the day. But eager to return to the unit for the advance from Sangatte along the coast, Gillan left it to the North Shores to round up the prisoners. Understandably, the North Shores rejected the Can Scot claim and reported the German garrison as surrendering to them alone.

A light cool rain was falling as 'A' and 'C' Companies started advancing along the coast road toward Calais. Lieutenant Colonel Crofton's plan called for the two companies to leapfrog each other. Major Schjelderup's 'C' Company led and immediately came up against stiff resistance. The roadside was heavily mined, and a series of blockhouses stretched from Sangatte all the way to Calais. Three miles from Sangatte, Fort Lapin also blocked the road. A slow, methodical advance was required, with each blockhouse taken in turn. Even when a blockhouse was cleared it remained a threat, as the Germans proved adept at infiltrating back into those that had been taken and left behind.[36]

Five hundred yards east of Sangatte, Schjelderup reported being under heavy fire from small-arms, mortars, and 75-millimetre guns. He asked for tank support, Flails and AVRES. Crofton sent the request to 7th Infantry Brigade, and Brigadier J.G. "Jock" Spragge ordered the armour to provide immediate support.[37] 'C' Company's advance slowed even more when a powerful flame-thrower opened up from one of the blockhouses. The Canadians were used to dealing out flame—not to being on the receiving end.[38] Major Brandon "Brandy" Conron's 'A' Squadron of the 1st Hussars soon arrived to provide direct and indirect fire against German positions.[39] The slow advance continued.

At 0805 hours, 'A' Company was held up again by two strongpoints dug into the beach sand left of the road. Once these were eliminated, 'C' Company leaped through and reached a junction where a road running north from Coquelles intersected the coast road. The Can Scots had advanced just short of two miles. As 'A' Company moved to the lead, Major Matthews realized "that swift progress could not be looked for." They were confined to the coastal road and very narrow frontages on either side, with heavy defences always just ahead. Matthews and Schjelderup paused to reorganize. With both companies growing weary, they decided to have a platoon from each tackle the next strongpoint—a farmstead beside the road. Once it fell, they hoped to have the remainder of 'A' Company dash through with one platoon going straight into Fort Lapin and the other pushing into the hamlet of Les Baraques. This hamlet was on the south side of the road, immediately opposite the fort.[40]

In the mid-morning, the clouds gave way to clear, sunny skies. At 0955 hours, two large formations from Bomber Command arrived. The smaller one, consisting of 191 bombers, struck Calais, while 341 bombers attacked the batteries at Cap Gris Nez. Between the two targets, a total of 3,648 tons of bombs were dropped during an operation that ended at 1155 hours.[41] Once again, there was intense flak. Lieutenant William Barrett of the 13th Field Regiment watched the planes pass through the flak, drop their bombs, and then make a wide turn over his gun area to head out over the channel. "About six of the bombers were hit and burst into flames. One of these fell near the gun area and exploded. Everybody wondered why the guns had not been called upon to fire a counter flak program like the one which had worked so well at Boulogne."[42]

Only one bomber over Cap Gris Nez was lost. From positions well back from the targets, 9th Canadian Infantry Brigade headquarters staff watched the raid with satisfaction. The brigade and its battalions had taken over the encirclement of the cape on September 23 and was busy preparing to put in a major attack on the batteries scheduled for September 29. Patrols went forward to investigate the bomb damage to enemy positions, but "apart from extensive cratering and damage to surface installations" could see little. Four German deserters were picked up. "Although they looked considerably shaken up, they reported that due to the depth of the gun positions the effect of the bombing raid could only be slight."[43]

Once the heavy bombers left, Typhoon fighter-bombers arrived and remained "extremely active" over Calais and its outer defences. Contact was maintained with 7th Brigade headquarters, so that the Typhoons "were on immediate call for any . . . targets. They certainly did a grand job."[44]

On the Sangatte–Calais road, the two Canadian Scottish platoons of 'A' and 'C' Companies selected by Matthews and Schjelderup to assault the next strongpoint struck in the early afternoon. Both were soon hotly engaged. "Houses, slit trenches, weapon pits and pillboxes were taken out with grenades, machineguns and the bayonet, the defenders fighting for the most part only until it was obvious that they would be killed or captured. For most the latter had the greatest appeal." The prisoners were sent back along the road to a POW cage at Sangatte. By 1900 hours, 'A' Company had gained the outskirts of Les Baraques—finding the entire place "completely flattened by bombing." As one platoon struggled through the ruins, the other hooked left to assault Fort Lapin.[45]

"After a brisk fight," Matthews wrote, "one fort was captured with some fifty to sixty [prisoners]. It was discovered, however, that the area consisted of not one, but several forts, so that the bulk of the defences had still to be overcome. Before this process, which they had begun so well, could be continued, the order was received to withdraw, since they were too near the target area of a proposed heavy bombing attack." The two companies withdrew a good distance to await the morning.[46] Despite the heavy fighting, Canadian Scottish casualties were quite low—one man killed and ten wounded.[47]

At 2030 hours, Brigadier Jock Spragge issued orders for September 27. The Can Scots were to continue their advance, take out Fort Lapin, and then break into Calais along the sea front. Having spent the day mopping up scattered opposition around Coquelles, the Royal Winnipeg Rifles would capture Fort Nieulay and rush a crossing of the Canal de la Rivière Neuve via the main road's still intact bridge. Farther south, the Regina Rifles would cross the inundated areas by boat and then fight their way due north into the city's factory district.[48] Before these attacks went in, there would be another heavy bombing raid to soften the German defences in seven specific targets. This required the forward troops of 7th Infantry Brigade to withdraw to a line about a mile and a half west of the city's outskirts.

As night fell on September 26, the progress of Operation Undergo was considered slow, but steady. "In a little more than a day and a half," one report stated, "great progress had been made against the formidable defences, both man-made and natural, of Calais. By midnight, 26/27 Sep, the division was able to report that the enemy was now back at his inner defences, and that 28 officers and 1,525 other ranks had been taken prisoner."[49]

WHILE EVENTS AT Calais had been developing favourably for the Allies on September 26, in the narrow salient from Eindhoven to Arnhem,

the fate of Market Garden had been sealed by further failure. With
1st British Airborne Division surrounded and clearly unable to break
through to the dwindling 2nd Para, 1st Parachute Brigade, force
trapped beside the road bridge at Arnhem, xxx British Corps commander Lieutenant General Brian Horrocks decided the situation was
hopeless. He ordered an evacuation by boat across the Nederrijn of as
many of the surrounded paratroops as possible to be carried out that
very night. As for the men at the bridge, no rescue was possible. The
rescue carried out by the engineers of 20th and 23rd Canadian Field
Companies and the British 553rd and 260th Field Companies succeeded in evacuating about 2,800 men. At 0545 hours on September
27, Operation Market Garden ended.

Even as late as September 25, Field Marshal Montgomery had remained confident that Market Garden could succeed. In a letter to his
son David's guardian, Montgomery wrote, "The autumn weather is
very wet and cold . . . I still live a caravan life in the fields but will very
soon have to take to the villages in order to get the men under cover.
I shall look forward to turning the German families out of the *best*
houses—very quickly!!" No sooner had this letter been penned than
Horrocks advised Dempsey that there was no prospect of reaching the
airborne division across the Nederrijn. The thought of establishing
billets within Germany anytime soon was gone.[50]

The day before Montgomery wrote his letter, General Eisenhower
had reminded him that "we need Antwerp." Clearly, First Canadian
Army could not possibly deliver up the clearance of both banks of the
Scheldt Estuary while its 3rd Infantry Division was fully engaged at
Calais. On the 26th, Montgomery responded to Eisenhower, concur-
ring that Antwerp was urgent, but simultaneously proposing another
hard push to the Rhine. Leaving the Canadians to open Antwerp,
British Second Army could punch out of the Nijmegen area of the
Market Garden salient to gain the northwest corner of the Ruhr. At
the same time, First U.S. Army could advance on Second Army's right
toward Cologne. The two armies would then converge to gain control
of the entire western part of the Ruhr. [51]

Such an operation would salvage something positive from Market
Garden's failure. Once Second Army struck out of Nijmegen, the

Germans would be forced to try to stop it. With First U.S. Army coming in from the other flank, Montgomery envisioned crushing many German divisions between them. Montgomery realized on September 27 that if the operation were to proceed, he would need First Canadian Army to "thrust strongly northwards on the general axis Tilburg–'s-Hertogenbosch, and so free the Second Army from its present commitment of a long left flank facing west." The Dutch town of 's-Hertogenbosch lay about fifty miles northeast of Antwerp, well east of First Canadian Army's current operational area. Rather than being able to concentrate forces on opening Antwerp, the Canadians would have to spread themselves even thinner.[52] The need for 3rd Infantry Division to finish its work at Calais and join the rest of II Canadian Corps in opening the Scheldt Estuary was consequently ever-more urgent.

[24]

An Unusual Battle

ROM 0830 TO 1105 hours on September 27, RAF heavy bombers pounded the western outskirts of Calais in support of 7th
Canadian Infantry Brigade's planned three-battalion attack. This time,
the bombers were protected by a thick counter-flak artillery program
that prevented German anti-aircraft gunners from causing serious
damage. One bomber was shot down, but some of the crew were observed parachuting safely into the German lines.[1] It was a major raid
involving 342 Lancasters dropping 1,718 tons of ordnance.[2]

As the bombers departed, Major Bill Matthews of Canadian Scottish
Regiment's 'A' Company and an artillery FOO sneaked up on Fort Lapin
to figure out a plan for attacking it. Reaching a suitable vantage point
required crossing an open stretch of sand dunes. As soon as the men
set out, German machine guns started "raking the area." Nobody was
hurt. When the FOO attempted to contact his regiment's headquarters
to arrange the supporting artillery, however, the wireless set failed.
With no time or means to rectify the problem, the Can Scots would
have to attack without artillery.

They did, however, have 'C' Squadron of the 1st Hussars.[3] In fact,
as Matthews and the dejected FOO returned to the start line, the
Shermans began blasting Fort Lapin from a farmyard just back of
where the Can Scots were formed up. Matthews and Lieutenant Colonel
Desmond Crofton were still trying to decide how to proceed when the

tankers—apparently thinking the original plan was still on—rolled toward the fort. The two Can Scots feared the tanks were going to go on alone but were unable to attract the attention of any crew commanders to stop them. Suddenly, the tanks lurched to a halt in the midst of the infantry. Matthews and other officers started shouting out directions for them to fire at targets identified during the reconnaissance. One of the fortified positions that together constituted Fort Lapin was set on fire by a shell.

Without the artillery, it was decided to delay the attack until after dark and then go in without the tanks in the hope of gaining some level of surprise. Major Matthews's 'A' Company again led with 'C' Company behind.[4] The platoon under 'A' Company's Sergeant Sandy Clarke crept up to the maze of barbed wire encircling one of the concrete forts. Clarke was a prairie farmer who considered himself a cowboy and proved he knew a thing or two about barbed wire. Despite being spotted by the Germans and subjected to heavy machine-gun fire, Clarke led his men in wriggling through the wire and reached the emplacement's steel doors. Wrenching them open, Clarke and his men chucked in hand grenades that flushed out some defenders.[5] The prisoners told Clarke that "the remainder would quit, given some encouragement."

Clarke led his platoon on to the next fort. As his men tackled that one, Matthews rushed a second platoon past to attack another fort beyond. He also sent 'A' Company's third platoon to secure the ruins of Les Baraques. The German prisoners had been right. Fort Lapin's remaining concrete emplacements fell easily. Among the prisoners was the fortress commander. Clarke's platoon also secured a hospital with its medical officer and patients. The third platoon met "sterner opposition" in Les Baraques, and only when 'C' Company reinforced it was the hamlet taken.[6]

The fortress commander, who was "neat and trimly dressed," took umbrage "at the lack of courtesy shown him by Canadians who had spent the last two days battling through fixed defences and fire from every type of German weapon to capture the place." When he insisted on surrendering to a general, Matthews said casually, "That's just fine, but unfortunately there are no General Officers handy, but after you have been searched you can go to a POW cage and perhaps you may find a couple there to do the right thing to." From the fort and hamlet, about 150 prisoners were taken.

With Fort Lapin silenced, nothing remained to prevent the Canadian Scottish Regiment from gaining the canal to force a crossing into the waterfront area of Calais. Behind the battalion, engineers set to work lifting the mines embedded in the coastal road. Many of these were the huge naval shells like those that had destroyed two tanks of the 1st Hussars the day before. Removing these shells proved impossible because the Germans had grouted them into place with cement in an upright stance. Each shell was about six inches in diameter, and the rounds were generally grouped in clusters of three. The only solution was to blow them in place, which required first evacuating nearby civilians from their homes. When the shells exploded, they often caused serious damage to adjacent buildings.[7] With the road cleared, trucks of the 8th Field Company joined the Canadian Scottish at the canal. The trucks carried kapok bridging and several collapsible canvas assault boats. Quick to assemble, a kapok bridge consisted of a series of buoyant cushions 6.6 feet long and just under 2 feet wide, filled with kapok. This light, cotton-like substance, obtained from kapok trees in Java, would allow the cushions to float even after being struck by multiple bullets. A simple wooden decking system of stringers enabled soldiers to then walk across the bridge single file. However, the maximum length of such a bridge was 150 feet, and it could be used only in still water. Any tidal or current flow or even moderate winds made crossing the bridge impracticable or dangerous.[8] Crofton planned to launch an assault crossing at midnight.[9] Not a single Can Scot died that day. One officer, Lieutenant A.C. MacKenzie, and six other ranks suffered wounds.[10]

TO THE RIGHT of the Canadian Scottish Regiment, the Royal Winnipeg Rifles had mounted their attack on Fort Nieulay with a squadron of 1st Hussars and the battalion's pioneer platoon Wasp carriers supporting 'A' and 'D' Companies. With its wide surrounding moat and thirty-three-foot-high heavily reinforced stone walls, the fort looked formidable. 'D' Company had taken a crack at the fort the night before, only to find it had no means of getting across the moat. When 'B' Company attempted to wriggle past the fort's flank, it came under heavy fire from shell-proof pillboxes built into the fortress walls and was driven back. Teeing up the September 27 attack, Lieutenant Colonel John Meldram hoped the Wasps and tanks would allow the Little Black Devils to bust through the main gate.[11]

"Obviously it was going to be an unusual battle," the Winnipeg regiment's historians wrote. "All the science of modern warfare . . . assembled to capture an ancient fort, with stone wall, a moat, and a drawbridge, but . . . still defended by resolute men."[12]

The attack went in at 1900 hours on the heels of an intense artillery barrage, with 'D' Company leading. "Corporal Red Prayzner and I were in the lead . . . stepping over dead comrades from the night before," Rifleman Stan Creaser recalled. "We elected to stay very close to our artillery cover and so we surprised about 8 or 10 enemy hiding in a house beside the road. They had left their machine-gun set up in the middle of the road. Our Lance Corporal Kevin White wanted the arrogant officer's pistol. When he reached for it the officer removed his helmet and started to swing it at Kevin. He changed his mind when I jabbed the Bren gun barrel into his face."[13]

Just before the fort, 'A' Company passed to the front. With a battery of medium artillery and smoke bombs fired by two sections of mortars, Lieutenant Gordon Embury's platoon closed on the bridge. Because of the covering fire and smoke, the platoon managed to get within two hundred yards of the bridge without drawing a response. Embury thought it looked like the German firing positions were unmanned. Dashing in under cover of the mortar smoke rounds, Embury's men quickly established a foothold in front of the bridge.

Coming up fast behind Embury's men were the three pioneer platoon Wasps with Sergeant Joe Roshick in the lead. Roshick drove onto the drawbridge, managed to break the gate down, and drove inside.[14] Rifleman Harold Prout was in one of the following Wasps. "Everything happened so fast. We just burst through the fortress gate and half of the Wasps went one way and half the other, and started to burn everything in sight, then withdrew to let the rifle [Companies] in to clean up the mess."[15]

When a German officer emerged from a building waving a white flag, Rifleman Walter Komarniski jumped off his carrier and approached him. While Komarniski was busy taking the man's pistol for a trophy, the officer said the fortress commander wished to surrender. "Well, where is the son of a bitch?" Komarniski snarled.

"My commander will receive your terms of surrender in his headquarters," the officer replied. He pointed toward an entrance leading to a dugout and gestured for Komarniski to enter. "You tell the son of a bitch if he doesn't come out of there, we'll burn him out," Komarniski said flatly. The rifleman soon took the fortress commander's surrender above ground.[16]

With Fort Nieulay subdued, 'B' Company under Major H.D. Knox passed by, as it had tried unsuccessfully to do the night before. Its objective was a bridge over the canal that was believed to be still intact. The company was slowed to a virtual crawl by almost constant minefields and shellfire coming from inside Calais. A little after midnight, the company veered off "the easily observed main road" and struck out cross-country. At 0450 hours and about six hundred yards short of the canal crossing, Knox's men were detected. Heavy machine-gun and mortar fire opened on them from the left flank and from Calais ahead. With casualties mounting rapidly, Meldram ordered Knox to withdraw. Meldram planned to try again for the bridge crossing after nightfall.[17]

AT 1930 HOURS on September 27, as the promised boats had failed to materialize, the Regina Rifles' 'A' Company waded into the morass of inundated fields and interconnected canals. Earlier in the day, Major Ronald Shawcross had been introduced to FFI member Henri Fontaine, who served as a guide. For about two hours, Shawcross and his men followed Fontaine "through salt water, brown sewer water and canals . . . In some places the water was so deep that I had to carry my runner/batman on my shoulders as he was 5'4" and he probably would have drowned . . . The water in places came up to my shoulders and we didn't smell pretty when we started and when we finished I guess we probably smelt even worse." Originally, the Reginas had hoped to reach the southern outskirts of Calais via a raised railway track, but it proved too heavily wired with mines and covered by machine guns.

So Shawcross and his men "snuck in through the back door, sewer and all." Fontaine guided them to a silk factory he had managed. The factory was located next to a section of the medieval wall encircling the old heart of Calais. 'A' Company established a defensive position between the wall and the factory, and then settled down for the night. The Germans appeared unaware of their presence.[18]

At dawn, Lieutenant Colonel Foster Matheson ordered 'D' Company to reinforce 'A' Company. Shawcross reported that he had lost one man killed patrolling beyond the factory position.[19] The Germans, however, still did not sense that the Reginas were nearby in force. Shawcross was happy to stay low and avoid trouble until more Reginas showed up.[20] By the afternoon, the Reginas had found an open road leading to the factory area. 'D' Company arrived, and it was also possible to move carriers up to distribute ammunition, food, and a rum ration. The Reginas were now literally on the doorstep of Calais and ready to break into it the next morning.[21]

While the Reginas' leading company had established itself in the southern outskirts of Calais, the Canadian Scottish Regiment had run into serious trouble crossing the canal. 'B' and 'D' Companies had kicked off a minute after midnight, with the intention to "carry the battle right through into the heart of the German defences."[22] This close to the harbour mouth, the canal widened and passed around either side of an artificial island on which the old fortification Bastion 11 stood. Across the canal, the citadel lay a short distance south of the intended landing point.

Major Earl English's 'B' Company carried the kapok bridge to the edge of the canal, with Major Dave Pugh's 'D' Company trailing. Nobody detected two old French tanks buried in the sand up to their turrets in front of Bastion 11 until they opened fire. The shells ripped diagonally across the road the two companies were on and shredded the kapok bridge. Both companies were divided in half by the incoming fire, with men behind unable to come forward and those ahead incapable of retreating. Bastion 11 burst into life as well, with an outpouring of shattering machine-gun and mortar fire.[23]

All semblance of order disappeared. The leading troops, desperate to get past the bastion, surmounted the canal "by the simple expedients of swimming, wading, using canvas boats, and by travelling Tarzan-like across on ropes," the battalion war diarist recorded. In this manner, most of 'D' Company got across, along with two 'B' Company platoons. But they found no respite. Instead, the men were now exposed to even heavier machine-gun fire, supplemented by 88-millimetre guns that "pinned them down where they were."[24] A storm of fire came from the bastion, from the citadel ahead, and from gun positions to the right. While some men dug slit trenches, most dived into the cover of bomb craters. Daylight found all of 'D,' 'C,' and 'B' Companies pinned down and scattered, the men in each crater unable to communicate with anybody else.[25]

Lieutenant Francis Norton's 'C' Company platoon was crammed into a single huge bomb crater. Any movement above ground level drew immediate fire from the French tanks. His men were soon rationing water, and there was no food. Shells and mortar rounds exploded almost constantly around the crater. Norton told his men to hunker down and sit tight. They could do nothing but hope to be rescued.[26]

At 0815 hours on September 28, the lieutenant commanding battalion headquarters' recce platoon slithered around to various vantage points and managed to report back to Lieutenant Colonel Desmond Crofton. The forward companies, he said, were pinned in place. 'A' Company was at Fort Lapin and enjoyed some freedom of movement. 'B' and 'D' Companies were entirely stranded. 'C' Company, pinned on the eastern edge of the ruins of Les Baraques, was only slightly less isolated. "The outlook was not altogether pleasant," the officer told Crofton. "The enemy had us just where he wanted us and it seemed we could do very little about it. But of course he was in no better positon. His forward elements were surrounded by our forward elements and vice versa."

Major Pugh's 'D' Company with part of 'B' Company had the added misfortune of being trapped within an old garbage dump that the bombing and shelling had churned into a foul mess. Pugh wanted to break out but could see no way to do so. To preserve the battery, the wireless set was only turned on once every hour to receive messages. About mid-morning, Crofton told Pugh to sit tight, and there was a rumour about some sort of truce. Pugh told his cold, wet, cramped, and hungry men to stay put.[27]

DURING THE MORNING of September 28, Bomber Command again visited Calais and Cap Gris Nez with a two-pronged raid. Calais was targeted by 194 bombers and the cape by 302, which dropped 855 tons.[28] The Cap Gris Nez bombing was Bomber Command's last step in supporting the pending attack by 9th Infantry Brigade, which was to start with first light at 0645 hours the next day.[29]

Shortly after the Calais strike, a French civilian arrived at Oberstleutnant Ludwig Schroeder's headquarters with a confused report that the Canadian divisional commander besieging the city wanted to speak with him. Schroeder's situation was deplorable. Contact with most of his garrison had been lost. He understood that the Canadians had seized Les Baraques and were closing from the southeast. Soon there would be fighting in the streets. The presence of twenty thousand civilians in the middle of a street battle struck him as an "embarrassing problem." He therefore thought a meeting to discuss evacuating the civilians a good idea.[30]

A few hours after this meeting with the French civilian, a Canadian II Corps Civil Affairs officer stationed at Ardres, a village about six miles southeast of Calais, heard a rumour that Schroeder wanted to surrender. The Civil Affairs unit forwarded a message to Schroeder stating that Major General Dan Spry was prepared to meet him at Le Pont sans Pareil, just north of Ardres, at 1000 hours on Friday, September 29. If Schroeder agreed to meet and all German fire ceased, the Canadians would "suspend attacks." Schroeder was to travel in a car bearing a white flag, and his safety and that of all occupants was guaranteed. An urgent response was requested so the Canadian troops could be ordered to stand down. Schroeder responded immediately that he agreed.[31]

At 2025 hours, 7th Brigade's Brigadier Jock Spragge ordered all three battalions to stand fast until further orders "and not to fire unless fired on." The brigade's war diarist considered this "an unusual message to be passed in the middle of battle . . . We were rather disappointed in this deal as it gave Schroeder time to change his guns around but there was nothing we could do about it for if we . . . continued to shell the city it would have made very nice propaganda for the Germans. However, we will get him yet and he shall pay for his truce. The front settled down into a very unnatural calm—and we laid plans for an all-out assault on the town."[32]

The meeting duly took place at 1000 hours on September 29, but Schroeder did not attend. He sent his senior artillery officer and three other officers. Right off the bat they told Spry the Germans were not prepared to surrender. Instead, they proposed that Calais be declared "an open city." After all, they argued, there were twenty thousand civilians currently "suffering from the bombing, shelling and shortage of food and medical supplies." Spry bluntly refused the proposal "on the grounds that the Boche were in the city and defending it." He would, however, agree to a truce lasting until 1200 hours on September 30 to enable the civilians to be evacuated.[33] At that time, all hell would be unleashed on Calais.

Later in the day, the senior Civil Affairs officer, 11 Canadian Corps Colonel J.J. Hurley, attended a conference in Calais, with Schroeder also in attendance. Although the meeting focused on the protocol for the evacuation, Hurley came away with the impression that the Germans would surrender "after a sufficient show of resistance has been made to make their surrender appear an honourable one."[34]

Immediately after his meeting with the Germans, Spry had called a conference to announce his instructions for the truce and to issue orders for the attack that would follow. As for the truce, the Canadians were confined to responding only to enemy weapons firing on them or active enemy patrols. No redistribution of men or resources would be allowed on the forward defence lines, but regroupings were planned before the truce could take place behind the lines. "We must not be first to fire before 301200 hours," Spry said.

When the truce ended, the attack would unfold in two phases. At 1400 hours on September 30, following a two-hour air attack by medium bombers and then rocket projectile–firing Typhoons, a ground attack would go in. From the east, 8th Infantry Brigade's Queen's Own Rifles would advance with two troops each of Flails, Crocodiles, and AVRES from the northeast. They were to secure the eastern bank of the canal running along that perimeter of the city. Meanwhile, 7th Infantry Brigade's battalions would take advantage of this diversion in whatever manner proved feasible. Approaching the city from the south, the Cameron Highlanders of Ottawa and the 17th Duke of York's Royal Canadian Hussars would press in as close as they could. All divisional artillery and two medium artillery regiments would provide support, including firing of smoke rounds to thicken a planned screen already created by the bombers having dropped incendiary bombs. The artillery plan was novel in that each regiment was assigned a specific area of the city that it would "sweep and search" with shells from 1300 to 1355 hours.

In the second phase, 7th Infantry Brigade would launch the main assault on the city. This attack would start at first light on October 1. Both the air support and artillery support plans would be the same as the day before.[35]

FOR 7TH INFANTRY Brigade, the truce was surreal. "Here we were wandering around in full view of the enemy and nothing happened—hard to get used to the idea but a good opportunity for us to conserve our strength," the brigade's war diarist wrote. Spry came in the late afternoon to discuss the forthcoming attack. He confessed to being "more than slightly put out by the whole affair and would cheerfully have killed Schroeder if he could have got his hands on him."[36]

While the truce allowed the Royal Winnipeg Rifles and the Regina Rifles a short rest period, it did nothing to improve the Canadian Scottish Regiment's situation. They were to stand fast and therefore could neither withdraw the trapped forward companies nor reinforce them. "It was as if two wrestlers, straining for mastery, were frozen in position, their muscles relaxed, but each retaining his hold on the other," the regiment's historian observed. "For the Canadian Scottish platoons stuck out on a limb, the unnatural calm, welcome in some way, still meant hours of waiting and watching without food."[37]

Schroeder had ordered his garrison to cease firing for the truce duration, but the German communication lines were so shattered, he doubted that many of his men had received word.[38] Likely this was why a German patrol moving toward Bastion 11 overran 'D' Company's No. 12 Platoon and took its men prisoner. As a number were wounded, a Can Scot medical orderly was later permitted to evacuate these back to the Canadian lines. When he passed the crater used by Major Dave

Pugh, the 'D' Company commander slipped him a note describing his plan to try breaking out come nightfall. Soon after sending the note, Pugh managed to creep from the crater over to a long concrete building behind his front that looked like it might serve as a good strongpoint for his men. Inside was a huge railway gun and some Germans, who fired at him. Pugh dashed back to the crater. During the regular hourly wireless checks, there was no acknowledgement from Lieutenant Colonel Desmond Crofton of Pugh's breakout plan. Pugh also had no idea whether there was a truce on or not.

Also cut off in the 'D' Company perimeter was a 'C' Company platoon commanded by Sergeant Armando Gri—a tough, competent soldier. Pugh decided Gri's platoon should lead the breakout, and they would do so by way of the railway gun building. Gri and his men slipped off into the darkness. Three-quarters of an hour later, the silence "was shattered by firing and shouting," Pugh said later. Gri "finally found an entrance to the main building and the platoon unearthed 105 Germans. These were shepherded back to the company area and gone over. We now had a problem as we wanted no part of them by daylight. An interrogation showed that the swamp between us and the battalion was the only feasible route out. The Germans would not file past their own area as the place was marked 'MINEN' [mines]. They were led into the swamp and after several tries a route was found waist high through the water . . . I reported to the C.O. . . . where the truce was confirmed."

Pugh duly returned to his company in the early-morning hours of September 30 and reported that once the truce expired, a final, large-scale attack was to begin. They would be joining the attack's second phase.[39]

To Fight or Not

WHILE NEGOTIATION OF the ceasefire and truce had been under way at Calais, September 29 brought the full-scale assault of Cap Gris Nez. For four long years, the powerful coastal batteries on this cape had threatened Allied shipping in the Dover straits and plagued the civilian population of Dover itself. When the guns had first started firing, Churchill had observed, "We have to fight for the command of the Straits by artillery, to destroy the enemy batteries, and to multiply and fortify our own."[1] The British batteries at Dover that included the two 14-inch guns, Winnie and Pooh, had duelled with the German batteries here for years—neither seriously damaging the other. Dover, however, had been hard hit, with more than two hundred civilians killed and hundreds more injured. About ten thousand buildings in and around the city were damaged or destroyed. Over four years, Dover was subjected to about a thousand attacks—an average of one every two days. As the Canadians closed on Calais, the commander at Cap Gris Nez had ordered a final barrage on Dover that unleashed fifty shells on September 26. Five civilians were killed, the last a sixty-three-year-old woman named Patience Ransley who was in a concrete-roofed shelter when a 16-inch shell struck and collapsed the ceiling on her.[2]

The German troops at Cap Gris Nez were mostly marines of the 242nd Naval Coastal Artillery Battalion and were believed to number between eight hundred and eleven hundred. As usual, this was an underestimate. They manned three main batteries. On the southern flank of the cape at Haringzelles, Battery Todt housed four 380-millimetre guns. At Floringzelle, on the cape's northeastern side, stood Battery Grosser Kurfürst with four 280-millimetre guns. On the western tip of the cape close by a lighthouse was Battery Gris Nez with three 170-millimetre guns. Both this battery and the one at Floringzelle could fire landward. All the guns were encased in massive reinforced-concrete and steel casemates impervious to anything but a direct hit by heavy shell or bomb. They were well protected by complex systems of minefields, electrified fences, cleverly concealed anti-tank ditches, some 88-millimetre anti-tank guns, many machine-gun posts in concrete pillboxes, and numerous 20-millimetre anti-aircraft guns.

Cap Gris Nez was to be taken by the familiar proven means—heavy aerial pre-bombardment and drenching artillery followed by armoured columns helping the infantry forward. Brigadier Rocky Rockingham planned to employ just two battalions—the North Nova Scotia Highlanders and the Highland Light Infantry. The latter, with the Flails of 'B' Squadron of the 1st Lothians and Border Yeomanry, two Crocodile troops, a troop of AVRES, and two troops of the 1st Hussars' 'B' Squadron, would attack on the right toward Floringzelle and Cap Gris Nez batteries. The North Novas had the 1st Lothians' 'C' Squadron under command, along with the same disposition of Crocodiles, AVRES, and 1st Hussars' 'B' Squadron tanks as the HLI's.[3] They were to take the Haringzelles Battery and a thick concrete fort at Cran-aux-Oeufs on the coast that housed the German headquarters. Artillery support was provided by 14th Canadian Field Regiment and the medium guns of 9th Army Group, Royal Artillery.[4]

Extensive reconnaissance identified strongpoints and determined the best routes through to objectives. While start lines for both battalions had been established behind a row of trees bordering a country road, it was all open, grassy ground to the various objectives, with the cape's high point by the lighthouse being fifty feet above sea level. The ground rose gradually from the road to this high point. After a dry summer, the ground was hard, making it difficult for the Flail chains to penetrate deeply.[5]

Precisely at 0635 hours, the artillery opened with a heavy bombardment. Ten minutes later, the infantry and armour emerged from the woods. It was a fine, clear day with excellent visibility, which meant the attackers were plainly visible to the gun positions. The North Nova Scotia Highlanders had 'D' Company to the right heading for one of the Haringzelles guns, and 'B' Company went for the other three on the left.[6] The 1st Lothians 'C' Squadron Flails led the way, creating a lane for each infantry company. Once Haringzelles fell, the Flails were to open a lane through to Cran-aux-Oeufs.[7] 'D' Company was again under command of Major Maurice Clennett, who had been slightly wounded during the Mont Lambert attack at Boulogne and had just returned to the battalion. Major Claude Abell commanded 'B' Company. Both companies were in arrowhead formation. On point and moving with the Flails in 'D' Company's sector was Lieutenant P.S. Carpenter's platoon. The other two platoons and Clennett's headquarters section held back as the Flails went about their slow work. Two streambeds, both dry, blocked the route. As each was reached, an AVRE loaded with fascines came forward to create an improvised bridge, over which the Flails and other armour crossed. In the long approach to the gun battery, Carpenter's platoon suffered heavy casualties, and just seven men were standing when the outer wire was gained. A blast of flame from a Crocodile brought immediate surrender.

To the right, Abell's 'B' Company followed a track and crossed one stream on an intact bridge that supported the weight of the tanks. The pace was still slow, and 'D' Company had already seized its gun by the time 'B' Company reached its first gun emplacement. Despite the din of gunfire and roar of Crocodile flame-throwers in 'D' Company's sector, the Germans here seemed oblivious to being under attack. That changed abruptly when an AVRE started pounding the concrete casemate with Petard rounds, and some of Abell's men rushed around to the open front from which the gun barrel protruded and chucked grenades inside. When the Petard started blasting its heavy bombs through window slits, the Germans surrendered. The other two gun positions quickly surrendered to avoid the grenade and Petard treatment.[8] By 0830 hours, the battery was silenced.

As the company secured the area, Abell decided to destroy a heavy mortar by lobbing a grenade down its tube. Normally a mortar was always empty, but this one had a live round inside that the grenade detonated. The resulting explosion killed Abell instantly.[9]

Right of the North Novas, the attack by the Highland Light Infantry ran into difficulty at first when the 'B' Squadron Flails stalled because bomb cratering had made the ground impassable. Trusting that the bombing had detonated all the mines, the Crocodiles and tanks of the 1st Hussars wove a tortuous route between craters and made it safely forward.[10] As the leading infantry with supporting Crocodiles closed on the Floringzelle battery, "white flags started popping up" and streams of surrendering Germans emerged.[11] The most westerly gun position—a turret completely encased in armour—continued to hold out. It seemed, however, that the German crew was unable to aim the gun, for its shots "went indiscriminately out to sea or inland." Finally, the section of Canadian engineers who had accompanied the infantry placed explosive charges on the turret top. After these detonated, the crew surrendered.[12]

Both battalions paused to reorganize for their second phases. 'C' Company of the North Novas was to advance to the Cran-aux-Oeufs headquarters. Lieutenant Colonel Foster Matheson came forward to discuss the operation with Captain L.C. Winhold. The advance would require crossing a long valley to where the headquarters stood on a small hill beside the shoreline.[13]

Earlier reconnaissance had revealed a minefield so dense that the 1st Lothians squadron commander decided the Flails must "flog the whole way." This stretch of ground had been so heavily churned by bombing that the soil was very loose, and the Flail chains were unable to penetrate deeply enough to detonate the mines. Instead, they tamped the soil down so that the mines were then exploded by the tracks of the Flails passing over them. The Flails were disabled one by one. "One," the squadron commander wrote, "was blown up and burnt out by a large calibre naval shell placed as a mine in the ground. This was dug in with the nose cap at ground level . . . the chains unluckily did not get a direct hit on the point of the nose, therefore it did not explode until the track pressed on it." Eleven Flails were knocked out, the last within two hundred yards of the objective.[14]

With this Flail firing its main gun in support, Winhold led a charge to the German wire across ground mercifully free of mines. Gaining an unoccupied trench, the North Novas raced into the headquarters area. Soon the entire garrison seemed to have surrendered and were being lined up in the open, when a machine-gun burst from a pillbox next to a radio tower hit one North Nova in both legs. One of the prisoners began shouting to the captain commanding the pillbox to surrender.[15] After blowing up the pillbox "in a most spectacular fashion," the captain and his men gave up.[16] It was determined later that the demolition destroyed instruments that controlled the firing of the coastal guns.[17]

The HLI had meanwhile headed for the cape battery at 1400 hours.[18] Nos. 1 and 2 Troops of the 1st Lothians' 'B' Squadron flailed ahead of the infantry.[19] They met only light opposition. The Germans at Battery Gris Nez, having watched the other batteries fall, were not inclined to fight. By 1800 hours, the battle for Cap Gris Nez was over. The HLI's Lieutenant Colonel Nicol Kingsmill and most of his headquarters staff arrived to inspect the battery around the lighthouse. Just short of the battery, the carrier triggered a mine. The battalion's adjutant, Captain C.D. Campbell, lost his right arm in the explosion, while Kingsmill's signaller suffered a broken leg and possible internal injuries.[20] Kingsmill was blown twelve feet from the carrier but landed unhurt.[21]

These were the last casualties suffered in what the army's official historian deemed "an inexpensive operation." The two Canadian battalions had forty-two total casualties, eight fatal.[22] Six of the dead were North Nova Scotia Highlanders, but the number of overall casualties was fairly evenly split.[23] About sixteen hundred Germans were taken prisoner, and no determination of killed was made. Although the 1st Lothians had many Flails knocked out, they reported no losses of men either wounded or killed.[24]

In the evening, the North Shores marched back to battalion headquarters at the coastal village of Audresselles. They were met on the outskirts by the battalion's pipe band, which escorted the tired men to a waiting dinner "in style."[25] Meanwhile, at another village, Bazinghen, the HLI also returned to billets. The battalion, Major R.D. Hodgins wrote, "is in high spirits after its successful effort today. Now the people in Dover can relax to a certain extent, knowing that the cross channel guns are silenced."[26]

WHILE CAP GRIS Nez was being taken on September 29, in Calais the civilian evacuation enabled by the uneasy truce had been in full swing. Both Canadian and German transport moved people out. "The German drivers, once out of the doomed city, had no desire to go back, and insisted on being taken prisoner." Lieutenant Colonel P.C. Klaehn, through whose lines the evacuation was passing, feared that permitting the Germans to desert might breach the truce. Divisional headquarters had "no such scruples." Particular delight was taken when Oberstleutnant Ludwig Schroeder's chauffeur deserted and the commander's "frantic request for [his] return went unheeded."

The evacuation was complete by the morning of September 30, and 3rd Division began teeing up the renewal of hostilities. At Le Pont sans Pareil, senior Civil Affairs officer Colonel J.J. Hurley met a final German delegation consisting of a major and two captains. They advised that the garrison was prepared to surrender at 1400 hours. Hurley replied that this was impossible because operations were going to be renewed immediately after the truce expired at noon. Major General Dan Spry confirmed this intent, adding "that the Hun, if they wished to quit, could march out with their hands up, without arms, and flying white flags in the normal manner."

At noon, the planned aerial bombardment began. This soon brought a German officer to the Cameron Highlanders of Ottawa's headquarters. Indignantly, he accused the Canadians of "a breach of faith." Klaehn gathered that the Germans had mistakenly thought their offer to surrender at 1400 had been accepted and Schroeder had ordered the men he could reach to lay down arms at that time. While Klaehn and the officer were talking, the planes departed and the artillery opened up as scheduled. Contacting Spry, Klaehn received permission to go into Calais and accept Schroeder's surrender if it was truly on offer. Taking a number of men in several vehicles, Klaehn headed into the city, only to have the small convoy fired on by Canadian artillery.[27] Klaehn's efforts to get this fire stopped came to nothing. Driving back the way he had come, Klaehn continued on the forty miles to divisional headquarters, where he angrily admonished the staff for going ahead with the artillery bombardment when the Germans clearly wanted to surrender. Receiving relatively grudging permission to continue trying to effect a general surrender, Klaehn ordered Major Bill Baird to take two machine-gun platoons of his 'C' Company and the German officer and head for Calais, which was just a mile and a half away.[28]

Even as the Cameron Highlanders of Ottawa were trying to effect the surrender, Calais was attacked from both the west and east. The Queen's Own Rifles advanced 'A' and 'B' Companies toward the city's eastern flank. As 'B' Company approached the outer ring of defences, its commander radioed headquarters. "We are completely surrounded—with white flags," he reported. 'C' and 'D' Companies passed through and by nightfall were well inside the outer defences, where more Germans were anxiously surrendering.[29]

On the western flank, the same scene played out as the Regina Rifles and Royal Winnipeg Rifles advanced. Having faced stiff resistance earlier, and with its 'D' Company still cut off, the Canadian Scottish Regiment expected a hard fight when 'A' Company led an assault at 1600 hours on Bastion 11 and a nearby fort. Captain S.L. Chambers's platoon attacked the bastion, which proved to be surrounded by an impregnable tangle of wire. But a section of M-10s of the 3rd Canadian Anti-Tank Regiment arrived just in time to rip a ten-yard gap in the wire. The M-10 gunners also smashed armour-piercing rounds through the heavy wooden door and silenced the two dug-in French tanks. Dashing through the wire breach, the Can Scots broke into the fort, only to find it empty. Hearing a lot of fire coming from the direction of the other fort, Chambers rushed to reinforce the platoon there and found that all the fire had been from Can Scot guns.

Lieutenant Colonel Desmond Crofton soon arrived. Seeing white flags fluttering all over the city to the north, he decided to keep punching through the harbour district. 'C' Company passed through 'A' Company, crossed a railroad bridge and, meeting little resistance, was soon beyond the citadel. This opened the way for 'D' and 'B' Companies to clear the citadel area. By 1900 hours, the Can Scots controlled most of the harbour and were knocking on the door of the headquarters of the Harbour Defence Garrison's commander, who offered to surrender to a senior officer. 'C' Company's Major Roger Schjelderup saw "no reason I would not be suitable for the job." Guided into the fortified headquarters by a German officer, Schjelderup soon found the commandant "standing rigidly at attention," along with five staff officers who were "also standing like ramrods." Schjelderup demanded that the commandant surrender the entire harbour garrison. Having no idea if Calais proper had surrendered, the commandant said in fluent English that he was "uncertain whether to fight or not." Schjelderup said Calais was surrendering, but the officer seemed disinclined to believe him. In front of this sharply turned-out German, Schjelderup realized he was but a "scruffy looking young Captain with my battledress torn, filthy and blood-stained." The two men were at an impasse. Schjelderup suggested that neither side fight the other while he arranged for Crofton to meet the commander. This was agreed.

At 0200 hours on October 1, Crofton arrived and met the commandant—a colonel—in his officer's mess. The colonel and eight other officers were all wearing their best uniforms complete with Iron Crosses. "The meeting was stiff and formal," but the colonel agreed to surrender his entire command at 0500 hours. At the appointed hour, 196 men and the eight officers were all lined up and marched into captivity.[30]

Back in Calais proper, meanwhile, the Cameron Highlanders of Ottawa's Major Bill Baird of 'C' Company had in the late afternoon of September 30 still been trying to link up with Schroeder. At 1830 hours, all Canadian artillery fire ceased and he was able to send a platoon leader along with a German officer to fetch the fortress commander. Half an hour later, Schroeder emerged in a convoy of two cars and was escorted to a farmhouse on the city's outskirts. Lieutenant Colonel C.P. Klaehn represented the Canadian side. Everything had been hurriedly "staged." Two chairs had been set on one side of a desk for the Germans and another chair on the opposite side for Klaehn. He stood behind the desk with an officer on either side of him as the Germans "walked in, clicked their heels and gave a smart Nazi salute minus the 'Heil Hitler.'" Klaehn and his officers returned a Canadian salute. Through an interpreter, Klaehn said he was ready to accept Schroeder's surrender, and that "all his men had to do was walk out with the white flag and they would be gathered in." If Schroeder surrendered now, all hostilities would cease. Schroeder agreed. The party then travelled to 3rd Division headquarters, but en route, the Canadians received a wireless message that they were to simply deliver Schroeder and the other officers to a POW cage. Major General Dan Spry had no wish to see Schroeder. "Thus was ended one of the tragic comedies that only war could produce," Cameron Highlanders of Ottawa war diarist Major Richard Ross concluded.[31]

Inside Calais, Regina Rifles 'A' Company's Major Ronald Shawcross had led his men toward the German flag fluttering over Schroeder's headquarters. They had passed from the factory district through a gate in the city's walls and had since been taking prisoners without any gunfights. Shawcross was tired and careless, walking straight up the centre of the streets with a long radio cord stretching back to where his two signallers followed with the No. 18 set. Finally, one of them said, "Sir, we don't care if you get killed but we don't want to be killed, how about staying on the edge of the road." Point taken, Shawcross complied. Soon the company reached Schroeder's headquarters and secured it. Shawcross took the commandant's flag and a gold sword as trophies.[32]

And so, Undergo ended with a series of small sputters rather than a dramatic bang. By 0900 hours, the entire city was secure. About 7,500 Germans were taken prisoner. How many had been killed was unknown. Canadian casualties had been startlingly light, under 300. Most of these were from 7th Brigade, with the Royal Winnipeg Rifles suffering 77 and the Regina Rifles 71, as compared to a total casualty count for 8th Brigade of just 29 among all battalions. Predictably, the port had been severely damaged by the bombings and German demolitions. It would not open until November as a ferry point for personnel moving between England and France.[33]

From his sickbed in England, Lieutenant General Harry Crerar sent a signal that was relayed without additional comment by Lieutenant General Guy Simonds to 3rd Division. "No matter how tough the job may be the [3rd Infantry Division] never fails," Crerar said. The division now faced a far tougher job than the one it had just carried out during these September days in the Pas de Calais. The day after the surrender of Calais, its battalions started marching ninety miles northward to the Leopold Canal. Here it joined the rapidly developing battle involving all of First Canadian Army to open the Scheldt Estuary. There was no time for rest, reinforcement, or regrouping. The division moved directly into combat. Although the Canadians would continue to suffer manpower shortages to war's end, their true Cinderella days were over. Hereafter, First Canadian Army was to be engaged in operations of critical importance to Allied operations in northwest Europe and, in the year to come, the march to victory over Germany. No longer would they be, or feel like, forgotten partners in the war's prosecution.

On October 1, Spry offered a message of thanks to all unit commanders involved in the division's battles to capture Boulogne, Calais, and Cap Gris Nez. "All ranks may take pride in the soldierly way in which these operations have been carried out. Some twenty thousand prisoners have been taken for which we suffered comparatively few casualties. As a result of our success, these ports will now be opened for heavy traffic for the maintenance of the Allied Armies in the advance into Germany. In years to come there will not be one of us who will not be glad to say of these battles, 'I was there.'"[34]

The Channel Ports in Memory

I N THE AFTERMATH, Regina Rifles' Padre Graham Jamieson stood in the church cemetery at Coulogne to oversee the burial of three of his regiment. The men had died near the village on September 28, but their bodies were not found for several days. When the local priest offered the church cemetery as an interim burial spot, Jamieson readily agreed. The dead were Lance Corporal Russel Leonard Finner and Riflemen Donald Melford Darby and Enery Louis Geddry. By the time of the funeral, the Reginas were gone—headed for the Breskens Pocket. The village's populace, however, turned out. As did the village's mayor.

"Seldom on this earth is there any joy which is not mingled with sorrow," he said in a short speech. "Thus today, although we are very happy, we must dim the brightness of our joy to take part in mourning and sorrow—the price of restored liberty.

"It is with deep feeling that I bow my head to the glorious remains of these courageous soldiers who have fallen on our soil. I do it on behalf of the municipal authorities of Coulogne and of the entire population. Rest in peace noble sons of Canada. May the soil of France lie lightly upon you. You lie at rest among our ancestors and near the French and English soldiers who found death on our soil in 1940.

"Your remembrance among us is assured and your more happy comrades who live to carry on the fight may rest assured that our hearts beat in unison with theirs so valiant. May they soon, victory having been assured and peace brought to the peoples of the world, be enabled to return to their beloved country and carry with them a mark of recognition of France's debt of gratitude to Canada."[1]

Today, the three men lie in Calais Canadian War Cemetery—along with 704 others. They are buried side by side. Rifleman Darby in 7D3, Lance Corporal Finner 7D4, and Rifleman Geddry 7D5. The row is at the back of the cemetery, a few in from the Cross of Sacrifice.

The cemetery has a unique entrance via a long, hedge-lined grass walkway that opens out as you approach the cemetery gates. Beyond the gates are rows of headstones with the Cross of Sacrifice at the back. Trees surround the cemetery, so despite lying next to the busy Route Nationale No. 1, it has a sense of peace, quiet, and separateness from the modern world beyond.

I visit the cemetery in the company of my Dutch friend and colleague Johan van Doorn on a pleasant spring day in April. Sunlight filters through a light, high haze to cast the cemetery in a golden hue. As per our custom, Johan and I walk the rows—noting names, ages, and the messages added to the headstones by loved ones who had seen their soldier go to war and never return. I do not yet know the story of the three Reginas, so take no more note of their headstones than the others. Respect is paid at them all.

When we arrived, three women were the only other visitors. One middle-aged, the other two younger—apparently a daughter and friend. The older woman explains that they had simply been passing on the way to Calais and were drawn in by the Commonwealth War Graves Commission signage. Now they linger, finding it difficult to leave without also walking past every headstone. The younger women wipe tears away now and then. One remarks on how young so many of the soldiers were. Often her own age. All this loss and sacrifice, she says.

At times, they pause and fumble with phones. Photos are taken, but there are no smiles. Their presence is being recorded—something to show friends and family. We were there; we remembered. "Thank you," the older woman says to me when Johan tells her I'm Canadian. I have encountered this before, so no longer feel awkward. No need to thank me, I wasn't there—I used to say that. But now I accept their sentiment. Learned this from a veteran who *had* been there—Sherry

Atkinson, who fought in Sicily. When Sicilians thronged him at remembrance ceremonies a few years back, he said, "It's not about me.
I'm just a symbol." The rest of us Canadians can serve as symbols as
well when those our soldiers liberated say thanks.

Soon after the women leave for Calais, we follow. For several days
now we have been touring *The Cinderella Campaign* battleground from
Chambois, where the Falaise Gap was closed, to the most northerly
port of Ostend in Belgium. Despite increased urban and industrial
sprawl, this battlefield remains remarkably intact. The port cities of
Calais, Boulogne, Dunkirk, and Le Havre suffered such extensive
bomb damage that a great deal of rebuilding was required. Except for
significant historical structures, there was little attempt at restoration,
so the cities reflect the stark architectural styles of the 1950s and 1960s.
Le Havre is an exception. In the lower city, a 133-hectare area of ruins
was reconstructed between 1945 and 1964 according to a precise architectural plan created by architect Auguste Perret. Although reliant on
the use of precast concrete modular frames, the resulting development
led to its being listed by UNESCO as a World Heritage Site—one of
only a few contemporary sites in Europe. To the east and north of the
rebuilt area, some neighbourhoods escaped destruction and retain
their nineteenth- and early twentieth-century charm.

As for monuments to the Canadian and British troops who fought
here or even other information on the channel port battles of September
1944, there is little to be found. The most impressive monument is
one to 1 British Corps on the start line for Operation Astonia. There
is a Churchill tank, a mock bridge over a section of anti-tank ditch, a
panel with crests providing the 1 Corps order of battle, and a brief description of the battle itself. Beyond the monument stretch farm fields
unchanged from 1944, so it is easy to visualize the British armour and
infantry advancing across them toward Le Havre.

Nothing on a similar scale has been developed by Canadians to
mark these battles. But there are smaller memorials to be found. At
Fort Nieulay on the outskirts of Calais, two small plaques are mounted
on the fortress wall near the entrance gate—one in French, the other
English. They commemorate the fort's capture by the Royal Winnipeg
Rifles on September 27 and were installed in 1994. Less easily found is

a small plaque at the base of the World War I monument in the village of Oye-Plage on the coast road between Calais and Dunkirk. It pays homage to the recce troops of 17th Duke of York's Royal Canadian Hussars (although the regiment is not identified) and FFI fighters who cut the coast road here and liberated the village on September 6. Immediately across the street from the St. Eloi Cathedral in Dunkirk stands a tower that today houses the city's tourism centre. On the side of the tower facing the cathedral is an impressive monument to the city's dead from the Great War. At the base on both flanks of the main memorial, plaques have been added to recognize the city's role in World War II. One is dedicated to the Canadian, Czech, and British units involved in besieging Dunkirk through to the German garrison's surrender at war's end. In Boulogne, within the citadel courtyard, two plaques relate the story respectively in English and French of how the Stormont, Dundas and Glengarry Highlanders gained entry to this bastion via a secret tunnel on September 18 and captured a garrison of two hundred Germans.

Although there are no monuments to mark them, the start lines for Operations Wellhit and Undergo are easily located, and the country-side is little changed from 1944. So it is easy to study the ground the Canadians crossed and fought on.

Because the German fortifications were so solid, many bunkers, casemates, and artillery-battery positions are still largely intact. Visitors standing by the pillboxes on Mont Lambert and looking down on the Canadian line of approach would find it sobering to see how exposed the troops would have been to the German guns. This is often the case at the various sites. All are worth visiting, but Mont Lambert, Fort de la Crèche, Cap Gris Nez, Cap Blanc Nez, and the partial remains of Battery Todt outside Sangatte should not be missed. One blockhouse of Battery Todt has been converted into a museum that includes a perfectly preserved 280-millimetre rail-mounted naval gun that once terrorized the citizens of Dover from here. On a clear day, it is possible to stand on the gun's catwalk, look along the barrel, and see the white cliffs across the channel. Inside the blockhouse is a treasure trove of military arms and equipment, as well as interpretative displays regarding the day-to-day life of the German garrison. Unfortunately, the museum curators have little to say about the battery's capture by Canadians.

As with the coastal ports area, Forêt de la Londe has changed little since the war, except for expansion of some communities that have been transformed into relatively upscale suburbs of Rouen. There is a well-known photo of Sergeant B. Shaw standing with a Bren gun on his shoulder looking from the ridge down to the Seine River with Rouen in the distance. I have stood in that same spot. Like the Canadians in 1944, Johan and I find Forêt de la Londe and immediately surrounding country a navigational maze. But the area is worthy of a visit to study the ground and also to discover the surprising number of monuments to the Canadians who passed through in a timeframe of less than a week. Finding some of these is a challenge, but on two occasions when we resorted to asking a local, he insisted on jumping into his car and guiding us to the exact spot.

In Rouen there are no monuments, but a major street was renamed Rue des Canadiens and intersects the Route de Rouen that is also the D38 highway. On the outskirts of Bourgtheroulde is a monument, featuring a somewhat abstract maple leaf, that reads, *A nos amis Canadiens morts pour que nous vivions libres*: "To our Canadian friends who died so that we could live free." It was installed on August 24, 2006, to commemorate the sixtieth anniversary of the town's liberation and stands next to a roundabout signed as the Rond Point des Canadiens. A short distance to the east of Bourgtheroulde is the village of Saint-Ouen-du-Tilleul, where an aged but still well-maintained monument recognizes the thirteen Canadians killed here between August 27 and 28. Each soldier's name, age, rank, and unit is given. Alongside the road running from Bourgtheroulde to Brionne near the hamlet of La Bouille, another monument commemorates the seven Canadians who died nearby. When this monument was erected is not indicated. Although quite weathered, it stands in a well-maintained plot with a hedge on three sides and a low wooden fence whose tops are carved into maple leafs facing the roadside. In the village of La Londe, there is also a monument to the eighty-six Canadians who died liberating it.

Finally, in the heart of the forest is another monument, that—because of its setting in the midst of the battleground and still-dense woods, as well as the sentiment expressed by its inscription—strikes me as the most poignant of all. Perhaps fittingly, it is also the hardest to find. Veterans such as South Saskatchewan Regiment's Charles "Chic" Goodman had told me about it, and he had even been present at its installation on October 22, 1994. But he described it as standing beside a narrow unpaved road that ran under one of the railroad overpasses. We spend a great deal of time driving up one country road and down another without any luck. Finally, somewhat exasperated, we pull into a parking lot not far from Orival to glare at our maps. The parking lot, it turns out, is a connection point to a vast network of bicycling, walking, and horseback riding trails that utilize the old forester paths that wind through the woods. And there on the map board detailing the trail network, a stop of interest is indicated: "Monument des Canadiens." A few minutes later, we are parked next to the railroad overpass. Wooden barriers block vehicles from entering the unpaved road, now named Route Forestière de Mont à la Chèvre. A short walk through the woods, and there it is.

At first glance, the monument is underwhelming. A rough slab of rock that looks like it was just pulled out of the ground somewhere nearby and then cemented into place. The inscription is highlighted with white paint. On this day there is a faded wreath that reads "Canada" lying on the gravel at its base. One of the Veteran Affairs' little lollipop sticks with a Canadian flag attached has been inserted into a crack on top of the rock. The flag is faded and brittle. Earlier it had a twin alongside, but its flag has crumbled away to leave just the little stem.

The inscription reads: *Qui que tu sois passant devant cette pierre souviens-toi ici les 26, 27, et 28 aout 1944 lors de durs combats de jeunes soldats canadiens ont fait le sacrifice de leur vie pour ta liberté.* This roughly translates as "Whoever you are, when you pass this stone, remember that on August 26, 27, and 28 during hard fighting, young Canadian soldiers sacrificed their lives for your freedom."

I have encountered many Canadians, Americans, and Britons who sometimes bitterly denounce the French for largely forgetting the sacrifices paid by their countrymen liberating France. Here in this isolated spot within dense woods is a monument installed not that long ago that speaks of a commitment to remembrance. I imagine

French families cycling along this path and coming to the monument, pausing to read the inscription and then to consider its message. At least some must go away with that message now inscribed in their minds and possibly their hearts. This is what makes war memorials important. They serve as portals to a time when the world was ablaze with the fire of war, and in spots like this forest, soldiers were fighting and dying. Were this stone not here, there would be no cause to pause and remember that sacrifice. Ultimately, whether it be the massive edifice of the Vimy Ridge Memorial or this simple stone, that is the role war memorials serve. It is what makes those we have worthy of preservation and encourages us to create new ones in other significant battlefield locations. "Your remembrance among us is assured," the Coulogne mayor said during the burial of the three Regina Rifles on September 28, 1944. Memorials like this one in Forêt de la Londe contribute to that assured remembrance.

APPENDIX A
PRINCIPAL COMMANDERS IN
THE CINDERELLA CAMPAIGN
(ONLY THOSE MENTIONED IN TEXT)

AMERICAN

Supreme Headquarters, Allied Expeditionary Force (SHAEF), Gen.
Dwight D. Eisenhower

Twelfth Army Group, Lt. Gen. Omar Bradley

First Army, Lt. Gen. Courtney H. Hodges

Third Army, Gen. George S. Patton

v Corps, Maj. Gen. L.T. Gerow

xix Corps, Maj. Gen. Charles H. Corlett

BRITISH

Chief of Imperial General Staff, Gen. Sir Alan Brooke

RAF Bomber Command, Air Marshal Sir Arthur Harris

Commander Twenty-First Army Group, Field Marshal Bernard
Law Montgomery

Twenty-First Army Group, Chief of Staff, Maj. Gen. Francis Wilfred
de Guingand

Second Army, Lt. Gen. Miles Dempsey

I Corps, Lt. Gen. John Crocker

xxx Corps, Lt. Gen. Brian Horrocks

6th Airborne Division, Maj. Gen. Richard Gale

49th (West Riding) Infantry Division, Maj. Gen. Evelyn Barker

51st (Highland) Infantry Division, Maj. Gen. Thomas "Tom" Rennie

79th Armoured Division, Maj. Gen. Percy Hobart

CANADIAN

First Army, Lt. Gen. Harry Crerar

II Corps, Lt. Gen. Guy Simonds
II Corps, Chief of Staff, Brig. Elliot Rodger
2nd Infantry Division, Maj. Gen. Charles Foulkes
3rd Infantry Division, Maj. Gen. Dan Spry
4th Armoured Division, Maj. Gen. Harry Foster
4th Armoured Brigade, Brig. Robert Moncel
4th Infantry Brigade, Brig. Fred Cabeldu
5th Infantry Brigade, Brig. W.J. "Bill" Megill
6th Infantry Brigade, Brig. Fred Clift, then Guy Gauvreau
7th Infantry Brigade, Brig. J.G. "Jock" Spragge
8th Infantry Brigade, Brig. Ken Blackader
9th Infantry Brigade, Brig. John "Rocky" Rockingham
10th Infantry Brigade, Brig. Jim Jefferson

GERMAN

Commander in Chief, West, Gen. FM Walter Model, then Gen. FM
    Gerd von Rundstedt, as of Sept. 4, 1944
Fifteenth Army, Gen. d. Inf. Gustav von Zangen
Commandant Fortress Boulogne, Gen. Lt. Ferdinand Heim
Commandant Fortress Calais, Obst. Lt. Ludwig Schroeder
Commandant Fortress Le Havre, Obst. Eberhard Wildermuth

APPENDIX B
THE CANADIAN ARMY IN
THE CINDERELLA CAMPAIGN
(COMBAT UNITS ONLY)

FIRST CANADIAN ARMY TROOPS
2ND ARMY GROUP, ROYAL CANADIAN ARTILLERY:
19th Field Regiment
3rd Medium Regiment
4th Medium Regiment
7th Medium Regiment

CORPS OF ROYAL CANADIAN ENGINEERS:
10th Field Park Company
5th Field Company
20th Field Company
23rd Field Company

II CANADIAN CORPS TROOPS
18th Armoured Car Regiment (12th Manitoba Dragoons)
6th Anti-Tank Regiment
2nd Survey Regiment
6th Light Anti-Aircraft Regiment

CORPS OF ROYAL CANADIAN ENGINEERS:
8th Field Park Company
29th Field Company
30th Field Company
31st Field Company

2ND CANADIAN INFANTRY DIVISION

8th Reconnaissance Regiment (14th Canadian Hussars)
Toronto Scottish Regiment (MG)

ROYAL CANADIAN ARTILLERY:
4th Field Regiment
5th Field Regiment
6th Field Regiment
2nd Anti-Tank Regiment
3rd Light Anti-Aircraft Regiment

CORPS OF ROYAL CANADIAN ENGINEERS:
1st Field Park Company
2nd Field Company
7th Field Company
11th Field Company

4TH CANADIAN INFANTRY BRIGADE:
Royal Regiment of Canada
Royal Hamilton Light Infantry
Essex Scottish Regiment

5TH CANADIAN INFANTRY BRIGADE:
Black Watch (Royal Highland Regiment) of Canada
Le Régiment de Maisonneuve
Calgary Highlanders

6TH CANADIAN INFANTRY BRIGADE:
Les Fusiliers Mont-Royal
Queen's Own Cameron Highlanders
South Saskatchewan Regiment

3RD CANADIAN INFANTRY DIVISION

7th Reconnaissance Regiment (17th Duke of York's Royal
    Canadian Hussars)
Cameron Highlanders of Ottawa (MG Battalion)

ROYAL CANADIAN ARTILLERY:
12th Field Regiment
13th Field Regiment
14th Field Regiment
3rd Anti-Tank Regiment
4th Light Anti-Aircraft Regiment

CORPS OF ROYAL CANADIAN ENGINEERS:
3rd Field Park Company
6th Field Company
16th Field Company
18th Field Company

7TH CANADIAN INFANTRY BRIGADE:
Royal Winnipeg Rifles
Regina Rifle Regiment
1st Battalion, Canadian Scottish Regiment

8TH CANADIAN INFANTRY BRIGADE:
Queen's Own Rifles of Canada
Le Régiment de la Chaudière
North Shore (New Brunswick) Regiment

9TH CANADIAN INFANTRY BRIGADE:
Highland Light Infantry of Canada
Stormont, Dundas and Glengarry Highlanders
North Nova Scotia Highlanders

4TH CANADIAN ARMOURED DIVISION
29th Armoured Reconnaissance Regiment (South
    Alberta Regiment)
10th Canadian Independent MG Company (New
    Brunswick Rangers)
Lake Superior Regiment (Motor)

ROYAL CANADIAN ARTILLERY:

15th Field Regiment

23rd Field Regiment (Self-Propelled)

5th Anti-Tank Regiment

4th Light Anti-Aircraft Regiment

ROYAL CANADIAN CORPS OF ENGINEERS:

6th Field Park Squadron

8th Field Squadron

9th Field Squadron

4TH CANADIAN ARMOURED BRIGADE:

21st Armoured Regiment (Governor General's Foot Guards)

22nd Armoured Regiment (Canadian Grenadier Guards)

28th Armoured Regiment (British Columbia Regiment)

10TH CANADIAN INFANTRY BRIGADE:

Lincoln and Welland Regiment

Algonquin Regiment

Argyll and Sutherland Highlanders of Canada

2ND CANADIAN ARMOURED BRIGADE:

6th Armoured Regiment (1st Hussars)

10th Armoured Regiment (Fort Garry Horse)

27th Armoured Regiment (Sherbrooke Fusilier Regiment)

APPENDIX C
CANADIAN INFANTRY BATTALION
(TYPICAL ORGANIZATION)

HQ COMPANY

No. 1: Signals Platoon

No. 2: Administrative Platoon

SUPPORT COMPANY

No. 3: Mortar Platoon (3-inch)

No. 4: Bren Carrier Platoon

No. 5: Assault Pioneer Platoon

No. 6: Anti-Tank Platoon
   (6-pounder)

'A' COMPANY

No. 7 Platoon

No. 8 Platoon

No. 9 Platoon

'B' COMPANY

No. 10 Platoon

No. 11 Platoon

No. 12 Platoon

'C' COMPANY

No. 13 Platoon

No. 14 Platoon

No. 15 Platoon

'D' COMPANY

No. 16 Platoon

No. 17 Platoon

No. 18 Platoon

L IKE MOST COMMONWEALTH armies, the Canadian Army used the British ranking system. Except for the lower ranks, this system differed little from one service arm to another. The German Army system, however, tended to identify service and rank throughout most of its command chain, and the ss ranking system was further complicated by the fact that many of its ranks harked back to the organization's clandestine paramilitary roots. The translations are roughly based on the Canadian ranking system, although many German ranks have no Canadian equivalent, and there is some differentiation in the responsibility each rank bestowed on its holder.

CANADIAN ARMY	GERMAN ARMY
Private, infantry	Schütze
Rifleman, rifle regiments	Schütze
Private	Grenadier
Gunner (artillery equivalent of private)	Kanonier
Trooper (armoured equivalent of private)	Panzerschütze
Sapper (engineer equivalent of private)	Pionier
Signaller (signals equivalent of private)	Funker
Lance Corporal	Gefreiter
Corporal	Obergefreiter
Lance Sergeant	Unteroffizier
Sergeant	Unterfeldwebel
Company Sergeant Major	Feldwebel
Battalion Sergeant Major	Oberfeldwebel
Regimental Sergeant Major	Stabsfeldwebel

CANADIAN ARMY	GERMAN ARMY
Second Lieutenant	Leutnant
Lieutenant	Oberleutnant
Captain	Hauptmann
Major	Major
Lieutenant Colonel	Oberstleutnant
Colonel	Oberst
Brigadier	Generalmajor
Major General	Generalleutnant
Lieutenant General	General der (service arm)
(No differentiation)	General der Artillerie
	General der Infanterie
	General der Kavallerie
	General der Pioniere
	General der Panzertruppen
General	Generaloberst
Field Marshal	Generalfeldmarschall
Commander in Chief	Oberbefehlshaber

APPENDIX E
ARMY DECORATIONS

THE DECORATION SYSTEM that Canada used in World War II, like most other aspects of its military organization and tradition, derived from Britain. Under this class-based system, most military decorations can be awarded either to officers or to "other ranks" but not to both. The Canadian army, navy, and air force also have distinct decorations. Only the Victoria Cross—the nation's highest award—can be won by personnel from any arm of the service or of any rank. The decorations and qualifying ranks are as follows.

VICTORIA CROSS (VC): Awarded for gallantry in the presence of the enemy. Instituted in 1856. Open to all ranks. The only award that can be granted for action in which the recipient was killed, other than Mentioned in Despatches—a less formal honour whereby an act of bravery was given specific credit in a formal report.

DISTINGUISHED SERVICE ORDER (DSO): Army officers of all ranks, but more commonly awarded to officers with ranks of major or higher.

MILITARY CROSS (MC): Army officers with a rank normally below major and, rarely, warrant officers.

DISTINGUISHED CONDUCT MEDAL (DCM): Army warrant officers and all lower ranks.

MILITARY MEDAL (MM): Army warrant officers and all lower ranks.

NOTES

For full source citations, see the Bibliography. Sources are listed under five headings: Books, Journal Articles, Websites, Unpublished Materials, and Interviews and Correspondence.

INTRODUCTION: NO TIME COULD BE WASTED
1. "Report on Op 'Wellhit,'" 1.
2. "Account of Ops in Boulogne Area 14/22," 1.
3. "North Shore (New Brunswick) War Diary," Sept. 1944, 12.
4. Bird, *North Shore (New Brunswick) Regiment*, 408–09.
5. "North Shore (New Brunswick) War Diary," Sept. 1944, 12.
6. Bird, *North Shore (New Brunswick) Regiment*, 410–11.
7. "Account of Ops in Boulogne Area 14/22," 1.
8. Hickey, *Scarlet Dawn*, 228.

PART ONE: PURSUIT TO THE SEINE

I GETTING ON WITH THE BUSINESS
1. Eisenhower, *Report by the Supreme Commander*, 62–64.
2. Zuehlke, *Breakout from Juno*, 413–41.
3. "An Account of Operations of Second Army," 182.
4. "Report No. 77," 5–9.
5. TNA:PRO WO 106/4356, 31.
6. Adams, *Battle for Western Europe*, 9.
7. Zaloga, *US Airborne Divisions in the ETO*, 67.
8. Nicholson, *Canadians in Italy*, 464.
9. Wilmot, *Struggle for Europe*, 454–57.
10. Stacey, *Victory Campaign*, 269.
11. Nicholson, *Canadians in Italy*, 493.
12. Wilmot, *Struggle for Europe*, 428–30.
13. Fraser, *Black Yesterdays*, 250.
14. "12th Manitoba Dragoons War Diary," Aug. 1944, 24.
15. Ibid., 24.
16. Fraser, *Black Yesterdays*, 250.
17. Hayes, *The Lincs*, 249–50.
18. TNA:PRO WO 106/4356, 4.
19. "Report No. 183," 3.

20. Zuehlke, *Tragedy at Dieppe*, 3.
21. "Headquarters, First Canadian Army War Diary," Aug. 1944, App. 16.
22. "Report No. 139," 7–8.
23. Hartigan, *Rising of Courage*, 244.
24. "Report No. 139," 14–15.

2 PRESS FORWARD

 1. "Report No. 139," 9.
 2. "Report No. 183," 16–17.
 3. Copp, *Fields of Fire*, 112.
 4. Dickson, *Thoroughly Canadian General*, 4–19.
 5. English, *Failure in High Command*, 192–93.
 6. D'Este, *Decision in Normandy*, 271–274.
 7. "Report No. 146," 29.
 8. "Report No. 183," 17–18.
 9. "Report No. 139," 9–10.
10. "Report No. 183," 18–19.
11. Lindsay, *So Few Got Through*, 54.
12. Horn and Wyczynski, *Paras Versus the Reich*, 155.
13. "Report No. 139," 10.
14. Ibid., 15.
15. Horn and Wyczynski, *Paras Versus the Reich*, 155.
16. "Report No. 139," 11.
17. Ibid., 15.
18. Crerar Papers, "Operations," 43.
19. Graham, *Price of Command*, 60–62.
20. Ibid., 109–10.
21. Ibid., 116–19.
22. Malone, *Portrait of War*, 199–200.
23. Crerar Papers, "Operations—Directives," 43.
24. Copp, *The Brigade*, 109–10.
25. "Sitreps 2 Cdn. Inf. Div. Aug. 44," 86.
26. "Op Logs 2 Cdn. Inf. Div. Aug. 44," 35.
27. "2nd Canadian Infantry Div. HQ War Diary," Aug. 1944, 6.
28. "5th Canadian Infantry Brigade War Diary," Aug. 1944, 8.
29. "Calgary Highlanders War Diary," Aug. 1944, 22.
30. "Black Watch War Diary," Aug. 1944, 10.
31. Bercuson, *Battalion of Heroes*, 107.
32. "Calgary Highlanders War Diary," Aug. 1944, 23.
33. "Lt. Col. Mark Tennant," *Calgary Highlanders* (website).
34. "Calgary Highlanders War Diary," Aug, 1944, 23.
35. Bercuson, *Battalion of Heroes*, 108–09.

3 IN EXTREMELY HIGH FETTLE

1. "Report No. 183," 22–23.
2. Lindsay, *So Few Got Through*, 64.
3. "Report No. 183," 23.
4. "Report No. 139," 11–12.
5. "Report No. 183," 23.
6. War Diaries for the 11th Hussars, *WWII: A British Focus* (website).
7. "Report No. 183," 24.
8. "Report No. 139," 16.
9. Ibid., 11–12.
10. Ibid., 16.
11. Ibid., 11–12.
12. Hartigan, *Rising of Courage*, 258.
13. "Report No. 139," 12.
14. Horn and Wyczynski, *Paras Versus the Reich*, 157–58.
15. "Report No. 139," 16.
16. Horn and Wyczynski, *Paras Versus the Reich*, 158.
17. Stacey, *Victory Campaign*, 279–80.
18. Zuehlke, *Breakout from Juno*, 360–61.
19. Fraser, *Black Yesterdays*, 248–49.
20. Caravaggio, "Commanding the Green Centre Line," 352–53.
21. "Lake Superior War Diary," Aug. 1944, 17.
22. Roberts, *Canadian Summer*, 75–76.
23. "Major General D.C. Spry," *Juno Beach Centre* (website).
24. "Report on Ops: Advance from Falaise," 1.
25. Roberts, *Canadian Summer*, 76.
26. "12th Manitoba Dragoons War Diary," Aug. 1944, 26.
27. "British Columbia Regiment War Diary," Aug. 1944, 19.
28. "Algonquin War Diary," Aug. 1944, 11.
29. "British Columbia Regiment War Diary," 19.
30. "12th Manitoba Dragoons War Diary," Aug. 1944, 26–27.
31. Stanley, *Face of Danger*, 183.
32. "12th Manitoba Dragoons War Diary," Aug. 1944, 27.

4 ON TO THE SEINE

1. "Report on Ops: Advance from Falaise," 2.
2. "12th Manitoba Dragoons War Diary," Aug. 1944, 28.
3. Spencer, *Fifteenth Field Regiment*, 123.
4. "Lake Superior War Diary," Aug. 1944, 16.
5. Stanley, *Face of Danger*, 183.
6. Spencer, *Fifteenth Field Regiment*, 123.
7. Stanley, *Face of Danger*, 184.
8. Spencer, *Fifteenth Field Regiment*, 123.
9. "Report No. 183," 11–12.
10. Stanley, *Face of Danger*, 184.

11. Foster, *Steady the Buttons*, 197.

   12. Spencer, *Fifteenth Field Regiment*, 123.

   13. "Lake Superior War Diary," Aug. 1944, 16.

   14. "Report No. 183," 11.

   15. "Stormont, Dundas and Glengarry War Diary," Aug. 1944, 22.

   16. "Report No. 146," 31.

   17. "Account of Attack on St. Germain," 1–2.

   18. Bercuson, *Battalion of Heroes*, 110–11.

   19. "Calgary Highlanders War Diary," Aug. 1944, 21–22.

   20. "Account of Attack on St. Germain," 2–3.

   21. "Calgary Highlanders War Diary," Aug. 1944, 21–23.

   22. "Report No. 183," 11–12.

   23. "8th Field Squadron War Diary," Aug. 1944, 11.

   24. "Report No. 183," 12–13.

   25. "8th Field Squadron War Diary," Aug. 1944, 11.

   26. "Report No. 183," 13.

   27. "12th Manitoba Dragoons War Diary," Aug. 1944, 29.

   28. "Report on Ops: Advance from Falaise," 3.

   29. Stanley, *Face of Danger*, 185.

   30. "4th Canadian Armoured Brigade War Diary," Aug. 1944, 15.

   31. "Lake Superior War Diary," Aug. 1944, 17.

   32. "12th Manitoba Dragoons War Diary," Aug. 1944, 29.

   33. "Report on Ops: Advance from Falaise," 3.

   34. Stanley, *Face of Danger*, 185.

   35. "12th Manitoba Dragoons War Diary," Aug. 1944, 30.

   36. "Report No. 183," 14–15.

   37. "Correspondence to 4 Cdn Armd Div," 1.

   38. Crerar Papers, "Ops 2 Cdn. Corps," 19–20.

   39. "Report No. 183," 36.

   40. Ibid., 27–28.

5 STRENUOUS EFFORTS BY ALL

   1. "Calgary Highlanders War Diary," Aug. 1944, 28.

   2. Bercuson, *Battalion of Heroes*, 114–15.

   3. "18th Canadian Field Ambulance War Diary," Aug. 1944, 14.

   4. "Calgary Highlanders War Diary," Aug. 1944, 29.

   5. Bercuson, *Battalion of Heroes*, 117.

   6. Copp, *Cinderella Army*, 24.

   7. "Calgary Highlanders War Diary," Aug. 1944, 29.

   8. "Account by Col. F.M. Mitchell," 1.

   9. "Account of the Capture . . . by Lt. Shea," 1.

   10. Copp, *The Brigade*, 91.

   11. Warren, *Wait for the Waggon*, 306.

   12. "Account by Col. F.M. Mitchell," 1.

   13. "Account of the Capture . . . by Lt. Shea," 2.

14. "Account by Col. F.M. Mitchell," 1.
   15. "Account of the Capture . . . by Lt. Shea," 1.
   16. Warren, *Wait for the Waggon*, 307.
   17. "Account of the Capture . . . by Lt. Shea," 2.
   18. "Account by Col. F.M. Mitchell," 2.
   19. "Black Watch War Diary," Aug. 44, 7.
   20. "Account by Col. F.M. Mitchell," 2.
   21. "Report No. 183," 37.
   22. Stacey, *Victory Campaign*, 284.
   23. "Report No. 63," 177–78.
   24. Ibid., 185–86.
   25. "Report No. 183," 39.
   26. Ibid., 30.
   27. Kerry and McDill, *History of the Corps*, 301.
   28. Rogers, *History of Lincoln and Welland Regiment*, 165–66.
   29. "Report No. 183," 31.
   30. Jackson, *Argyll and Sutherland Highlanders*, 104–05.
   31. Cassidy, *Warpath*, 147–49.
   32. Jackson, *Argyll and Sutherland Highlanders*, 105–06.
   33. "Report No. 183," 32.
   34. Kerry and McDill, *History of the Corps*, 302.
   35. "Regina Rifles War Diary," Aug. 1944, 16.
   36. Kerry and McDill, *History of the Corps*, 302.
   37. "Regina Rifles War Diary," Aug. 1944, 16–17.
   38. Roy, *Ready for the Fray*, 299–300.
   39. "Report No. 183," 33.
   40. Roy, *Ready for the Fray*, 300–01.
   41. "Report No. 183," 34.
   42. Ibid., 32–33.

6 THE QUICKEST WAY TO WIN
   1. "Report No. 69," 6–11.
   2. Stacey, *Victory Campaign*, 286.
   3. "Report No. 146," 34–35.
   4. "Report No. 69," 8–9.
   5. "Report No. 146," 34–35.
   6. "Report No. 183," 49–50.
   7. Wilmot, *Struggle for Europe*, 434–36.
   8. Adams, *Battle for Western Europe*, 86–87.
   9. Ibid., 41–42.
   10. Ellis, *Defeat of Germany*, 72.
   11. Adams, *Battle for Western Europe*, 44.
   12. Ibid., 47.
   13. Blumenson, *Breakout and Pursuit*, 632–33.
   14. Ellis, *Battle of Normandy*, 459–61.

15. Wilmot, *Struggle for Europe*, 468–69.
16. Ellis, *Battle of Normandy*, 462–64.
17. TNA:PRO WO 106/4356, 26–30.

7 A GREAT SPOT TO BE AMBUSHED
1. "Report No. 146," 34–35.
2. "Report No. 69," 8–10.
3. "Report No. 146," 36.
4. "11 Canadian Corps Intelligence Summaries," no. 42.
5. "2nd Canadian Infantry Div HQ War Diary," Aug. 1944, Ops Log, 542.
6. Ibid., Ops Log, 551.
7. "Report No. 183," 39.
8. Ibid., 45.
9. "Report No. 146," 36.
10. Nicholson, *Gunners of Canada*, 333.
11. "Report No. 146," 36.
12. "Royal Hamilton Light Infantry War Diary," Aug. 1944, 13.
13. "Report No. 183," 40.
14. McIntyre, "Pursuit to the Seine," *Cdn. Mil. Hist.*, 59–63.
15. Antal and Shackleton, *Duty Nobly Done*, 470.
16. McIntyre, "Pursuit to the Seine," *Cdn. Mil. Hist.*, 63–65.
17. "Essex Scottish Regiment War Diary," Aug. 1944, 11.
18. "Report No. 183," 41–42.
19. "Royal Regiment of Canada War Diary," Aug. 1944, 38.
20. Blackburn, *Guns of Normandy*, 463.
21. "Royal Regiment of Canada War Diary," Aug. 1944, 38.
22. "4th Canadian Infantry Brigade War Diary," Aug. 1944, 20.
23. "Report No. 183," 41.
24. "Essex Scottish Regiment War Diary," Aug. 1944, 11.
25. "Report No. 183," 41–42.
26. "Royal Regiment of Canada War Diary," Aug. 1944, 39.
27. "South Saskatchewan Regiment War Diary," Aug. 1944, 11–12.
28. "6th Canadian Infantry Brigade War Diary," Aug. 1944, 23–24.
29. Queen-Hughes, *Whatever Men Dare*, 122.
30. "Account of Capt. Bruce Marshall," 1.
31. "6th Canadian Infantry Brigade War Diary," Aug. 1944, 24.
32. "Queen's Own Cameron Highlanders War Diary," Aug. 1944, 10.
33. Portugal, *We Were There*, vol. 5, 2491.
34. "Account of Capt. Bruce Marshall," 1.
35. "6th Canadian Infantry Brigade War Diary," Aug. 1944, 22.
36. "Report No. 183," 45–46.
37. Ibid., 46.
38. "South Saskatchewan Regiment War Diary," Aug. 1944, 12.
39. Portugal, *We Were There*, vol. 5, 2491–92.
40. "Sherbrooke Fusiliers War Diary," Aug. 1944, 13.

41. Grant, *Carry On*, 90–91.

42. "Report No. 183," 46.

43. "South Saskatchewan Regiment War Diary," Aug. 1944, 12.

8 A NIGHTMARE

1. "Royal Regiment of Canada War Diary," Aug. 1944, 40–41.

2. Goodspeed, *Battle Royal*, 472–73.

3. "Royal Regiment of Canada War Diary," Aug. 1944, App. 3, 1.

4. "Essex Scottish War Diary," Aug. 1944, 11.

5. McIntyre, "Pursuit to the Seine," *Cdn. Mil. Hist.*, 68–69.

6. "Essex Scottish War Diary," Aug. 1944, 11–12.

7. Stacey, *Victory Campaign*, 290.

8. "Royal Regiment of Canada War Diary," Aug. 1944, 42–43.

9. "Royal Hamilton Light Infantry War Diary," Aug. 1944, 13–14.

10. Brown, Brown, and Greenhous, *Semper Paratus*, 265–66.

11. "2nd Canadian Infantry Div. HQ War Diary," Aug. 1944, Ops Log, 552.

12. "South Saskatchewan Regiment War Diary," Aug. 1944, 12–14.

13. "Queen's Own Cameron Highlanders War Diary," Aug. 1944, 12.

14. "Calgary Highlanders War Diary," Aug. 1944, 33.

15. "Report No. 183," 44.

16. "South Saskatchewan Regiment War Diary," Aug. 1944, 15–16.

17. Stacey, *Victory Campaign*, 292.

18. "Queen's Own Cameron Highlanders War Diary," Aug. 1944, 12.

19. Stacey, *Victory Campaign*, 292.

20. McIntyre, "Pursuit to the Seine," *Cdn. Mil. Hist.*, 14.

21. "Report No. 183," 34–35.

22. "Canadian Scottish Regiment War Diary," Aug. 1944, 30.

23. Rogers, *History of the Lincoln and Welland Reg.*, 168.

24. "Lincoln and Welland Regiment War Diary," Aug. 1944, 12.

25. Rogers, *History of the Lincoln and Welland Reg.*, 168.

26. "Canadian Scottish Regiment War Diary," Aug. 1944, 30.

27. "Argyll and Sutherland Highlanders War Diary," Aug. 1944, 11.

28. "South Alberta Regiment War Diary," Aug. 1944, 22–23.

29. Fraser, *Black Yesterdays*, 262–63.

30. Jackson, *The Argyll and Sutherland Highlanders*, 106.

31. "Algonquin Regiment War Diary," Aug. 1944, 12.

32. Reid, *Named by the Enemy*, 197.

33. "Royal Winnipeg Regiment War Diary," Aug. 1944, 7.

34. Stacey, *Victory Campaign*, 293.

35. "Highland Light Infantry War Diary," Aug. 1944, 6.

36. "9th Canadian Infantry Brigade War Diary," Aug. 1944, 12.

9 LIKE INK ON A BLOTTER

1. TNA:PRO CAB 44/253, "Chapter 11 (Part 11)—The Enemy," 1.

2. "Report No. 69," 10–13.

3. Stacey, *Victory Campaign*, 294.
4. "Report No. 183," 50.
5. Ibid., 52–53.
6. "Report No. 69," 16.
7. "Advance of 30 Corps Across R. Seine," 4–5.
8. "Report No. 69," 16.
9. "Report No. 77," 12–15.
10. Stacey, *Victory Campaign*, 301–02.
11. Dickson, *A Thoroughly Canadian General*, 327.
12. "Report No. 146," 38–39.
13. "Report No. 183," 58–59.
14. Crerar Papers, "Correspondence with Field-Marshal Montgomery," 66.
15. "Report No. 183," 59.
16. Roberts, *Canadian Summer*, 81.
17. "Canadian Grenadier Guards War Diary," Sept. 1944, 1.
18. "4th Canadian Armoured Brigade War Diary," Sept. 1944, 1.
19. Roberts, *Canadian Summer*, 82.
20. Duguid, *History of the Canadian Grenadier Guards*, 289.
21. Hershell Smith interview.
22. Duguid, *History of the Canadian Grenadier Guards*, 289.
23. Hershell Smith interview.
24. Lord Shaughnessy Obituary, *The Telegraph*.
25. "Canadian Grenadier Guards War Diary," Sept. 1944, 1.
26. "10th Canadian Infantry Brigade War Diary," Sept. 1944, 1.
27. Rogers, *History of the Lincoln and Welland Reg.*, 169.
28. "Report No. 183," 60.
29. "7th Canadian Infantry Brigade War Diary," Sept. 1944, 1.
30. "9th Canadian Infantry Brigade War Diary," Sept. 1944, 1.
31. Pavey, *Historical Account of 7th Canadian Reconnaissance Reg.*, 88.
32. TNA:PRO WO 179/2769, 1.
33. Bennett, *Ultra in the West*, 135.
34. "La liberation de Dieppe," *Présentation des sites de Jean Delamare* (website).
35. "Report No. 69," 14–15.
36. "Report No. 183," 60.
37. Crerar Papers, "Operation 'Fusilade' and 'Astonia'," 33–34.
38. "Report No. 69," 14–16.
39. Ibid.
40. Copp, *Cinderella Army*, 44.
41. "Report No. 183," 60–61.
42. Stacey, *Victory Campaign*, 300.
43. "Report No. 183," 62–63.
44. TNA:PRO ADM 234/363, 37.
45. "Report No. 183," 62–63.
46. "Report on Op Astonia," 2.
47. "Report No. 183," 62–63.
48. "Report No. 146," 39.

PART TWO: THE DAYS OF UNCERTAINTY

10 LET US GET ON WITH THE WAR
 1. Butcher, *My Three Years with Eisenhower*, 654–55.
 2. Montgomery, *Normandy to the Baltic*, 162.
 3. Ibid., 153.
 4. Adams, *Battle for Western Europe*, 102–03.
 5. TNA:PRO WO 179/2769, "General Staff, App. 4."
 6. Montgomery, *Normandy to the Baltic*, 162.
 7. Adams, *Battle for Western Europe*, 94.
 8. Butcher, *My Three Years with Eisenhower*, 659.
 9. Hamilton, *Monty: The Field Marshal*, 20–22.
 10. TNA:PRO WO 106/4356, 23–24.
 11. Crerar Papers, "Correspondence with Field-Marshal Montgomery," 79.
 12. Ibid., 74.
 13. Ibid., 77–78.
 14. "Report No. 183," 61–62.
 15. Crerar Papers, "Correspondence with Field-Marshal Montgomery," 77–78.
 16. Hamilton, *Monty: The Field Marshal*, 20.
 17. Crerar Papers, "Correspondence with Field-Marshal Montgomery," 70.
 18. Bennett, *Ultra in the West*, 147.
 19. Stacey, *Victory Campaign*, 301.
 20. "Report No. 69," 20–21.
 21. TNA:PRO WO 205/1020, "Interrogation Reports German Generals," 5.
 22. "Report No. 183," 67–68.
 23. TNA:PRO ADM 234/363, 30–33.
 24. "Operations of the Coastal Forces," *Captain Class Frigate Association* (website).
 25. "17th Duke of York's Royal Cdn. Hussars War Diary," Sept. 1944, 2.
 26. "6th Canadian Anti-Tank Reg. War Diary," Sept. 1944, 1.
 27. Heintzman, *History of the Sixth Anti-Tank*, 24.
 28. "17th Duke of York's Royal Cdn. Hussars War Diary," Sept. 1944, 2.
 29. "9th Canadian Infantry Brigade War Diary," Sept. 1944, 2.
 30. "6th Canadian Anti-Tank Regiment War Diary," Sept. 1944, 2.
 31. Pavey, *Historical Account of 7th Cdn. Reconnaissance Reg.*, 67.
 32. "6th Canadian Anti-Tank Regiment War Diary," Sept. 1944, 3.
 33. Pavey, *Historical Account of 7th Cdn. Reconnaissance Reg.*, 67.
 34. Heintzman, *History of the Sixth Anti-Tank*, 25.
 35. "17th Duke of York's Royal Cdn. Hussars War Diary," App. 5, 4.

11 TROUBLE GALORE
 1. Crerar Papers, "Operations—Directives," 54.
 2. Ibid., 53.
 3. Graham, *Price of Command*, 178.
 4. Crerar Papers, "Operations—Directives," 57.
 5. Stacey, *Victory Campaign*, 310.
 6. De Guingand, *Operation Victory*, 328–30.

7. Crerar Papers, "Operations 2 Cdn. Corps," 17.
8. "Second Canadian Infantry Div. HQ War Diary," 3.
9. "Report No. 183," 78.
10. Copp, *Cinderella Army*, 34–35.
11. "4th Canadian Infantry Brigade War Diary," Aug. 1944, 23.
12. "Canadian Scottish Regiment War Diary," Aug. 1944, 31.
13. "Calgary Highlanders War Diary," Sept. 1944, 5.
14. "Report No. 183," 78.
15. "14th Canadian Hussars War Diary," Sept. 1944, 3.
16. "12th Manitoba Dragoons War Diary," Sept. 1944, 5.
17. Henry, *Regimental History of 18th Armoured Car Regiment*, 35.
18. "12th Manitoba Dragoons War Diary," Sept. 1944, 5–6.
19. Roberts, *Canadian Summer*, 83.
20. "Report No. 146," 53–54.
21. "Report No. 137," 10–11.
22. "Report No. 146," 53.
23. "Black Watch Regiment War Diary," Sept. 1944, 3.
24. Bercuson, *Battalion of Heroes*, 127.
25. "5th Canadian Infantry Brigade War Diary," Sept. 1944, App. 13, 112–13.
26. Hunter, "Unit History of I CDN FD PK COY," 2.
27. Charles Barrington Bourne, "Canadian Army Overseas Honours and Awards," *National Defence and the Canadian Forces* (website).
28. "Calgary Highlanders War Diary," Sept. 1944, 7–8.
29. Copp, *The Brigade*, 120.
30. "Account of Régiment de Maisonneuve," 2.
31. "Report No. 183," 78.
32. Copp, *The Brigade*, 120.
33. Marchand, *Le Régiment de Maisonneuve*, 128–30.
34. "Le Régiment de Maisonneuve War Diary," Sept. 1944, 2.
35. "Calgary Highlanders War Diary," Sept. 1944, 8.
36. Bercuson, *Battalion of Heroes*, 129.
37. Marchand, *Le Régiment de Maisonneuve*, 5, 131.
38. Bercuson, *Battalion of Heroes*, 129–30.
39. "Calgary Highlanders War Diary," Sept. 1944, 9.
40. "5th Canadian Infantry Brigade War Diary," Sept. 1944, App. 13, 118.
41. Bercuson, *Battalion of Heroes*, 130–31.
42. "Calgary Highlanders War Diary," Sept. 1944, 10.
43. "Toronto Scottish Regiment (MG) War Diary," Sept. 1944, 3.
44. "5th Canadian Field Regiment War Diary," Sept. 1944, 2.
45. "Calgary Highlanders War Diary," Sept. 1944, 10.
46. Bercuson, *Battalion of Heroes*, 132.
47. "Calgary Highlanders War Diary," Sept. 1944, 10–11.
48. Ibid., 10–12.
49. "Black Watch War Diary," Sept. 1944, 3–4.
50. "2nd Canadian Infantry Div. HQ War Diary," 3.

51. Roberts, *Canadian Summer*, 84–87.
52. McGregor, William, correspondence with author.
53. "2nd Canadian Infantry Div. HQ War Diary," 3.
54. "Les Fusiliers Mont-Royal War Diary," Sept. 1944, 2.
55. "6th Canadian Infantry Brigade War Diary," Sept. 1944, 3.
56. "Les Fusilliers Mont-Royal War Diary," Sept. 1944, 2.
57. Buchanan, *March of the Prairie Men*, 38.
58. "South Saskatchewan Regiment War Diary," Sept. 1944, 6.
59. "6th Canadian Infantry Brigade War Diary," Sept. 1944, 3.
60. "2nd Canadian Infantry Div. HQ War Diary," 3.
61. "South Saskatchewan Regiment War Diary," Sept. 1944, 6.
62. "Queen's Own Cameron Highlanders War Diary," Sept. 1944, 4.

12 FATEFUL DECISIONS

1. Montgomery, *Memoirs of Field-Marshal Montgomery*, 274.
2. Wilmot, *Struggle for Europe*, 488.
3. Adams, *Battle for Western Europe*, 129.
4. Hinsley, *British Intelligence in the Second World War*, 378–79.
5. Ambrose, *Supreme Commander*, 518.
6. Wilmot, *Struggle for Europe*, 489.
7. Butcher, *My Three Years with Eisenhower*, 662.
8. "Report No. 162," 9.
9. Stacey, *Victory Campaign*, 319–20.
10. Wilmot, *Struggle for Europe*, 481–82.
11. Ellis, *Defeat of Germany*, 22–23.

13 BOLD RUTHLESS ACTION

1. "Report No. 184," 3.
2. TNA:PRO WO 171/259, 2.
3. Crerar Papers, "Operation 'Fusilade' and 'Astonia'," 23.
4. TNA:PRO WO 171/500, App. C, 1.
5. Crerar Papers, "Operation 'Fusilade' and 'Astonia'," 20–23.
6. TNA:PRO WO 171/664, 2–3.
7. TNA:PRO WO 205/1020, "Wildermuth," 1–3.
8. TNA:PRO ADM 234/363, 33.
9. TNA:PRO WO 205/1020, "Wildermuth," 7.
10. TNA:PRO ADM 234/363, 33–34.
11. "21 Army Group—Op Reports, Astonia," 2.
12. "Narrative of the Capture of Le Havre: Operation Astonia," 2.
13. "21 Army Group—Op Reports, Astonia," 2.
14. TNA:PRO WO 205/1020, 3–8.
15. TNA:PRO WO 171/664, 4.
16. TNA:PRO WO 205/1020, 7–8.
17. TNA:PRO WO 171/664, 4.
18. "21 Army Group—Op Reports, Astonia," 2.

19. "Narrative of the Capture of Le Havre: Operation Astonia," 2.
20. "The Story of 34 Armoured Bde," *Royal Tank Regiment Association* (website).
21. TNA:PRO WO 171/664, 3.
22. "Narrative of the Capture of Le Havre: Operation Astonia," 2.
23. Williams, *Long Left Flank*, 57.
24. "Narrative of the Capture of Le Havre: Operation Astonia," 3.
25. Margry, "The Capture of Le Havre," *After the Battle*, 7.
26. "Narrative of the Capture of Le Havre: Operation Astonia," 3.
27. Margry, "The Capture of Le Havre," *After the Battle*, 7.
28. Delderfield, "Confidential Report on the Recent Bombing of Le Havre," 69.
29. TNA:PRO WO 171/664, 10.
30. TNA:PRO WO 205/1020, "Interrogation, Wildermuth," 8.
31. TNA:PRO WO 171/500, App. C to Int. Summary No. 59, 1–2.
32. "Narrative of the Capture of Le Havre: Operation Astonia," 4–5.
33. Tonner, "The 'Ram' Kangaroo," *MilArt* (website).
34. "Narrative of the Capture of Le Havre: Operation Astonia," 4.
35. TNA:PRO WO 171/500, "Report on Operation Astonia, Part II," 1.
36. "Report No. 184," 6.
37. "Narrative of the Capture of Le Havre: Operation Astonia," 6–7.
38. "Report No. 184," 6.
39. Margry, "The Capture of Le Havre," *After the Battle*, 7–9.
40. Stacey, *Victory Campaign*, 334.
41. TNA:PRO WO 171/643, App. B, 5.

14 FLAILS TO THE FRONT
1. TNA:PRO WO 171/500, App. LL to Int. Summary No. 58, 1.
2. "21 Army Group Op Reports—Astonia," 3.
3. Margry, "The Capture of Le Havre," *After the Battle*, 9.
4. "21 Army Group Op Reports—Astonia," 3.
5. Margry, "The Capture of Le Havre," *After the Battle*, 9.
6. "Narrative of the Capture of Le Havre: Operation Astonia," 14.
7. Delderfield, "Confidential Report," *Canadian Military History*, 74.
8. TNA:PRO WO 205/1020, 9.
9. TNA:PRO WO 171/500, 1.
10. TNA:PRO WO 171/841, 15–17.
11. Margry, "The Capture of Le Havre," *After the Battle*, 11.
12. TNA:PRO WO 171/841, 18–19.
13. Margry, "The Capture of Le Havre," *After the Battle*, 10.
14. TNA:PRO WO 171/500, 1–2.
15. TNA:PRO WO 171/841, 20–21.
16. "Narrative of the Capture of Le Havre: Operation Astonia," 16.
17. Ibid.," 16.
18. Margry, "The Capture of Le Havre," *After the Battle*, 11.
19. "Narrative of the Capture of Le Havre: Operation Astonia," 16.
20. Margry, "The Capture of Le Havre," *After the Battle*, 11.

21. Ibid., 16.
22. "Narrative of the Capture of Le Havre: Operation Astonia," 16.
23. Margry, "The Capture of Le Havre," *After the Battle,* 16.
24. "Narrative of the Capture of Le Havre: Operation Astonia," 17.
25. TNA:PRO WO 171/650, 9.
26. "Narrative of the Capture of Le Havre: Operation Astonia," 17.
27. TNA:PRO WO 171/500, App. D(II), 1–2.
28. TNA:PRO WO 171/858, App. J, 13.
29. "Narrative of the Capture of Le Havre: Operation Astonia," 18.
30. TNA:PRO WO 171/858, App. J, 10–13.
31. "Narrative of the Capture of Le Havre: Operation Astonia," 19.
32. "21 Army Group Op Reports—Astonia," 16.
33. TNA:PRO WO 205/1020, 10.
34. "21 Army Group Op Reports—Astonia," 16.
35. TNA:PRO WO 205/1020, 9–10.

15 TRIFLING OPPOSITION
1. "Narrative of the Capture of Le Havre: Operation Astonia," 10.
2. Margry, "The Capture of Le Havre," *After the Battle,* 20.
3. "Report No. 184," 9.
4. TNA:PRO WO 171/500, App. O(I), Part II, 6.
5. "Narrative of the Capture of Le Havre: Operation Astonia," 24.
6. "21 Army Group Op Reports—Astonia," 16–17.
7. Margry, "The Capture of Le Havre," *After the Battle,* 22.
8. "Narrative of the Capture of Le Havre: Operation Astonia," 22.
9. "Report No. 184," 9.
10. Ibid., 19.
11. Margry, The Capture of Le Havre, *After the Battle,* 22.
12. "Narrative of the Capture of Le Havre: Operation Astonia," 24.
13. Ibid., 20.
14. Margry, "The Capture of Le Havre," *After the Battle,* 20.
15. "Narrative of the Capture of Le Havre: Operation Astonia," 20.
16. TNA:PRO WO 171/664, 12.
17. "Narrative of the Capture of Le Havre: Operation Astonia," 20.
18. "21 Army Group Op Reports—Astonia," 17.
19. TNA:PRO WO 171/664, 12.
20. Margry, "The Capture of Le Havre," *After the Battle,* 20.
21. TNA:PRO WO 171/664, 12.
22. "Narrative of the Capture of Le Havre: Operation Astonia," 20.
23. Margry, "The Capture of Le Havre," *After the Battle,* 20.
24. TNA:PRO WO 171/664, 12.
25. Margry, "The Capture of Le Havre," *After the Battle,* 20.
26. "21 Army Group Op Reports—Astonia," 18.
27. "Narrative of the Capture of Le Havre: Operation Astonia," 20–21.
28. Margry, "The Capture of Le Havre," *After the Battle,* 21.

29. "Narrative of the Capture of Le Havre: Operation Astonia," 22.
30. TNA:PRO WO 171/500, App. O(I), Part II, 4–5.
31. TNA:PRO WO 171/500, App. D(I), I.
32. TNA:PRO WO 171/500, App. O(I), Part II, 5.
33. Margry, "The Capture of Le Havre," *After the Battle*, 20.
34. TNA:PRO WO 171/500, App. O(I), Part II, 5.
35. TNA:PRO WO 205/1020, 10.
36. "21 Army Group Op Reports—Astonia," 21.
37. TNA:PRO WO 171/500, App. O(I), Part II, 6.
38. Margry, "The Capture of Le Havre," *After the Battle*, 23.
39. "Narrative of the Capture of Le Havre: Operation Astonia," 25.
40. Margry, "The Capture of Le Havre," *After the Battle*, 24.
41. TNA:PRO WO 171/643, App. E, 2.
42. "21 Army Group Op Reports—Astonia," 21.
43. TNA:PRO WO 205/1020, 10–11.
44. TNA:PRO WO 171/643, App. D, 2.
45. Margry, "The Capture of Le Havre," *After the Battle*, 27.
46. Montgomery, *Normandy to the Baltic*, 168.
47. "Report No. 184," 10.
48. Margry, "The Capture of Le Havre," *After the Battle*, 27.
49. "Air Support Reports," 2.
50. "21 Army Group Op Reports—Astonia," 23.
51. Margry, "The Capture of Le Havre," *After the Battle*, 30–31.
52. "21 Army Group Op Reports—Astonia," 24–26.

16 A LOT TO CRACK
1. TNA:PRO ADM 202/99, 3–4.
2. "Report No. 184," 11.
3. TNA:PRO WO 171/858, 4.
4. TNA:PRO ADM 234/363, 34.
5. Margry, "The Capture of Le Havre," *After the Battle*, 31.
6. "Report No. 183," 79–81.
7. Buchanan, *March of the Prairie Men*, 38.
8. "South Saskatchewan Regiment War Diary," Sept. 1944, 7.
9. Buchanan, *March of the Prairie Men*, 38.
10. "6th Canadian Field Regiment War Diary," Sept. 1944, 3.
11. South Saskatchewan Regiment War Diary," Sept. 1944, 7–10.
12. Meanwell, *I Battalion: The Essex Scottish Regiment*, 46.
13. *History of Third Canadian Light Anti-Aircraft Regiment*, 32–33.
14. "Essex Scottish Regiment War Diary," Sept. 1944, App. 13, 2.
15. Buchanan, *March of the Prairie Men*, 38.
16. South Saskatchewan Regiment War Diary," Sept. 1944, 9–10.
17. "2nd Canadian Infantry Div. HQ War Diary," 4.
18. "Les Fusiliers Mont-Royal War Diary," Sept. 1944, 3.
19. Queen-Hughes, *Whatever Men Dare*, 129–30.

20. "Report No. 183," 81–82.
21. "4th Canadian Infantry Brigade War Diary," Sept. 1944, 10.
22. "Report No. 183," 81–82.
23. "Account of a Two Coy attack Spycker," 1–2.
24. "Black Watch War Diary," Sept. 1944, 5.
25. "Report No. 183," 80.

17 THEY COULD HAVE BLASTED US

1. "Queen's Own Cameron War Diary," Sept. 1944, Battle of Bray-Dunes, 1.
2. Hossack, *Mike Target*, 22.
3. Blackburn, *Guns of Victory*, 12.
4. "4th Canadian Infantry Brigade War Diary," Sept. 1944, 10.
5. "Royal Regiment of Canada War Diary," Sept. 1944, 16.
6. Brown, Brown, and Greenhous, *Semper Paratus*, 272.
7. "Report No. 183," 92–94.
8. Stacey, *Victory Campaign*, 336.
9. Dickson, *A Thoroughly Canadian General*, 344–45.
10. TNA:PRO WO 106/4356, 19.
11. "Queen's Own Cameron War Diary," Sept. 1944, Battle of Bray-Dunes, 1.
12. Ibid., App. 17, 11.
13. Frank Kean Breakey, "Canadian Army Overseas Honours and Awards," *National Defence and the Canadian Forces* (website).
14. "Queen's Own Cameron War Diary," Sept. 1944, Battle of Bray-Dunes, 1.
15. "South Saskatchewan Regiment War Diary," Sept. 1944, 11–12.
16. "4th Canadian Infantry Brigade War Diary," Sept. 1944, 11.
17. "2nd Canadian Field Company, RCE, War Diary," Sept. 1944, 3–4.
18. "Royal Regiment of Canada War Diary," Sept. 1944, 17–18.
19. "Royal Hamilton Light Infantry War Diary," Sept. 1944, 10.
20. Goodspeed, *Battle Royal*, 487.
21. "Royal Regiment of Canada War Diary," Sept. 1944, 18–19.
22. Blackburn, *Guns of Victory*, 16.
23. "Royal Regiment of Canada War Diary," Sept. 1944, 18–19.
24. "14th Canadian Hussars War Diary," Sept. 1944, 9.
25. TNA:PRO WO 171/528, 16.
26. "1st Czech Independent Armoured Brigade Group, Hist. Notes on Ops," 1.
27. White, *On All Fronts*, 193.
28. "1st Czech Independent Armoured Brigade Group, Hist. Notes on Ops," 2.
29. White, *On All Fronts*, 202–04.

PART THREE: THE PAS DE CALAIS BATTLES

18 A LOST OUTPOST

1. Ellis, *Defeat of Germany*, 29–34.
2. "Capture of Boulogne—Sep 44," 3.

3. "Report No. 184," 19.
4. Ibid., 21–22.
5. "Capture of Boulogne—Sep 44," 2–3.
6. "Reports, Appreciations, etc., Report on Boulogne Harbour," 1.
7. TNA:PRO WO 205/1020, 1–4.
8. Stacey, *Victory Campaign*, 337.
9. TNA:PRO WO 205/1020, 4–6.
10. "8th Canadian Infantry Brigade War Diary," Sept. 1944, 5.
11. "Report on Op 'Wellhit' capture of Boulogne Fortress," 1.
12. "Report No. 184," 25.
13. "Air Support 3 Cdn. Inf.," 3.
14. "Report No. 184," 20.
15. "8th Canadian Infantry Brigade War Diary," App. 4, 9.
16. "Report No. 184," 23.
17. TNA:PRO WO 171/858, 5.
18. TNA:PRO WO 171/1801, App. Op Wellhit, 1.
19. "Report No. 184," 23.
20. TNA:PRO WO 171/858, 5.
21. TNA:PRO WO 171/879, App. A, 1.
22. "Report on Flame Action by Wasps," 1.
23. "Report No. 184," 23.
24. Ross, *History of the 1st Battalion Cameron Highlanders*, 63–64.
25. Portugal, *We Were There*, vol. 4, 1821.
26. "Report on Op 'Wellhit' capture of Boulogne Fortress," 12.
27. Portugal, *We Were There*, vol. 4, 1822.
28. "Royal Marine Siege Regt., Detailed Narrative," 5.
29. TNA:PRO WO 205/1020, 6.
30. "Report No. 146," 48.
31. TNA:PRO WO 205/1020, 6.
32. "Report No. 146," 48.
33. Bird, *North Shore (New Brunswick) Regiment*, 215.
34. "Report No. 146," 48.
35. TNA:PRO WO 205/1020, 6.
36. "Report No. 184," 22.
37. Stacey, *Victory Campaign*, 338.
38. TNA:PRO WO 179/2769, App. 21, 1.
39. "Report No. 184," 21–24.

19 A HARD DAY'S FIGHTING
1. Rockingham interview.
2. Stacey, *Victory Campaign*, 339.
3. "Account by Capt. W.S. Hamilton RCCS on bombing of Boulogne," 1.
4. Galbraith, "Operation 'Wellhit': The Capture of Boulogne," *After the Battle*, 6.
5. TNA:PRO WO 205/1020, 7.
6. "Air Support Reports," 4–5.

7. Stacey, *Victory Campaign*, 339.
8. "Account of Ops in Boulogne . . . by Lt. Col. JE Anderson," 2.
9. "North Shore (New Brunswick) War Diary," 12.
10. Bird, *North Shore (New Brunswick) Regiment*, 413–16.
11. Fenton Edgar Daley, "Canadian Army Overseas Honours and Awards," *National Defence and the Canadian Forces* (website).
12. Bird, *North Shore (New Brunswick) Regiment*, 413–14.
13. "Account of Ops in Boulogne . . . by Lt. Col. JE Anderson," 2.
14. "Royal Marine Siege Regt., Detailed Narrative," 7.
15. "Information re: Dover Guns," 4.
16. McAndrew, *Liberation*, 38.
17. "Operation Wellhit: Capture of Boulogne Fortress," 17.
18. "Le Régiment de la Chaudière War Diary," Sept. 1944, 9.
19. "8th Canadian Infantry Brigade War Diary," Sept. 1944, 6.
20. Castonguay and Ross, *Le Régiment de la Chaudière*, 288–90.
21. "Story of Battle of Boulogne by 10 Cdn Armd Regt (FGH)," 2.
22. Ibid.
23. *Vanguard: Fort Garry Horse*, 72.
24. "Le Régiment de la Chaudière War Diary," Sept. 1944, 10.
25. "Story of Battle of Boulogne by 10 Cdn Armd Regt (FGH)," 3.
26. TNA:PRO WO 171/1801, App. E, Operation Wellhit, 2.
27. Robert Richards, "Canadian Army Overseas Honours and Awards," *National Defence and the Canadian Forces* (website).
28. Joseph Etienne Ouellet, "Canadian Army Overseas Honours and Awards," *National Defence and the Canadian Forces* (website).
29. Barnard, *Queen's Own Rifles of Canada*, 225.
30. Martin, *Battle Diary*, 77–78.
31. Barnard, *Queen's Own Rifles of Canada*, 225.
32. Martin, *Battle Diary*, 79–81.
33. "Account by Lt. Col. Rowley," 2.
34. Boss and Patterson, *Up the Glens*, 122.
35. "Account by Lt. Col. Rowley," 3.
36. "Report No. 184," 25.
37. Bird, *No Retreating Footsteps*, 217–18.
38. "Msgs—2 Cdn Corps, Report on Flame Action by Wasps," 1.
39. "Report No. 184," 25.
40. Pavey, *Historical Account of the 7th Reconnaissance Rgt.*, 71.
41. "Msgs—2 Cdn Corps, Report on Flame Action by Wasps," 1.
42. "North Nova Scotia Highlanders War Diary," Sept. 1944, 7.
43. "Account by Lt. Col. Rowley," 3.
44. "Report No. 184," 25–26.
45. Stacey, *Victory Campaign*, 341.

20 PROCESS OF WINKLING OUT

1. Boss and Patterson, *Up the Glens*, 122.
2. "North Nova Scotia Highlanders War Diary," Sept. 1944, 8.
3. Ross, *History of the 1st Battalion Cameron Highlanders*, 65.
4. "Cameron Highlanders of Ottawa (MG) War Diary," Sept. 1944, App. 'C' Coy, 3.
5. "8th Canadian Infantry Brigade War Diary," Sept. 1944, 6.
6. Bird, *North Shore (New Brunswick) Regiment*, 418.
7. "Account of Ops in Boulogne . . . by Lt. Col. JE Anderson," 2–3.
8. Castonguay and Ross, *Le Régiment de la Chaudière*, 290–91.
9. Barnard, *The Queen's Own Rifles of Canada*, 226.
10. Martin, *Battle Diary*, 81–82.
11. "Queen's Own Rifles War Diary," Sept. 1944, 5.
12. Barnard, *The Queen's Own Rifles of Canada*, 226.
13. "Story of Battle of Boulogne by 10 Cdn Armd Regt (FGH)," 3.
14. Bird, *No Retreating Footsteps*, 219–20.
15. Ritchie McVean Grainger, "Canadian Army Overseas Honours and Awards," *National Defence and the Canadian Forces* (website).
16. TNA:PRO WO 171/858, App. A, 2–3.
17. "Report No. 184," 28.
18. "Account by Lt. Col. Rowley," 4.
19. "Report No. 184," 29.
20. Portugal, *We Were There*, vol. 3, 1249–1250.
21. "Account by Lt. Col. Rowley," 4.
22. "Highland Light Infantry War Diary," Sept. 1944, 11.
23. "Report No. 184," 29.
24. "Cameron Highlanders of Ottawa (MG) War Diary," Sept. 1944, App. 'C' Company, 4–5.
25. "Cameron Highlanders of Ottawa (MG) War Diary," Sept. 1944, App. 8, 3.
26. Murray Stanley Dickson and Charles Alexander Spratt, "Canadian Army Overseas Honours and Awards," *National Defence and the Canadian Forces* (website).
27. "Cameron Highlanders of Ottawa (MG) War Diary," Sept. 1944, App. 8, 3–4.
28. Couvrette, "A Tale of Survival," *Ottawa Citizen*.
29. "Cameron Highlanders of Ottawa (MG) War Diary," Sept. 1944, App. 8, 3–4.
30. Ross, *History of the 1st Battalion Cameron Highlanders*, 65.
31. "Cameron Highlanders of Ottawa (MG) War Diary," Sept. 1944, App. 8, 3.
32. Kerry and McDill, *History of the Corps*, 326.
33. "Report No. 184," 30.
34. "Highland Light Infantry War Diary," Sept. 1944, 10–11.
35. "Galt Father Hears Two Sons Killed," *Toronto Star*.
36. "Highland Light Infantry War Diary," Sept. 1944, 10.
37. "9th Canadian Infantry Brigade War Diary," Sept. 1944, 8.
38. "Report No. 184," 31.
39. TNA:PRO WO 171/858, App. J, 20–21.
40. Ibid.
41. Stacey, *Victory Campaign*, 342.

42. "Operation Wellhit: Capture of Boulogne Fortress," 22.

43. "Account by Lt. Col. Rowley," 4.

44. "Joseph Greenblatt Correspondence," letter 52.

45. Whitsed, *Canadians: A Battalion at War*, 117–18.

46. "Operation Wellhit: Capture of Boulogne Fortress," 23.

47. "Report No. 184," 33.

21 ANOTHER FORTRESS FINISHED

1. "Stormont, Dundas and Glengarry Highlanders War Diary," Sept. 1944, 13.

2. "Account by Lt. Col. Rowley," 4.

3. "North Nova Scotia Highlanders War Diary," Sept. 1944, 10.

4. "Queen's Own Rifles War Diary," Sept. 1944, 6.

5. "Report No. 184," 33.

6. "Le Régiment de la Chaudière War Diary," Sept. 1944, 13.

7. "Stormont, Dundas and Glengarry Highlanders War Diary," Sept. 1944, 13.

8. Boss and Patterson, *Up the Glens*, 123.

9. "Account by Lt. Col. Rowley," 4–5.

10. Boss and Patterson, *Up the Glens*, 123.

11. "Account by Lt. Col. Rowley," 5.

12. Boss and Patterson, *Up the Glens*, 123.

13. Bird, *North Shore (New Brunswick) Regiment*, 419–20.

14. "Operation Wellhit: Capture of Boulogne Fortress," 23.

15. "Report No. 184," 33.

16. "Queen's Own Rifles War Diary," Sept. 1944, 6.

17. Barnard, *Queen's Own Rifles of Canada*, 226.

18. Stacey, *Victory Campaign*, 348.

19. Castonguay and Ross, *Le Régiment de la Chaudière*, 292.

20. Bird, *North Shore (New Brunswick) Regiment*, 420–22.

21. Boss and Patterson, *Up the Glens*, 123–24.

22. "Highland Light Infantry War Diary," Sept. 1944, 12.

23. "Msgs—2 Cdn Corps, App. D," 2.

24. "Operation Wellhit: Capture of Boulogne Fortress," 25.

25. "Story of Battle of Boulogne by 10 Cdn Armd Regt (FGH)," 5.

26. Bird, *No Retreating Footsteps*, 228–29.

27. "Story of Battle of Boulogne by 10 Cdn Armd Regt (FGH)," 5.

28. "North Nova Scotia Highlanders War Diary," Sept. 1944, 10.

29. "Report No. 184," 34.

30. "Operation Wellhit: Capture of Boulogne Fortress," 26.

31. "North Nova Scotia Highlanders War Diary," Sept. 1944, 11.

32. Bird, *North Shore (New Brunswick) Regiment*, 422.

33. "Account of Ops in Boulogne . . . by Lt. Col. JE Anderson," 3.

34. Bird, *North Shore (New Brunswick) Regiment*, 422–24.

35. "Account of Ops in Boulogne . . . by Lt. Col. JE Anderson," 4.

36. "Operation Wellhit: Capture of Boulogne Fortress," 25.

37. "Report No. 184," 34.

38. "Queen's Own Rifles War Diary," Sept. 1944, 7.

39. Barnard, *The Queen's Own Rifles of Canada*, 227.

40. "Story of Battle of Boulogne by 10 Cdn Armd Regt (FGH)," 7.

41. "Report No. 184," 36.

42. "Stormont, Dundas and Glengarry Highlanders War Diary," Sept. 1944, 15.

43. "Story of Battle of Boulogne by 10 Cdn Armd Regt (FGH)," 7.

44. "Report No. 184," 36.

45. Rockingham interview.

46. "Report No. 184," App. E.

47. TNA:PRO WO 205/1020, 7.

48. "9th Canadian Infantry Brigade War Diary," Sept. 1944, 10.

49. Ibid., 7.

22 WITH GREAT BOLDNESS AND EFFICIENCY

1. "Report No. 184," 38.

2. "Report No. 146," 50.

3. Stacey, *Victory Campaign*, 345.

4. "Report No. 184," 40.

5. "Account of Assault on Calais by Maj. M.H.V. Matthews," 1.

6. "Report No. 184," 41.

7. "Siege and Capture of Calais," 2.

8. Stacey, *Victory Campaign*, 346.

9. "Report No. 184," 41.

10. Stacey, *Victory Campaign*, 346.

11. TNA:PRO WO 205/1020, 1–4.

12. TNA:PRO AIR 25/717, App. 4, 1–2.

13. "Report No. 184," 43.

14. "Op 'Undergo' Hy Bomber Effort," 1.

15. "Operation Undergo, Misc Bomber Command Messages," 14.

16. "Report No. 184," 43.

17. "Operation Undergo, Misc Bomber Command Messages," 31.

18. "Report No. 184," 43.

19. Nicholson, *Gunners of Canada*, 350.

20. Portugal, *We Were There*, vol. 4, 1822.

21. "Report . . . on use of smoke in Op 'Undergo'," 1.

22. "Report No. 184," 43.

23. "Report . . . on use of smoke in Op 'Undergo'," 1–4.

24. Barrett, *History of 13 Canadian Field Artillery*, 76.

25. "Report No. 184," 44.

26. "Operation Undergo, Misc Bomber Command Messages," 17.

27. "Air Support," 11–12.

28. "Personal Diary of Brig. N.E. Rodger," 20–24 Sep.

29. "Report No. 184," 44–45.

30. "Operation Undergo, Misc Bomber Command Messages," 16.

31. "7th Canadian Infantry Brigade War Diary," Sept. 1944, 23.

32. Hall interview.
33. "3rd Canadian Infantry Division War Diary," Sept. 1944, App. 41, Serial 43.
34. Guy Granville Simonds, "Canadian Army Overseas Honours and Awards," *National Defence and the Canadian Forces* (website).
35. Crerar Papers, "Correspondence with Lt-Gen G.G. Simonds," 35.
36. Luxton, *1st Battalion, the Regina Rifles*, 50.
37. "Regina Rifles War Diary," Sept. 1944, 18.
38. "North Shore (New Brunswick) War Diary," Sept. 1944, 15.
39. Bird, *North Shore (New Brunswick) Regiment*, 426–27.

23 WE WILL FIGHT

1. "Regina Rifles War Diary," Sept. 1944, 18.
2. Stacey, *Victory Campaign*, 349.
3. "Regina Rifles War Diary," Sept. 1944, 18.
4. "Operation Undergo, Misc Bomber Command Messages," 11–12.
5. Stacey, *Victory Campaign*, 349.
6. Nicholson, *Gunners of Canada*, 352.
7. TNA:PRO WO 171/858, App. J, 18.
8. "North Shore (New Brunswick) War Diary," Sept. 1944, 16.
9. Bird, *North Shore (New Brunswick) Regiment*, 427–28.
10. "North Shore (New Brunswick) War Diary," Sept. 1944, 15.
11. Castonguay and Ross, *Le Régiment de la Chaudière*, 295.
12. "North Shore (New Brunswick) War Diary," Sept. 1944, 16.
13. Bird, *North Shore (New Brunswick) Regiment*, 428–31.
14. "North Shore (New Brunswick) War Diary," Sept. 1944, 16–18.
15. Bird, *North Shore (New Brunswick) Regiment*, 428.
16. "7th Canadian Infantry Brigade War Diary," Sept. 1944, 23.
17. Shawcross, *What Was It Like?*, 204.
18. Luxton, *1st Battalion, the Regina Rifles*, 51.
19. "Royal Winnipeg Rifles War Diary," Sept. 1944, 8.
20. Reid, *Named by the Enemy*, 200.
21. Kuppers, *Perspectives*, 43.
22. "Royal Winnipeg Rifles War Diary," Sept. 1944, 8.
23. Kuppers, *Perspectives*, 43.
24. Bruce Edward Caw, "Canadian Army Overseas Honours and Awards," *National Defence and the Canadian Forces* (website).
25. Kuppers, *Perspectives*, 43.
26. "Royal Winnipeg Rifles War Diary," Sept. 1944, 8.
27. Bruce Edward Caw, "Canadian Army Overseas Honours and Awards," *National Defence and the Canadian Forces* (website).
28. "Royal Winnipeg Rifles War Diary," Sept. 1944, 8.
29. "1st Hussars Regiment War Diary," Sept. 1944, 7.
30. Conron, *History of the 1st Hussars Regiment*, 104.
31. "1st Hussars Regiment War Diary," Sept. 1944, 7–8.
32. "Canadian Scottish Regiment War Diary," Sept. 1944, 16.

33. "1st Canadian Armoured Personnel Carrier Squadron War Diary," Sept. 1944, 6.

34. "Canadian Scottish Regiment War Diary," Sept. 1944, 16.

35. "Canadian Scottish Regiment War Diary," Oct. 1944, App. 10, 1.

36. Roy, *Ready for the Fray*, 310.

37. "7th Canadian Infantry Brigade War Diary," Sept. 1944, 25.

38. "Account of Assault on Calais by Maj. M.H.V. Matthews," 3.

39. "1st Hussars Regiment War Diary," Sept. 1944, 8.

40. "Account of Assault on Calais by Maj. M.H.V. Matthews," 3.

41. Stacey, *Victory Campaign*, 350–53.

42. Barrett, *History of 13 Canadian Field Artillery*, 78.

43. "9th Canadian Infantry Brigade War Diary," Sept. 1944, 11.

44. "7th Canadian Infantry Brigade War Diary," Sept. 1944, 25.

45. Roy, *Ready for the Fray*, 311.

46. "Account of Assault on Calais by Maj. M.H.V. Matthews," 3.

47. "Canadian Scottish Regiment War Diary," Sept. 1944, 16.

48. "7th Canadian Infantry Brigade War Diary," Sept. 1944, 25.

49. "Report No. 184," 47.

50. Hamilton, *Monty: The Field Marshal*, 91.

51. Pogue, *Supreme Command*, 297.

52. Crerar Papers, "21 Army Group, General Operational Situation," 1–3.

24 AN UNUSUAL BATTLE

1. "Report No. 184," 47–48.

2. Stacey, *Victory Campaign*, 350.

3. McNorgan, *The Gallant Hussars*, 188.

4. "Account of Assault on Calais by Maj. M.H.V. Matthews," 3–4.

5. "Canadian Scottish Regiment War Diary," Oct. 1944, App. 10, 2.

6. "Account of Assault on Calais by Maj. M.H.V. Matthews," 4.

7. Kerry and McDill, *History of the Corps*, 329.

8. "UK Military Bridging—Floating Equipment," *Think Defence* (website).

9. Roy, *Ready for the Fray*, 312–13.

10. "Canadian Scottish Regiment War Diary," Sept. 1944, 18.

11. "Royal Winnipeg Rifles War Diary," Sept. 1944, 9.

12. Tacoma and Wells, *Little Black Devils*, 172.

13. Kuppers, *Perspectives*, 31.

14. Tacoma and Wells, *Little Black Devils*, 172.

15. Portugal, *We Were There*. vol. 6, 3083.

16. Reid, *Named by the Enemy*, 202.

17. "Royal Winnipeg Rifles War Diary," Sept. 1944, 9–10.

18. Shawcross, *What Was It Like?*, 205–06.

19. "Regina Rifles War Diary," Sept. 1944, App. 4, 15.

20. Shawcross, *What Was It Like?*, 206.

21. "7th Canadian Infantry Brigade War Diary," Sept. 1944, 27.

22. "Canadian Scottish Regiment War Diary," Sept. 1944, 18.

23. Roy, *Ready for the Fray*, 314.

24. "Canadian Scottish Regiment War Diary," Sept. 1944, 18.
25. Roy, *Ready for the Fray*, 314.
26. Norton interview.
27. Roy, *Ready for the Fray*, 314–15.
28. Stacey, *Victory Campaign*, 353.
29. "9th Canadian Infantry Brigade War Diary," Sept. 1944, 12.
30. TNA:PRO WO 205/1020, 5.
31. "Report No. 184," 48–49.
32. "7th Canadian Infantry Brigade War Diary," Sept. 1944, 27.
33. "Report No. 184," 49.
34. Stacey, *Victory Campaign*, 351.
35. "Report No. 184," 49–50.
36. "7th Canadian Infantry Brigade War Diary," Sept. 1944, 28.
37. Roy, *Ready for the Fray*, 315.
38. TNA:PRO WO 205/1020, 6.
39. Roy, *Ready for the Fray*, 315–16.

25 TO FIGHT OR NOT
1. Stacey, *Victory Campaign*, 352.
2. "The Guns of Cap Gris Nez," *Military History Now* (website).
3. "Report No. 184," 50.
4. Stacey, *Victory Campaign*, 355.
5. "Report No. 184," 51.
6. Bird, *No Retreating Footsteps*, 236.
7. TNA:PRO WO 171/858, App. J, 21.
8. "Account of attack on Cap Gris Nez by Lt-Col D.F. Forbes," 2.
9. Bird, *No Retreating Footsteps*, 238.
10. TNA:PRO WO 171/858, App. J, 22.
11. "Highland Light Infantry War Diary," Sept. 1944, 16.
12. TNA:PRO WO 171/858, App. J, 22.
13. Bird, *No Retreating Footsteps*, 238.
14. TNA:PRO WO 171/858, App. J, 21.
15. Bird, *No Retreating Footsteps*, 239–40.
16. "Account of attack on Cap Gris Nez by Lt-Col D.F. Forbes," 2.
17. Bird, *No Retreating Footsteps*, 240.
18. "Highland Light Infantry War Diary," Sept. 1944, 16.
19. TNA:PRO WO 171/858, App. J, 22.
20. "Highland Light Infantry War Diary," Sept. 1944, 16.
21. "9th Canadian Infantry Brigade War Diary," Sept. 1944, 13.
22. Stacey, *Victory Campaign*, 352–54.
23. Bird, *No Retreating Footsteps*, 241.
24. TNA:PRO WO 171/858, App. J, 21.
25. Bird, *No Retreating Footsteps*, 240.
26. "Highland Light Infantry War Diary," Sept. 1944, 16.
27. "Report No. 184," 53.

28. "Cameron Highlanders of Ottawa (MG) War Diary," Sept. 1944, 15.
29. Barnard, *Queen's Own Rifles*, 229.
30. Roy, *Ready for the Fray*, 317–19.
31. "Cameron Highlanders of Ottawa (MG) War Diary," Sept. 1944, 15.
32. Shawcross, *What Was It Like?*, 207.
33. Stacey, *Victory Campaign*, 352.
34. "Report No. 184," 54.

EPILOGUE: THE CHANNEL PORTS IN MEMORY
1. Luxton, *1st Battalion, the Regina Rifles*, 51–52.

BIBLIOGRAPHY

Abbreviations: AHQ–Army Headquarters. CAB–Records of the Cabinet Office. CMHQ–Canadian Military Headquarters. CWM–Canadian War Museum. DHH–Director of Heritage and History. DND–Department of National Defence. LAC–Library and Archives Canada. NARA–National Archives of the United States. PRO–Public Record Office (U.K.). TNA–The National Archives of the U.K. UVICSC–University of Victoria Libraries Special Collections. WO–War Office (U.K.).

BOOKS

Adams, John A. *The Battle for Western Europe–Fall 1944: An Operational Assessment.* Indianapolis: Indiana University Press, 2010.

Ambrose, Stephen E. *The Supreme Commander: The War Years of General Dwight D. Eisenhower.* Jackson: University Press of Mississippi, 1999.

Antal, Sandy, and Kevin R. Shackleton. *Duty Nobly Done: The Official History of the Essex and Kent Scottish Regiment.* Windsor, ON: Walkerville, 2006.

Barnard, W.T. *The Queen's Own Rifles of Canada, 1860–1960: One Hundred Years of Canada.* Don Mills, ON: Ontario Publishing Company, 1960.

Barrett, William W. *History of the 13 Canadian Field Regiment.* N.p., 1945.

Bennett, Ralph. *Ultra in the West: The Normandy Campaign of 1944–45.* New York: Charles Scribner & Sons, 1979.

Bercuson, David. *Battalion of Heroes: The Calgary Highlanders in World War II.* Calgary: Calgary Highlanders Regimental Funds Fdn., 1994.

Bird, Will R. *North Shore (New Brunswick) Regiment.* Fredericton: Brunswick Press, 1963.

———. *No Retreating Footsteps: The Story of the North Nova Scotia Highlanders.* Hantsport, NS: Lancelot Press, 1983.

Blackburn, George G. *The Guns of Normandy: A Soldier's Eye View, France 1944.* Toronto: McClelland & Stewart, 1995.

———. *The Guns of Victory: A Soldier's Eye View, Belgium, Holland, and Germany, 1944–45.* Toronto: McClelland & Stewart, 1996.

Blumenson, Martin. *Breakout and Pursuit: United States Army in World War II—The European Theatre of Operations.* Washington, D.C.: Center of Military History, United States Army, 1993.

Boss, W., and W.J. Patterson. *Up the Glens: Stormont, Dundas and Glengarry Highlanders, 1783–1994.* Cornwall, ON: The Old Book Store, 1995.

Brown, Kingsley Sr., Kingsley Brown Jr., and Brereton Greenhous. *Semper Paratus: The History of the Royal Hamilton Light Infantry (Wentworth Regiment), 1862–1977.* Hamilton, ON: RHLI Historical Assoc., 1977.

Buchanan, George B. *March of the Prairie Men: A Story of the South Saskatchewan Regiment.* Weyburn, SK: S. Sask. R. Orderly Room, 1958.

Butcher, Harry C. *My Three Years with Eisenhower: The Personal Diary of Captain Harry C. Butcher, USNR.* New York: Simon & Schuster, 1946.

Cassidy, George L. *Warpath: The Story of the Algonquin Regiment, 1939–1945.* Markham, ON: Paperjacks, 1980.

Castonguay, Jacques, and Armand Ross. *Le Régiment de la Chaudière.* Lévis, QC: N.p., 1983.

Conron, A. Brandon. *A History of the 1st Hussars Regiment: 1856–1980.* N.p., 1980.

Copp, Terry. *The Brigade: The Fifth Canadian Infantry Brigade, 1939–1945.* Stoney Creek, ON: Fortress, 1992.

———. *Fields of Fire: The Canadians in Normandy.* Toronto: University of Toronto Press, 2003.

———. *Cinderella Army: The Canadians in Northwest Europe, 1944–1945.* Toronto: University of Toronto Press, 2006.

De Guingand, Francis. *Operation Victory.* London: Hodder & Stoughton, 1960.

D'Este, Carlo. *Decision in Normandy: The Unwritten Story of Montgomery and the Allied Campaign.* London: Penguin, 1983.

Dickson, Paul Douglas. *A Thoroughly Canadian General: A Biography of General H.D.G. Crerar.* Toronto: University of Toronto Press, 2007.

Duguid, A. Fortescue. *History of the Canadian Grenadier Guards, 1760–1964.* Montreal: Gazette Printing, 1965.

Eisenhower, Gen. Dwight D. *Report by the Supreme Commander to the Combined Chiefs of Staff on Operations in Europe of the Allied Expeditionary Force, 6 June 1944 to 8 May 1945.* London: His Majesty's Stationery Office, 1946.

Ellis, L.F. *The Battle of Normandy.* Vol. 1 of *Victory in the West.* London: Her Majesty's Stationery Office, 1962.

———. *The Defeat of Germany.* Vol. 2 of *Victory in the West.* London: Her Majesty's Stationery Office, 1968.

English, John A. *Failure in High Command: The Canadian Army and the Normandy Campaign.* Ottawa: Golden Dog Press, 1995.

Foster, Robert M., et al. *Steady the Buttons Two by Two: Governor General's Horse Guards Regimental History, 125th Anniversary, 1872–1997.* Ottawa: Governor General's Foot Guards, 1999.

Fraser, Robert L. *Black Yesterdays: The Argyll's War.* Hamilton: Argyll Fdn., 1996.

Goodspeed, D.J. *Battle Royal: A History of the Royal Regiment of Canada, 1862–1962.* Toronto: Royal Regt. of Canada Assoc., 1962.

Graham, Dominick. *The Price of Command: A Biography of General Guy Simonds.* Toronto: Stoddart, 1993.

Grant, D.W. *Carry On: The History of the Toronto Scottish Regiment (MG), 1939–1945.* Toronto: N.p., 1949.

Hamilton, Nigel. *Monty: The Field Marshal, 1944–1976.* London: Hamish Hamilton, 1986.

Hartigan, Dan. *A Rising of Courage: Canada's Paratroops in the Liberation of Normandy.* Calgary: Drop Zone, 2000.

Hayes, Geoffrey. *The Lincs: A History of the Lincoln and Welland Regiment at War.* Alma, ON: Maple Leaf Route, 1986.

Heintzman, G.T., W.A. Hand, and E.H. Heeney (eds). *History of the Sixth Anti-Tank.* Toronto: 6 Canadian Anti-Tank Regiment Royal Canadian Artillery, 1946.

Henry, C.E. *Regimental History of the 18th Armoured Car Regiment (XII Manitoba Dragoons).* Deventer, Netherlands: Nederlandsche Diepdruk Inrichting, 1945.

Hickey, R.M. *The Scarlet Dawn.* Campbelltown, NB: Tribune, 1949.

Hinsley, F.H. *British Intelligence in the Second World War: Its Influence on Strategy and Operations.* Vol. 3, part II. London: Her Majesty's Stationery Office, 1988.

The History of the Third Canadian Light Anti-Aircraft Regiment from 17 August, 1940, to 7 May, 1945, World War II. N.a., n.p., 1945.

Horn, Bernd, and Michel Wyczynski. *Paras Versus the Reich: Canada's Paratroopers at War, 1942–45.* Toronto: Dundurn, 2003.

Hossack, Ken. *Mike Target.* Ottawa: N.p., 1945.

Jackson, H.M. *The Argyll and Sutherland Highlanders of Canada (Princess Louise's), 1928–1953.* N.p., 1953.

Kerry, A.J., and W.A. McDill. *History of the Corps of Royal Canadian Engineers.* Vol. 2 (1936–46). Ottawa: Military Engineers Assoc. of Canada, 1966.

Kuppers, Alex W. *Perspectives: Royal Winnipeg Rifles.* Royal Winnipeg Rifles Assoc., B.C. Branch, 2003.

Lindsay, Martin. *So Few Got Through.* London: Collins, 1946.

Luxton, Eric, ed. *1st Battalion, the Regina Rifles Regiment, 1939–1946.* Regina: The Regt., 1946.

Malone, Richard S. *A Portrait of War: 1939–1945.* Don Mills, ON: Collins, 1983.

Marchand, Gérard. *Le Régiment de Maisonneuve vers la victoire, 1944–1945.* Montreal: Les Presses Libres, 1980.

Martin, Charles Cromwell. *Battle Diary: From D-Day and Normandy to the Zuider Zee and VE.* Toronto: Dundurn, 1994.

Meanwell, R.W. *1 Battalion: The Essex Scottish Regiment, 1939–1945—A Brief Narrative.* Aldershot, U.K.: Wellington Press, 1946.

McAndrew, Bill. *Liberation: The Canadians in Europe.* Montreal: Éditions Art Global, 1995.

McNorgan, Michael R. *The Gallant Hussars: A History of the 1st Hussars Regiment, 1856–2004.* Aylmer, ON: Aylmer Express, 2004.

Montgomery, Bernard Law. *The Memoirs of Field-Marshal the Viscount Montgomery of Alamein, K.G.* London: Collins, 1958.

———. *Normandy to the Baltic.* Germany: British Army of the Rhine, 1946.

Nicholson, G.W.L. *The Canadians in Italy, 1943–1945.* Vol. 2 of *Official History of the Canadian Army in the Second World War.* Ottawa: Queen's Printer, 1957.

———. *The Gunners of Canada.* Vol. 2. Toronto: McClelland & Stewart, 1972.

Pavey, Walter G. *An Historical Account of the 7th Canadian Reconnaissance Regiment (17th Duke of York's Royal Canadian Hussars) in the World War, 1939–1945.* Montreal: Harpell's Press, 1946.

Pogue, Forrest C. *Supreme Command.* Washington, D.C.: U.S. Government Printing Office, 1954.

Portugal, Jean E. *We Were There: The Navy, the Army and the RCAF—A Record for Canada.* 7 vols. Shelburne, ON: Battered Silicon Dispatch Box, 1998.

Queen-Hughes, R.W. *Whatever Men Dare: A History of the Queen's Own Cameron Highlanders of Canada, 1935–1960.* Winnipeg: Bulman Bros., 1960.

Reid, Brian A. *Named by the Enemy: A History of the Royal Winnipeg Rifles.* Winnipeg: Royal Winnipeg Rifles, 2010.

Roberts, James Alan. *The Canadian Summer: The Memoirs of James Alan Roberts.* Toronto: University of Toronto Press, 1981.

Rogers, R.L. *History of the Lincoln and Welland Regiment.* Montreal: Industrial Shops for the Deaf, 1954.

Ross, Richard M. *The History of the 1st Battalion Cameron Highlanders of Ottawa (MG).* N.p., n.d.

Roy, Reginald. *Ready for the Fray: The History of the Canadian Scottish Regiment (Princess Mary's), 1920 to 1955.* Vancouver: Evergreen Press, 1958.

Shawcross, Ronald Gendall. *What Was It Like? A Rifleman Remembers.* Victoria, BC: Trafford, 2004.

Spencer, Robert A. *History of the Fifteenth Canadian Field Regiment, Royal Canadian Artillery: 1941 to 1945.* New York: Elsevier, 1945.

Stacey, Charles P. *The Victory Campaign: The Operations in North-West Europe, 1944–1945.* Vol. 3 of *Official History of the Canadian Army in the Second World War.* Ottawa: Queen's Printer, 1960.

Stanley, George F.G. *In the Face of Danger: The History of the Lake Superior Regiment.* Port Arthur, ON: Lake Superior Rgt., 1960.

Tacoma, Bruce, and Eric Wells. *Little Black Devils: A History of the Royal Winnipeg Rifles.* Winnipeg: Frye Publishing, 1983.

Vanguard: The Fort Garry Horse in the Second World War. Doetinchem, Netherlands: Uitgevers-Maatschappij, 'C. Misset, 1945.

Warren, Arnold. *Wait for the Waggon: The Story of the Royal Canadian Army Service Corps.* Toronto: McClelland & Stewart, 1961.

White, Lewis M., ed. *On All Fronts: Czechs and Slovaks in World War II.* New York: Czechoslovak Society of Arts and Sciences, 1991.

Whitsed, Roy. *Canadians: A Battalion at War.* Mississauga, ON: Burlington Books, 1996.

Williams, Jeffrey, *The Long Left Flank: The Hard Fought Way to the Reich, 1944–1945.* Toronto: Stoddart, 1998.

Wilmot, Chester. *The Struggle for Europe.* London: Collins, 1952.

Zaloga, Steven J. *US Airborne Divisions in the ETO, 1944–45.* Oxford, U.K.: Osprey Publishing, 2007.

Zuehlke, Mark. *Breakout from Juno: First Canadian Army and the Normandy Campaign, July 4–August 21, 1944.* Vancouver: Douglas & McIntyre, 2011.

————. *Tragedy at Dieppe: Operation Jubilee, August 19, 1944.* Madeira Park, BC: Douglas & McIntyre, 2012.

JOURNAL ARTICLES

Caravaggio, Angelo N. "Commanding the Green Centre Line in Normandy: A Case Study of Division Command in the Second World War." *Theses and Dissertations (Comprehensive)*, paper 1075, Wilfrid Laurier University, 2009.

Couvrette, Paul. "A Tale of Survival." *Ottawa Citizen*, Nov. 10, 2012.

Delderfield, R.F. "Confidential Report on the Recent Bombing of Le Havre." *Canadian Military History*, vol. 20, no. 4 (Autumn 2011): 69–74.

Galbraith, Ian. "Operation 'Wellhit': The Capture of Boulogne." *After the Battle*, no. 86, 1994: 1–23.

"Galt Father Hears Two Sons Killed in Action 3 Days Apart." *Toronto Star*, Oct. 5, 1944.

Margry, Karel. "The Capture of Le Havre." *After the Battle*, no. 139, 2008: 2–31.

McIntyre, Doug R., "Pursuit to the Seine: The Essex Scottish and the Forêt de La Londe, August 1944." *Canadian Military History*, vol. 7, no. 1 (Winter 1998): 59–72.

WEBSITES

"Canadian Army Overseas Honours and Awards (1939–45)." *National Defence and the Canadian Forces.* DHH, DND. www.cmp-cpm.forces.gc.ca/dhh-dhp/gal/cao-aco /index-eng.asp.

"Find War Dead." *Commonwealth War Graves Commission.* www.cwgc.org/find-war -dead.aspx.

"La liberation de Dieppe." *Présentation des sites de Jean Delamare.* Accessed Sept, 12, 2016. http://delamarejean.free.fr/dieppe_1944/liberation.html.

"Lieutenant Colonel Mark Tennant." *The Calgary Highlanders.* Accessed Apr. 6, 2016. www.calgaryhighlanders.com/history/highlanders/personalities/tennant.htm.

"Lord Shaughnessy." Obituaries. *The Telegraph.* Accessed Sept. 14, 2016. www.telegraph.co.uk/news/obituaries/1431696/Lord-Shaughnessy.html.

"Major General D.C. Spry." Canada in the Second World War. *Juno Beach Centre.* Accessed Apr. 22, 2016. www.junobeach.org/canada-in-wwii/articles/major-general -d-c-spry/.

"Operations of the Coastal Forces Control Frigates." *Captain Class Frigate Association.* Accessed Sept. 29, 2016. www.captainclassfrigates.co.uk/ops/coastcom.html.

"The Guns of Cap Gris Nez—Hitler's Four-Year Artillery Bombardment of Southern England." *Military History Now.* Accessed Feb. 16, 2017. http://militaryhistorynow .com/2016/02/12/the-guns-of-cap-gris-nez-hitlers-four-year-artillery-bombardment -of-southern-england/.

"The Story of 34 Armoured Bde." *The Royal Tank Regiment Association.* Accessed Jan. 3, 2017. http://www.royaltankregiment.com/9_RTR/History%20of%2034%20Armd %20Bde.htm.

Tonner, Mark W. "The 'Ram' Kangaroo Armoured Personnel Carrier, Part 1." *MilArt: Articles on Canadian Militaria.* Accessed Dec. 30, 2016. https://servicepub .wordpress.com/2014/10/16/the-ram-kangaroo-armoured-personnel-carrier-part-1/.

"UK Military Bridging—Floating Equipment." *Think Defence*. Accessed Feb. 15, 2017. www.thinkdefence.co.uk/2011/12/uk-military-bridging-floating-equipment/.

"War Diaries for the 11th Hussars (Prince Albert's Own)." (1944.) *WWII: A British Focus*. Accessed Apr. 11, 2016. www.warlinks.com/armour/11_hussars/11huss _44.php.

UNPUBLISHED MATERIALS

"Account by Capt. W.S. Hamilton, RCCS, on bombing of Boulogne." 235C3.4091(D1), RG24, LAC.

"Account by Col. F.M. Mitchell of the Capture of Bourgtheroulde by the RHC 26 August 44." 145.2F15011(D1), DHH, DND.

"Account by Lt. Col. Rowley, SD&G Highrs: The Attack on Boulogne." 145.2S8011(D4), DHH, DND.

"Account of a Two Coy Attack Spycker by 'B' and 'C' Coys, RHC, Given by Maj. Pinkham, OC, 'C' Coy." 145.2R15011(D5), DHH, DND.

"Account of Assault on Calais by Maj. W.H.V. Matthews." 145.2C4011(D2), DHH, DND.

"Account of attack on Cap Gris Nez by Lt-Col D.F. Forbes." 145.2N2011(D1), DHH, DND.

"Account of Capt. Bruce Marshall (Camerons of Canada) in the Forêt de la Londe, 27–30 Aug 44." 145.2Q1011(D4), DHH, DND.

"Account of Ops in Boulogne Area 14/22 Sep 44 by Lt. Col. JE Anderson." 145.2N3011(D1) N. Shore R., DHH, DND.

"Account of the Attack on St. Germain La Campagne on 23 Aug 44 by Fus MRS as given by Maj. Dextraze." 145.2F10H(D7), DHH, DND.

"Account of the Capture of Bourgtheroulde by RHC, 26 Aug. 44, by Lt. Shea, 10." 145.2R15011(D2), DHH, DND.

"Account of the Régiment de Maisonneuve at Bourbourgville and Bergues by Capt. Fafard, Adjt." 145.2R6011(D7), DHH, DND.

"Advance of 30 Corps across R. Seine to Brussels & Antwerp." 225B30.013(D1), RG24, LAC.

"Air Support." 215C1.(D251), RG24, LAC.

"Air Support Reports." 215C1.099(D16), RG24, LAC.

"Air Support 3 Cdn. Inf." 215C3.099(D1), RG24, LAC.

"Algonquin Regiment War Diary," Aug. 1944. RG24, LAC.

"An Account of the Operations of Second Army in Europe: 1944–1945." 215B2.013(D7), RG24, LAC.

"Argyll and Sutherland Highlanders War Diary," Aug. 1944. RG24, LAC.

"Black Watch War Diary," Aug. 1944. RG24, LAC.

"Black Watch War Diary," Sept. 1944. RG24, LAC.

"British Columbia Regiment War Diary," Aug. 1944. RG24, LAC.

"Calgary Highlanders War Diary," Aug. 1944. RG24, LAC.

"Calgary Highlanders War Diary," Sept. 1944. RG24, LAC.

"Cameron Highlanders of Ottawa (MG) War Diary," Sept. 1944. RG24, LAC.

"Canadian Grenadier Guards War Diary," Sept. 1944. RG24, LAC.

"Canadian Scottish Regiment War Diary," Aug. 1944. RG24, LAC.

"Canadian Scottish Regiment War Diary," Sept. 1944. RG24, LAC.

"Canadian Scottish Regiment War Diary," Oct. 1944. RG24, LAC.

"Capture of Boulogne—Sep 44." 215C1.013(D31), RG24, LAC.

"Correspondence to 4 Cdn Armd Div—re: El Beuf and Mantes Gassicourt and Abbeville area." 245C4.012(D3), RG24, LAC.

Crerar Papers. "Correspondence with Field-Marshal Montgomery, 3 Feb. 42–14 Jul. 45." 958C.009(D172), MG30, vol. 2, LAC.

———. "Correspondence with Lt-Gen G.G. Simonds, 2 Cdn Corps 29 Nov. 43–26 Jun 45." 958C.009(D169), MG30, vol. 2, LAC.

———. "Operation 'Fusilade' and 'Astonia.' Period 27 Aug. 44–11 Sep. 44." 958C.009 (D38), MG30, vol. 2, LAC.

———. "Operations—Directives—First Canadian Army—Period 22 Jul. 44–20 Sep. 44." 958C.009(D89), MG30, vol. 2, LAC.

———. "Operations 2 Cdn. Corps—Period 15 Aug 44 to 16 Oct 44." 958C.009(D54), MG30, vol. 2, LAC.

———. "21 Army Group, General Operational Situation and Directive." 958C.009(D65), MG30, vol. 2, LAC.

"18th Canadian Field Ambulance War Diary," Aug. 1944.

"18th Canadian Field Company, RCE War Diary," Sept. 1944. RG24, LAC.

"8th Canadian Infantry Brigade War Diary," Sept. 1944. RG24, LAC.

"8th Field Squadron, RCE War Diary," Aug. 1944. RG24, LAC.

"Essex Scottish Regiment War Diary," Aug. 1944. RG24, LAC.

"Essex Scottish Regiment War Diary," Sept. 1944. RG24, LAC.

"5th Canadian Field Regiment War Diary," Sept. 1944. RG24, LAC.

"5th Canadian Infantry Brigade War Diary," Aug. 1944. RG24, LAC.

"5th Canadian Infantry Brigade War Diary," Sept. 1944. RG24, LAC.

"1st Canadian Armoured Personnel Carrier Squadron War Diary," Sept. 1944. RG24, LAC.

"1st Czech Independent Armoured Brigade Group, Hist. Notes on Ops." 285ŽC1.013(D1), LAC.

"1st Hussars Regiment War Diary," Sept. 1944. RG24, LAC.

"14th Canadian Hussars War Diary," Sept. 1944. RG24, LAC.

"4th Canadian Armoured Brigade War Diary," Aug. 1944. RG24, LAC.

"4th Canadian Armoured Brigade War Diary," Sept. 1944. RG24, LAC.

"4th Canadian Infantry Brigade War Diary," Aug. 1944. RG24, LAC.

"4th Canadian Infantry Brigade War Diary," Sept. 1944. RG24, LAC.

"Headquarters, First Canadian Army War Diary," Aug. 1944. RG24, LAC.

"Highland Light Infantry War Diary," Sept. 1944. RG24, LAC.

Hunter, Maj. C.C. "Unit History of 1 CDN FD PK COY RCE and 2 CDN INF DIV BR PL RCE." 143.2FI011(D1), DHH, DND.

"Information re: Dover Guns." Documents from 540 Coast Regiment, RCA. 934.013(D9), RG24, LAC.

"Joseph Greenblatt Correspondence." Archival Collection CN: 19990209-002, DOCS MNU 58A 1155-3-6, CWM.

"Lake Superior Regiment (Motor) War Diary," Aug. 1944. RG24, LAC.

"Le Régiment de la Chaudière War Diary," Sept. 1944. RG24, LAC.

"Le Régiment de Maisonneuve War Diary," Sept. 1944. RG24, LAC.

"Les Fusiliers Mont-Royal War Diary," Sept. 1944. RG24, LAC.

"Lincoln and Welland Regiment War Diary," Aug. 1944. RG24, LAC.

"Msgs—2 Cdn Corps." 142.91S2092(D1), DHH, DND.

"Narrative of the Capture of Le Havre: Operation Astonia." 225B1.013(D1), RG24, LAC.

"9th Canadian Infantry Brigade War Diary," Aug. 1944. RG24, LAC.

"9th Canadian Infantry Brigade War Diary," Sept. 1944. RG24, LAC.

"North Nova Scotia Highlanders War Diary," Sept. 1944. RG24, LAC.

"North Shore (New Brunswick) War Diary," Sept. 1944. RG24, LAC.

"Op Logs 2 Cdn. Inf. Div. Aug. 44." 235C2.015(D8), RG24, LAC.

"Op 'Undergo' Hy Bomber Effort." 235C3.095(D1), RG24, LAC.

"Operation Undergo, Misc Bomber Command Messages." 692.019(D1), DHH, DND.

"Operation Wellhit: Capture of Boulogne Fortress." 235C3.013(D2), RG24, LAC.

"Personal Diary of Brig. N.E. Rodger." 19950071-004, MANU 58A1 114.1, CWM.

"Queen's Own Cameron Highlanders War Diary," Aug. 1944. RG24, LAC.

"Queen's Own Cameron Highlanders War Diary," Sept. 1944. RG24, LAC.

"Queen's Own Rifles War Diary," Sept. 1944. RG24, LAC.

"Regina Rifles War Diary," Aug. 1944. RG24, LAC.

"Regina Rifles War Diary," Sept. 1944. RG24, LAC.

"Report No. 63, Manpower Problems of the Canadian Army in the Second World War." AHQ, DHH, DND.

"Report No. 69, The Campaign in North-West Europe: Information from German Sources, Part III—German Defence Operations in the Sphere of First Canadian Army (23 Aug–8 Nov 44)." AHQ, DHH, DND.

"Report No. 77, The Campaign in North-West Europe: Information from German Sources, Part IV—Higher Direction of Operations from Falaise Debacle to Ardennes Offensive (20 Aug–16 Dec 44)." AHQ, DHH, DND.

"Report No. 137, Enemy Air Attack and the Canadian Army in the United Kingdom, 1943–45: The V-Weapons." CMHQ, DHH, DND.

"Report No. 139, The 1st Canadian Parachute Battalion in France (6 June–6 September 1944)." CMHQ, DHH, DND.

"Report No. 146, Operations of First Canadian Army in North-West Europe, 31 Jul–1 Oct 44." CMHQ, DHH, DND.

"Report No. 162, Canadian Participation in the Operations in North-West Europe, 1944, Part III: Canadian Operations in July." CMHQ, DHH, DND.

"Report No. 183, Canadian Participation in the Operations in North-West Europe, 1944, Part IV: First Canadian Army in the Pursuit (23 Aug–30 Sep)." CMHQ, DHH, DND.

"Report No. 184, Canadian Participation in the Operations in North-West Europe, 1944, Part V: Clearing the Channel Ports, 3 Sep-6 Feb 45." CMHQ, DHH, DND.

"Report on Flame Action by Wasps." 142.91S2092(D1), DHH, DND.

"Report on Op Astonia." 225B1.013(D1), RG24, LAC.

"Report on Op 'Wellhit' capture of Boulogne Fortress, 17–22 Sep 44." 235C3.013(D2), RG24, LAC.

"Report on Ops: Advance from Falaise to Calais by 7 Cdn Recce Regt-22 Aug/5 Sep 44." 141.4A7013(D1), DHH, DND.

"Report . . . on use of smoke in Op 'Undergo.'" 142.96009(D10), DHH, DND.

"Reports, Appreciations, etc." 212C1.3009(D102), RG24, LAC.

"Royal Hamilton Light Infantry War Diary," Aug. 1944. RG24, LAC.

"Royal Marine Siege Regiment, Detailed Narrative." 200G1.013(D2), RG24, LAC.

"Royal Regiment of Canada War Diary," Aug. 1944, RG24, LAC.

"Royal Regiment of Canada War Diary," Sept. 1944. RG24, LAC.

"Royal Winnipeg Rifles War Diary," Sept. 1944. RG24, LAC.

"11 Canadian Corps Intelligence Summaries," Aug. 1944. RG24, LAC.

"2nd Canadian Field Company, RCE, War Diary," Sept. 1944, RG24, LAC.

"2nd Canadian Infantry Division Headquarters (G Branch) War Diary," Aug. 1944.
    RG24, LAC.

"2nd Canadian Infantry Division Headquarters (G Branch) War Diary," Sept. 1944.
    RG24, LAC.

"17th Duke of York's Royal Canadian Hussars War Diary," Sept. 1944. RG24, LAC.

"7th Canadian Infantry Brigade War Diary," Sept. 1944. RG24, LAC.

"Sherbrooke Fusiliers War Diary," Aug. 1944. RG24, LAC.

"Siege and Capture of Calais," 215C1.013(D32). RG24, LAC.

"Sitreps 2 Cdn. Inf. Div. Aug. 44," 235C2.013(D10). RG24, LAC.

"6th Canadian Anti-Tank Regiment War Diary," Sept. 1944. RG24, LAC.

"6th Canadian Field Regiment War Diary," Sept. 1944. RG24, LAC.

"6th Canadian Infantry Brigade War Diary," Aug. 1944. RG24, LAC.

"6th Canadian Infantry Brigade War Diary," Sept. 1944. RG24, LAC.

"South Alberta Regiment War Diary," Aug. 1944. RG24, LAC.

"South Saskatchewan Regiment War Diary," Aug. 1944. RG24, LAC.

"South Saskatchewan Regiment War Diary," Sept. 1944. RG24, LAC.

"Stormont, Dundas & Glengarry Highlanders War Diary," Aug. 1944. RG24, LAC.

"Stormont, Dundas & Glengarry Highlanders War Diary," Sept. 1944. RG24, LAC.

"Story of Battle of Boulogne by 10 Cdn Armd Regt (FGH)." 141.4A10013(D3), DHH, DND.

"10th Canadian Infantry Brigade War Diary," Sept. 1944. RG24, LAC.

"3rd Canadian Infantry Division War Diary," Sept. 1944. RG24, LAC.

TNA:PRO ADM 202/99. "4th SS Brigade War Diary, Sept. 1944."

TNA:PRO ADM 234/363. "No. 49: Campaign in North-West Europe June
    1944–May 1945."

TNA:PRO AIR 25/717. "No. 84 Composite Group, Appendices."

TNA:PRO CAB 44/253. "Chapter 11 (Part 11)–The Enemy (Army Intelligence)."

TNA:PRO WO 106/4356. "21 Army Group Directives." Vol. 11, M519 20/9/44.

TNA:PRO WO 171/259. "G-Branch HQ, 1 Corps," Sept. 1944.

TNA:PRO WO 171/500. "49 Infantry Division War Diary," Sept. 1944.

TNA:PRO WO 171/528. "51st Infantry Division War Diary," Sept. 1944.

TNA:PRO WO 171/643. "34 Tank Brigade War Diary," Sept. 1944.

TNA:PRO WO 171/650. "56 Infantry Brigade War Diary," Sept. 1944.

TNA:PRO WO 171/664. "146 Infantry Brigade War Diary," Sept. 1944.

TNA:PRO WO 171/841. "22nd Dragoons Regiment War Diary," Sept. 1944.

TNA:PRO WO 171/858. "1st Lothians and Border Yeomanry War Diary," Sept. 1944.

TNA:PRO WO 171/879. "147th Regiment Royal Armoured Corps War Diary," Sept. 1944.

TNA:PRO WO 171/1801. "6th Assault Regiment, RE War Diary," Sept. 1944.

TNA:PRO WO 179/2769. "General Staff, Headquarters 3 Canadian Infantry Division," Sept. 1944.

TNA:PRO WO 205/1020. "Interrogation Reports German Generals."

"Toronto Scottish Regiment (MG) War Diary," Sept. 1944. RG24, LAC.

"12th Manitoba Dragoons War Diary," Aug. 1944. RG24, LAC.

"12th Manitoba Dragoons War Diary," Sept. 1944. RG24, LAC.

"21 Army Group Op Reports." 215A21.013. RG24, LAC.

INTERVIEWS AND CORRESPONDENCE

Hall, A.C. Vassar. Interview by Chris D. Main, Victoria, June 7, 11, and 15, 1979. UVICSC.

McGregor, William. Correspondence with author. Apr. 23, 2017.

Norton, Francis. Interview by Tom Torrie, Victoria, Aug. 28, 1987. UVICSC.

Rockingham, John Meredith. Interview by Reginald H. Roy, Qualicum Beach, BC, July 11, 1979. UVICSC.

Smith, Hershell. Interview by Chris Bell, Victoria, Sept. 2, 1982, and Aug. 30, 1983. UVICSC.

INDEX OF FORMATIONS, UNITS AND CORPS

ABOUT THE AUTHOR

THE CINDERELLA CAMPAIGN is the twelfth volume in Mark Zuehlke's critically acclaimed Canadian Battle Series—the most extensive published account of the battle experiences of Canada's Army in World War II. The series is also the most exhaustive recounting of the battles and campaigns fought by any nation during that war to have been written by a single author. These best-selling books continue to confirm Zuehlke's reputation as the nation's leading popular military historian. In 2006, *Holding Juno: Canada's Heroic Defence of the D-Day Beaches* won the City of Victoria Butler Book Prize.

He has written six other historical works, including *For Honour's Sake: The War of 1812 and the Brokering of an Uneasy Peace*, which won the 2007 Canadian Author's Association Lela Common Award for Canadian History.

Recently, Zuehlke has turned his hand to graphic novels, working with Renegade Arts on a number of projects based on Canadian history. In 2012, he was the co-author of *The Loxleys and the War of 1812*, and in 2013 wrote the script for a sequel, *The Loxleys and Confederation*.

Also a novelist, he is the author of the popular Elias McCann series, the first of which—*Hands Like Clouds*—won the 2000 Crime Writers of Canada Arthur Ellis Award for Best First Novel.

Zuehlke lives in Victoria, British Columbia, and is currently working on his next Canadian Battle Series book, which will detail the last battles fought by Canadians in the Italian Campaign during the fall of 1944 and winter of 1944–45. In 2015, he published a companion volume to the Canadian Battle Series—*Through Blood and Sweat: A Remembrance Trek Across Sicily's World War II Battlegrounds*—a memoir of his experiences in July 2013 when, over twenty days, Zuehlke and a small contingent of Canadians marched 350 kilometres to retrace the routes taken by 1st Canadian Infantry Division through Sicily in 1943. On the web, Zuehlke can be found at www.zuehlke.ca and Mark Zuehlke's Canadian Battle Series Facebook page.